Trigger Warning

This is an honest and raw account of my journey with anorexia nervosa, so it documents a lot of disordered behaviours and thoughts. I have omitted as many numbers and specifics as possible, while still providing an accurate insight into the mind of someone with anorexia nervosa - part of the reason I wrote this is to educate carers and clinicians. If you are in a fragile state of mine and are easily triggered, I strongly recommend you do not read this. If you are in a healthier frame of mind - by which I mean almost completely recovered and able to look at the doctored photos of Victoria's Secret models without feeling the slightest twinge of longing or guilt - but don't want to know specific numbers or exercise accounts, I have highlighted these paragraphs and identified the category of triggering content. If you need to, please cover these paragraphs with your hand to stop your curious, wandering eyes from seeing anything potentially damaging.

Early years

I think I had a relatively happy childhood. I have incredibly loving parents, who will do almost anything for me if I need it. Even when we were younger, Adam and I got on reasonably well, as siblings go. I went to nice schools, though I struggled to find many friends with whom I felt I could be myself, without being judged, until the end of high school. Mum and Dad spent hours driving Adam and me to various musical activities and, until I got very sick with Chronic Fatigue Syndrome, (CFS), I excelled at both violin and school. I should have been happy and had a very healthy self-esteem.

And that was the case, until I became too sick with CFS to concentrate during violin practice or at school, and consequently stopped winning competitions and topping the class. Mum and Dad always told us that being a good person was more important than being clever. Every time they read our school reports, without fail, they would turn to the last page, which contained the teachers' feedback on our behaviour. It became a joke in our house, that they always said "This is the most important page. More important than your marks." While I trusted that Mum and Dad truly believed this, my observations of the world told another story.

Eavesdropping on adult conversations, books and television shows taught me that clever, hardworking people went on to have interesting, fulfilling jobs and earned enough to support themselves. People who weren't as intelligent, or who were lazy at school, became checkout chicks and road workers — occupations I deduced to be subtly looked down upon. And, sadly, you don't usually get a high-paying job, and therefore comfortable life, simply by being kind. Without questioning it — why would I, when I was surrounded by evidence to support the benefits of intelligence? — I based my self-worth on doing well at music and school. Sure, I knew I was a nice person, and usually did the right thing, but I didn't base my self-esteem on my kindness. So, when people stopped praising me for doing well musically and academically, I turned to the other thing for which I was praised: being thin.

Society had taught me that being thin is a good thing, something to aspire to. And I was thin. I was proud of it, as though it was a virtue. I saw thinness as proof of self-control. Only people who eat too much or are lazy are overweight, right? At the same time, I knew I was naturally thin because the rest of the family was. But I saw that as a virtue too, in the same way that people who are born clever or musically gifted are celebrated. They don't have to work for those genes; it's just ancestry and luck.

Contents

Trigger Warning	3
Early Years	4
Triggers	9
Year 12	14
Gap Year	20
Heathgrove	26
After Heathgrove	32
Maudsley	39
Escape	48
Hobart Year 1	57
New Zealand	62
Hobart Year 2	66
USA	78
Summer	85
Hobart Year 3	89
Hobart Post Uni	104
China	121
Perth	125
Europe	132
Tour	143
Post Europe	148
Auditions and Work	151
Touring	163
More Auditions and Work	167
Siobhan	175

Governor	184
Continuing Recovery	200
Slipping	210
Sick	217
Back to Uni	220
2020	224
Realisations and Confusion	232
Autism	237
Tales of Exhaustion	242
Work and Uni	252
Autism Assessment	261
Marissa and Malnutrition	270
Crash	279
Refeeding	286
A New Perspective	294
Wisdom Teeth and Another Assessment	303
Panic Attacks	309
Thank You	323
Recommended Books & Social Media Accounts	323

Although I was proud of my small build, I always felt that it wasn't enough. Mum and Adam are also very slim and I often wondered if they were thinner than me. Looking back I realise how much thought I put into this. People often commented on how thin I was, but if ever someone remarked upon Adam's small build without acknowledging me, I wondered if I was skinny enough to deserve a mention. I knew I was thin and was therefore proud, but I was never sure if I was thin enough to be truly worthy as a person.

Mum often talked about how we were a slim family and I heard in her voice — or thought I heard — the unspoken but widely-accepted belief that thinness is the superior body-type. But I always wondered if I was as slim as her and Adam, and if not being so made me a lesser person her eyes. When Adam first went into hospital after being diagnosed with type one Diabetes, the doctor had commented on how thin he was. They were worried he had lost weight due to ketosis, and was possibly in Ketoacidosis, which isn't uncommon for newly diagnosed type one diabetics.
"Didn't she look at the rest of us and see that we're all slim? Hannah not so much, but Adam and I…" Mum said afterwards. She often said things I took to mean that she and Adam were thinner than I was. Maybe she meant no such thing. Maybe I interpreted it incorrectly. Only in hindsight do I realise how sensitive and insecure I must have been, for an offhand remark to have affected me so deeply; how much I overanalysed and needed external validation in order to feel worthy.

This is probably a good time to discuss fatphobia. I am very aware that I am speaking as someone who has never been anywhere near plus size - even if, at times, I felt that I was. My understanding of the term 'fatphobic' has two main definitions, both of which encompass a variety of nuances.

1. The phobia of other fat people which, in my experience, is less a fear and more a judgement and dislike of fat people. I'm talking about kids making fat jokes and teasing fat kids; adults who should know better, who are still making fat jokes; people commenting on celebrities or friends who have "let themselves go" and put on weight; consciously choosing to leave a fat person out of a conversation or friendship group; the list goes on.

2. The phobia of being fat. I know that a lot of fat people find this fear offensive, and I understand why. Of course it is offensive to know that someone else doesn't want to be like you! However, regardless of our individual values, society is fatphobic. Most of us are very aware that, unfortunately, being fat increases our chances of being a target for bullying. Therefore, out of self-preservation, we do not want to be fat.

I learnt this very early on. As an insecure child trying to fit in, I watched, listened and internalised anything that may help me to do so. I saw fat kids being bullied and blamed for farting; fat people in movies and television being the comic relief, pitied, or shown to be greedy or lazy. I never wanted to be ridiculed in that way. The few times a family member joked about how much I had eaten I was mortified. I felt like a worthless, disgusting, smelly slug. Just as some immigrants hide their cultural roots in an attempt to fit in and avoid racism, I knew I never wanted to be fat, because of the bullying and ostracism that would accompany it. I was very aware of my thin privilege and wanted to keep it.

Whatever anyone actually said or meant, I grew up with these beliefs:
1. Being thin is a virtue. It is proof of self-control and a genetic predisposition which is to be admired.
2. Being overweight is proof of laziness and a lack of self-control. It is disgusting.
3. I am not as thin as Mum and Adam. Therefore I am disgusting.

A lot of these thoughts and thinking patterns became semi-subconscious, and I came to accept them as normal, without ever challenging them. Maybe, because I was excelling at school and musically, I still felt good enough about myself to be ok. I may not have been quite thin enough but at least I was good at school and music.

When I was nine years old I started showing early signs of CFS, however we didn't know what it was until much later. I didn't notice that I was feeling more tired, or that I was getting sick more often because it was gradual. Mum and Dad noticed but didn't know the cause, which scared them. I had been very sick as a baby and Mum was terrified I was going to have health problems throughout my life — little did she know how accurate her fears were!

One symptom I definitely did notice was severe abdominal bloating after eating. I remember it starting at the end of my ninth year, over the Christmas holidays. I thought I was getting fat because it happened after I ate — and food makes you fat, right? My tummy was sticking out and I knew the food was in there. It was around this time that I saw part of a cartoon Adam was watching. One of the characters ate a lot of food very quickly, causing his stomach to balloon out. To me, this one scene confirmed my hypothesis. Eating was causing my tummy to poke out. Let's not forget that I was only nine, trying to work out what was happening to my body, with an existing fear of being fat and wondering if I already was. Ironically, I never told anyone my tummy had started sticking out after I ate, because half of me knew that I wasn't actually fat, and I worried that Mum and Dad would think I was anorexic if I showed them my tummy and told them I thought I was getting fat.

I did, however, try to stop the bloating from happening. I noticed that when I ate less I bloated less, so I tried to eat less. I wasn't incredibly strict with myself though — not like I was years later — and I remember often giving in to my cravings and then making excuses to the inner critic that told me I was greedy and lacked self-control. I also started exercising. Nothing extreme, just going for walks and sometimes running up and down the length of my bedroom in the morning — being very careful to step as lightly as possible so no one heard. I don't think my family were aware of my indoor running or thought anything of the walks.

When I was about 11 I noticed that, if I sat on a chair wearing short shorts, I could see my thighs flatten and squash together. I thought it looked horrible. I first noticed during an orchestra rehearsal and immediately started worrying others would see and think I was fat. Squishing my legs together in an attempt to make them look thinner didn't work. Looking around at others in the orchestra, I tried to see if their legs had also flattened out, but was also conscious I might look like a pervert, staring at people's legs. I also couldn't look down at their legs from the same position as I was viewing my own — directly above — so it was hard to tell if theirs looked the same. Eventually, I discovered that, if I sat on the edge of my chair, with the bare part of my legs surrounded by air, they wouldn't be able to flatten. I have always sat the same way since unless my legs are under a table where I, and no one else, can see them and feel disgusted.

I was in my teens when I noticed that my quadriceps and the skin above my kneecaps wobbled a bit when I walked. Again I was incredibly self-conscious and worried others would think I must be greedy and lazy if I had fat that wobbled. I had grown up thinking that if someone had so much fat that it wobbled, they must have a lot of it! In fact, I thought having any fat on your body was unhealthy. Even before social media, we were bombarded with advertisements demonising fat, which was reflected in television, movies, and the conversations of our own friends and family. As a teenager observing everything in an attempt to make sense of a world in which I felt I didn't quite belong, I deduced that having zero body fat was the ultimate goal. The models in advertisements looked like they had almost achieved that. Given this belief, I was horrified when I saw my legs wobbling. I was disgusted with myself and assumed others would be too. I tried to tense my legs when I walked to stop the wobbling, but it made my gait stilted and awkward. Somehow I discovered that, if I slightly bent my knee as my leg met the ground, my muscles would tense enough to reduce the wobble, making it much less noticeable. I assumed that, as walking in this way also caused me to use my muscles more, it would help burn off the offending, wobbling fat. In hindsight, I think the wobble was actually caused by my leg muscles — not fat — moving around as my feet jolted against the ground. Whatever the cause, walking like that became a habit, and still is.

It wasn't until I was 13 that I realised it wasn't fat, but gas, making my tummy poke out after eating. It was the summer holidays and I was sitting on the couch in the lounge room with mum and dad. They were doing their weekly cryptic crossword and I was reading. Dad has had problems with his digestion since he was a teenager and would sometimes mention that he had a sore tummy or was bloated. On this occasion, he showed Mum and me his protruding belly and I realised that that was what had been happening to me. "So am I!" I said, and showed them my bloated tummy. I went on to tell Mum and Dad that I had been bloating for a while, though I didn't specify that by "a while" I meant four years.

Soon after, Mum took me to the GP, after which followed a succession of appointments with various — unhelpful but expensive — specialists. It took a year or two for me to be diagnosed with CFS and multiple food intolerances. During this time I became increasingly tired and sick. I was unable to concentrate on music or schoolwork; I often had such severe stomach pains that I couldn't stand upright, and sometimes collapsed to the floor if the pain spasmed; my eyes had dark rings around them; I had strange, thick, eczema-like dandruff; and other delightful symptoms of my body's inability to function as it should. After I was diagnosed with CFS, Gilbert, a good friend from school, said I had looked so sick he had worried I had cancer. He hadn't said anything in case I didn't want to talk about it.

Even after diagnosis, it took me a few years to recover, as we tried all sorts of — mostly ineffective — treatments. Not a lot is known about the causes and treatment of CFS, possibly because a lot of Doctors don't believe it exists; that it's just laziness. Due to my lack of concentration, I was no longer topping the class in tests and I didn't always win when I entered violin competitions, which felt like a punch in the guts every time. Musical and academic achievements had been my main source of self-esteem for as long as I could remember, and now they were gone. My only fallback, being thin, was more unreliable than ever, with my bloated stomach making me look, from my perspective, as though I had a gut.

Triggers

Before I was diagnosed with CFS I lost weight. While we were eliminating food, to work out what was causing all my digestive problems and tiredness, my diet became very restricted. Not because I was trying to restrict my intake; but simply because, in order to work out which foods were causing the problems, I had to go back to a very basic diet and re-introduce foods one by one. At some point, my GP, Maisie, decided I needed to put on some weight and suggested I make a Nutella-esque spread to put on my grain-free, milk-free, everything-free muffins. As milk and cocoa were restricted by the diet, she suggested combining margarine, icing sugar and carob — cocoa's less popular sibling. Though this concoction was a far cry from delicious Nutella, it was one nice thing I could eat. I spread it on my muffins with increasing thickness. I also scooped quite a bit out of the tub on my finger while I was preparing said muffins. I was probably eating at least half a cup of margarine each day in the form of 'carob spread.'

I didn't think anything of it. Even though I had a vague idea about calories, from attempting to make sense of a few nutrition labels when I was nine, I didn't track them and had no idea how many I was meant to be consuming each day. I knew that eating more was related to weight gain, but also knew that I didn't put on weight easily. I was aware of more fat on my tummy, an area of my body that I monitored closely due to the bloating, but also didn't know what was fat and how much was air.

One night, Mum, Dad and I went shopping to find something nice for me to wear to a school dance. I had never bought anything new for a dance; I always just chose a favourite outfit from what I already owned. But mum said she wanted to get me something nice, that I'd had a tough few years always feeling sick, and I deserved a treat. I felt it was unnecessary to buy new clothes, but was also excited at the prospect of finding something nice. I didn't realise until years later that it was the norm for most girls to buy a new outfit for these events. We were having trouble finding a dress that fit properly, didn't gape at the neckline, and was loose enough to hide my bloated tummy. Eventually, we found one that Mum agreed was safe for me to bend over in, without giving everyone a view all the way down to my navel. I liked the design and colour, but could still see my belly poking out in the mirror.
"I can still see my bloated tummy though," I said to Mum. "I don't want to have to worry about that at the dance."
"I don't think it's all bloating. It looks like some of it is fat," she replied, frowning slightly. "You've been having a lot of that carob spread, haven't you?"

And that was the turning point. I interpreted her frown as thinly-veiled disgust. Was she telling me off for eating unhealthily or did she just think I was greedy? In hindsight, I know Mum was just being matter-of-fact. But I had always held her up as the epitome of thinness, correctness and self-control. I yearned for her approval, which I had half-doubted for a long as I could remember, even though she made a point of telling me that she loved me every day. Because it was Mum who had noticed and announced the fat — which society had taught me was shameful — I was mortified, embarrassed and ashamed. I felt that everything I had always related to being overweight — greed, laziness, a lack of self-control, selfishness — traits that I already feared I possessed — had been exposed within me. I knew I had to get rid of that fat as soon as I could. I needed it gone now! A few months later, Mum said that she saw my face after she spoke those innocent words and wanted to take them back straight away. But she couldn't. I had heard them. It was too late.

I want to make it very clear that I do not blame Mum at all. She meant no malice and has never suggested I lose weight. At the time, I was too shocked and insecure to realise those words were simply a non-judgemental observation; a stating of facts. However, I was already wondering if I was fat and found most comments triggering. I was also always on the lookout for danger — signs that people didn't like me or that I had unwittingly committed a social faux pas. The reason Mum's words had such a profound effect on me was because she was my Mum; my main role model. She always did the right thing, worked incredibly hard, and was thin; therefore, to me, her words were gospel. From my perspective, her words confirmed my fears to be true.

I was 15 at the time. It isn't unusual for girls to feel insecure about their bodies in their teenage years. The next day, I started decreasing the amount of carob spread I used until, after a few weeks, I was spreading it thinner than Vegemite. I stopped having a glass of milk with my breakfast. I stopped eating potato chips, which were one of the few nice things I could enjoy on my restricted diet. Mum and Dad noticed and both spoke to me on different occasions.

Dad brought it up one morning while we were driving to school.
"So, Mum and I have noticed that you've started eating less."
"Mmm," I feigned disinterest, while anxiety entered my belly.
"Remember Maisie said you need to be gaining weight?" He glanced over at my poker face. "That's not going to happen unless you eat more, is it?"
I responded with another murmur.

"Now, I don't know if you're worried about how you look. You probably don't want to talk about this with your boring old Dad, but I've been told that when most women lose weight, they lose it from their breasts first. And, now I can speak from experience — boys like breasts."
I think we were both mortified. I gave another "Mmhmm," before Dad turned the radio volume back up. He probably thought I was trying to lose weight to impress boys, not to impress Mum.

Although Mum and Dad were worried about my decreased food intake, I was only restricting half-heartedly. It wasn't until a year later that I felt I took weight loss seriously. I became much more aware of my body that year though, having had my fears that I was fat and gross affirmed — in my eyes — by Mum that night in the changing room. I compared myself to others even more than I had before. When I was about ten, I started to feel vaguely gross and dirty when I was near people with clear skin and neat hair. I assumed they wouldn't want to be near me, in case contact would infect their perfection, so I always made sure I didn't stand too close to them. If I saw someone who was thinner than me, I would feel like a lesser person, and would feel an intense yearning in my belly, to be as thin as them. After Mum's words, all these thoughts and feelings became much louder. I became hyper-aware of my own flaws and anyone who was thinner than me.

In the middle of the next year, when I was 16, my second last year of school, most of the music students in years 10, 11 and 12 went to Europe for about three weeks. We went to Italy, Hungary and France, performing in outdoor concerts and churches. I'd say there were at least 130 of us on tour. I went to a music specialist school and about a third to half of the students in each year group played an instrument and were a member of at least one of the bands, orchestras or choirs. I remember spending a lot of time comparing myself to other girls on the tour. I was around other people my age for over half my waking hours during term, but on tour, it was almost all the time and at every meal. Of course I paid more attention to the girls I labelled "perfect" in my head — those with "perfect" skin, hair that always looked nice, thin arms and flat bellies. I noticed that they ate less than me — possibly restricting a bit due to their own body image concerns or social pressure — and how delicately they seemed to eat. I was seeing them all of the time; a constant reminder of what I wasn't, but so desperately wanted to be.

When I got home I made rules for eating and I stuck to them. I did push-ups and sit-ups in my room every morning, and went for a 20-minute power walk every afternoon. I told myself that what I was doing was healthy, not yet fully comprehending my obsession. I exercised to lose weight, not to be healthy, and felt very anxious if anything prevented me from going for my walk. I also started deliberately eating a lot less, measured out my food and got very stressed if someone made me food that was different to what I felt I needed, in order to lose weight. Dad had always made up my lunchbox for school, but I started doing it myself so that I could spread exactly the right amount of peanut paste and honey on my rice cakes, not use any butter and definitely not add anything extra!

Maisie, my GP, had been weighing me at every appointment because I was meant to be putting on weight, so she saw the number dropping. I had been happy to put on weight when she told me I needed to the year before. I felt proud that I needed to because it meant that I was naturally underweight. Now I regretted following her instructions, especially my liberal use of the carob spread. I was having weekly appointments at that stage, so she could monitor the CFS, so she noticed declining weight quite early. At each appointment when my weight dropped, she asked me what was happening. I always replied, with affected flippancy, that I hadn't been as hungry, or that I just wasn't sure why I'd lost weight. Mum, who took me to the appointments, jumped in to tell Maisie I had been exercising and measuring my food. I told them that I enjoyed the walks and was trying to be healthy, and that I was measuring my food to make sure I was eating enough. I hated lying to answer their questions, but I was scared to admit the truth.

On top of often feeling tired, hungry and cold, having to evade Mum and Dad's questions about food, and pretending everything was normal, I was trying to understand my emotions. I wanted to stop worrying about everything I ate but, in my new mindset, that felt impossible. I hoped that, once I had lost the weight I had gained before the tour, I would be able to eat normally again. But Mum, Dad and Maisie kept getting in the way of my losing weight. And even without their probing questions, restricting my food was exhausting. There were many times that I wanted to curl on the floor and sob, but I couldn't give myself that rest time. I had to keep moving, or at least remain standing.

This phase of restriction only lasted about two months, during the school term following music tour. One day during the next holiday break, Mum asked if I had eaten morning tea.
"Nah, I wasn't hungry," I replied, attempting nonchalance.
Mum sighed. I knew that sigh. It was a dangerous sigh; the sigh that always preceded an angry outburst. My response had caused two months of bottled-up stress to erupt — Mum couldn't hold it in anymore. She yelled about how I had been restricting and exercising and that I didn't need to lose weight. I am

always frightened when Mum yells, but this time it was also cathartic; she scared me into sobbing and admitting that I had been trying to lose weight. Perhaps my tears caused Mum to soften and calm down, or maybe she had just run out of steam.
"Is this because of what I said, that night in the changing room?" She asked gently.
I nodded.
She sighed again, but this sigh wasn't angry; it was filled with sadness and despair. "You know I didn't mean you're fat, don't you?"
I nodded again.
"I regretted those words as soon as they left my mouth, and when I saw your face fall…"
"I know, I know you didn't mean it like that. But I do have fat on my tummy and I hate it. It looks horrible and it makes the bloating even worse. I thought if I could at least lose the fat, it would help…"
I cried some more, while Mum comforted me. When I had calmed down a bit, she raised the subject of eating more. I began to wail in fear. After that night in the changing room I had got it into my head that any weight I gained would be fat — thanks diet culture. I hadn't thought about athletes who gain muscle mass. When I voiced this fear to Mum, she explained that I would gain weight as a mixture of fat and muscle, whatever my body needed. I felt much better and started eating more. I continued to exercise everyday though, including the push-ups and sit-ups I did in my room before my walks.

One day soon after Mum yelled at me, Dad and I googled the calories in some of the food I was eating, to check that I was eating enough. Because I wasn't eating much "normal" food, because of my food intolerances, Dad wanted to find out how many calories my substitute foods contained, so we could compare them to "normal" food like bread. This is good information to know if it's being used for the right reasons. It didn't take me long to start checking the number of calories in all of my food. At first it was out of interest and to check that I was eating enough, but it didn't take long for my curiosity to become unhealthy and obsessive. And so began the calorie counting that has persisted since.

My eating was ok for the rest of that year. I put on a bit of weight — probably a mixture of fat and muscle — and felt ok about it because the amount of fat I could pinch on my belly didn't increase. I was more conscious of what I was eating, in terms of how sugary or fatty it was, and deliberately ate less of those foods. For example, I only allowed myself to drink diet soft drinks. If there was only regular soft drink available, I wouldn't have anything.

Year 12

During the summer holidays, I went to two music camps. On the whole, I had a wonderful time, made some great friends, had lots of fun adventures exploring Melbourne, Canberra and Sydney, and played fantastic music. For the first week of the second camp, I was sharing a room with another girl, which meant I had to make sure I did my sit-ups and push-ups while she was in the shower so she wouldn't see. Even though I was eating well and feeling mostly ok about how I looked, I knew I would feel guilty and anxious if I didn't do those exercises. I was still scared to have more than an iota of fat on my tummy. I had been relieved that, although I had put on a bit of weight, I still had very little fat on my tummy. I had lost it between the night in the changing room and the day Mum yelled at me, and it hadn't come back. I checked it every morning by pinching it between my fingers. Partway through the music camp I noticed my fingers gripping more fat — though who knows if it was my imagination — and I felt disgusting. I hated myself for it. But I told myself I could turn things around. I just had to eat healthier. I had been slightly freer with my eating while I was away, so I tightened my rules. One morning I googled the calories in vodka, on the computer in the lobby of the apartment building where we were staying, while trying not to let anyone see what I was doing, because I had drunk some the night before.

When I got home I continued to restrict junk food and, at some point, started looking at the fat content on food labels. I reasoned that, if I reduced the amount of fat I ate, I would reduce the amount of fat on my body. Food and exercise advertisements, television shows, movies, adults and health education at school had taught me that having too much fat on my body is bad. It also taught me that eating too much fat is bad. Why else would there be low-fat options for so many foods? It's hard to avoid hearing people talking about trying to reduce their fat intake, even in casual conversation. I knew there were good fats and bad fats, but assumed that the good fats were just slightly better than the "bad" fats. Surely no fats were actually good. My black-and-white thinking led me to conclude that, if eating too much fat was unhealthy, then I would be healthier if I removed all fat from my diet. And if having too much body fat was unhealthy, I would aim for the opposite. I didn't want to have any fat rolls, especially on my tummy, even if I was bending over. In an episode of The Big Bang Theory, Howard mentioned having three percent body fat. That seemed like a good goal.

Google told me that 10-30 percent of our daily calories should come from fat. I decided to aim for 10% or less. Since, by this stage, I was eating less than the daily recommended caloric intake, I was constraining myself to 16 grams of fat per day. I couldn't avoid fat at dinner, because Mum and Dad cooked for us all and used oil. One night while I was helping Mum cook, I took note of how much oil she used. Later that night I calculated how much fat I had consumed, once it was divided between the four of us. I was horrified that I was getting a whole ten grams in one meal! It felt like such a waste. I carefully restricted and calculated my fat intake for the remainder of the day so that I stayed below my goal. I only spread a small amount of peanut paste on my rice cakes, so that it would only add three grams to my daily quota. At some point, I eliminated the peanut paste and only allowed myself to use honey or Vegemite. No margarine, obviously.

I found a variety of yoghurt that only had one gram of fat per 100 grams and ate it as part of my breakfast every morning. I weighed out 100 grams one day, when no one else was at home to see, then counted how many semi-heaped teaspoons it took to serve out that amount. I needed to make sure I wasn't eating more than 100 grams, but also knew I couldn't weigh it every morning with Mum and Dad watching — Mum had seen me weighing something earlier and told me to stop. One week I only got seven or eight serves out of the 1 litre tub, instead of ten, and became excessively anxious because it meant that I had been having more than one gram of fat for breakfast. I was worried I had gained fat on my body. I also felt guilty for being greedy and eating more. I remember trying to hide my distress, while Mum and Dad made light of it, saying I must have enjoyed it.

I was still having trouble with my digestion, bloating whenever I ate, though it was much better than a few years earlier, thanks to the elimination of certain foods and my CFS improving. Maisie introduced us to the FODMAP[1] diet, wondering if an inability to digest certain sugars could be the cause of my gut problems. I followed the diet for about a month, however it was very restrictive, especially combined with my existing food intolerances. I was hungry and tired a lot of the time and the bloating didn't improve - if anything it was worse - though I think that was more due to hunger and the placebo effect of my monitoring it more closely. Although I was only on the diet for about a month, I lost weight and unintentionally decreased my food intake, which I found hard, mentally, to reverse when I stopped the FODMAP diet.

Year 12 is stressful for most, to varying degrees. I was almost certain I wanted to study music at university. My first choice of university had a very low

---

[1] Fermentable Oligosaccharides, Disaccharides, Monosaccharides And Polyols.

TER[2] cut-off, so I could have sailed through doing easy subjects. I wanted to do my best though, partly to keep my options open and partly just to see how well I could do. Eating properly would have helped. Not having CFS would also have helped. Because I had CFS I was only doing five subjects instead of the usual six, only four of which were TEE:[3] Chemistry, Applicable maths, English, TEE Music and non-TEE Music. Though my workload was lighter than it could have been, the combination of CFS, inadequate nutrition, stress about food and exercise, and perfectionism made that year incredibly stressful. A few years after high school, one of my closest friends commented that I had been pretty relaxed that year. I was shocked. I thought it had been obvious that I was close to breaking. But, looking back, I realised that I had never voiced my stress. I didn't have time. I was too tired. I just kept my head down and worked because that was the only way to get through.

That year Siena, one of my best friends, started a long struggle with clinical depression and anxiety. At that age, I thought depression was being sad all of the time. I didn't understand why some days she would get angry at me and ignore me. Or why, when she stayed up late baking cupcakes to give to everyone at school, and the next morning found that they had all collapsed, she threw them around the kitchen and was inconsolable for the whole day. I worried about Siena, so I sat with her during lunch or recess while she cried; tried to get through to her when she was silent; and roamed the school trying to find her when she ran away in tears, even though I was exhausted and my body was screaming at me to eat. I put her needs first because I thought it was more important than whatever I was going through. What was I going through anyway? Surely I didn't have anorexia. People with anorexia think they're fat. I didn't think that. I just wanted to be a bit thinner and didn't want fat on my tummy. Or my thighs or arms, come to think of it. But I knew I wasn't fat.

So I continued as I had been, gradually eating less and researching the macronutrients and calorie content of any food that didn't come in packaging, on which the nutritional information was printed. I developed a very real fear for a growing number of foods.

One day during a choir rehearsal our conductor, (who is a wonderful person and would never encourage unhealthy weight loss or negative body image),

---

[2] Tertiary Entrance Rank. This has been replaced by ATAR (Australian Tertiary Admissions Rank).

[3] Tertiary Entrance Exam. In Western Australia, students need to pass at least four TEE subjects to be considered for acceptance into a University.

retold a story from one of her conductor friends. After a concert this friend had conducted, a woman came up to her and said she had enjoyed watching her because she had absolutely no back fat. As the conductor, she had her back to the audience for most of the concert, so this woman had ample time to scrutinise her back. Our conductor was saying that she had never even thought about back fat, and was now hyper-aware of it, to the extent that she checked how her back looked when she tried on concert clothing. I had never considered back fat, nor had the rest of the choir. But now it was on my mind. I added back fat to my list of body checks. A few weeks later as I was standing, (standing, not sitting, to burn extra calories wherever I could), on the train platform one morning, on my way to school, I subtly checked the amount of fat on my hips, tummy and now back. I was so proud, when my fingers found bone just beneath the skin on my back, with no layer of fat, that I felt butterfly wings of excitement in my belly. Yes, I was cold, tired and hungry and I hated going for power walks when I was already exhausted, but at least I had no back fat!

At some point during that year, I started running the flat and downhill sections of my circuit instead of power walking. I felt I should be walking for at least 30 minutes, because of the "Find Thirty"[4] campaign, but it only took 15 minutes to power walk around the property and I didn't want to go around twice because I got bored, tired and also had to fit in homework and violin practice. I also reasoned that there was a long, steep, uphill section, which was far more gruelling than walking on flat ground. When I started running parts of the track I could do two laps in 20 minutes, which I figured would burn as many calories as walking it, even though it took less time. Though I worried I was wrong.

One day in winter it was dark when I got home from my after-school rehearsal and Mum said it wasn't safe for me to go for my walk. Skipping the exercise caused a huge amount of anxiety. I scrutinised my body in even greater detail the following morning, to check that missing my walk hadn't caused me to gain any fat. To ensure I wouldn't continue to miss my exercise on the days I got home late, I moved it to the morning. I knew this would seem strange and obsessive to Mum and Dad, who had already noticed that something was up. In an attempt to excuse my strange behaviour, I told them I enjoyed it and it energised me for the day. I knew they only half believed me, but they didn't stop me. Maybe they reasoned that a 20-minute walk wouldn't burn up too

---

[4] The Heart Foundation, funded by the Western Australian Department of Health, launched the Find Thirty campaign to encourage adults to be more active for good health.

much energy and hoped my obsessive behaviours would end when I finished school. Ironically it was also dark in the early mornings because I was getting up at 5:30 am. Dad came with me on those days, for safety. Because he was there I couldn't run, which made me anxious and worried. He didn't want to run and also said it was too dark to do so safely without the danger of tripping over loose rocks. Needless to say, I absolutely would have run if he hadn't been there, but I had to settle for power walking. He often commented on my fast pace and sometimes had to ask me to slow down.

I really felt the cold that winter. There were three main reasons:
1) I was losing body fat and muscle, which deprived me of my own natural, portable blanket of sorts.
2) I wasn't consuming enough energy to keep myself warm. I had put my body in an energy deficit, so it was forced to prioritise: organs were allocated just enough to keep working; my muscles took as much as they could for my obsessive exercise, unnecessary standing and general movement, such as walking between classes. My body kept me as warm as it could while also trying to keep me alive.
3) I was deliberately making myself cold to force my body to burn more energy as it worked to make me warmer. A friend had made an innocent comment the year before about how, if his body was cold, his metabolism would speed up to warm him. I remembered that and used it to my advantage — or so I thought. I have since been told that, unless we are exposed to much lower temperatures — colder than a Western Australian winter — the body doesn't burn much more energy keeping us warm. We just feel cold. Mum and Dad noticed that I was avoiding dressing warmly and that I was feeling the cold, even though I denied it. They forced me to wear tights to school under my skirt or shorts. I took them off as soon as I got to school and froze for the rest of the day.

Near the end of the year, I started two new treatments for CFS and, very quickly, one or both of them worked — we still don't know which. Some people suggested it was placebo, but I disagree. I had tried so many treatments and supplements by this point that I didn't have much hope that anything would help. However, after both treatments, I had much more energy and the brain fog caused by the CFS was gone. One night, I was studying for a chemistry test and was shocked that, at 9 o'clock, I wasn't at all tired, I understood everything, I could concentrate and I wasn't stressed. I topped the year on that test. It was the beginning of term four, just in time for my final exams. The CFS symptoms continued to gradually diminish as the term progressed and had probably disappeared by the end of the year. It's hard to know when exactly, because it was gradual and I had forgotten what a normal amount of energy felt like. I was also tired from not eating enough, which added to the confusion.

Mum had spoken a few times about her own experience restricting her food when she was in years 11 and 12. She had had an incompetent physics and chemistry teacher and resorted to teaching herself the curriculum. She started restricting her food and sometimes gave her dinner to the family dog if she was eating in her room while she worked. She lost a noticeable amount of weight during those two years, but felt ok about eating more when she finished her year 12 exams. We both hoped that would happen for me too. But it didn't. After exams finished I continued my exercise regime and couldn't convince myself to eat more. I tried and had long arguments with myself inside my head, but I didn't want to deal with the huge amount of anxiety and guilt I knew eating more would cause.

I was scared about missing my daily exercise when I went on leavers. I was actually relieved that Mum and Dad, who worried that a group of 17-year-olds staying in a house together with an unknown amount of alcohol was a recipe for all sorts of trouble, only allowed me to go for two days. It meant that I could exercise the morning I left and in the afternoon when I got back home. I went for a run as soon as I got home, telling Mum I had restless legs and was looking forward to it. In truth, I would have felt guilty and anxious until I had done it. I was also tired and wanted to do it before I became even more tired.

Gap Year

In January of the following year, I went on a music camp in Canberra. I had been to the same camp twice before and had a great time playing some of the most exciting and emotive orchestral repertoire written. Young musicians from all over Australia auditioned to be accepted into the camp, so the standard was high and I got to make friends from other states.

I was worried about what I would be given to eat at camp. We stayed in the university accommodation, which provided our meals. On previous camps, the kitchen had had trouble catering to my many food intolerances. This year I was more worried about being served food that was high in calories and fat. I knew I wouldn't be able to request the specific low-fat yoghurt I ate at home. I would need to be flexible and work with what they had. I felt as though I was feeling my way through a dangerous obstacle course blindfolded when I ate the yoghurt they gave me, because I couldn't read the nutritional information or measure it out. They gave me eggs for protein, which terrified me, because eggs contain fat. I was torn between wanting to eat all of the food they gave me — bigger portions than I served myself at home — because I was hungry and tired, and being scared to gain weight if I ate more. Being tired and hungry was preferable to being abused by the voice in my head for eating more.

Being on camp was triggering because it seemed that at least half the people there were thinner than me. This was probably largely due to me always being on the lookout for people who were thinner than me. I have since learnt that there are a lot of musicians who, due to the pressure of their profession and a predisposition for perfectionism, develop eating disorders, so who knows how many of the thin people I noticed were also restricting their food? Being around thin people made me even more conscious and critical of my body than I already was. I felt I was fat and disgusting; my yearning to lose weight became even stronger and all-consuming than when I was at home, which resulted in extra food restriction. Two friends with whom I spent a lot of time on that camp were also very slim. I don't know how our bodies actually compared but, at the time, I thought they were thinner than me, and would therefore think I was gross and not want to be around me. Those two people also became good friends very quickly that year, and were closer with each other than the rest of the group. I assumed this was because they were the thinnest and most beautiful people in our group and therefore belonged together.

I had decided to take a gap year before starting university. There were three reasons for this:
1) Mum recommended it because, as I had been so sick for most of high school, it was more stressful than it should have been, and I could probably do with a break.
2) I needed to earn money to buy a car so that I could drive to uni. We lived 13km from the nearest train station so I would need a car just to get there.
3) Adam had taken a gap year and he had lots of fun.

My plan work-wise was to audition for a casual position[5] with the state professional Symphony Orchestra, (SO), teach a few students privately, play whatever gigs I was offered and get a casual shop job. I did all of these things and loved playing with SO. I didn't love my job working in a frozen yoghurt kiosk, but I hadn't expected to. The 50 percent discount was nice though, and the eating disorder loved that I was on my feet all day. I deliberately walked back and forth while offering passersby yoghurt samples, instead of standing still, to burn more calories. Working also meant fewer breaks to eat, which meant I was forced to skip snacks. I didn't need to use my own willpower to stop myself from eating; I wasn't allowed a break and therefore couldn't eat.

I tried to catch up with friends as much as I could, but it was hard to coordinate with their university or work timetables. I didn't have my licence yet — I did three tests early on in the year and was so nervous I failed — so I was restricted to public transport and Mum and Dad's kindness. I continued my morning exercise and energy deficit food plan, which gradually became more restrictive as the year progressed. I wasn't aiming to eat less, but if I ate less one day, due to a lack of appetite or time, then I would be scared to return to my previous quota the following day. I had read that the metabolism slows down when a person eats less, so I worried that, after eating less one day, it would have slowed down, and eating more the next day would make me put on weight. So I gradually spiralled down.

I had been seeing Maisie, the GP, semi-regularly since I was 14, initially to help treat the CFS and then to keep an eye on things when I started losing weight. I had fortnightly, then weekly appointments, as my weight dropped. They were always stressful. Either my weight would have increased slightly and I would worry and feel guilty, or it would have dropped and I would be told off by Maisie and grilled about what I was eating.

---

[5] I would be called in to work if they needed a full string section or if a violinist was sick.

Eventually, I admitted that I was struggling emotionally and felt it would be helpful to talk to a psychologist. Maisie started trying to probe into my emotions, attempting to fill the role of psychologist herself. I was angry. I didn't want to talk to her about it; she was the bitch who told me off each week for losing weight. I wanted to talk to a psychologist, not her.

I continued to restrict my food and increase my exercise as the year progressed. I became more anxious around food and avoided sitting wherever possible. I had read online that we should only really be seated for a few hours each day, so I tried to follow that rule, even when my legs felt so weak I had to constantly focus on preventing them from folding beneath me. The only times I could sit without anxiety was if I was reading or eating. I tried to stand if I was talking to people or watching television, and read in the car as much as possible. I had read somewhere else online that sitting consumed less energy than standing, but reading used more than watching television or doing nothing.

In April, Maisie recommended I start taking anti-anxiety medication to help me eat more. I didn't want to for two reasons:
1) I worried that they might work so well that I felt ok about eating more and gaining weight, which terrified me.
2) She mentioned that I may feel nauseous during the first few days of taking them. I was worried that might stop me from doing my morning exercise if it was bad.

I said I didn't want to, but Mum and Dad wanted me to try anything that might help. I wasn't yet 18, so legally they could decide for me, especially as Maisie could argue that I wasn't of sound mind. Dad said they wouldn't play the "under 18 card," but if I didn't agree to take the anti-depressants they would stop driving me to the train station. This meant I wouldn't be able to get to work, let alone see my friends. I took the lesser of two evils — the anti-anxiety tablets. At least I could still get out of the house, where I could exercise and restrict my food. I didn't end up experiencing any nausea, but they didn't help my anxiety either.

They did sink me into a pit of all-consuming despair for a few days though, a week after I started taking them. I was angry, since they were meant to help with depression, and it came during a weekend that should have been fun. Mum, Dad, my friend Lucy, and I had gone to Fairbridge Festival, which was usually my favourite weekend of the year. It's a music festival held on a big rural property about an hour's drive from our house. I had been to the festival a few times as a child, when it was much smaller, but it had since grown to accommodate about ten venues, acts from around the world, a long road lined with interesting market stalls, an assortment of food trucks and a variety of activities for children and adults throughout the day. A lot of festival-goers camped overnight in the paddocks onsite, using the opportunity to luxuriate in the relaxed atmosphere and feeling of community. We drove home each night, because it wasn't too far, and Mum and Dad felt the drive was worth it for a proper bed and a warm shower.

I was at my lowest on the last day of the festival. It was the most depressed I had ever felt, but it was confusing because I wasn't feeling depressed about anything in particular. Everything just seemed so hopeless. I had never felt so despondent and miserable, which is ironic, since I had been slowly starving myself for over a year by this point. By early afternoon, I couldn't deal with being with Lucy anymore — not because it was her; I wasn't up to being with anyone. I went to the toilet and then walked off on my own. About ten minutes later, she sent me a text message:

'Lo?

I ignored it. I couldn't pretend to be ok anymore. I needed to be alone. We found each other by chance a few hours later. By the last night of the festival, I was feeling a tiny bit more positive, but I was also embarrassed and worried about how Lucy had perceived the situation, and if it had been awkward for her.

A few weeks later, Maisie said I needed to stop running because it was putting too much stress on my heart. When I said I enjoyed the exercise in the morning, she said I could go for a gentle walk. In my mind, Maisie was being mean for trying to stop me from losing weight. How could running be bad for me anyway? I walked until I rounded the corner of the driveway, in case Mum or Dad was watching, and then started jogging. A few weeks later, Mum started sitting outside in the cold while I went for my "walk." She told me she was worried I might collapse and wanted to make sure I came back. I was annoyed at her for trying to make me feel guilty, and deliberately didn't speak to her when I walked past her sitting on the bench.

It was around that time that I heard strange vocal sounds coming from Mum and Dad's bedroom one night. It sounded like one of them was either in pain or crying, so I went to check if everything was ok. Mum was sobbing and Dad was trying to comfort her.
"What's wrong?" I asked.
"Mum's just a bit sad, it's ok," Dad replied.
"Why? What's happened?"

"Worried about you," Mum choked out.
"Why?" I knew the answer, but I didn't want to hear it.
"Don't... want... to... lose... you," Mum forced out between sobs.
"It's ok, I'm going to be ok." I was trying to believe it myself. I wouldn't let myself get too far.
"Don't... want... you... to... die."
"I won't Mum, I won't. I'm going to be ok." Seeing Mum in such a state scared me. I didn't want her to be hurting because of me. But nor did I know how I could possibly convince myself to eat more. Mum calmed down a bit — or pretended to for my sake — and I went back to bed.

I hadn't known what I wanted for my 18th. Mum and Dad said that, as it's a milestone age, I could have a bigger present and party. Adam had asked for a new bed, as we had both had the same beds since we transitioned from the cot. Mum and Dad assumed I would want the same, but I had no interest in a bed.

At some point, the idea of having my own dog popped into my head. It would be wonderful to have a dog that was just mine, not the family's; my own little buddy. I wasn't sure what Mum and Dad would think, but they thought it was a great idea — Mum was possibly more excited than I was. After reading about different crossbreeds on the Harry's Practice website, I decided to get a toy Cavoodle.[6] They're intelligent, social, loving and I wanted a dog that was small enough for me to pick up and cuddle. I named him Noddy after my favourite cartoon when I was a child.

I thought it would be nice to take Noddy on my run/walks in the morning. I hadn't thought it through too well though. Little Noddy was far too small to keep up with me. He also got tired very quickly because he was only eight weeks old. I ended up picking him up and power-walking the rest of the way, which made me anxious for the rest of the day because I hadn't run the flat sections. Believe me, I tried, but Noddy didn't like being jolted around so I stopped for his sake. My guilt at not running and the fear of gaining weight as a result made it a tough decision — the eating disorder or Noddy's comfort. I'm glad I chose Noddy.

(BMI)

Not long after I turned 18, my BMI dropped below 15

---

[6] At the time, I didn't know dog shelters are always desperate for people to adopt abandoned dogs, otherwise I would have done that instead.

Maisie sighed and, as she looked from her calculator, I could see tears in her eyes.
"Your BMI is now less than 15. We're going to have to call Heathgrove Hospital and see if they have a bed for you."
My stomach dropped. I tried to sound confident as I protested. "You can't force me to go, I'm over 18."
"Well, if your BMI is under 15 and you refuse hospitalisation, you can be sectioned under the Mental Health Act. You would be taken to Graylands Hospital[7] until a bed becomes available at Heathgrove. And let me tell you, Graylands is not a place you want to be."
I hadn't realised there was a law that could force hospitalisation.
Maisie continued, unnecessarily I felt. "If you resist being taken to hospital, the police will come to your house and will be permitted to handcuff you, if they feel it is necessary. And that will go on your criminal record."
She seemed so smug and unsympathetic. Maybe she thought I was vain or unnecessarily stubborn, which is a common view of people with anorexia. I later learned that medical students only spend a few hours learning about eating disorders at university. Most of what Maisie was taught, at least 30 years earlier, has since been disproven.

Heathgrove is only one hospital in Perth with an inpatient program for eating disorders, so we were told we would have to wait about a week for a bed to become available. In the meantime, the hospital offered us an appointment with Dr P, the psychiatrist in charge of the eating disorders ward. Maisie said he was very good, so I went to the appointment with a positive mindset.

"So why are you here?" Dr P asked abruptly, once we were seated.
I looked to Mum and Dad to answer. I felt awkward talking about anything to do with my emotions, nor didn't understand why he was asking. He headed up the eating disorders program there; wasn't it obvious?
"No, I want to know why *you* think you're here," he patronised, as though I was being naughty.
"I think... people say... my doctor... I think I might have Anorexia...?" I mumbled.
After my embarrassing admission, I was permitted to sit and nod for the remainder of the appointment, as Dr P described the treatment program with a complete lack of empathy or sensitivity.

---

[7] A public mental health in-patient facility.

I assumed I was perceiving things differently because I was scared to eat more and gain weight. However, once we were out of the building, Dad said "Was it just me or was he incredibly rude and unfriendly?"
Mum agreed and I was relieved. We complained about him on the way home, but for some reason maintained the belief that going to hospital would result in my recovery.

I was playing with SO that week and had gone to see Dr P straight after rehearsal. During the appointment, he said I needed to take it easy because my heart had shrunk and would be quite weak. I took this to mean no exercise, which was terrifying.
"Hannah has work this week playing with an orchestra. Should she stop that?" Dad asked.
"Yes. All that moving about will be putting strain on her heart," Dr P replied.
"She's meant to be performing this weekend. Is she ok to do that or should she pull out?"
"No, she needs to stop right away." He turned to me. "Your heart is very weak. It's not safe for you to do much more than sit and read, ok?"
I was gutted. I had been especially excited for this concert, because Richard Tognetti was conducting, and would also be performing a Concerto with the orchestra. This was neither the first nor the last of many things I would miss out on due to anorexia nervosa (AN).

Heathgrove

The mental health clinic at Heathgrove Hospital called about a week later to inform us that a bed had become available. I was in two minds about going to hospital. I was terrified of eating more and being recovered — being happy at a higher (healthy) weight was a state of being for which I simultaneously yearned and found revolting. The thought of being at a higher weight in my current mindset was scary and repulsive, so even though I wanted to believe that I could accept myself at that weight, I found the idea of acceptance disgusting. However, hospitals are meant to make you well again, right? And Maisie had said Heathgrove was a good place to go. While her own attempts to treat my food restriction had been harmful, I still believed that, as a doctor, she would have reliable intel on the hospital's treatment program. I figured they must have really good psychologists and methods that would help me see things differently, so I would be able to eat without feeling guilty and hating myself.

I was also proud that I needed to go to hospital, that I had been so good at losing weight that I had made myself sick enough to need hospitalisation. It was truly a triumph to have demonstrated such willpower when exercising and restricting food. Though I didn't want to die, I felt that dying from AN would be the ultimate triumph, a hero's death. I understood why warriors in books and movies set in ancient times wanted "a hero's death" on the battlefield. The other main positive, in my mind, about hospital was that I would find out who my true friends were. Surely only my true friends would want to visit me. I was so insecure I doubted that anyone liked me very much. I felt my friends endured my presence but wouldn't miss me if I wasn't around. This would put my friendships to the test.

The first few hours in hospital were a combination of scary and surreal. I had an interview in my room with Karen, the nurse who was assigned to me for the afternoon. The only thing I remember was her asking if I had a history of violence.
I chuckled. "Well when I was —" I saw her look up, worried, until I continued "— about three, apparently I almost strangled my older brother."
When Mum and Dad laughed, she gave a small, forced, chuckle. She continued to look worried and confused until Mum and Dad explained the story.

Everyone on the eating disorder program ate together, at set times. At dinner, my first meal, the rest of the group was very friendly. I automatically compared myself to the smaller patients and felt I wasn't thin enough. I felt ok about eating though, because everyone else was and they were still very slim.

After each main meal, we had to sit for half an hour in the lounge. This was partly to mimic real life, in which people might sit and chat after a meal, but mostly to stop anyone from purging or exercising.
"What are you in for?" One girl asked, when we were all seated on the couches.
I was unsure what she meant at first. Wasn't it obvious? We were all in the ED program.
"Anorexia," I mumbled self-consciously — I still hate the word; it feels so abrasive with the 'x.' For the next 30 minutes, the rest of the group asked me about myself and answered my questions about the hospital. I learned quickly that some of the others were much sicker than I was and had been so for longer, with multiple hospital admissions. The ED voice in my head told me I wasn't sick enough and needed to do better.

Everyone in the ED group was kind and welcoming. I came to learn that this is true of almost everyone with an ED. Those who aren't outwardly warm usually are inside. It is the illness, and often harmful, involuntary "treatment," that has made them rigid, scared, jaded or introverted, and which may cause them to seem abrupt or cold. In truth, they are consumed with self-hatred and are doing their best just to get through each day. And so, though we all had a screaming demon inside our heads, we tried to help and support anyone in the group who was having a particularly bad day, and commiserated after difficult meals.

There must have been about 20 other patients in the mental health ward aside from our group, which numbered around ten, give or take a few depending on the day. We had three meals and three snacks together every day in the dining room, supervised by two nurses, one at each end of the table. The other patients on the ward could eat whenever and wherever they wanted, as long as they didn't miss the food trolley. Our meals were timed, to teach those of us who try to make meals last as long as possible, to savour the food, to eat at a normal pace. Others in the group felt anxious at meals and wanted them to be over as soon as possible. Everyone felt this balancing act. None of us wanted to be the first to finish, for fear that everyone else would think we were greedy — though there was one girl who found meal times so stressful that she ate as fast as she could and spent the rest of the time fidgeting, desperate to get out of the dining room. However, no one didn't want to be last, to have everyone watching us eat, and be the only person stopping those who felt anxious from leaving the table. We also couldn't risk not having finished our food at the end of the time limit, as anything left un-eaten would be written in our notes.

The nurses sat at the table with us for a few reasons. Someone had to time the meal and it was more normal for them to sit with us than time us while watching from the corner, or put a stopwatch on the table. They also wanted to normalise the whole experience of eating, with casual conversation and no diet talk. Most of them meant well, but having them there often made everyone more anxious, because it was a reminder of where we were and what we were doing. Lastly, and most importantly, they were there to check our plates afterwards to see what we had left uneaten, and to make sure we didn't hide or throw away any food.

In my first week, I saw another girl do a little trick with her butter that made it look like she had used half of it, when in fact she hadn't used any. I use this trick for the remainder of my stay. Another friend told me that, when he ordered a muesli bar for his snack, he would bring a similar bar in his pocket, which had ten calories less, and swap them when no one was looking. It was the same brand so the nurses never realised. I developed my own tricks to hide unused salad dressing and other food I was scared to eat, though I had to be very careful because some nurses watched very closely.

One girl, Maeve, was particularly skilled at hiding food. She was very sick, physically and mentally, and terrified to eat. Maeve would hide food in her baggy sleeves before transferring it into her shoes at most meals. One day after lunch, another patient, Talia, told the nurse that she had seen Maeve hiding food in her shoes. I'm not sure why Talia dobbed her in. I agree that the nurses needed to be made aware, for Maeve's health, however, I felt Talia's action was driven more by jealousy than goodwill. Perhaps she yearned for Maeve's sleight of hand, or her own ED was berating her for not being as dedicated to avoiding food as Maeve obviously was. Talia said it was unfair on the rest of us, for Maeve to get away with hiding her food, but I disagreed; we all had our little tricks for hiding small amounts of food. Maeve was called out from the lounge where we were sitting and searched. It didn't take the nurses long to find the hidden food. They watched her like a hawk at meals after that and sometimes brought an extra nurse to the table. I was quietly glad, because it was easier for me to hide food for the next few days, while the nurses were focusing on Maeve.

At the end of my first week one girl, who I hadn't spoken to much, came to my room to give me a big fluffy pink ball. She explained that it was a travelling ball and each owner passed it on when they were discharged, usually to someone who was struggling or needed some extra love — or something fluffy to hug. It was her last day and she thought that, as I was new, I probably needed it. I can't say that having the ball helped me, but it was lovely of her to choose me and I did feel a bit special, which may have helped in a small way.

Most of the time the ball sat in my room and was sometimes the topic of conversation when friends or family visited. For a few days I used it to exercise. I jogged on the spot and side-stepped while kicking it against the wall. I figured it would get my heart rate up and be a bit of fun. I was kicking it hard, because I wanted to work my leg muscles. After two or three days of this, Harry, whose room was on the other side of the wall into which I had been kicking the ball, sidled up to me while we were waiting outside the dining room for a meal.
"Have you been exercising in your room?" He asked quietly.
I didn't know what to say. Would he tell the nurses? Reading the panic on my face, he rephrased his question.
"Have you been doing anything that would make a thumping sound?"
"Oh yeah I've got this fluffy ball… I kick it against the wall when I'm bored," I mumbled, in an attempt to make it sound innocent.
Harry nodded knowingly.
"Because I can hear it—"
"Oh sorry. I didn't realise it was loud. I can stop—"
"No, it's ok, it doesn't bother me. But if I can hear it, they can probably hear it in the nurses' station. You want to be careful…"
"Oh, gosh, thank you. I assumed it would be quiet enough…"
I still appreciate Harry's warning. I stopped my weak excuse for soccer practice and found a quieter form of exercise.

On weekdays we had two 90-minute group therapy sessions. I found the group setting difficult to navigate. I never knew how much of myself to reveal, scared to share my darkest thoughts with people I had only just met. I worried they would think there was something intrinsically wrong with me, or that I wasn't as dedicated to my ED as they were. Talking as a group also meant no one received more than a few minutes of individual attention, even if they didn't mind sharing their private thoughts with the group. Sometimes it was good just to talk things though, and it filled the time. I found art therapy to be the most helpful. We also did occupational therapy, general group therapy, nutrition education and a particularly boring and pointless session called 'Me and My Family'.

I think 'Me and My Family' was aimed at people whose families had a part in causing or exacerbating their eating disorder, or who were generally unsupportive. I'm not aware of anyone who found it helpful though. We all dreaded Thursday afternoons, usually sitting in awkward silence while the woman — was she even a psych? Who knows — asked us leading questions that no one understood or related to. One day she got us to assume specific poses of family members, based on the descriptions she read out, as though they were caught frozen in motion, or posing for a family portrait. We were all confused and embarrassed at having the rest of the group looking at us. Afterwards, she tried to lead a discussion about the characters in the families, in the hope that someone would identify with them. None of us did and she became forceful, asking people directly what they thought. That was probably the worst session and we were all bewildered afterwards.

When I left I gave the fluffy, pink ball to Maeve, with whom I had had a lot of good chats. She left a few weeks after I arrived, not because she was ready, but because she was struggling a lot, hardly eating and, for some reason, her psychiatrist allowed her to leave. A few weeks later, she came back, and we became good friends. Maeve was even sicker when she came back, having returned to her restrictive eating habits while she was at home — hence the food-hiding — so I decided she was a good recipient for the ball.

After Heathgrove

Going back into the real world after hospital was strange. I didn't feel ready. "Well, no one ever feels ready, do they?" Dr P said briskly. "You just need to go for it. Remember, moving forward."[8]
I just had to take the plunge. That made sense.
"Also, we aah need your bed for another patient. There was a misunderstanding and she's come a day early, so…" he left the sentence hanging.
Well, that decided it. Nice to know I was more than just a number…

We went out to dinner that night. I'm not sure if Mum and Dad intended it as a celebration or didn't want us to have dinner too late, as I was discharged in the evening. In a way it was exciting to be out, but I felt overwhelmed by the number of people in the restaurant. I felt self-conscious of my size and compared myself to Adam and the diners.

I felt awkward going back to work and seeing people again too. Partly because it took a little while to get used to going out again and partly because I wondered if people who knew me would notice that I had gained weight. I didn't know who had been told that I had been in hospital having treatment for AN, or what they thought about it. Everyone who knew was supportive, but I'm a very private person and didn't want anyone but close friends and family to know.

A few weeks after I left Heathgrove, Mum and I went to a performance Adam was in at uni[9] and saw Peter, his violin teacher, with whom I had had a few lessons before I went to hospital. Peter knew I had been in hospital and had called me while I was there, which I had really appreciated.
"It's wonderful to see you, that you're out," he said.
"Thanks," I saw awkwardly, embarrassed at the reference to my mental health.
"You're looking well, and not very different."
I nodded and offered a small smile, unsure how to respond.
"Just a bit fatter," he chuckled.
I knew he meant well, so I pretended to laugh along with him. As soon as Peter was gone, Mum turned to me.

---

[8] Julia Gillard ousted Kevin Rudd while I was in Heathgrove and was often heard saying "Moving Forward" in speeches, which Dr P had adopted when talking about our recovery.

[9] He did a Bachelor of Music, majoring in violin performance.

"Don't worry, you're not fat! He didn't mean you're fat."

(Weight and calories)

Before I had even left hospital, I decided I would lose three kilos as fast as possible, then maintain that weight — 47kg. I chose 47kg because I had held that weight for a while the previous year, before spiralling down further, and had been able to tolerate my body at that size. I chose my own meals when I got out of hospital, except dinner, which we ate together as a family, so I decreased my daily intake to 1200 calories — I had read that my metabolism would slow down if I ate less than that - and went for a half-hour brisk walk each day. I knew alarm bells would go off in Mum and Dad's heads if I started running again. I figured that my metabolism would be faster than usual after eating so many calories in hospital, so if I cut back my calories abruptly, it would stay fast for a while and I would lose weight quickly — this was based on what little information I had managed to find on the internet. I don't know how long it took for my metabolism to slow down, but I lost a kilo a week.

I was proud of what I saw as an achievement, however Dr P, Mum and Dad were not. Even without knowing my weight, Mum and Dad knew I wasn't eating enough because they saw most of my meals. I thought Dr P would be impressed when he weighed me at my first appointment after leaving Heathgrove, such was the extent of my delusion.

Though I had lost weight as fast as I had gained it in hospital, a clear sign that I had reverted to my disordered habits, Dr P directed the conversation to my acne.
"Would you like a prescription for Roaccutane?" He asked.
"It's not that bad, is it?" I asked, self-consciously. I knew Roaccutane was one of the strongest acne medications.
"Weeeell you've got quite a lot of pimples and I can also see some scarring, which won't go away. Best to deal with it now so you don't get more scars."
Great thing to say to someone with such terrible self-esteem they starved themselves until their heart was close to giving out. I knew it wasn't uncommon for Roaccutane to cause depression, but Mum soon found out it can also cause anorexia. Different to anorexia nervosa, anorexia is a loss of appetite. Not a helpful symptom for someone battling AN. Needless to say, I never took Roaccutane, but his suggestion still baffles me.

A few weeks after I left Heathgrove, my name finally reached the top of the waiting list at the Centre for Clinical Interventions (CCI) which, at the time, was the best place for outpatient ED treatment. There is always a long waiting list because it is free and there aren't enough psychologists trained in ED to cater to the high demand of patients. As I had lost weight so fast, Mum and Dad wanted to take control of my meals[10] straight away, but Adelle, the psychologist CCI had assigned to me, convinced them to give me the opportunity to prove that I could gain the weight back myself first.

I really did my best. The ED voice was screaming at me not to eat more but I knew that, if I didn't, Mum and Dad would take over and make me do it anyway. I started drinking Fortijuice, the high-calorie drinks I drank in hospital, with my main meals, but I also decreased the calories in the meal to balance it out. I probably increased my overall intake a small amount, but not enough to gain any weight. I was scared to eat more because I knew I would hate myself at a higher weight. They gave me four weeks to gain back the weight I had lost. At the end of that time, I had only maintained my weight, so Mum and Dad took full control of my meals.

I don't remember much of this time. There were lots of arguments between me, Mum and Dad, and I hated seeing my weight go up. They monitored all of my meals, which meant meeting with them during breaks at SO and when I was out with friends, which was awkward.

When I had a belated joint birthday party with Michael, one of my closest school friends, Mum and Dad wouldn't let me choose what I wanted to eat, even for one night. I was furious. I had to eat the dinner they had made for me, instead of the party food I had enjoyed planning and cooking. They said I could have party food as well, but why on earth would I willingly eat extra? I felt they must have had no understanding of what I was feeling if they thought the ED would allow me to eat extra food.

Other than the birthday party I only have vague memories of eventually going along with the meals, even though I hated them, Mum and Dad, and myself; family therapy, which was unproductive and traumatic; getting my period for the first time in my life; and gradually being handed back control of my meals. By the time I started university, I was allowed to eat all but breakfast and dinner by myself.

In January the following year, some friends invited me to go to the movies with them. Rosie, the friend who had organised the get-together, wanted to see Black Swan.

---

[10] For them, this meant choosing all of my meals and snacks and watching me eat, so I couldn't hide or throw away any food.

"We're going to see a ballet movie," said Gilbert, the only male in the group, in disgust.
I had seen the trailer and it looked interesting. We hadn't been watching for long when we realised it is anything but a girly ballet movie. I later found out that the genre is 'Psychological Thriller.'

I maintain to this day that the movie is very well made. I felt uneasy watching it and discovered later that my friends felt the same. The topic was too close to home for me. A few times it is hinted that Nina, the main character, has a history of disordered eating and bulimia, which has resulted in a strained and tense relationship with her mother. In one scene the mother tries to make Nina eat a piece of cake, which she declines. Nina tries to make excuses without causing an argument, but the mother gets angry and starts yelling at her. Another theme throughout the movie is the company director's attempts to help Nina let go of her perfectionism and to be more expressive in her dancing. I had been having similar conversations with Peter about my violin playing — though that is where the similarity ends; Peter never bullied, pressured or sexually assaulted me!

As I sat in the dark theatre surrounded by people, I began to feel more and more uncomfortable, and slightly claustrophobic. I just wanted the movie to finish. I felt trapped. I wanted to leave but didn't want to bother anyone by pushing past them. One moment I was watching the scene in which Nina peels back the skin from around her fingernail; the next my friends were leaning over me, asking if I was ok. I didn't know what had happened.
"You had a seizure!" Gilbert whispered.
"What?"
"Do you need some fresh air?"
"I'll take her outside."
"I'm ok, I can go by myself. You don't want to miss the movie," I protested groggily.
"It's ok. Come on."
I walked out of the cinema with Siena, and she led me to the bathroom. I still didn't know what had happened. I felt dizzy and groggy, as though I had dozed off.

I felt slightly better after washing my face. I wasn't looking forward to watching the rest of the movie, but I didn't want Siena to miss out, since she had bought a ticket. When we came out of the bathroom, the rest of the group — Rosie, Mel and Gilbert — were waiting.
"Are you ok?" Rosie asked.
"I think so. Just kinda groggy, I dunno. What happened?" I asked.

"You just suddenly went limp. Then you started breathing really loud, then it looked like you were having a fit for a few seconds. Then you opened your eyes," Gilbert said matter-of-factly.
Odd, I thought. I would tell Mum and Dad when they came to pick me up.
"Do you want us to take you to the hospital?" Gilbert asked.
"One of us can drive you," Rosie offered.
"Nah I'm fine. Let's go back in. I don't want you to miss the movie." I was just a bit tired. I didn't need to go to hospital.
"Now you have to be honest about this, it's really important. Has anything like this happened to you before?" Gilbert asked seriously.
"No." I hadn't fainted since I was ten.
Gilbert and Rosie in particular were quite worried, and kept trying to convince me that what had happened was potentially serious and that I should go to a hospital. Eventually I agreed to go. I still felt bad that they would all miss the end of the movie. A few days later, they told me they were grateful for an excuse to leave, as they had also been feeling uncomfortable.

While Mel drove us to Royal Perth Hospital, I called Mum and Dad to tell them what had happened. They met us in the Emergency Department. I told the nurses and doctors in Emergency what had happened, with some help from Gilbert and Rosie, and they did some blood tests. The results determined that I hadn't had a seizure. At the time, I was slightly disappointed; a seizure was more interesting than fainting. The doctor explained that I had probably fainted because I was feeling tense and claustrophobic. Usually, when people faint, they fall to the ground, bringing their brain level with their heart. However, as I was already sitting, my brain remained above my heart. My body then fitted in an attempt to bring my brain lower, but this didn't work and, for some reason, I regained consciousness. In short, I was physically fine, but still very troubled emotionally.

Being at uni was positive in that I was with my friends a lot, studying something I mostly enjoyed, and with a purpose. But I was incredibly insecure about my appearance, and being around others my age, who I assumed were judging me based on my weight — I was still below the healthy BMI range but I felt enormous — meant I always felt self-conscious. One friend in particular was, and still is, a tiny human. So thin. To this day I wonder if she has some form of disordered eating. I used to feel huge and ugly around her and had no idea why she wanted to be friends with me.

I wanted to have full control of all my meals. Partly because I felt I should at that age; partly to have the freedom to go out with friends; but mainly because I wanted to lose weight. I kept asking Adelle about it — at this point we were doing family therapy every second week and individual sessions every other — and eventually, she suggested another trial. I had a month to show I could take charge of my meals and not lose weight. If I succeeded I could continue to make my own food choices and eat without supervision. She also suggested setting a minimum weight to which I could drop during that month, since weight fluctuates and I had been eating more than most people to maintain my current weight.

I knew it was my chance to prove I could do it on my own, but I was also desperate to lose weight. My discomfort, self-consciousness and self-loathing in that bigger body was all-consuming. I was disgusted with myself and assumed everyone who saw me was too. I decided to lose weight as fast as I could, while staying just above the minimum weight we had set. Then I could keep control but not look and feel quite so horrible.

Mum and Dad soon noticed that my intake had dropped. They had been watching me like a hawk whenever I ate for a few years. It was a stressful month because I knew they were watching me closely while pretending they weren't. They also made comments, which they attempted to veil as innocent remarks, about how much I was eating. I dropped about a kilo each week, so I was on track to reach the minimum weight Adelle had set by the end of the month — success! The ED voice was proud.

When Adelle weighed me, I was just above the minimum. I thought I was safe and set to go. Mum and Dad had other plans. They told Adelle that I had drastically cut back my intake and clearly set out to lose weight. It was true, but I hadn't dropped below the minimum. That was the deal! Mum and Dad told me they were going to take back full control of my meals. They had gone back on their word — to be fair, so had I, but I had stayed above that minimum weight! — but I didn't have much choice. They were my parents, I still lived at home, I didn't have my driver's license yet and the train station was about 13 kilometres away, so there wasn't much I could do.

During the appointment, Mum and Dad told Adelle and me that they had decided to treat me using the Maudsley method.[11] They also wanted to get me to a higher weight than I had been before the one-month trial. They wondered if my body's optimum weight was higher than we had originally thought, and that my brain hadn't healed because I had never reached that weight. Their plan was the result of hundreds of hours of research, reading academic papers

---

[11] It's a form of Family Based Therapy, considered by many professionals to be one of the most effective treatment models. Google it.

and speaking with other carers on online forums. I understand and agree with this theory — it has been scientifically proven — however, it ignores the emotional aspect. If the emotional issues that triggered the eating disorder aren't resolved, the patient won't fully recover. I tried to explain this to Mum and Dad, but they didn't believe me. They said it was the eating disorder trying to fool them, or that I only believed that because my brain wasn't healed. They thought all my worries would go away when I had been at a higher weight long enough for my brain to heal. We spent the rest of the appointment arguing and reached no resolution.

Straight after the appointment with Adelle, we went to Adam's house. He had been in Europe for about 10 weeks with his girlfriend and had flown in that afternoon. When I hugged him I burst into tears. I tried not to, because I didn't want him to have to deal with my problems when he'd just arrived home to what should have been a happy reunion, and was probably jet-lagged. "Sorry, I'm sorry, I didn't want to do this," I repeated, through my tears and snot. "It's ok," he said, as he hugged me, even though he didn't know why I was crying — though he probably had an idea.

Maudsley

The next ten months were probably the most horrible time of my life to date — worse than when I was starving myself and exercising at every opportunity. All of my meals were chosen by Mum or Dad and they watched me the entire time I was eating. No exceptions.

Instead of using Fortijuice to get in extra calories, Mum and Dad made me eat lots of oily, energy-dense food. I think this was because they wanted my diet to contain a higher fat content than the drinks would provide, as this would apparently help my brain heal. Sometimes I felt sick from eating so much rich food. The volume of food meant I was rarely hungry, but I ate because I knew there was no other option.

Breakfast was the biggest meal. I had a few thick pancakes, which were fried in oil twice, then spread with butter and honey or maple syrup; scrambled eggs with cheese, swimming in oil; and a smoothie made with yoghurt, fruit, seeds, nuts, honey and oil. Mum always tried to pour in the oil when I was out of the room, but one day I caught her, and what I had suspected was confirmed. I was angry they were forcing me to eat such a ludicrous amount for breakfast. They would never have let me eat a meal so high in fat and sugar every day a few years earlier.

For morning and afternoon tea, dessert and supper, they gave me some sort of cake, slice, muffin, or creamy yoghurt, everything chosen for its high fat and calorie content. Most of the food was quite nice, I have to admit, but I didn't let on at the time. I didn't want to give Mum and Dad the pleasure of seeing me enjoy food. I wanted to make Maudsley as hard for them as possible, even though I could never make them suffer as much as I was. I found some of their recipe pages and saw that Mum had written down how many calories and grams of fat in each portion. Lunch and dinner were relatively normal; some sort of curry or pasta, though always a generous serving.

I was eating much more than was normal, even for a growing teenage boy. I tried calculating my daily calories many times, but I never knew exactly how much oil went into everything, especially breakfast. At every opportunity, I reminded Mum and Dad that I was eating much more than either of them, but they always said I needed to, for my brain to heal. They often added, patronisingly, that food was my medicine and they were doing this because they loved me. That always made my blood boil.

We had countless stand-offs and arguments, particularly in the first month or two. There was a lot of yelling and uncontrollable sobbing on my part. Sometimes we sat at the table for hours after they had finished their dinner while I refused to eat something. Eventually, I decided it wasn't worth the time. I had tested them and learnt that they wouldn't back down. I loathed Mum and Dad at every meal — while simultaneously hating that I hated them, and not wanting to hate them — but decided it was better to just eat and get away from them than cause a fuss to annoy them.

Adam decided to move home when he found out what was involved in Maudsley and how unhappy I was. I will always be grateful to him for his selflessness. He had been living with his best friend close to the city, so moving home meant living further away from his friends and work, which meant spending more on petrol, while still paying rent — he still slept at the rental every few nights if he had an early morning or late night. He wasn't home a lot because he still had a life to live, but it was much better when he was there. Mum and Dad decided to enforce half an hour of family time after dinner, in an attempt to repair and build our relationship. We would either play a game or chat. I found it patronising and it felt like an additional punishment, even though I understood their aim. I was glad when Adam was there.

Because I was at uni for most of the day, Mum and Dad came in to eat with me. They didn't seem to understand quite how humiliating this was for me. I didn't want to tell my friends I had an eating disorder, another thing Mum and Dad didn't understand. In my opinion, having an eating disorder is a very personal issue, so I told as few people as possible. Michael was the only friend at uni who knew. I tried to hide from my other friends that I was having lunch with my parents, which was very hard. Mum and Dad made no effort to be discreet when they came to uni, even though I explained my feelings to them many times. They always said it was the eating disorder "thriving on secrecy" that was driving my decision and that I was lying when I explained my reasons. They were annoyed that I insisted on meeting them in their car, instead of at the cafe, and that sometimes I was late meeting them because I was trying to find an excuse to leave my friends. I often said I was going to practise, before sneaking away to meet Mum or Dad.

Once I walked around with some friends for 20 minutes or more, hoping they would stop following me so I could meet Mum. She kept messaging and calling, before coming into the music building to look for me. She found us in the foyer and glared at me from the balcony above. She looked ready to march over and grab me, thinking I had been purposefully avoiding her — as if I thought that would work after months of their obsessive monitoring.

After the first few months, Mum and Dad sometimes allowed Adam or my grandparents to monitor a meal or snack if they were available and willing. I obviously preferred anyone to Mum and Dad, and they knew that. Though I was angry at them for making me so unhappy, I also knew that they were only adhering so strictly to the Maudsley regime because they desperately wanted me to be well and happy. They weren't doing it as punishment, so if they could make it easier for me, they would.

When Michael asked if he could be one of the people Mum and Dad trusted to monitor my eating, they agreed — though Dad had a serious talk with him and made it very clear that, if I didn't finish my food, they would expect him to report back to them. I am still incredibly grateful to Michael, for being so mature, caring and selfless. He was willing to have a deep and potentially awkward discussion with Dad, and possibly put himself in a difficult position with me if I didn't eat, to help remove some of the distress from my life. He still thinks his offer was the obvious thing for him to do, as a friend. We used to eat together most of the time before I started Maudsley, and he was happy to hang out again.

Michael monitored a lot of my meals after that. It gave me much more freedom, allowing me to be out with friends during meal times if he was there. I never made a fuss about my food because I didn't want to put him in an uncomfortable position.

There was one time, however, when Michael had to "report" me to Mum and Dad. They had started giving me nuts and dried fruit as a snack sometimes and, as Michael would be monitoring it, I had taken the container of food to uni. I was always on the lookout for ways to decrease my food intake — and am also not a huge fan of Brazil nuts, which they had given me. I had considered throwing away portions of food on the way to uni before — if Mum or Dad were meeting me they would bring the food, but if I was eating with Michael I would bring it — but they always gave me pre-sealed food, like small yoghurts. On the way to uni, I took about half of the nuts and dried fruit out of the container and threw them away. I wondered if they had told Michael how much they had put in the container, but didn't think even they would be that pedantic. When I opened the container to eat, I thought Michael looked unsure for a moment, but then the moment was over. I told myself I had imagined or misinterpreted it. When I noticed him sending a text as I was eating, I wondered if Mum and Dad had actually specified the amount of food, and he had noticed that it was less. Surely not. Apparently, they had. When Mum met me for lunch that day she brought a slice of cake along with with my normal meal.

"Why do I have to eat that as well?" I asked sullenly.
"Because you didn't have all of your morning tea," she replied, with an edge to her voice.
"What? Yes I did!" I pretended to be offended.
"No, you threw half of it away," Mum said, with a meaningful look.
I ate the cake. I didn't want to have a stand-off at uni. Mum and Dad never gave me another chance to meddle with a snack or meal, but I wouldn't have taken it even if they had. I hadn't ever wanted to put Michael in that position. I had thrown away the food that day thinking he wouldn't know, and therefore wouldn't have to tell Dad. Still deceptive, but I hadn't thought it would be at Michael's expense.

Mum was spending a lot of time on an online forum for carers of people with eating disorders during this time. The tab was almost always there on her internet window. I can't remember why I first looked at the site myself; maybe she had been talking about it. Reading through the posts from parents and carers angered me. None of them understood. They didn't see their children as people anymore, they only saw an eating disorder. I'm sure my judgement was clouded by anger, but I think there was also some truth to my interpretation.

It didn't take long to find Mum's account. I read some of her posts, which made me angrier than those by other carers. How dare she talk about me online! I started checking what she was writing every week or so. A few times she realised I had found her posts and made new accounts. I guessed the password to her final account, which allowed me to read private messages she had received and sent to other forum members. Reading them made me furious, but being sneaky allowed me to feel a small amount of accomplishment.

It's hard to describe how I felt during the ten months we did Maudsley. I enjoyed having energy and eating nice food, but felt simultaneously guilty for enjoying it and not putting up more of a fight. The ED voice told me I should try harder to prevent the weight gain, either by exercising whenever Mum and Dad weren't around or running away from home. But I knew that, even if I exercised enough to counter all the food I was eating, they would just give me more food, or watch me more closely so I couldn't exercise. And running away seemed extreme, even though I was 19. I'm not someone who breaks the rules.

I often thought about the possibility of just living in my car at uni. There were even showers there, which anyone could use. There was a fridge in the cafe where I could store food, a microwave, and practice rooms I could sleep in if my car was cold or uncomfortable.

I looked on Gumtree for spare rooms in share houses. I wasn't working much aside from SO, which was about one week each month. I wouldn't be able to pay rent without going into my savings, which I didn't want to do. The ED voice told me I should spend as much money as necessary to be thin again, but that fought with the part of me that felt incredibly anxious spending money. I responded to one advertisement and went to the house to meet the people already living there. I had used a notebook that I kept in my bedroom, to plan a day and time to meet them. It was tricky to find a window when I had enough time to walk to the house and back, outside of class and meeting Mum or Dad to eat. A few days later, I found a post from Mum on the forum, saying that she had found my notes planning the times. I was furious that she had been going through my things. But I also understood her fear. The people in the house were nice, but they decided to give the room to someone else because I didn't have a solid plan for paying rent. Can't blame them.

I hated what Mum and Dad were doing, even though I knew they meant well. Part of me hated them for it, while another part felt bad for hating them. Sometimes I yelled at them, and I never made an effort to be good company when they came to meet me. If anything I was deliberately sullen. I felt they didn't deserve any better, since they were knowingly making my life horrible. At the same time, I felt horrible for how I was treating them. I knew my behaviour was hurting them and I hated myself for that. I was conflicted.

I became even more self-conscious of my body. My high fat, high calorie diet had, unsurprisingly, caused me to put on weight. I thought I looked horrible and fat and assumed others thought so too. I also assumed they would think I was fat[12] because of laziness and greed, and therefore wouldn't want to be friends with me. I was grateful my current friends still wanted to be around me, and was shocked when anyone seemed to be interested in talking to me.

Because I had gained weight, I didn't feel comfortable wearing many of my clothes. I definitely didn't want to wear anything remotely figure-hugging, but also didn't want to buy new, looser clothes. This was partly because I didn't want to spend the money, but mostly because I hoped I would be smaller again soon — I didn't want to give in to Mum, Dad, Maudsley and this bigger body that I hated.

---

[12] My BMI was still near the bottom of the "healthy" range but it was the heaviest I had ever been and I felt enormous.

Mum or Gran bought me a pair of shorts one day which were a bit bigger, very comfortable, but also very daggy. I felt safer wearing them though — safe from scrutiny — because they were loose and came down to my knees. I wore these every day for about six months. I washed them on the weekends and put them in the dryer, so I could wear them again straight away. I worried people would notice I was wearing the same shorts every day and think it was dirty, unhygienic and gross — as well as fat, lazy and greedy. I tried to think of an explanation in case anyone asked. The best I came up with was that I owned more than one pair, or washed them overnight. Luckily no one ever asked, but I still wonder if anyone noticed.

I doubt that anyone who wasn't immediate family, or one of my closest friends, could have guessed that I was struggling with a serious mental health condition. They probably thought I was shy — or maybe grumpy — and didn't care much for fashion, without giving much thought to my size. I kept my emotions inside when I was at uni, work or around other people. I had to. I felt I had to. However, one day at uni, I couldn't hold it in anymore. There was too much grief and self-loathing inside me, that it came spilling out while I was talking to Michael. Luckily we were in a practice room, so no one else could see — I probably would have held it in if we had been in public.

I told him how much I hated myself, how horrible and ugly I thought I looked, and that I didn't know how much longer this would all go on — would it be years? My unhappiness and hopelessness was squeezing me; I couldn't escape. He was his usual understanding, caring self, but he honestly couldn't understand why I hated myself. He told me how much he valued my friendship and enjoyed hanging out, but I couldn't make myself believe him. I always wondered why he wanted to be friends with me, to be honest. He was such a fun person, everyone liked him, while I was an awkward, boring, ugly, scared nobody.

"Don't take this the wrong way," Michael said, after some thought, "but you sound a bit like one of those religious people. You know, there's no evidence that god exists, but they believe in him so strongly. You can show them proof of evolution and dinosaurs and he doesn't even answer their prayers, but they still believe. You're like that."
He was absolutely correct. He'd hit the nail on the head.
"Sorry if I've offended you," he said uncertainly.
"No, not at all. You're absolutely right." I just didn't know how to convince myself. I had been trying for so long, gathering evidence that I wasn't a bad person, or fat, but I just couldn't make myself actually believe it.

It was around that time that businesses started advertising discounts on coupon apps such as Scoopon. A uni friend told me about it and the thought of getting big discounts appealed to me, so I downloaded the app she used. I used to scroll through the deals when I was bored at home or in a lecture. Most required spending more than I wanted to in order to get a discount, but I got a small dopamine hit seeing '70% off' written, before reading the fine print. One day I saw a deal for discount liposuction. I had daydreamed about magically removing the fat I had gained in the past year and may have briefly considered liposuction, but never seriously. I felt it was cheating to have it removed surgically, instead of doing the hard work myself. I assumed it was expensive too. But with the discount, it came to about $150, though I didn't read the fine print.

I googled liposuction, to see what was involved, and seriously considered getting it done. Apparently, I would need to stay overnight after the operation, which would be a problem since Mum and Dad were monitoring my meals and always knew where I was. I was also a little scared, because the operation sounded serious. Fears aside, if I got the operation, I would need to come up with a good story to explain to Mum and Dad why I had disappeared for over a day, and face the consequences; or move out of home before I got the operation, so they couldn't stop me and wouldn't know what I was doing. In the end, I decided not to attempt the covert expedition. Getting surgery felt too big and serious. It also felt like cheating. And I was scared to defy Mum and Dad.

After about eight months Mum, Dad and Adelle decided I could start having one unsupervised snack each day. I worked out how many years it would take, at a rate of eight months per meal or snack, for me to have full control back — I would be 24! In defiance, I always skipped the snack that was unsupervised. Unfortunately, it had no effect on my weight, probably because I was eating so much at my other meals. All I achieved was hunger between meals, which I usually attempted to quell with a diet Coke.

A short time after I was granted this small freedom, Mum and Dad decided that Mum and I should go on a holiday together, to try to heal our relationship. I was dreading it. It was obvious I was more hostile towards Mum. From my point of view, this was valid — she did most of the research that informed their decisions around my "treatment," spent lots of time reading other carers' posts in the forum, didn't eat very much and rarely finished her meals, always leaving some food on the plate. Mum and Dad blamed my hostility towards Mum on the eating disorder but, even before I started restricting my food, we had never gotten on like the Gilmore Girls.

We went to Balingup[13] and stayed in a cottage for the weekend. I had hoped I might be granted more freedom with my food, but Mum brought down my snacks and some meals for both of us, which she had cooked in advance. I was determined to be grumpy, unfriendly, talk to Mum as little as possible, and generally give her a horrible weekend. I felt she deserved it.

We actually had quite a nice weekend. I'm sure there were times when I was grumpy, probably at meals, but I don't remember the specifics. We went on some walks, visited the horses and goats on the property where we were staying, looked in the pretty, crafty shops in Bridgetown, ate delicious pumpkin soup with surprisingly decent gluten-free bread for lunch, and even had fish and chips for dinner one night — I wasn't really scared of the fat in the deep-fried food because it was no more than what I had been consuming for the past eight months. I had decided to make the weekend hell for Mum, but I think we both had a nice time.

A few days after we got back to Perth, I asked if I could have another snack unsupervised, since the weekend had gone well."No, sweety," Mum said, her tone dripping with sadness and sympathy, which infuriated me. "Your brain hasn't healed enough yet."
I was furious. "It's never going to heal when you're making me so miserable!"
"Hannah, we're doing this because we love you. We understand it's hard for you to make the decision to eat yourself, so we're making it for you."
She continued with her Maudsley speech, which I had already heard far too many times. I was seething. I had tried so hard. I had let my guard down. I had been nice to Mum all weekend, even though she had been making my life hell. And I got nothing. Just the same lecture about my brain chemistry and how much they loved me.

I started to think about moving out of home again. However, I had discovered, thanks to the online forum, that Mum and Dad had put a tracker in my car, so they would know where I was if I went awol. They were using Adam's old iPhone with the Find My Friends app turned on. According to Mum's post, they were taking it out of my car every few nights to charge it. I had tried to find it once or twice, with no success. There's a lot I don't know about cars though, so I figured there must be another secret spot I didn't know about. Maybe it was even underneath the car.

---

[13] A beautiful, small town a few hours South of Perth.

I can't remember what made me become more serious about moving out. Maybe it was a mixture of things. I was only allowed to eat — or not eat — one snack unsupervised; and, even after the trip to Balingup, I wasn't given any more freedom. I had also been preparing to audition for the Australian Youth Orchestra. If I was successful I would get to take part in two seasons of rehearsals and concerts — the first in the eastern states in February the following year; the second in Europe later that same year. Mum and Dad had said that, even if I passed the audition, they wouldn't let me go unless I was in a much healthier place mentally. That definitely impacted my decision to move, because there wasn't much point passing the audition if I couldn't accept the offer.

I organised to visit my friend Steve one weekend, in the small window of time I had between meeting Mum or Dad for meals. He had agreed to help me look through my car for the iPhone. We searched the car thoroughly — under the seats, in the join between the seat back and bottom, the dark areas under the glove box and around the pedals, in the glove box, under the floor mats, in any nooks in the boot, in the bag of tools for changing tyres, under the boot mat, around the spare tyre and any area underneath the car that we could see. We didn't find anything. In the end, Steve said it mustn't be there anymore. I wondered if it was stitched into the seats, but the stitching still looked perfect. Surely they wouldn't unpick and restitch the stitching every time they charged the phone!

Escape

That afternoon, Steve and I talked about me moving out. He encouraged me to do it, but I was still hesitant. I didn't want to hurt Mum and Dad, I was scared, I was worried about money and I didn't know if I would be able to have any sort of relationship at all with my family if I moved out. Steve suggested asking Mel, a friend from school, if anyone was using the spare room in the house she rented with her boyfriend. It felt like a big step, actually contacting someone and asking for a room. But I did it. Mel was understanding, partly because she's just a lovely person, and also because of her experiences with her own family. She said she was happy for me to take the room. She gave me her address, told me how much the rent was and said she would talk to her boyfriend, Kyle, but she was pretty sure he would be fine with me moving in. She was so calm about it all, as though it was a normal situation, which helped me to start believing I might actually be able to make it happen. Mel and I stayed in touch over the next few days. I was still in two minds, but I made a list of what I would take with me if I plucked up the courage to move out.

I can't remember what it was that made me decide that I was definitely going to move, or how I chose the day. I sent Mel a message saying that, if I didn't chicken out or get caught, I would come the next day. She was, again, very understanding, and said they would leave a key in the meter box and that she may or may not see me the following afternoon. I was so grateful for her understanding and trust, leaving a key out and trusting me to be alone in their house.

Even though I was 20, I knew Mum and Dad would stop me from moving out, physically if need be. I only had small windows of time between meeting them, so I had to plan my movements carefully. I left for uni after breakfast to practise — I often practised there instead of at home, partly to get away from the house; partly to see my friends and partly to annoy Mum and Dad, because it meant they had to drive there to meet me — agreeing to meet Mum at a designated time and place for morning tea. But I didn't go to uni. I parked down the road and around a few corners, read my book and stressed for an hour or so. I nearly chickened out many times but I knew that, if I gave into my fear when I had come this far, I would probably never pluck up the courage again. I knew approximately when Mum would need to leave to meet me, but I called the house a few times to check she had left. The first time I called she answered — I hung up, hoping she would assume it was a prank call — so I was glad I checked.

When I was almost certain she had left, I drove back home to get my things. I only packed the necessities, but I deemed my goose down doona a necessity. It was July after all. I was packing as fast as I could because I knew Mum would be expecting to meet me in about 30 minutes.

As I drove away from the house for the second time that day, I had nervous, scared butterflies in my tummy and couldn't believe what I was doing. I wasn't someone who broke the rules. My acts of defiance towards Mum and Dad had only ever been small and relatively insignificant, like buying ice cream or chocolate at school. What was I doing? Would I be able to have a relationship with Mum and Dad or Adam after this? Would they call the police? I knew, thanks to the online forum, that they had talked about contacting the police if I ran away. I was still worried the tracker was somewhere in my car too. After I had been driving for about 15 minutes though, I felt free and happy. The scared butterflies transformed into happy, excited ones. As I drove along Tonkin Highway I realised I felt relaxed and excited. I was smiling.

The positive feeling didn't last long. Mum messaged, then called, but I didn't answer because I was driving. When I didn't answer she called a few more times. Adam called too — I assumed she asked him to, hoping I would answer his call. I called Mum as I sat in my car in the driveway of Mel's house, having just arrived, sobbing and apologising for worrying her, but also refusing to come home or tell her where I was, for which I also apologised.

Mum was surprisingly calm. "I expected you might do this at some point.
"I'm sorry to make you worry," I sobbed. "Are you ok?"
"I'm ok. I'm with Adam at the moment and I'll call Dad again soon," she assured me. "Are you ok?"
"Yeah, I'll be alright."
"Do you have a place to stay?"
"Yeah. I'm going to rent with friends."
"Ok. Where are you?"
"I can't tell you." I was aware that my voice sounded awkward as I struggled to stand up for myself.
"Why not, Hannah?"
"Because I don't want you to make me come home."
"Ok. You know we're worried about you because we love you, don't you?"
"Yes, but I can't tell you. I can't go back home." I started sobbing again.

Adam called me later, and tried to convince me to go back home. Talking to him was calming, but he didn't change my mind. I was scared — of what

Mum and Dad would do, of hurting them, of the unknown — and felt very alone, but I wasn't giving up on my newfound freedom yet.

I found the door key, brought my things inside, looked around the house a bit and unpacked the few possessions I had brought. Dad and Michael called at some point. Gilbert messaged too, because Mum and Dad had started calling my friends to ask if they knew where I was. Once I had settled in as much as I could, I practised. I knew it was an odd thing to do on such a strange and emotional day, but I figured I should get on with things. I was practising when Mel got home.

We hadn't seen each other much since she moved to a different school in year 10. Mel had moved around a lot, I had been sick, it wasn't easy for me to get around until I got my licence, and we had both had a lot going on. I had been wondering if she would think it was odd or rude that I had asked to rent with her and Kyle. But I was paying rent and had made it very clear that I would understand if they didn't want me to live with them. Mel was nothing but welcoming and understanding; I was relieved. I think she felt a bit awkward too, but we both tried to act as though there was nothing odd about the situation. Kyle came home a bit later and Mel introduced us properly. We had briefly met at a friend's wedding a few years before but had barely spoken. He seemed like a nice guy.

Coincidentally, it was Gilbert's birthday that day and he had invited a few of us out for drinks at the Irish club. I hadn't been sure if I would be up to going. I felt uneasy and worried after a very stressful day, so I decided to go, hoping I would have fun and that it would help take my mind off everything. I also didn't want to third wheel on Mel and Kyle.

I was glad I went. It was good to get out and see Gilbert. We spoke about what had happened that day and how I was feeling. At some point, he bought a jug of lemonade to share. Usually, I wouldn't have even considered having any, unless it was diet lemonade. But I hadn't had dinner, so I reasoned that the calories balanced out.

Dad called the next day to ask if I would be open to having a family meeting. I had guessed they would want to do something like this. I knew it would be hard, stressful and awkward, but I wanted to have a good relationship with them. Unfortunately, there was no way to achieve that without having at least a few awkward discussions first. We arranged to meet at uni because it was neutral ground and I would be there to practise anyway — my practice schedule was becoming increasingly rigid, especially with the audition approaching.

We met a day or so later, in one of the cafes. For most of the meeting Mum, Dad and Adam tried to convince me to come home. I held my ground. I reasoned it was unlikely they would try to force me physically, since we were in public.
"What if I come to uni to meet you for all your meals, instead of Mum and Dad," Adam offered.
That was unexpected. "But you have to work."
"Well, I live pretty close to here and you know how flexible my working hours are." He grinned. It was handy working for your best friend's dad. Even still, I was astounded by his generosity. But I didn't want to be monitored at all — and yes, I also wanted to eat less so I could lose some weight. I hated how I looked and felt. I needed to lose weight as soon as possible! They spent about an hour trying to persuade me to move home, but I didn't budge from my position. Eventually, Dad decided there was no point discussing things any further. When I left, I saw Mum put her head in her hands in despair. I felt horrible. I knew I was causing her pain and worry. But I wouldn't go back home to live under their rule.

Our family had been having a semi-regular Sunday dinner for a year or so at this point. It was very casual — our family is rarely formal — and as Dad put it, "come if you're free, unless you've got a better offer." Usually Mum's parents — Gran and Grandad — Adam and his girlfriend, Avril, came. Dad made it clear when we met at uni, that he was keen for me to continue coming to family dinners. I wanted to go too, but was worried they would take my car keys and make me stay.

It took Mum and Dad about a week to find out where I was living. The day I moved out I had told Michael that I was living with Mel. When Dad called him, hoping he would know where I was, Michael told him. He had to make a quick decision when Dad called. When he started supervising some of my meals he promised Dad he wouldn't lie to him, so when Dad asked if he knew where I was living, Michael told him the truth. They found out Mel's address from the mother of another school friend, Farwa. Farwa messaged me soon after Mum and Dad had called her Mum, apologising profusely. Her Mum had been worried about me and yelled at her. Farwa hadn't known what to do, so she told her Mum the address, but felt terrible. I forgave her immediately. I understood how she felt and I knew she had been put in a tricky position. I was scared Mum and Dad would come take me home, but they didn't. Maybe they just wanted to know, in case they saw me losing weight, or I cut off contact.

I cut back on my food as soon as I moved out. Partly because, as Mum and Dad had been trying to hold my weight much higher than it naturally sat, they had been making me eat much more than the average person. Partly because I desperately wanted to lose weight as fast as possible, without restricting too much — not a lot of weight; I just wanted to lose what I had gained since starting Maudsley. And partly because I felt I didn't want to spend too much money.

I have been careful with money since I was about six years old, when the only money I had were the odd coins I found under sofa cushions or in corners at home, which probably fell out of Mum or Dad's pockets, and which I really should have given back. I remember once proudly showing Gran the six dollars I had saved.
"And do you think you'll buy with that?" She asked.
I didn't have an answer; I was just proud of how much I had saved. I put the coins back in my little purse.

Growing up in a one-income house, with Mum and Dad paying for Adam and me to learn violin — an expensive hobby — I had observed how to be careful with money. I knew the difference between necessities and treats. Going out for a meal, even buying a drink at a cafe, had always been a special and rare occasion. I spent my own money with the same care, for which Mum, Dad, Gran and Grandad praised me. In high school, I started thinking about studying overseas after I finished my Bachelor's in Perth. I also wanted to buy a better violin when I had saved up enough. I knew both would cost a lot. Even if I studied in Germany, where university fees are very low, I would need money to cover rent and food for a few years. I had saved as much as I could since I started working in my gap year. Saving had become a habit.

I had wondered for a few years if the anxiety I felt when spending money, especially unplanned or large amounts, was abnormal. Whenever I considered buying something when I was much younger, the decision always felt huge, as though making the "wrong" choice would negatively impact the rest of my life.
"Do you want to take a walk and think about it?" Mum often asked me. I once spent about half an hour sitting on the floor of a department store, repeatedly comparing the pros and cons of my shortlist of wallets. I counted the pockets, zipped sections, size, overall look, material and price, while Mum patiently browsed nearby. Worrying about spending money when I had just moved out

and didn't have much regular income didn't seem unreasonable. Though I had a decent amount saved up, it was intended for overseas study and a new violin, so I didn't want to have to dip into it if I could avoid it.

Even so, I knew that I considered spending money the same way I thought about eating food. In my head I often worded eating as "spending calories," in the sense of using up some of my daily quota of allowed calories — I had started counting again as soon as I moved out. And I felt a similar anxiety when it came to spending money, as I did when I considered eating something additional or different. But I told myself they couldn't be linked. I had never heard anyone else talk about it. I assumed it was something strange about me, and was therefore embarrassed to talk about it, even with Adelle. There were a lot of things I didn't tell her because I was worried that she would judge me.

As I proved that I could look after myself, was still eating and was happier, Mum and Dad started to trust me and the tension eased. And I was genuinely happier. I had more freedom, was able to see my friends more, and allowed myself to enjoy food instead of resenting Mum and Dad every time I ate. And yes, I was happy I was losing weight, too which allowed me to hate myself a little bit less.

A few days after I moved out, Adam received some very exciting news. He had started a choir that year, which I sang in, and we had been invited to perform in Carnegie Hall with other choirs from around the world. We would sing together as one big choir, conducted by Eric Whitacre, a composer whose music we had sung and loved. Unfortunately, though we had been invited, we would need to cover all of our own costs, so most of our choir couldn't afford to go. At first, I wasn't going to either, because of the cost, but then Adam decided he was going. I was sick of seeing him go on exciting overseas trips while I had to stay home because Mum and Dad were monitoring my meals. Seeing Adam's excitement made me excited too and for once no one could stop me going. America was nowhere near the top of my travel bucket list, but singing in Carnegie Hall would be amazing. And as I researched, I found more and more exciting things to see and do there. So, while I was paying rent and living expenses on a very low income, I was also saving for an overseas holiday. I planned my food consumption and petrol usage meticulously, so I would be able to afford the trip without dipping into my savings.

About a month after I moved out, I started having appointments with Craig, a clinical psychologist from Sydney, via Skype. Unbeknownst to me, Mum and Dad had been in touch with Craig's practice before I moved out. It had taken a while to sort out payment and Medicare since we weren't seeing each other face to face. Craig was well-known in the eating disorder world and often spoke at national conferences. A psych I saw a few years later was very excited to hear him talk at a conference and even referred to herself as a fangirl. He was a nice guy and we got on well, but I felt he was trying to be cool; the good cop to Mum and Dad's bad cop. When he asked how everything was going, how much I was eating and how I felt about food, I omitted truths that I knew were disordered, and sometimes lied. I was surprised that he believed me. I thought he would have learned to identify ED lies, given that all of his clients had some form of eating disorder. Apparently not.

I had been nearing the end of my period when I moved out. I didn't get the next one, or any more. I lied to anyone who asked about it, including Krish, (my childhood GP; we stopped seeing Maisie after I got out of Heathgrove), Mum, Dad and Craig. I had cut my food back but not too much, and my weight was still above what it was when my period started. I assumed stress had caused it to stop.

And I was very stressed. Aside from my strained relationship with Mum and Dad after moving out, uni was incredibly busy that semester. I had my audition for AYO and a few big uni productions for which I needed to rehearse and perform. This was on top of my own personal practice, classes and work. I was at uni from 8 am until the evening most days. When we had rehearsals for shows we wouldn't finish until around 10 pm. A lot of my friends had a similar schedule, but without the stress of family, money, living out of home, an eating disorder and extreme perfectionism. Siena was also struggling with her mental health and I was one of her main supports. Helping her and her boyfriend took a lot of time and mental energy, not that I resented her for a second.

It was an exhausting semester — emotionally, physically and mentally. But it was also wonderful to be able to spend more time with my friends and have a better relationship with Mum and Dad, as they came to trust me. I ate quite well most of the time, however, my fear of spending money usually resulted in me skipping dinner when I had late nights at uni — which made the ED voice happy. Sometimes I ate some chocolate for dinner, or mulberries from the tree at uni when it was fruiting season. My energy and concentration were usually still ok, probably because it didn't happen too often. But it definitely wasn't a healthy decision and the eating disorder loved it. The ED voice congratulated me every time I missed dinner. I felt so good, as though I was doing something really worthy. I was beginning to feel pure again. The eating disorder was slowly gaining strength.

I made it through the semester and was relieved when the holidays came. Not long after my final exam, Peter, (my violin teacher), called to tell me his contract at the university hadn't been renewed for the following year. Though he had been head of strings there for five years, his wife, dogs, house and life were in Hobart. He would move back there and hoped to teach at the University of Tasmania. He was considering flying to Perth a few times during semester to teach his students here — there were more than ten of us — or to teach us online.

The other option was for me to transfer to the University of Tasmania and finish my degree there. Someone would be replacing him in Perth but we didn't yet know who. I could move to the University of Western Australia, which was the only other university in Perth that offered a music degree, but would need to repeat second year, which I had just finished. It was a big decision. I considered staying in Perth and learning from the new violin teacher on staff, whoever that may be, or Dorothy, who had taught me through my teenage years. But I wasn't happy at my current university. That semester I had been bullied by a senior staff member and my practice time had been stolen by rehearsals for concerts that only benefited the vocal students we were accompanying. I wanted to keep learning from Peter. It had taken me 18 months to understand his cryptic way of explaining things, but I was finally making some really exciting progress, which I wanted to continue.

In the end, I decided to move to Hobart for my third year. Quite a few other friends were moving to continue learning with Peter, so I would have friends there. I was apprehensive when I spoke to Mum and Dad about it, but they were surprisingly supportive. They definitely would have preferred me to stay in Perth, but I think they knew how much I wanted to learn from Peter, and I had proven that I could look after myself. They were worried about a relapse, especially since I wasn't completely recovered, so we spoke about seeing a GP regularly in Hobart. They also spoke to Peter about their worries. But I was moving to Hobart! I was very excited about the adventure and also felt it could be a new start of sorts — while also being very aware that thinking of something as a "fresh start" is a common trap; however, I had moved out, was still healthy and maybe the new setting and new friends would help me start again, not as shy, awkward Hannah, but as happy, adventurous Hannah, who had moved states to focus on violin. And yes, the disordered part of me was looking forward to losing a bit more weight without Mum and Dad around to notice.

Before the next year of uni started, I went to America! Since it was such a long and expensive flight from Perth, I decided to go to Canada before New

York. We have distant relatives in Toronto, including my Grandad's cousin, who loves music. He was excited to learn, a few years earlier, that Adam and I played violin and had sent us discs filled with his favourite classical music. I had emailed him and spoken to him on the phone a few times and wanted to meet him. I never thought I would, as he was in his eighties and lived so far away, but now I had an opportunity.

My eating was pretty good on the holiday. It helped that food was cheap and the portions were large. The ED voice was happy when I walked a lot or ate less on some days, and I was still roughly counting calories. But I mostly ate what I wanted and had a great time.

Hobart Year 1

I moved to Hobart not long after I got back from New York. My great Aunty Chrissie and Kath, my second cousin, were visiting from Belfast, so I stayed in Perth an extra week or two, to spend time with them. I flew out of Perth around midnight and landed in Hobart at about seven or eight in the morning. I had arranged to stay with Julie and Parvati — friends from Perth, who had moved there in February — until I found a place of my own. They had a spare room and a blow-up mattress. They also kindly picked me up from the airport.

Staying with Julie and Parvati was great. They were so welcoming, inviting me to join them to cook dinner, get groceries and watch movies. I was worried I would be third-wheeling but they didn't seem to mind. They were also full of helpful information about Hobart, uni and work, which they were very happy to share.

I didn't feel very hungry for the first two weeks I was there, though I'm not sure why. I was usually hungry for snacks between meals, whether I ate them or not, even when I was at my lowest weight. But now I wasn't. And I didn't see Julie or Parvati eat between meals, so I felt that I shouldn't either, since I wasn't hungry anyway. They had scales in the bathroom, so I started weighing myself in my underwear in the morning before I showered. I was excited to see the number decreasing; about a kilo each week. One morning I did a happy dance because my weight had gone down again and I was feeling ok about how my body looked.

Peter's wife, Maria, was the head of food and beverage at the Museum of Old and New Art, (MONA), which was already a major tourist attraction in Hobart. She had organised waitressing jobs there for some of Peter's other students, who had arrived in Hobart before me. I had considered auditioning for casual work with the Tasmanian Symphony Orchestra but decided against it. Though it was a great job, practising orchestra parts and being in rehearsal for SO had taken away from my personal practice time when I was in Perth, and I wanted to really focus on my playing while I was in Hobart. So Maria found me a job at MONA too.

My first shift was in The Source, their fancy restaurant, serving breakfast. I only ate something small before I left home that day, because the ED voice told me not to eat too early. My shift started at eight, so I had to get a bus around seven — MONA is about ten kilometres from Hobart CBD, but the bus service isn't great. I was very hungry and tired by the time I finished my shift, but the chefs put out leftover food for us to eat when we were cleaning up and vacuuming. What a treat! I was estimating the calories in the food on offer, to make sure I didn't eat "too much," but also very grateful for such delicious — and free! — food. The girl who trained me was happy with how I had worked, and I continued to work well. I worked at MONA for the three years I was in Hobart.

I found a share house to live in after three weeks. It was on the main street with four other people I didn't know, but everyone kept to themselves, which suited me wonderfully. The electricity costs were also included in the rent, so I could use the heater as much as I wanted. Everyone had warned me that electricity was expensive in Tasmania. Julie and Parvati had used the heater very sparingly, opting for extra layers of clothing instead. Mum and Dad posted my big, warm doona over the first week I was there because I was freezing at night. It was a relief to know I wouldn't be cold at home anymore.

Unfortunately, semester had already started when I got to Hobart and I had neither auditioned nor enrolled. I had hoped I would be able to audition online or transfer without an audition, but politics at the University of Tasmania, (UTas), prevented this. When I decided to go to the USA I thought I would be continuing uni in Perth, so missing the first few weeks of the semester wouldn't have been a problem, but it was different with a new university. I would have to audition in the mid-year holidays and start in semester two. I was disappointed, because I had hoped to only be in Hobart for a year, but there was nothing I could do about it. For the rest of the first semester, I practised for my audition, worked at MONA, had lessons, explored Hobart and settled in.

When I had been working at MONA for a month or so, I started getting more shifts. These were primarily in the Wine Bar, where the other Perth violinists worked. I preferred it there because it was much less formal than The Source, where I was never sure how to interact with the guests. In the Wine Bar it was more casual and busy and I mostly just delivered food, cleared plates and did the dishes. I could also work longer shifts that didn't start so early in the day.

The eating disorder loved it when I worked in The Source because I got a lot of exercise taking orders, delivering food, taking used dishes to the kitchen and cleaning after service. It loved the Wine Bar even more. I had to walk faster, didn't get a break to eat morning or afternoon tea, sometimes didn't get a lunch break if it was busy and, if I did, I was usually given vegetable soup, which I estimated to be relatively low in calories — others had bread with their soup but I am gluten intolerant. I could have brought food with me, or eaten more before my shift, but the ED voice told me I shouldn't worry, that I should be more carefree with food — if carefree meant not worrying if I sometimes ate less. During my first year there, I made myself a milky coffee before I started the shift, or in the afternoon when it had quietened down, but at some point the eating disorder made me stop that too. I was exhausted and ravenous when I finished my shifts, from power walking all day and eating little, and the eating disorder loved it. It would have been smarter for me to audition for TSO. Though playing with them would have taken away from my practice time, I wouldn't have had to work as many hours as I was at MONA, to earn the same amount. But I couldn't bring myself to give up all the exercise I was getting.

For most of my time in Hobart, I was having two or three violin lessons a week. One week, when I was getting close to me mastering something important, I had four or five. Peter was only paid to give us about 13 hours of lessons each semester, but he gave most of us three or four times that. He was very generous. Because we had lessons every two to four days, as needed, none of us had a regular lesson time. Sometimes I would have a lesson on a Saturday or Sunday before work, then he would drive me in — I wouldn't have made it in time if I took the bus. I am forever grateful for this generosity. It took up at least another 40 minutes of his day, driving me there and back, not to mention petrol costs, for which he never accepted a cent. He did this for other students too. Maybe he didn't mind taking us in because it meant he could also see Maria, who worked at MONA almost everyday, and get a free coffee and croissant. Even so, it was incredibly kind. The days when I had a lesson before work were even more exhausting though. Lessons with Peter were mentally and emotionally intense and I usually needed a rest afterwards. However, this wasn't possible when I went straight to work, particularly as he often lost track of time during lessons and we had to rush to MONA, arriving just on time or slightly late. The eating disorder gave me more praise at the end of these days though, because I had worked hard, proved the strength of my willpower and probably burned even more calories.

I also did a lot of walking outside of work, without really trying. I hadn't brought my car over, the bus service was average and, since I lived in the city, most places were within walking distance — I should point out here that I considered three or four kilometres each way "walking distance." The only time I used the bus was to get to MONA or Peter and Maria's house; there was no point in using it to get around the city because it was faster to walk. Once I started uni, I walked at least eight kilometres on most days. I didn't do any extra exercise in the morning, as I had before hospital, but the eating disorder was happy I was getting a lot of steps in.

During that first year, I was still eating a decent amount of food. I forget what my exact calorie limit was, but it was more than 1500 per day. I was counting calories and had rules concerning what times I was allowed to eat, but I didn't feel like I was restricting. My aim was to eat enough, but not "too much;" I didn't want to gain weight.

On one of my explorative outings, I found an ice cream shop down the road from me, that made exciting sundaes. I wanted to have one as a treat after my uni audition, which was around midday, but couldn't consider having it in addition to lunch. Nor could I allow myself to have such a big afternoon tea. I decided to make the sundae my lunch. It was about the right number of calories for lunch anyway. Having a sundae for lunch isn't the best life choice, but I don't think it would be unusual for someone my age to do it every so often. However, I don't deny that my reasoning for doing so was absolutely disordered. But it was the only way I could allow myself to have a treat without guilt. And yes, I did enjoy it.

Because I lived so close to everything and could usually come home for meals, even if I had morning and afternoon classes at uni, I had gotten into the habit of not bringing food with me anywhere. In truth, it wasn't just a habit; it was the eating disorder being sneaky, which I told myself was me being disorganised, which is a monumental lie because I am anything but. I had also stopped carrying a bag with me, because my coat, which I wore most of the year due to Tasmania's cold climate, had big pockets, which held my phone and wallet — all I needed. It was nice not needing to carry a bag, and it became almost a challenge for me, to bring as little as possible when I went out, so I wouldn't need one. Sometimes I would bring an apple in my violin case or some chocolate in my pocket, but usually I brought nothing. The eating disorder loved that I sometimes skipped snacks or had a meal late because I had been out with no food.

Because of my anxiety around spending money, it was very rare that I would buy food out, even if I was starving and exhausted. It was usually just snacks that I missed, rarely entire meals, but my rule of not carrying food with me contributed to my gradual slide into more disordered thinking and restrictive eating.

Sometimes someone might offer me food too, at work or uni or at a party, and I didn't want to have already eaten, because then I couldn't allow myself to have what was on offer, which was usually more interesting than what I would have given myself to eat. It became my habit to hope there would be food on offer wherever I was going, especially if I would be out for a while. I knew that sometimes there wouldn't be, but the ED voice told me to be more carefree and take a chance — I was only allowed to be carefree about possibly eating less though, never more. I might get tired or hungry if there was no food, but I'd had lots of practice struggling through tiredness and hunger, and I enjoyed the ED voice's congratulations and the feeling that I was doing something worthwhile, for the greater good. As I gradually became more restrictive in my day-to-day eating, I became more focused on food and was more affected by the tiredness and hunger if there was no free food on offer. I was always on the lookout for free food, even if I wasn't hungry or tired yet. Free food also meant I wasn't eating food I had bought myself, which was a win, since spending money made me anxious.

Overall, that first year in Hobart was positive. Near the end of the year, not long after moving in with Harriet and Rose, two friends who also learnt with Peter, I sat on the floor of my bedroom and realised that year had been my favourite year since 2001. I had continued seeing Craig, the psychologist from Sydney, for a few months via Skype, but at some point, we agreed that there was no need. All of the worries and problems I shared with him were normal life problems, seemingly unrelated the eating disorder. He didn't know how much the eating disorder was loving the exercise, that I was counting my calories and that my period had stopped when I moved out of home the year before and hadn't returned. My weight had dropped a bit, but not too much, otherwise Mum and Dad would have been on my case.

I went home for the summer holidays. I hadn't been back all year and I was really looking forward to it. Dad had visited twice but I hadn't seen the rest of my family since I left in April. It was great to be back. I stayed with Mum and Dad, as I had done for the few weeks between returning from America and leaving for Hobart. It was nice to be able to enjoy their company, without suspicion or anger. I knew my eating was a bit restrictive and worried they would notice, so I made sure the meals they saw me eat looked normal. I always aimed to be out of the house for some meals too, while seeing friends, so they wouldn't see everything I ate in a day.

New Zealand

We had planned a family holiday to New Zealand in January. Mum and Dad had met there so it was a special place for them. They had always wanted to take Adam and I there, but the cost, Mum's fear of flying, and then my eating disorder, had prevented us. In my first year of uni, Mum did a fear of flying course, but she still found flying very stressful and scary. However, she felt the fear was worth it, to go to New Zealand again.

A few weeks after I left Heathgrove, I contracted some sort of virus. I felt nauseous and vomited a few times, so I was feeling particularly hopeless about life. On this rare occasion, I let my guard down with Mum and cried. My overwhelming despair and grief — I was out of hospital but still far from recovered; I hated myself even more than before I was admitted — was such that I couldn't hold it in any longer. I looked up at the calendar on my wall, which was filled with beautiful pictures of Venice.
"I just want to be well again and go to Venice."
Mum was surprised.
"You want to go to Venice?"
"Yeah." I started to cry quietly. "It's so beautiful and magical. I loved it there. I want to travel and enjoy life, like Adam."
Mum considered this. I think she sensed the change in my demeanour; she was talking to the real, raw, vulnerable Hannah.
"Ok, how about we make a deal of sorts," she began. "I know how scary it is for you to eat more, but it will be worth it when you're out the other side. And flying is terrifying for me. I know it's a different type of fear to yours, but it's big enough that I haven't been able to fly for about twenty years. I know there are courses you can do to overcome fear of flying, I'd need to look into it… But if you can confront your fears and recover, I'll do a fear of flying course and then we can go on holiday as a family to celebrate. Maybe not to Venice — I don't know that we could afford that — but maybe we could go to New Zealand. Dad and I have always wanted to take you and Adam there."
I wanted to be excited, but I had no idea how to stop hating myself and my body.

Mum kept her promise and did the fear of flying course. On the last day, the group flew to Kalgoorlie[14] and back. She wasn't cured — she was still very anxious during the flights — but she had done it. She and Dad repeated the Kalgoorlie flight together about six months later, as the instructor had recommended that they continue to face their fear until it was gone. We didn't

---

[14] About an hour from Perth by plane.

go to New Zealand though, because it wouldn't have been any fun while we were doing Maudsley. Then I moved out.

At some point during that first year in Hobart, I brought up the possibility of a family holiday to New Zealand. Finally, I was excited about it. I knew I wasn't fully recovered, but my eating was ok, and I was well enough to (mostly) enjoy life. We planned the trip together, though Mum did most of it, as she and Dad knew the best places to visit.

On January 14 we flew to Christchurch, stopping in Sydney. Mum had been feeling increasingly anxious about flying in the lead-up to the trip. The night before we left, while we were packing, I put some lavender oil in her oil burner, in an attempt to relax her, even just a little. However, I didn't know I needed to add carrier oil, so the moisture evaporated quickly, leaving the residue to burn, which added to Mum's stress. Luckily we had relatively smooth flights. And Adam kept Mum distracted with sudokus.

New Zealand was mostly great, though it was harder for me to hide my slightly disordered eating while we were living in each other's pockets. Before hospital I focused on avoiding fat, as well as restricting calories. However, a lot of people in the eating disorders group in hospital also feared carbohydrates, which had rubbed off on me. Mum and Dad noticed this soon after I got out of hospital, when I repeatedly left uneaten rice on my plate. From then on, they made sure I ate a full serving of carbohydrate at every meal. I reacted to their pedantry, coming to fear carbohydrates even more and — partly from stubbornness, partly from fear — avoiding it whenever I could. I had started eating rice again when I moved out but had been eating less near the end of the previous year — the ED voice tried to convince me that it was too much hassle to cook. Since Mum and Dad saw all of my meals in New Zealand I felt trapped, and was always on guard to hide uneaten rice, burn extra calories through exercise, or make an excuse for not finishing my meal.

We did a lot of walking on the trip, exploring towns and going on hikes. I wasn't walking as much as I did in Hobart though, and I was very aware of this. One day I insisted that we walk up a nearby hill, at the top of which was an observatory and cafe. I was excited to see the observatory but was mostly driven by my need to exercise. Mum often gets earaches when it's very windy — by the beach or at high altitudes — which happened that day. I pretended I didn't hear her when she complained of being in pain. I pretended I was encouraging her to keep going, so she could enjoy the view from the top. The truth was that I was scared to turn back because I thought I would put on weight if I didn't do a long walk that day. I don't know if she saw through my act. I felt she did, and was worried she would call me out, but she didn't. We got to the top, enjoyed the view, had something to eat, and then walked down again. I don't think any of us enjoyed ourselves until we were lower down, away from the wind.

I found travel days stressful too because we didn't exercise as much. We had been buying nuts, dried fruit, fresh fruit and chocolate, to snack on between meals. I introduced the family to Whittaker's chocolate since it's a New Zealand company and Dad especially was loving it! As much as I also loved it, I felt guilty having more than one or two squares at a time. On driving days I felt bad having any at all.

One day in Queenstown, Adam and I did a zip-lining course down the big mountain. We took the gondola to the top and zipped down over six lines. I was terrified until the sixth line, which I absolutely loved — and wanted to do the whole course again! The bush was gorgeous too. In the afternoon, when we decided we would all explore separately, I decided to walk up the mountain. I wanted to spend more time in the bush, enjoy the view from the top of the mountain, and use the exercise to "earn" an ice cream from a place I'd seen in the town. The walk was beautiful, but less enjoyable than it could have been because I was walking for the sake of burning calories, not enjoyment.

When I got back to the hostel where we were staying, I wasn't really hungry, which annoyed me. Eating when I'm really hungry is so much more satisfying than when I'm only a little hungry. Being hungry makes me feel like I've really earned the food, which was why I had done the hike. In retrospect, I think I was constipated. I really wanted the ice cream though, so I went anyway. Mum came too, but I got annoyed because she wasn't walking as fast as I wanted to. I had a tiny feeling of hunger in my tummy and I wanted to eat before it went away. The ice cream wasn't even very good. It had been listed as one of the highlights of Queenstown but it was actually quite tasteless. I was annoyed with myself and the ice cream shop and felt it was a waste of calories.

Later in the afternoon, Adam announced that he wanted to go out for a really nice dinner. I didn't. I still wasn't hungry and I had just had two scoops of ice cream. If we went out for a nice dinner I needed to know in advance, so I could eat less during the day. But I couldn't say any of that. I tried to change his mind, but he had found a place that apparently served really good wine, so he couldn't be swayed. I ordered a green curry, the only thing on the menu that didn't contain wheat, about which I complained. Partly because I felt it was selfish of Adam to choose a restaurant he wanted to go to with no regard for my food intolerances, but mostly because I was scared of the rice, calories and the guilt that would follow. I felt guilty and conflicted the whole time I was eating. Each bite brought me joy, which was closely followed by guilt, then indecision as to whether or not to have another forkful.

I also needed to hide my lack of period. I had known I would need to hide the truth over the summer since Mum and Dad would notice the absence of used pads in the bin. I worked out lies I could tell Mum and Dad, should they ask. I was going to say it had come while I was staying with a friend — she and I had stayed at her parents' holiday house for a few days — then again in New Zealand, where they might not see the pads if I disposed of them in public toilets. I knew Mum especially would be watching, so I had to be prepared. They never asked me about it, but a few years later Mum said she had wondered when we were in New Zealand.

Overall the holiday was great. It was wonderful to be together as a family without too much distrust from Mum and Dad, no anger or arguments, relatively good energy, and the relaxed, semi-carefree feeling a holiday allows. It wasn't completely carefree though; I still have to hide aspects of my eating from Mum and Dad, and worried on the days when we did less exercise.

Hobart Year 2

I was excited about my second year in Hobart. Now that we were living together, I envisioned Harriet, Rose and I becoming best friends, sharing secrets, living that carefree uni life, making music all day, and finding freedom in my own violin playing. I told myself I would be less tight with my money; buy things I considered to be a luxury, like eggs and peanut paste, and sometimes buy myself a coffee or meal out.

Unfortunately, this did not happen. I had the best intentions with Harriet and Rose. I tried to be spontaneous and social, but being around them for so much of the time I was home was exhausting. Navigating everyday life activities such as making breakfast, putting away groceries and just chatting with them, was stressful. I didn't know what to say, I felt I was being awkward, It was hard to concentrate on making conversation while doing everyday tasks, and I didn't want to disagree with anything or bring up my dislike for doing the majority of the dishes, in case they thought I was being a bitch. I didn't realise at the time quite how much it was affecting me. Other friends spoke about needing their own space and not wanting to talk to housemates or family in the morning, so I thought what I was feeling was normal. I didn't understand that the reason others don't want to have conversations in the morning is because they're still sleepy. Not because they don't know what to say at any time of day; feel that the silence is awkward and blame themselves; their brain freezes and they get butterflies while they try desperately to think of something appropriate to say, assuming the other person thinks they're socially awkward or just plain weird, all the while trying to look normal.

I was still in the habit of not taking food with me when I went out, challenging myself to bring the bare minimum and fit everything in my jacket pockets. Consequently, I continued to miss snacks and have very late meals if I was out. Contrary to my intention, I still wasn't allowing myself to buy food to eat while I was out. Aside from the cost, I enjoyed meals so much more if I had to wait for them. 'Agony and ecstasy' has always been a big part of my eating disorder. "If I miss this snack I'll enjoy the next meal so much more." Or "If I eat less now I can eat more later when we go out." Or, probably the eating disorder's favourite: "if I eat less now, I'll feel good about having restricted."

I continued to work at MONA, where I ate nowhere near enough and power-walked for most of my shift. It wouldn't have been hard for me to eat more, even without bringing my own food. I could have had a hot chocolate with my soup at lunch, eaten more cheese when it was offered, or had a fruit juice, soft drink or milky coffee during the afternoon, but I deliberately didn't. The ED voice's favourite advice — "You'll feel good for restricting later" — was playing on repeat.

I made little effort to wear warm clothes at work. The uniforms weren't designed for Hobart's cold temperatures, but others wore singlets or thermals underneath the nylon tops, with trousers. I didn't wear anything underneath on my top half and wore leggings, or a skirt and tights. Again, it was partly the thought that I would feel a sense of achievement for struggling through the cold and burning extra calories to stay warm — if that actually happened. But I also told myself that, if I had survived the previous weekend, I could do it again. And if others didn't need to wear extra layers — not everyone wore extra layers — then I shouldn't either. I liked seeing how thin my legs were when I saw my reflection. It made me feel that my hunger, cold and tiredness were worth something; I was doing something good.

I had almost no reprieve from the cold for the next two years. In my first year, I had a wonderful heater in my bedroom and used it as much as I needed, as bills were included in my rent. For the next two years, bills were additional and in that second year, we lived in a very cold house. It was drafty, with visible gaps beneath the doors that led outside, and a chimney that wasn't covered at the top.

There were two portable heaters in the house, but three of us, and it took a long time to heat up a room since the hot air escaped under the doors. We talked about how to heat the house when it started to get cold and agreed it was unfair for one person to be without a heater, especially since we were splitting the power bill equally. We also didn't want to have two heaters running all day, as none of us was earning much. We decided to practise at uni, where there were heaters in most of the practice rooms, and save our money.

In many ways this made sense. However, I rarely took food with me to uni, so I was missing even more snacks than before — I made sure I was home for main meals. I also burnt more energy walking to and from uni to practise, which the eating disorder loved. Around the middle of the year, I started taking small amounts of food to uni, but it wasn't enough, so my concentration suffered. I felt slightly light-headed most of the time when I was practising. I tried to always practise just after meals, when I would (hopefully) have more energy. This didn't always work though. Sometimes I had to do something else after a meal, such as go to a class or rehearsal. At other times, something unexpected would come up, preventing me from practising, which caused me a huge amount of stress and annoyance. Often I wasn't eating enough at each meal to give me enough energy anyway, even immediately afterwards. I didn't know what else to do though. It was better than practising at other times when I was even more tired. And I had spiralled down too far to start eating more, though I spent hours arguing with the ED voice, trying to convince it to allow me to eat more without feeling guilty.

As I am intolerant to gluten, corn and potatoes, my main source of carbohydrates is rice. I can also have quinoa, but the price tag meant I didn't even consider buying it. I usually cooked up some brown rice — I legitimately prefer brown to white — every few days, to have with lunch and dinner. Brown rice is about twice the price of white, but a one or two-kilo bag lasted me a few weeks, so I didn't have to talk myself into spending the extra too often. I knew the extra dollar shouldn't have even been a problem — yes, brown rice is about twice the price of white, but one dollar times two is still only two dollars. I was worrying about one dollar!

One day, when I went to the shops to buy a few things, including a new bag of brown rice, I couldn't talk myself into spending the extra dollar. I tried, I really did. I tried to convince myself while I walked the aisles finding the other things I needed. When I compared the price of brown and white rice my stomach dropped and I felt dizzy. I was scared, but I picked up the packet of brown rice anyway. I could do this, then I wouldn't need to for another month or more. I almost got to the check-out. While I was waiting in the queue, I turned around and put the rice back on the shelf. I told myself I could make do without. I would eat more protein or something. I didn't really need carbs anyway. I had seen lots of carb-free recipes online and the keto diet was taking off. If other people could survive without carbohydrates, then I could too.

I had chosen a very challenging program for my recital that semester and I was proud that Peter had trusted me to pull it off. I was excited and wanted to do the music justice with a great performance. I wanted to impress Peter in lessons, show him how hard I was working, and that I was capable, but felt I always fell short. This was partly because I *was* falling short. I could hardly concentrate when I practiced because I was lightheaded and tired, and in lessons we often misunderstood each other. I was also nervous whenever I played for him. And, even though I usually tried to have my lessons soon after a meal, I was usually tired and unable to concentrate properly. I was often cold too, which made my fingers numb and my muscles tense. This happened when I practised at home too, or in a practice room with no heater, which made progress even slower or non-existent.

Most people find Peter a little odd, because he is. Eccentric in a wonderful way. Intimidating too, though he tries very hard not to be. We all felt less intimidated by him in Hobart; he was more relaxed there, with Maria and their dogs. We all noticed his change in mood, and decrease in cigarettes. But lessons were still stressful and I wasn't quite grasping the full meaning of his words, try as I might. Intellectually, I understood how to change my technique, but anxiety prevented me from relaxing, which impaired my dexterity and mental clarity. These difficulties, and how to overcome them, filled my thoughts almost constantly and caused a lot of stress, tears and exhaustion. Violin and the eating disorder had become the most important things in my life, but the eating disorder prevented me from excelling at violin. What a paradox!

The stress leading up to my recital was all-consuming. I had no head space for anything else. About four days before, I was so constipated that just the thought of eating made me feel sick. However, not eating only increased my exhaustion. Rose recommended grating a tablespoon of fresh ginger and eating it with honey. I was scared to have "too much"[15] honey but followed her advice and it got things moving — TMI. From then on I always made sure I stocked up on fresh ginger the week before a recital.

Luckily, my recital was the first one for the day, at 9 am, which meant I could get it over with early, and didn't run the risk of it being delayed if they were running late. I had hardly slept the night before my recital the previous semester, so I was glad it would be over by the time my lack of sleep caught up with me. I figured I could survive on adrenaline until about midday, but would crash soon after, so an afternoon recital would have been even more of a struggle.

I played as well as I could have hoped in the circumstances. My pieces hadn't been perfect when I practised them, so I knew they wouldn't be in performance either. Overall it went quite well, and I didn't have any big memory slips. I was tremendously relieved and happy afterwards, and excited for the following semester — I had decided to stay in Hobart to do Honours. I watched three friends' recitals after mine, which left me absolutely exhausted. The same thing had happened two years previously. I was so tense on their behalf, willing them to play well and not have any memory slips, that it drained my own mental energy. I also hadn't eaten enough for breakfast, as usual, and was wrecked from my own recital.

---

[15] From the perspective of the calorie-counting eating disorder

We went to a bar nearby to celebrate after my friends' recitals. Two of the friends had just finished Honours, so they were completely finished. There were quite a few of us there having drinks and some people ordered food to share. I was either scared of or allergic to the food they ordered, and couldn't convince myself to spend money ordering my own food. Harriet — who had performed after me that morning — and I had decided a few weeks prior that we would have a cocktail to celebrate being finished for the semester. Because of the cost and the calorie content of a cocktail, there was no way I could allow myself to eat or buy any food. Though I was exhausted, and stressed about money and calories, I still enjoyed the celebrations. I knew I had earned it and was relieved my recital was over.

I stayed in Hobart for the next two weeks, because the Dark MoFo festival,[16] staffed by MONA, was happening. MONA needed all the staff they could get and I was happy to work long shifts and earn extra money. The museum was busier than usual — a lot of people fly down from Melbourne and Sydney for Dark MoFo — so it was exhausting work, especially as I wasn't eating enough. The eating disorder loved that I was running around at work and often missed lunch because we were too busy for anyone to have a break.

It was June, so the daily maximums were usually single-digits, (Celsius), but a lot of the Dark MoFo events were outside. Maybe because it was cheaper, or maybe because the organisers thought it would create a more festive atmosphere. Whatever the reason, the result was me being tired and cold — even more than usual — for almost all of my waking hours, but feeling that my suffering was for the greater good, because that's what the ED voice told me — the greater good being strength of will and weight-loss.

Though I worried about what Mum and Dad would think of my eating and how I would hide the lack of it, I was relieved to go home. It would be warmer, I wouldn't have to work and I wouldn't need to be completely self-sufficient. I could almost return to the relative simplicity of being a child. Almost. And I wouldn't have the stress of living with housemates who, while lovely people, caused me to feel a low-level, but constant, anxiety.

I don't remember much of that holiday. It was nice to catch up with friends and relax a bit, but I had to work even harder to hide how little I was eating, because my intake had decreased since the summer. To most people, it probably looked like a healthy diet, but Mum and Dad were watching more

---

[16] Dark MoFo celebrates pagan rituals, mythology, dark, like, life and death through music, art, food and film.

closely and had a deeper understanding of food and nutrition. Most of the time, my allergies provided the perfect excuse for me to eat different food to others. For example, if I didn't eat pasta or bread, none of my friends would have thought anything of it, because they knew about my gluten intolerance. Most didn't realise this meant I wasn't eating any carbohydrates and was cutting about half the calories from my meal. It's interesting how many people just look at the volume of food instead of the actual food, unless it's obviously rabbit food — raw carrots, celery, lettuce etc. But I knew Mum and Dad would notice the lack of carbohydrates in the meals I prepared myself, my avoidance of oils and fats, and the lack of snacks between meals. I planned my days so I was away from them during meals as much as possible. But I knew they were watching, especially Mum.

A few days before I flew back to Hobart, Mum and Dad sat me down to have a chat about my eating. I denied any deliberate restriction and said I had been stressed, sometimes didn't have time to eat snacks and sometimes just wasn't hungry. I'm pretty sure they saw right through my lies. They asked if we were using the heaters in our house too, because they had noticed that spending money made me anxious. Dad had visited during the first semester, so he knew how cold our house was, and that we hadn't used the heaters during his stay. I denied the anxiety around money and said that we practised at uni where it was warm, rugged up a bit at home, and were fine. Although I staunchly denied that the ED voice was in control, the outcome of the discussion was that I would start seeing a psychologist they had found in Hobart. They thought seeing a female psych face-to-face might be more helpful than my online sessions with Craig.

Knowing that Mum and Dad were becoming more involved added to my stress and, from then on, the eating disorder was often on my mind. Up until then, I had tried to tell myself it wasn't too bad — I was counting calories and restricting, but almost always trying to convince myself to eat more. Having said that, I felt pure joy seeing the number on the scale go down and my clothes become looser. However, my declining weight became a stressor, instead of something of which I could be proud, and made me question my meagre food intake. While questioning the ED voice was a step in the right direction, the conflicting emotions increased my stress even more.

For the first few weeks back in Hobart, I made a huge effort to try to act like a normal person around Harriet and Rose. However, it didn't take long for the constant acting and attempts to decipher the true meaning of their words, to wear me out. I often stayed in my room if I could hear them in the kitchen or living room. It wasn't that I didn't want to talk to them; I just felt uncomfortable and the effort it took to appear normal was stressful and exhausting. I often worried they thought I was weird, socially awkward, annoying, obsessive, or just didn't like me. When I wasn't worrying, I was wondering how to fit in with what they were doing, how to not annoy them, if the silence was awkward, if I was talking too much, if they thought I ate too much… One day I was so stressed that I couldn't stop thinking about them — questioning the meaning behind everything they had said; analysing my actions and how they could have been interpreted as offensive. I couldn't concentrate on my practice so, in the end, I gave up and went home. Luckily Harriet and Rose were both out. Before I got to my room I was crying and, once inside, I was sobbing uncontrollably. I felt utterly hopeless. I didn't know what to do. I felt trapped. I didn't feel I could talk to either of them about it because I couldn't articulate my confusing thoughts and feelings. I just cried myself out and then went to work.

Alanna, the new psych, was good, but ultimately unhelpful. We talked around and around the topic of weight gain and eating more, but I was terrified to put on weight — and therefore terrified to eat more. I didn't want to hate myself again. I understood, logically, that the people who cared for me wouldn't love me any less if I gained weight, but I couldn't make myself truly believe it. And I was too stressed about my violin playing, finances and housemates, to focus on recovery. Though, even without these external stressors, I don't think I would have been able to persuade myself to eat more. I convinced myself to eat a little bit more for a few weeks, but when I saw my weight increase — either because of a fluctuation or a genuine increase in muscle or fat I will never know — I freaked out and returned to my previous food rules.

Our main two topics of discussion were Alanna trying to help me with my violin technique, in an attempt to help remove that stress; and debating Mum and Dad's involvement and pressure. Though she meant well, cared a lot and gave me a lot of time, none of it was helpful. Her advice on violin playing — she was an amateur musician but not a violinist — wasn't helpful, because the root of my problems were anxiety, which caused muscle tension; and a lack of concentration, caused by food restriction. Nor did our conversations about Mum and Dad's involvement lead to any resolution. Alanna understood that I didn't want them involved, but we had agreed that they would be — though I had been forced to agree. We talked about how stressful it was for me to feel they were always watching, and brainstormed other possible arrangements that would work for everyone. But there was no arrangement that would satisfy everyone. I didn't want Mum and Dad to be told my weight and they wanted me to come home and do Maudsley again.

Near the end of the semester, during which my weight had continued to decline, Dad said he was going to visit, to casually monitor my meals for a few days, so I could prove to him that I was eating enough. I flat refused. I argued that him being in the house and obviously watching, would make me too stressed, particularly with my recital only a week or so after he proposed to visit. That much was true. It made me stressed just thinking about having him in the house, worrying about him being bored, or being in the way of Harriet and Rose, and cooking for both of us. It definitely would have affected my practice, which was the second most important thing in my obsessive life. When Dad offered to rent a room or house nearby I insisted it would still be too stressful — though, with that arrangement, it would mostly be because he would see what I ate. I also didn't want him paying for accommodation in addition to his flights. I felt guilty whenever they spent money looking after me; I felt they shouldn't need to anymore.

Alanna suggested a compromise: She and I could meet for every meal one day on a weekend. Then I wouldn't need to worry about having Dad around for a few days, or his flight costs. It was very generous of her to give up her whole day. She said she would have been in the area anyway, to go to the markets and do some shopping, but I think she was trying to ease my guilt. We met for breakfast, lunch and dinner. Alanna suggested I eat my snacks by myself, so I wouldn't need to interrupt my practice to come meet her. I was more than happy with this arrangement, and skipped them. No one was watching, and I knew I would be eating more than usual at my main meals that day. I had to be able to prove to Alanna that I could eat a normal amount.

And I did. Mum, Dad and Alanna had all been of the view that, if the ED voice was loud enough, it wouldn't allow me to eat an adequate amount, even if only for one day. I had had the same worry. But maybe the sick part of me understood that finishing my meals with Alanna was the lesser of two evils. I didn't doubt that Dad would fly over and drag me back to Perth or, at the very least, physically stop me from returning to Hobart the following year to do my final semester of Honours, if I didn't pass the test with Alanna. Skipping the snacks also helped me to feel ok about finishing my meals.

Mum, Dad and Adam flew to Hobart at the end of the semester to watch my recital and see a bit of Tasmania. They arrived two nights before my recital — there was no point in them coming earlier because I would be too busy practising and stressing to spend time with them. The day before my recital — their first day in Hobart — I met them for breakfast, lunch and dinner. They explored Hobart in between meals while I practised.

(Food)

I had the 9 am recital again, which I didn't mind, as I was still waking up multiple times throughout the night. I had been brainstorming with the ED voice for about a month to work out what to eat for breakfast on the morning of my recital. I needed something that would give me enough energy to carry me through my warm-up and the performance, taking into account a heavy dose of nerves, which saps my energy — I often wondered exactly how many calories anxiety used! I didn't want to eat "too much" though, because I wanted to be able to enjoy a celebratory meal afterwards. In the end, I decided on two eggs with vegetables — my customary breakfast at this point was homemade natural yoghurt, with some fruit and a small amount of nuts. To me, eating two eggs was momentous, but I had convinced the ED voice I would need the energy to get through an hour-long recital, preceded by an hour of anxious warming up. "Hmmm looks delicious," Adam commented sarcastically, as he walked through the kitchen to get to the bathroom.[17] I had hoped he wouldn't see what I was eating, but he wanted to get to uni early enough to set up his recording equipment and test the acoustics — I had asked him to record my recital and he loves playing with sound equipment — so he left the house soon after me. I offered to make him breakfast, since he was getting up so early, and took great pleasure in smelling the Nutella as I spread it on his toast. My body screamed at me to eat it, but the ED voice warned me of the guilt that was sure to follow if I did, and permitted me to lick only the tiniest smudge from my finger.

Unsurprisingly, my recital felt like a marathon and I was exhausted at the end. Adrenaline allowed me to concentrate just enough to avoid any big mistakes, so I made it through as well as I could have hoped. Again, finishing was a huge relief and I was proud of what I had achieved — though the healthy part of me knew I could have played much better if I hadn't been starving myself all year. Mum, Dad, Adam, and a few friends had come to watch, so we went to Salamanca[18] for coffee afterwards. I had planned to invite everyone back to our place for cheese, crackers and celebration, but one friend was determined to have a coffee — he's Italian and very serious about his coffee. It was only about 10.30 am when we got to the cafe, and I hadn't been eating snacks for quite a while, so eating at that time, even while celebrating, was out of the question — I tried to convince the ED voice that eating something small

---

[17] He was staying on our couch because there wasn't room for him at Mum and Dad's Airbnb.

[18] The trendy strip of cafes, restaurants, bars and shops near the water.

wouldn't make me put on weight, but I couldn't be sure that was true. I decided it was better to be hungry and avoid the guilt that would follow eating. I was exhausted and my stomach felt empty, having eaten breakfast three and a half hours earlier and barely slept the night before. However, I knew we would go out for lunch as a family, and I wanted to be able to enjoy that without guilt. I said I wasn't hungry and watched everyone else eat, trying to imagine how their food tasted.

It was nice to have lunch afterwards with just the four of us. There had been about ten of us at the cafe, which I found overwhelming after the initial excitement. We walked around Hobart for the rest of the day; Dad and I showed Mum and Adam some of our favourite places from his previous visits. For dinner, we made use of the fancy cheeses I had intended to share after my recital, with the addition of crackers, some dip and chopped vegetables. We ate at Mum and Dad's Airbnb, where I luxuriated in the joy of heating. Even though it was November, it was still cold in Tasmania. The day before, we had noticed there was snow on the top of Mount Wellington — you can see the white top from sea-level — so Mum, Dad and Adam had driven up and seen falling snow for the first time! We still weren't using the heating in our house, but Mum and Dad had theirs cranked up — bliss. My muscles could finally un-tense. It was a nice dinner, I was relieved my recital was over, and I felt safe with my family in the warmth. But the lack of vegetable volume with which I usually filled myself up worried me. I ate most of the carrot sticks, with just enough dip to be able to taste it, as little cheese as I could bear, balancing hunger and guilt, and as few crackers as I could get away with — I knew Mum and Dad would be watching.

The next day we went to Bruny Island, mostly to go on the famous Bruny Island cruise. We had only heard wonderful things about the cruise and it had won a few tourism awards. We had to leave the house by 7 am, as it takes about two hours to get to Bruny Island from Hobart. The eating disorder only allowed me to eat breakfast after 8 am, a rule I had broken the day before due to my early recital. That had caused a lot of anxiety and internal turmoil, but I had argued with the ED voice for weeks beforehand, reasoning that I needed to eat earlier to give my best performance. Aside from the happiness of my friends and family, being thin and achieving my musical goals were the two most important aspects of my life, so it was a tough decision, but luckily violin won. However, I did not deem my enjoyment of the cruise to be nearly as important as giving my best performance in recital. The magical time of 8 am came as we were in the car, waiting in line to drive onto the ferry that would take us to Bruny Island. Maybe because I had risen earlier than usual and had had a tiring day the day before, I had been feeling even more ravenous and light-headed than usual for at least an hour. I was relieved when it was time to eat. I had brought my breakfast in a jar and began eating in the car.

"What have you got there?" Mum asked, attempting a casual, conversational tone.

"Just some yoghurt and fruit and cereal and nuts," I replied, also attempting a casual, bored act, while worrying where Mum's questioning would lead.

"Is that breakfast?" Again, the camouflaged probing.

"Just a snack. Second breakfast!" I joked.

I don't think she believed me. Adam remained quiet. I don't know if he was also suspicious. I had told him that I ate breakfast while he was having a shower that morning but, even at the time, I wasn't sure if he believed me.

I was still hungry and lightheaded after eating — breakfast rarely satisfied my hunger, though I never stopped hoping it would. The hunger, tiredness and dizziness remained for the rest of the day, even after lunch. I had been looking forward to the cruise, and I enjoyed it as much as I could, but it was hard to be interested in the scenery and wildlife when I was tired and cold — the low temperature was intensified by the sea spray and wind chill as we sped through the water. I was sad and disappointed that my eating habits had prevented me from enjoying the experience. The rest of the day on Bruny Island was also shadowed by the eating disorder. I found it difficult to choose something to eat for lunch, as everything on the menu was energy-dense, and was too scared to eat ice cream made with the famous Bruny Island berries. I think Mum and Dad noticed my mood and anxiety around eating but thankfully didn't say anything.

Adam flew back to Perth the next day, as he couldn't afford to take more time off work. I was grateful he'd spent the money for such a short trip, just to see my recital. Mum and Dad stayed another five days and the three of us saw as much as we could of Tasmania. I had only been out of Hobart once, as I hadn't brought my car over from Perth. I had gone to Launceston earlier that year for a choir performance, but had only been there a few hours. Other than that, the furthest I had been from the Hobart CBD was MONA, which was about 10km away.

I had been looking forward to the trip for two reasons: Firstly, I had wanted to see more of Tasmania for a long time. I had seen friends' photos, read and talked about where to go, and now I was finally going to do it. It was a good way to celebrate finishing a busy semester. Secondly, after the stress of living with Harriet and Rose all year, I was looking forward to getting away. I was anxious about what I would eat with Mum and Dad watching, but was still naive enough to think the change of scenery and break from violin practice would allow me to be more carefree.

It was the opposite. At every meal, I was hyper-aware of Mum and Dad watching me. Mum often commented about how much and what I was eating. She tried to use a casual tone of voice but, to my hyper-alert mind, it was a poorly-camouflaged interrogation. I was also worried about my lack of exercise, which made me feel even more guilty about eating. I usually walked everywhere in Hobart out of necessity, but on our brief holiday, we spent a lot of time in the car, driving between towns, so I was sitting much more than usual.

We had some fun times, but it was always an effort for me to pretend I was enjoying myself, to stay upright and continue walking, and to pretend I wasn't chilled to the bone, while my body was screaming at me to find somewhere warm to sit down and rest. My compulsive need to move as much as possible was ever-present; I was always looking for an opportunity to exercise. I pretended I wanted to go for extra walks to see the scenery, to walk places instead of driving — "to get some fresh air," though I longed for the warmth of the car — or to walk further when we went on bush walks. I pretended to be happy, to prove to Mum and Dad that I was ok and enjoying myself, instead of stressed and exhausted. Luckily there were no arguments on the holiday. Maybe Mum and Dad had decided not to say anything because they didn't want to ruin the experience or our relationship, or maybe I gave a believable performance. I know I didn't completely deceive them, but nor did I reveal just how bad things had become.

USA

Only a few days after Mum and Dad flew home, I flew to Dallas, Texas. I had joined the Southern Gospel Choir not long after I moved to Hobart because some friends from Perth were in it, Maria, Peter's amazing wife, was one of the directors, and I love gospel music. It was organised and run by the university but members of the public could also join. At the beginning of the year Andrew, the choir's main director, announced a tour to North America, where we would get to sing with genuine gospel choirs — we were very aware that we were a bunch of mostly white Australians trying to make that amazing gospel sound. The choir and uni did some fundraising, but we had to cover most of the cost ourselves. I strongly considered not going, and saving my pennies for travel and lessons in Europe when I had finished Honours, but in the end I decided to go. I would probably never get the opportunity to sing with a proper gospel choir again, and I had a lot of savings anyway. I had been really looking forward to it. I needed a break from working at MONA, the stress of living with Harriet and Rose, and my suffocating daily routine. I also hoped that America's lower food prices, the break from practice and work, and the holiday mindset, would allow me to bend my normal food rules, and get my eating back on track.

As on my recent holiday with Mum and Dad though, my hopes remained hopes. I had genuinely intended to improve my eating on that trip. Part of the problem with making my own food was that I knew all of the ingredients and was scared to vary them — partly because of my strict food rules and partly because I felt anxious about spending more money than was absolutely necessary. I bought the cheapest food possible, splitting my shopping between a fresh produce market and Woolworths. I remembered the price of everything I bought and knew that fruit and vegetables were cheaper at the market, whereas non-perishables were cheaper at Woolworths. Sometimes I also took a longer walk to Coles, for things that were cheaper there than at Woolworths. I often looked at the online catalogues for all three shops, to check what was on special and compare prices. I didn't mind eating food cooked by others, unless it was obviously calorie dense, because I didn't know exactly how much of each ingredient was present. Though I generally needed to control everything, a big part of me still wanted to feel comfortable eating more, so I tried to eat food made by others as much as possible. I would have eaten out more in Hobart if I hadn't felt so anxious spending money. I hoped that the combination of the USA's cheaper food, and the generous daily budget I had set myself — much more than I allowed myself to spend at home — would enable me to eat lots of delicious food. I wouldn't know the exact ingredients or quantities, preventing me from counting calories, which would allow me to relax my food rules, rewrite some neural pathways and turn this relapse around.

Unfortunately, my plan was thwarted by two unforeseen developments. The first was the presence of corn in almost all of America's processed food. I don't know how I avoided it when I was there the year before; it's in almost everything. I have a lot of food sensitivities which cause various forms of stomach discomfort and corn is one of the worst. This unintentional consumption of corn caused me to be very constipated for most of the tour. I went a week with no bowel movements until a friend gave me a laxative. Even after that, they were few, far between, small and forced. TMI, you're welcome. In hindsight, it's likely the constipation was also caused, in part, by stress. Though I had much more free time than usual, we still had rehearsals, I had to adapt to different, changing living spaces, I was around people most of the day, and was sharing a room with someone I didn't know very well at all. I thought my roommate was really cool, but always worried that she found me boring and annoying. We had been given the choice of choosing our roommate or being assigned one and I had chosen to be assigned one, so I could meet someone new.

The chronic constipation ruined my appetite. Though I wasn't at all hungry, I made myself eat some fruit for breakfast. I genuinely wanted the scrambled eggs and strange crunchy bacon from the hotel buffet, but felt sick when I ate. I wanted to try the exciting flavours of coffee at Starbucks — as we were there in November there were all sorts of tacky pumpkin and cinnamon-flavoured offerings — but had little appetite for main meals, let alone snacks or drinks. Somehow, my energy was mostly ok, which is lucky given how little I was eating — even less than when I was in Hobart.

Because I wasn't eating as much, I also wasn't buying as much food. I was spending much less than I had planned, which the ED voice loved. I quickly returned to my non-holiday mindset of aiming to spend as little as possible each day. If I spent ten dollars one day, because I had only bought a small amount of food, I would feel guilty if I spent more the next, and would avoid it if possible. I started calculating how much money I could save if I continued the tour on this new budget. The anxiety I already felt spending money, coupled with my amended daily budget, which I imposed with my usual rigidity, prevented me from spending more on food on the rare occasions when I had an appetite. Even when food was provided for us, free of charge, the thought of eating more than I had been on previous days — when constipation had spoiled my appetite — made me feel guilty. So I didn't.

Being constipated caused my already strict food rules to become even tighter. Or rather, the eating disorder took advantage of the constipation and used it as an excuse to eat even less. Overall the tour was great fun, but the fun was diluted by feeling sick, fat, lethargic and uncomfortable from being constipated; tired from not eating enough, when the lack of food eventually took its toll; the challenge of navigating food choices with full bowels and the ED voice screaming in my head; and the stress of cohabiting with someone I didn't know well and who I assumed resented me.

Earlier in the year, when I confirmed my participation in the tour, I decided to do some solo travel afterwards. It seemed a waste to spend so much on the airfare and only stay for the ten-day choir tour. Staying longer would cost more, but I had learnt to be a very thrifty traveller, from my trip to Canada and the USA the year before. I decided that the relatively small sum it would cost me to stay an extra two weeks would make the whole trip more worthwhile. I booked hostels in LA, San Francisco and Vegas, buses between the cities, and started planning my daily itinerary.

While travelling with the group and following the timetable added stress in some ways, it was also reassuring to know there were friends and adults I could turn to if I really needed help. Which is probably why, at the end of the tour, when most of the group was getting ready to leave for the airport and I was preparing to leave for a hostel on the other side of town, I began to feel very alone and worried. I burst into tears in the hotel foyer, as I was hugging my friends goodbye. Maria saw and came over to give me a big hug. I felt a bit better after letting the tears out and knew I would probably be fine once I was on my way to my new accommodation. It was just a combination of the unknown, being surrounded by emotional people heading home, and Andrew's dramatic warnings of the dangers of LA.

Near the end of the tour, I became optimistic that traveling solo would be less stressful. I wouldn't need to worry about rehearsals, concerts, or sharing a room with someone I didn't know very well. And in some ways it was, but it was replaced by the stress of looking after myself and finding my way around unfamiliar cities. I had hoped that the freedom to choose where and when I ate would help the constipation, and it did to some extent, but my bowel movements remained slow until I got back to Hobart. However, my goal of spending as little as possible each day remained, even though I was now buying all of my meals — during the tour one or two meals were provided each day, which we had paid for in the initial tour fee. I had been thinking about this near the end of the tour and decided that, since I had already saved money from eating less, I could spend more while travelling alone. A perfectly logical thought. However, during my first day alone, the part of me that became extremely anxious whenever I spent money, suggested that I continue spending as little as possible, so I could add what I saved to the Europe fund. So I did.

I balked at the cost of my Disneyland ticket but managed to talk myself into spending the money. I was even more anxious than usual about spending money for the next few days though. I didn't buy any souvenirs there and couldn't bring myself to pay for a proper lunch. Whereas in the city I could have bought a meal for about $10, in Disneyland everything was at least $20. In the end, I decided to get an ice cream sundae because it was $9. This may seem like an odd choice for someone with AN, but the somewhat healthy part of me reasoned that 1. A few scoops of ice cream contained roughly the same number of calories as I would usually have for lunch; 2. I hadn't had morning or afternoon tea that day and hadn't for most of the trip; and 3. I would be walking around all day, burning calories. I'd had a small breakfast too. I didn't really enjoy the sundae. The ice cream was cheap and tacky, and the ED voice berated me the entire time I was eating, demanding that I stop and throw the rest away. It guilted me after I finished and, though I reminded myself of my three well-reasoned arguments, I accepted its reprimands and vowed to do better next time. Unfortunately I was still hungry afterwards, but I couldn't allow myself to eat anything else.

My next stop was Las Vegas. My main reason for going there was to see the Grand Canyon, but I was also curious to see the Vegas strip. On the first day, I was overtired from a mostly sleepless overnight bus trip. For me, this often means feeling hyper for most of the day until I completely crash. I had fun exploring the strip, walking through fake Venice, fake Broadway and depressing rooms filled with a maze of slot machines and chain-smoking gambling addicts, with dead eyes and bad skin. I could feel myself getting sick that night but told myself that I wasn't — this placebo tactic often holds off colds for me. I was definitely sick when I woke up the next morning though. I assumed I was run down from a busy few weeks or had possibly contracted it from someone on the crowded Greyhound bus I had taken from LA. A decent night's sleep may have kept the sickness at bay, but I had been woken multiple times during the night by drunk roommates coming in.

Unfortunately, I remained sick for my entire stay in Vegas. I had hoped to take advantage of the cheap/free drinks there and try all the cocktails, but decided it was best not to drink, as I wanted to get better as quickly as possible. Though I was sick I still did a lot of walking, partly because I wanted to make the most of my time there and partly, of course, because the ED voice told me to. It was a kilometre from my hostel to the edge of the strip, where most of my exploration took place. As in Disneyland, a lot of the eateries weren't cheap, however, I found a supermarket where I could buy cheap, prepackaged salads.

On the second day, I went on a bus trip to the Grand Canyon. It was still dark when we left, as it takes about four hours to get there. I got up around 6 am, which was more of a struggle than usual, due to another night of drunken interruptions and the fact that I was still sick. It was worth it though. We had a few hours there to walk the length of the South Rim. The entire walk was mind-blowing. I kept taking photos, but none could capture the vastness, the huge-ness, of the Canyon. I joked many times afterwards that I came to understand why it's called the *Grand* Canyon. Walking the Rim and seeing the canyon is still one of my favourite travel experiences and I think everyone should go at some point in their life if they are able. It was hard to tear my eyes away from the view. Needless to say, the ED loved the walk. I still worried about sitting on the bus for so long each way though.

I don't remember what I ate that day but it wouldn't have been much. The bus stopped at a shop on the way to the canyon, so we could use the toilet, stretch our legs and get something to eat. It was the kind of shop that sold overpriced, tacky souvenirs, junk food, drinks and other non-perishables — nuts, dried fruit, chocolate etc. The junk food scared me, as did the non-perishables, as they were often nutrient-dense — though most foods are nutrient-dense compared to the vegetables with which I tried to fill most of my diet.

The next day the Black Friday sales started. I was confused because, to me, Black Friday was when the 13th day of the month landed on a Friday. I asked my roommates what it was all about but, being half drunk and excited to be in Vegas, all I had been able to ascertain was that there were bargains to be had. I walked to a nearby collection of outlet stores, having been told it was a good place to go for Black Friday deals. The overcrowded outdoor mall confirmed this. I was excited to do some shopping for myself and buy Christmas presents and souvenirs for my friends and family. It only took about ten minutes for me to become overwhelmed by the crowds and depressed by everyone's greed and lack of consideration. None of the shoppers cared about anyone else. I was constantly dodging people and being squished as they pushed past me. I couldn't get answers or help from shop assistants, as they gave preference to people who were ready to make a purchase or were more pushy than me.

I had seen a Ghirardelli shop near the entrance, selling what looked like decadent milkshakes, and decided to have one for lunch. As with the ice cream in Disneyland, I reasoned that the calories were probably about the same as a normal lunch for me — I also skipped morning tea, just in case I had underestimated the number of calories in the milkshake, and so I could enjoy it without guilt. Unfortunately, the milkshake contained more ice than I was expecting, and was therefore not as tasty and creamy as I had hoped. The excess of ice meant less calories, but how much less? I was still hungry and tired afterwards, but worried that, if I had "spent" my lunch allowance of calories on the milkshake — I yearned to know the exact number of calories — eating more would put me "over the limit," which terrified me.

I gave up on the sales after an hour or two. All the shops were too crowded for me to look at anything properly and I was becoming more depressed the longer I was there. I wanted to explore the arts district anyway, which happened to be near the outlet mall. It didn't take long for my mood to improve once I retreated to the kinder atmosphere of quiet streets, greenery and small shops selling handmade crafts. It was mostly the people there that helped. They were happy to talk to me and answer my questions, even if I didn't buy anything. One man even explained the origin of the Black Friday sales to me. I stayed in the area as long as I could, soaking up the tranquillity. The peaceful vibes were restoring me emotionally. That day I learned that the concrete jungle of Vegas is not for me. One day was enough for me to marvel at what humans can build, before the people there ruined it.

After Vegas, I went to San Francisco. Everyone had told me that San Fran has a great vibe and lots of culture. I didn't find either, though possibly because I was busy worrying about calories and money and starting to feel hungry and tired. My constipation was improving, and I had gotten over whatever sickness I had in Vegas, but my plan to eat food more freely had gone out the window less than a week into the trip. Now I had to stick to the reduced amount I had been eating when I was constipated — partly because of my amended food rules and partly because of my new goal to spend as little money as possible.

That isn't to say I didn't have fun in San Francisco, Vegas or LA; just not as much as I could have. I went to the Golden Gate Bridge, but couldn't convince myself to pay to hire a bike to ride across. I walked, which took longer and used more energy. I also walked everywhere else in the city. My roommate on the gospel tour said she bought a tram pass because the hills were so steep. And they are. But I didn't buy a pass. Mostly because of the cost — though I didn't look into how much it actually cost — but it quickly became a disordered compulsion. Once I had walked up a few hills, instead of taking the tram, I had to continue to do so. And the ED voice congratulated me for my willpower each time.

I booked a bus tour to Yosemite. Similar to the trip to the Grand Canyon, they made one stop each way, so we could buy food and go to the toilet. As in Nevada, I was scared to eat the cheaper, higher calorie foods, but also scared to buy a more expensive safe food, like a salad. I had brought some snacks with me in my bag, but I was still hungry and tired after eating, because I had deliberately brought the bare minimum, to prevent myself from eating "too much." The day trip was fun, but it rained most of the time and was cold. I tried to make the most of it though, and see as much as I could. I took photos of myself smiling and trying to look like I was having fun. I asked another tourist to take a photo of me in front of a waterfall. I put my arms up in the air in feigned joy, so I would have a memory of myself living the dream while, in truth, I was cold, tired and could feel the effort of holding my arms up sapping my energy.

On my last day, I finally went to The Cheesecake Factory and bought myself a cheesecake for lunch. I had assumed The Cheesecake Factory was a mythical restaurant that only existed in the Big Bang Theory, but at some point, I learnt that it's real and there are lots of them. I looked through the menu on their website, hoping to go there for lunch or dinner. However the meal prices were much higher than I felt comfortable paying, so I immediately scrapped that idea. Instead, I turned to the desserts. I looked through the cheesecakes carefully, making a shortlist and weighing up the pros and cons of each. In the end, I chose one called 'Adam's Reece's Cheesecake.' I was very excited to eat it. I bought one to take away and brought it back to eat in the foyer of my hostel, while I waited for my shuttle to the airport. The cake was my lunch, as I couldn't fathom eating one as a snack without feeling disgusted at my greed. Unfortunately, I wasn't hungry when I got back to the hostel with my much-anticipated cake. I was probably still a bit constipated. And sometimes, when I'm excited about a special meal, the anxiety caused by my anticipation, and my need for it to be perfect, spoils my hunger. Or maybe, because I had restricted my food earlier in the day to make up for the cheesecake, my digestion had slowed down and wasn't giving me hunger cues. Whatever the reason, I was disappointed by my lack of hunger, after looking forward to this treat for so long and planning it so carefully. I ate it anyway, feeling guilty the entire time. Maybe I wasn't hungry because my body didn't need the food. Maybe I would put on weight from the unnecessary calories. I was greedy for eating when I wasn't hungry, just because I wanted a treat.

Summer

I stayed in Hobart for about two weeks before flying back to Perth for the summer holidays. During the first week, I took part in an orchestral training program, organised by the university. I spent the second week working, practising and cleaning up the house for our final inspection. Rose was moving to Milan the following year, while Harriet and I both planned to stay another six months in Hobart. I would finish Honours mid-year and planned to go to Europe to do some auditions and have lessons afterwards. We had been speaking to other friends at uni about finding a house to rent together the following year.

While cleaning didn't require the intense mental concentration demanded by violin practice, it was physically exhausting. Harriet and I were also working at MONA most days, during which I power-walked around the Wine Bar, delivering meals and clearing tables, for six or more hours, sometimes with no break. The night before we moved out, our neighbours invited us over for dinner. They were lovely, laid-back art students we had come to know during the year. One of them made a delicious vegan lasagne, however, I was unfortunately intolerant to most of the ingredients, as it was full of pasta and soy cheese. I went to bed with a gaping hole in my stomach that night, so it took me a long time to get to sleep. I had spied my last tin of tuna in our neighbours' pantry, which Rose must have given them when she took over what was left in our pantry earlier in the day. I had planned to eat it with lunch the following day. I felt it would be rude to ask for it back, though, in hindsight, they probably wouldn't have minded.

The next day Bill — a uni friend with a car — and I took Harriet's and my belongings to his house, to store over the summer. It was very kind of him to let us stack boxes in his living space and to take the time to help move everything. It was exhausting, carrying everything out of the house, making it fit in his car, and making conversation with Bill on the drive. He's a lovely guy, and easy to talk to, but I was still hungry from the night before and stressed about everything I needed to do that day.

Harriet, Rose and I had planned to meet at a cafe when I got back from Bill's. We had been talking about going there together for over a year and had never made it. I never bought food out, not even coffee, so I was nervous about how I would deal with the situation. Harriet and Rose both knew I was very careful with money, but didn't realise quite how anxious it made me, because I covered the truth with lies and omissions as much as I could. I brought some chocolate to share, hoping they would buy some food and we would share everything. Unfortunately, I ended up feeling awkward about bringing chocolate to a cafe, where I should have been buying their food. I worried what the owners would think if they saw, or if Harriet and Rose would think it was rude. I tried to rectify the situation by saying it was the type of chocolate we all loved and had sometimes shared throughout the year, and thought it would be fitting to share a block one last time. To avoid buying a coffee, I said I didn't want any more caffeine and just wanted chocolate. I don't think they believed me, but I stuck to my story. Unfortunately, neither Harriet nor Rose bought food, only coffee, so I only ate two or three squares of chocolate, because I was scared to eat any more. That was my lunch. I flew home that afternoon.

The summer holidays were not great. As on previous visits, I ate away from home as much as possible, or when Mum and Dad were out. I couldn't avoid them at every meal though, so they quickly saw how restricted my eating had become. And they probably guessed that I was avoiding eating with them. Mum made lots of unsubtle comments about what I was eating and pretended to innocently offer me more, or different, food. I don't remember a lot from that summer, except that I had to be very secretive with food, I was always worried Mum would mention the eating disorder or make me eat something scary, and I generally felt quite anxious when I was at home.

"Can you, Mum and I have a chat about your health?" Dad asked one day.
"Yeah?" I replied, feigning disinterest while butterflies suddenly took flight in my tummy.
I was pretty sure I knew what they would say, and I wasn't wrong.
"How do you think your eating is going?" Dad asked, when the three of us were seated.
"Ummm ok? I know it could be better, but I'm working on it," I mumbled. I knew it was highly unlikely they would believe me, but it was worth a try.
"We can tell, just by looking at you, that you lost weight in America. Do you want to tell us what happened there?"
"I told you. There was corn in everything. I was really constipated most of the time. I ate as much as I could, but usually I felt sick… I've been eating normally since I got back, but I guess it hasn't been enough for me to gain back the weight I lost." I attempted to appear worried about the weight loss, but I was secretly pleased.
"We've seen what you eat though. It's mostly vegetables. Maybe a bit of protein, but never any carbohydrate except at dinner, when we cook. And even then, you leave most of the rice on your plate," Mum replied. The agitation in her voice scared me.
"I'm sick of always having rice," I lied.

Their probing and my lies took us in circles, while Mum's voice rose and I felt increasingly trapped.
"We don't want you to go back to Hobart next year," Dad said eventually. "It wouldn't be safe. You're not well enough."
My stomach dropped.
"It's because we love you," Mum said, her voice dripping with sickly sweet sympathy.
I was furious at her for using that line again. She always used it as her trump card, but it only fanned my burning rage. I rolled my eyes.
"If you loved me, you would let me go back so I have a chance to recover and be happy, instead of staying here. I won't recover here; I'll only get worse!" I knew I sounded like a self-entitled teenager.
"You had all of last year to turn things around and you only got worse," Dad reasoned.
"That's because I knew Alanna was reporting back to you. It made me too stressed to eat. If you'd just leave me alone I could have recovered by now."
"Come on, we were on the other side of the country. It'd be hard to leave you alone much more than we have been," dad replied, exasperated.
"You were seeing Alanna all year and your eating has only become more restricted. The Ed's in control," Mum said. I hated it when she used the 'ED' acronym, as though it was an inside joke and she was in the know.

Mum and Dad wanted me to go to a treatment centre in Ohio, which had a high recovery rate. They would pay for everything. The average stay was about a month, so they assumed it would be similar for me. When I was discharged, I could return to Perth, practise eating properly in the real world, and go back to Hobart when I was ready. There was no way I was going to agree to that. I felt I needed to continue working on my violin playing; it was a compulsion. I was also in a rush to finish uni and get on with life. I felt going to the treatment centre would waste precious time. We argued for a long time, Mum and I fluctuating between being angry, stressed, sad and calm, while Dad remained steady and pragmatic. Eventually, I convinced them to allow me to return to Hobart, but with extra supports in place.

I had to see Beth, my GP, every week, where I would be weighed, have my pulse and blood pressure taken, and provide a urine sample, to prove I wasn't water loading — which I had been. Dad was going to come visit not long after I got back, to meet with Beth and Alanna in person. They wanted Beth to tell them my weights each week, so they knew what was going on and I had some accountability. This was what I feared most. Up until now, I had only had to deal with Beth and Alanna's concern when weight went down. They couldn't do much until my BMI dropped below 15, which is the somewhat arbitrary number at which a person can be hospitalised against their will. But if Mum and Dad decided my weight was too low, I wouldn't have been surprised if they flew to Hobart and physically dragged me onto a plane back to Perth. However, I was also worried that they wouldn't allow me to go back to Hobart if I didn't agree to their terms. Again, it wouldn't have surprised me if they physically restrained me if I tried to leave the house to go to the airport. Luckily, they suggested a compromise: Beth wouldn't tell them my weight unless it dropped below a certain number. The number they chose was higher than I wanted, but it was better than them knowing my exact weight every week. I still had hope that I could turn this relapse around. Even though we had come to an "agreement" I knew Mum and Dad — especially Mum — were worried that I was returning to Hobart. The atmosphere in the car was tense as we drove to the airport. I was relieved to get away.

Hobart Year 3

Harriet and I had been looking at rentals in Hobart over the holidays, but it was hard to apply when we couldn't be there in person, let alone commit without seeing the place. After sharing links from realestate.com.au for a few weeks, we decided to wait until we got back to Hobart to find a place. This meant finding a temporary place to live. Harriet was going to stay with her boyfriend's family, so I asked Facebook if anyone had a room. Luckily Carrie, a uni friend from Adelaide, was coming back a few weeks after me, so her room was free and she was happy for me to use it. I'm still incredibly grateful to her for her generosity and for trusting me with her things. Her housemate, Ying, who I had never met, let me in the first night and gave me Carrie's key. She was lovely and spent most of her time studying in her room. I was glad because it took away the stress of conversing with someone I didn't know well.

The airport shuttle bus dropped me in Hobart early in the evening, but Ying couldn't meet me at the apartment until about 9 pm. I had an hour or two to kill and also needed to get dinner. It made sense to go to a restaurant for dinner, especially as I had my suitcase and violin with me. However, there was no way I could convince myself to pay for a restaurant meal, so I got some tinned vegetables and a small tub of cottage cheese from Woolworths and ate in the foyer of the shopping area.

The next morning I was tired and hungry from the stress of the previous day. I hadn't bought any groceries the night before, because my hands were full with my luggage. Though I was very hungry, moderately lightheaded and had shaky legs, I walked to Woolworths, got some groceries and came back to eat breakfast. Uni hadn't started yet, so I spent most of those two weeks practising, working at MONA, having lessons and trying to find a home for the next six months.

As promised, Dad came to visit almost two weeks later. I had to move out of Carrie's room while Dad was there because Ying had a friend coming to stay in the room. I still hadn't found somewhere to live long-term, but another friend came to the rescue. Jan, another violinist from Perth, worked and lived in the boarding house at a private school in the city. Her role was to supervise the boarders, help them with their homework, and be someone they could come to for help and support. The school was looking for someone else to work alongside her and I had applied for the job. It would be perfect. It would give me a place to live, a job — I wouldn't need to work at MONA anymore — and my meals would be provided. The healthy part of me was excited about the meals — I wouldn't have to stress about spending money on food; I usually found it easier to eat proper meals if I hadn't prepared them myself and therefore didn't know all of the ingredients; and apparently, the food was delicious — they had a proper chef! The interview wasn't for another week or so but Jan said that, as school hadn't yet started for the year, I could stay there for a bit. We were both hoping I would get the job anyway, and continue living there. Luckily Dad had hired a car, so he drove my luggage and me to the boarding house.

Luckily, Jan kept to herself. I had worried we might be sharing a room or that we'd be around each other a lot but, like me, Jan seemed to prefer being alone. I slept in one of the student dorm beds and hardly saw her except when I arrived back at the school after being out, as she had to unlock the door to let me in. Unfortunately, the chef wasn't back yet, but there was a small kitchen. I didn't want to risk bothering Jan by cooking on the stove and I feel awkward cooking when others are watching anyway, so I stuck to food I could eat cold or microwave — frozen or tinned vegetables, yoghurt, tinned tuna and cottage cheese. It was a long walk up a steep hill from the nearest supermarket to the school, so I planned my shopping trips around work and practice and carefully rationed my food so I wouldn't run out before I had the time and energy to tackle the hill again. Unfortunately I had to leave the school after five days, when some boarders returned early.

Again I was lucky. When I mentioned to Harriet that I needed to move again, she said that Myf, a friend from MONA, was looking to rent out her backyard studio for short stints. I messaged Myf, who was happy to let me stay until I found a place. One morning before work, in light rain, I walked my suitcase, violin and small handbag the few kilometres to Myf's house. Unfortunately, this included another very steep hill. Myf lived on the aptly-named Hill Street, which must have been one of the steepest streets in Hobart.

"What do you want to do food-wise?" I asked Myf that afternoon. "Do you want to eat together or should I do my own thing?"
"Oh, I hadn't thought about it." I was shocked anyone could be so carefree about the cost of food. "I've already started preparing the chicken for dinner tonight so do you want to eat with us?"
Should I offer them money? I never bought fresh meat because it was more expensive than eggs and lentils, so I was worried about how much money Myf might expect me to contribute for my share.
"Do you want me to pay extra rent, to cover food then, if we share?" I asked.
Did they want to share, or was this hospitality just for my first night?

"Let's just play it by ear. You buy what you need and we'll do our usual shop and we can share."
I guess this is what most people would do; people who don't get stressed every time they have to spend money, don't buy almost exactly the same food every week because it's the cheapest available, and ration themselves so it lasts the whole week. But Myf's relaxed approach didn't give me a definite answer. How much would we be sharing each other's food? Should I cook every few days? Are they just being polite? Do they want me to move out now? Are they already regretting agreeing to let me stay?

Myf and Jack were truly wonderful hosts, but I found it very stressful living with them. I had to go into the house to use the kitchen or bathroom, and Myf was often there — she lived there after all. Each time I went in we would have a chat, which was lovely, but I always worried I was bothering Myf, and felt anxious about taking long breaks from practice. I timetabled my practice regimentally and got stressed if anyone or anything forced me to break the routine.

I muddled through my time there, questioning everything I said and did and staying in the studio as much as possible. This meant I often stayed there instead of going inside to get food when I was hungry. But I didn't know how to act when I went inside. I felt awkward eating with them too. I often felt awkward eating with others, unless there was a big group of us, allowing me to fade into the crowd.

"Have you ever had an eating disorder?" Myf asked me one night when Jack was out.
"Yes," I replied, shocked, feeling my face flush. "Why do you ask?"
"I've just noticed you eat very carefully, slow and neat. And you're so skinny."
"Oh, that's not the eating disorder. I just feel a bit uncomfortable eating with you and Jack because it's your house and I worry I'm imposing…" I felt awkward admitting to my discomfort but decided to take a risk and speak truthfully. I don't think Myf believed me.
"I used to have anorexia, when I was about thirteen, so I notice the signs in other people" she said.
I was shocked. Myf was always so happy; it had never occurred to me that she may not have always been that way.

"I did the 40-hour famine, so I lost a bit of weight. Then when it was over and I could eat again, I felt guilty," Myf explained.

Mum had told me about another girl who had developed AN after doing the 40-hour famine, so I wasn't surprised. For her and Myf, the weight loss had been enough to trigger the eating disorder.

"I had a book where I wrote down everything I ate each day and how much I weighed. I was just eating vegetables — small amounts of broccoli and carrots — but I never reached my target weight; I've just got big bones."

I wondered why Myf never reached her goal weight if she was eating as little as she said. I didn't know then that some people's bodies naturally sit at a higher weight and will never drop into the anorexic BMI range without suffering organ failure. Myf and I had a good heart-to-heart that night. I never would have guessed she'd had AN. She seemed so carefree around food.

At some point during my two weeks with Myf and Jack, I mentioned to another work friend, Ann, that I was going to look at a rental that afternoon. I had been looking on Gumtree and going to meet people advertising rooms since I got back to Hobart, but it was hard to find people who wanted someone for only five or six months. Ann said she was looking for someone to sublet her room while she was away for a few months for work. Conveniently she lived a few minutes walk from Myf and Jack. I had met Ann's housemates briefly the year before at her birthday party, but she suggested I come over for dinner, so we could get to know each other — and they could decide if they liked me enough to live with me.

They were happy for me to move in and I did so a few days later. Ann wasn't leaving for another week or two, but they had a makeshift spare room outside, attached to the shed, which I could use. I was keen to move and finally settle, even if it meant living in a shack. It was exciting living in a little cubby house, looking out into the garden. Luckily it wasn't too cold yet, because it wasn't insulated. A few days later, Bill brought over my boxes of belongings from his house and I started to settle in.

It was a beautiful house, with lots of wood furnishings and a decent-sized backyard. My housemates were lovely. It was nice to live with older people who were more mature and settled in life. Christie was a paralegal and had become friends with Ann after they met in a meditation class. Hans was a lovely carpenter from Berlin, who was always up for a chat and with whom I had lots of fascinating conversations. He was separated from his partner, Katherine, but they had a young daughter together, Lina. Hans always had a special smile on his face when he talked about Lina.

Mum and Dad came to visit not long after I moved in, while I was still sleeping in the shack. Ann was away for the weekend so she was happy for them to stay in her room. The only thing I remember from their visit was the three of us chatting to Hans one afternoon. He was telling us about growing up in West Berlin, when the wall was still up, and how he was so lucky to be on the Western side. He said he used to play football with the American soldiers. He was trying to explain the geography to Mum and Dad and, lacking pen and paper, breathed on the window to fog it up and drew a map with his finger. I had no idea where in Europe Germany was, and was too tired to pay attention. I had been restricting my food all day, while pretending to be happy and energetic, because Mum, Dad and I were going out for dinner.

Unfortunately, Hans moved out a few days after I moved into Ann's room, as he had bought a warehouse, which he was going to transform into a house. He had been subletting his room from John, who had been diving in Antarctica for six months. John arrived after midnight, so I met him the next morning. I tried not to ask him too many questions about his research and Antarctica — when Ann told me he was doing a PhD in Marine Biology, and I said I was excited to hear all about it, she politely, but somewhat firmly, suggested I give him time to rest before bothering him with all my questions. About a week after I moved into her room, Ann's work brought her back to Hobart for a few days. I asked if she wanted to stay in her room while she was back, but she said "No," before changing the subject, so I assumed her employer was providing accommodation. It turned out she was staying with us, in John's room. I had wondered if they were together, from the way she spoke about him, but she had never actually come out and said it, so I didn't ask.

Uni semester started about a week later. I knew it would be busy, with even more repertoire than usual to learn, but I had started learning it while I was in Perth. I had practised two to three hours a day in Perth — though Mum kept telling me to take more time off — and had come back to Hobart earlier to start lessons again, so I thought I was on track. I had also gone back to basics for a month or so, to focus on fixing some bad habits in my technique, which had been causing me trouble for a few years. It was mostly to do with holding unnecessary tension while I was playing, so I had to break that habit while teaching myself how to make the necessary movements without clenching my muscles. I was somewhat surprised and also proud that I had achieved this.

I had two options for my Honours project at UTas: I could perform a 50-minute recital and write a thesis or perform a 50-minute recital and record and edit another 20-minute performance of additional repertoire. I chose the recording project, as writing a thesis didn't interest me, and I could use the recording for orchestral auditions. I had chosen to record the first two movements of Mozart Concerto No. 5, as most orchestral auditions require a

Mozart Concerto. I only needed the first two movements because that filled the 20 minutes.

In the first week of the semester Collette, the head of strings, announced that she wanted to give students the opportunity to perform a concerto with the orchestra. I truly felt that this year would be about recovery and putting everything into music, so I asked to perform the Mozart Concerto. Collette agreed but asked me to perform the entire concerto — three movements instead of two. I love the third movement, but I already had so many notes to learn and, though I was feeling positive, I was also already stressed. When I voiced this, she suggested asking another violinist at uni to play the third movement. I could leave the stage after the second movement and he could walk on to play the third. He is a brilliant violinist, but I felt that if he could learn the third movement on top of his recital repertoire, then I should also be able to. I felt I would be letting myself down if I didn't rise to the challenge, so I agreed to perform all there movements.

(Food rules, food and exercise)

Every morning, unless I was working, I got up at 7 am, had a shower and breakfast, then practised for two hours, while I felt fresh. After practice my tired, hungry brain struggled through whatever written work I needed to do for uni, until 1 pm, which was the earliest I allowed myself to eat lunch. I did more uni work or other chores after lunch, then practised for another two or more hours after dinner.

For a few days early in the year, I wasn't hungry after my shower so, not wanting to waste time, I practised until I was hungry, then had breakfast. It felt good to have done some of my practice before I ate; eating felt like a reward for my work. After a few days of this, the ED quickly changed the rules; I wasn't allowed to eat breakfast until 9 am at the earliest. Some days I was ravenous, lightheaded and could barely concentrate while I was practising. I willed myself to focus, but there's only so much you can achieve with a malnourished body and brain, even with the strongest willpower. I still practised — I would have been overcome with guilt if I hadn't — but it wasn't productive, especially as the year progressed, my body became weaker, and my brain shrunk.

A month or so into semester, I noticed that John and Christie relaxed after dinner, having done all their work during the day. I started to wish that I could relax at night too. It was harder to make myself go back to my room to practise, knowing they were in the lounge room chatting. Practising after dinner also forced me to have a half-decent dinner, so I would have enough energy to concentrate — though my dinners were becoming less substantial, making my nighttime practice as much of a struggle as it was in the morning. I reassessed my routine; if I did all my practice during the day it wouldn't matter if I ate less for dinner. I liked going to bed a bit hungry and I would feel good for eating less. I was often tired after my insubstantial lunch, and even more so later in the afternoon. I moved my nighttime practice session to the morning, continuing after breakfast with almost no break, until I had lunch.

When the clock allowed me to finish, I walked to the local shop — down and up steep Hill Street each way — with weak legs, an empty stomach and varying degrees of lightheadedness, to buy food to make lunch. I made multiple trips to the shop each week; partly because it caused me less anxiety to spread out my spending, and also out of necessity, as I had to carry whatever I had bought on the walk home. Eating lunch was always a relief and felt like a huge reward that I had worked hard to earn. I was usually still hungry when I finished eating though.

Fitting meals around my uni timetable and lessons was always tricky. Luckily I didn't need to go into uni as much that semester, as most of my workload was self-directed. I was especially appreciative of this, as I had to walk up a very steep hill to get home from uni. I planned my days to avoid walking up the hill more than once a day, though the ED voice congratulated me on the days I made two trips. Unfortunately, I had a one-hour class at 9 am once a week, where we learnt about recording and editing. If I ate breakfast before I left I would need to eat at 8 am, which would leave me feeling guilty all morning. It would also mean a longer gap between breakfast and lunch, during which I would become hungry, and the ED voice would berate me for allowing myself to eat early.

I planned my mealtimes so they were spaced evenly throughout the day to avoid long stretches of time without eating. Food was the highlight of my day and it had to be perfect. I made sure I was hungry before eating because it allowed me to enjoy the meal so much more. I went to the toilet just before I ate, so I would be as empty as possible and wouldn't feel the discomfort of a full bladder during the meal. I always sat in the same place for breakfast and lunch, with the understanding of flexibility at dinner, and used my favourite cutlery and crockery. I preferred to eat alone, so I could watch part of a movie or tv show and not need to concentrate on having a conversation — I could relax completely.

(Food rules)

I spent a lot of time working out the best time to have breakfast — before or after the 9 am class. I considered bringing it with me and eating at uni, just before class, but then I wouldn't be able to brush my teeth afterwards and might have to talk to someone while I was eating, which would mar the experience. It also meant that when I got home from class and needed to practise — the class was also ruining my practice schedule — I wouldn't have eaten for over two hours and would have just walked up the hill. I would be hungry and tired and practice would be even harder than usual. I decided to eat breakfast when I got home, after class, around 10.30 am. I was always ravenous and lightheaded during the class and had to constantly force myself to focus. I spent most of the class yearning for food and imagining myself eating delicious fear foods. The walk home after class, up the hill, was exhausting. I was often so impatient to get home and eat that I continuously imagined myself a few metres further up the footpath than I actually was.

The first time I went to see Beth that year, my weight had increased slightly. I felt like a failure, but she said it would make Mum and Dad happy to know the number and asked if I minded her telling them. I agreed, hoping it would lessen their worry and get them off my back a bit. I tried to tell myself that my weight may not have actually gone up. My appointments were at different times of the day, so it was hard to compare weights. I was also still water loading before my appointments and drank different amounts each time, depending on how full my bladder was and if Beth was running late — I often had to wait about an hour, which made water loading a balancing act combined with a guessing game. It was very stressful. I wanted to get at least a litre in, but if I drank it too early and had to wait a long time, I would be busting during the appointment. A few times I couldn't hold it in and had to go to the toiler before my appointment, then drink another litre as quickly as I could. I used to worry that the reception staff would report to Beth that I was drinking, and tried to sit where they couldn't see me easily, and drink when they were busy talking to other patients.

Giving the urine sample was another hurdle, as I had to do this before Beth weighed me. A dipstick told her its concentration, from which she could get an idea of how much I had been drinking. There were two obstacles here: Firstly, as I had to collect the sample before being weighed, I had to wee a bit, then stop! This is difficult enough at the best of times but with a full bladder, it takes constant concentration and a strong pelvic floor. I had to work hard not to squirm for the rest of the appointment, as I struggled not to wet myself. The second problem was that the dipstick told Beth how diluted my urine was.

Each time she commented on the dilution, I feigned innocence, saying I hadn't drunk any more than usual and no, I didn't need to go to the toilet. Maybe there was something wrong with the dipstick? Was there a chance the test wasn't accurate for everyone? I don't know if she believed me but Mum saw right through my lies. I continued to deny water loading though. It would be worse if I admitted to it, and I couldn't stop it, or my weight might drop below the number we had agreed upon before I left Perth.

Every month or so, Peter and Maria would invite all of Peter's students over to their house for "family dinner." Harriet and I always looked forward to the conversation — which included stories of Peter and Maria's travels, strange people they had worked with, famous violinists, and Peter's childhood and boarding school antics — seeing Peter and Maria relaxed, the warmth of their fire and a really good meal. By chance, they organised a dinner on my birthday. I wasn't sure if it was deliberate or a coincidence, and I mentioned this to Mum and Dad. Unbeknown to me, they ordered a big cake from a bakery in Hobart, which they knew I liked, and asked Peter to pick it up so we could all share it after dinner. It was one of those fancy cakes which are delicious and also a work of architectural art. There was a lot of chocolate meringue, nuts and various types of chocolate ganache. It was delicious. I had had it once before. There were only five or six of us there that night, so we didn't make much of a dent in the cake. Peter and Maria didn't want any and no one else wanted to take any home, so I went home with about two-thirds of a huge cake, planning to share it with John and Christie. There wasn't room in the fridge for my big cake, so I left it on my bedroom floor that night. It was only a few degrees anyway, and the cake was full of sugar, so it wouldn't go off.

(Food)

I had every intention of sharing the cake with Christie and John. I love making delicious food for others, but the part of me that constantly stressed about money, worried that they would eat it faster than me — I knew I would only allow myself to eat a tiny amount each day — and I would miss out. The next morning while I was practising before breakfast, my hunger got the better of me and I broke off a small piece of the chocolate meringue to eat. It was delicious and I was so hungry that I broke off a few more pieces to eat. I immediately felt horribly guilty for giving in to my hunger and worried that I would gain fat from the extra calories. The ED voice ordered me to eat less at breakfast to make up for my indulgence. At that time, my breakfast included a poached egg, so I reasoned that, as I had just eaten meringue, I shouldn't have an egg that day. All debts repaid. I allowed myself to eat a few more pieces of meringue since I would be having less at breakfast. This became a habit. I would eat some of the cake — I allowed myself to have some of the ganache too, though I felt guilty every time — but omit the egg from my breakfast. I continued until the cake was all gone. This took a few weeks, but the cold May weather and sugar stopped it from going off. When the cake was finished, I continued to omit the egg from my breakfast. I couldn't convince myself to start buying eggs again, and the actions required to poach an egg seemed too time-consuming. The ED voice told me it was too much hassle to cook an egg, but I knew it was lying.

Near the end of semester, I mentioned my plan to go to Europe in a text message to Mum. She and Dad knew I wanted to go later that year, to have lessons with different teachers and hopefully find someone to learn from for a year or so, but they always changed the subject when I brought it up. This time, however, she said I couldn't go because I wasn't well enough. I knew that, legally, there was nothing they could do to stop me from going, but it wouldn't have surprised me if they physically prevented me from going to the airport — Dad had done so when I tried to leave the house to go to uni a few years earlier, when we were doing Maudsley.

I considered planning the trip without telling them, then sneaking out at night and taking a taxi to the airport, but I was scared to defy them. Moving out had been scary enough; I didn't know if I had the courage to sneak off to Europe without telling them. I also didn't want to pay for a taxi to the airport. I knew a taxi fare was pocket money compared to my airfare, accommodation and everything else. However, I was so anxious about spending money that a taxi fare, on top of travel costs, felt like too much. I also considered flying to Europe from Hobart, so Mum and Dad wouldn't be able to stop me, but my passport was in Perth and, though I was angry and disappointed, I didn't want to worry them. I argued with Mum via text, saying that I would be able to eat better when I didn't have the stress of uni and she and Dad watching me. She said that if I couldn't eat properly at home then it would be even harder in a foreign country, especially with my food intolerances and fear of spending money — I continued to deny having a fear of spending money but I don't blame them for not believing me.

Mum and Dad wanted me to come home when I finished uni, to live with them. They wanted to control my meals until I put on weight and recovered. Only then would they allow me to go to Europe. But I didn't want to be twiddling my thumbs in Perth while we did Maudsley again — I knew that just eating more and gaining weight would help me recover anyway — it felt like a waste of precious time. And I truly believed that being away from home, in Europe, would help my eating. I thought I would be more relaxed spending money, as I had been in Canada and the USA two years earlier, and therefore allow myself to buy more food — I knew this hadn't worked out in the USA the previous year, but I blamed the constipation. I also thought that buying food out, which had been prepared by someone else, would allow me to eat more without feeling guilty. If I put on weight it would be slow — hopefully so slow that I wouldn't notice. I knew I could have done this in Hobart too — Alanna and I talked about it a lot in our sessions — but knowing the number of calories in my food and my fear of spending more money felt like a literal, physical, barrier inside my mind, preventing me buying more nutrient-dense food. Money aside, work, lessons and simply not being hungry at times, stopped me from eating, even when I wanted to.

I was furious with Mum and Dad, especially Mum, since she had been the one to tell me I couldn't go. I was angry because they had been trying to take back control of my eating for years, and had only made it worse. I felt that, if they would just leave me alone, I could get better in my own way. And because Mum was telling me what I could and couldn't do, as though I was a child, when I was almost 23. There was no way I was going back to Perth at the end of the semester to do Maudsley again. I needed to keep working on my violin playing anyway. If not with teachers in Europe, then with Peter. Consumed by hurt and resentment, I stopped messaging and calling Mum and Dad. Mum started sending me a message every day, saying how much she loved me, which both annoyed and saddened me. But I didn't allow myself to reply.

A day or two after Mum told me I couldn't go to Europe, I was in the kitchen making a cup of tea, thinking about the conversation and my options. Ann, who was in Hobart for a short visit, came into the house from the backyard, where she and John had been sitting.
"Have you decided where you're going in Europe?" She asked, while the kettle boiled.
I had to tell her the truth; she would find out eventually anyway.
"Mum and Dad don't want me to go," I sighed.
"But… isn't that your decision? It's your money, and you've saved enough, haven't you?"
"Yeah but… they're just worried about me travelling alone. They don't trust me," I half-lied, rolling my eyes. Ann didn't know I had AN and I wanted to keep it that way. I worried people would treat me differently if I told them.
"Didn't you stay in America by yourself after the tour last year though?" She asked, trying to understand the seemingly sudden change in Mum and Dad's attitude.

"Yeah but… this will be longer and… they don't speak English… They're just being stupid," I mumbled.

The tears I had been blinking back began to fall. Ann was so wonderfully and effortlessly understanding and comforting.

"I need to find somewhere else to stay now too," I said through my tears. "I don't want to go back to Perth but you'll need your room back soon."

"That's ok, I can stay in John's room," she replied easily.

"What? No, you don't have to do that. You'll want your own space."

Surely it was too soon for them to make that commitment. How naive of me.

"No, it's ok, I want to. I probably would have anyway," she assured me.

It didn't take much to convince me, because I wanted to believe it was ok for me to stay there. I was relieved, but continued to worry about what Mum and Dad might do. When I told them I was staying in Hobart, would Dad would come over and force me to come back to Perth?

There was a wonderful gas heater in our lounge, which Ann, John and Christie happily used when it was cold. Every time they switched it on, I felt a knot in my stomach; I was worried about the gas bill. I never turned it on myself, opting to rug up in a beanie and dressing gown instead. I did all my practice at home that year, to save time and avoid walking up the hill on the way back from uni. There was a small, portable, oil heater in my room, but I only used it once or twice for about half an hour, before worrying that continued use would cost too much. I felt that, since it was only me using the heater, it would only be fair for me to pay a larger portion of the energy bill, which scared me even more. So, to keep things fair and spend as little as possible, I didn't use the heater. Instead, while it was less than ten degrees outside — and not much warmer inside — I dressed in tracksuit pants, a thick dressing gown, a beanie and fingerless gloves. I also drank about one cup of tea every hour in an attempt to warm myself up. I was still so cold I constantly had tension in my shoulders — which didn't help my violin playing — and varying degrees of numbness in my fingers. Unless I was in the lounge room at night, when someone else turned on the heater, or under my thick doona at night — though sometimes not even then — I was uncomfortably cold. The type of cold that prevents you from relaxing and distracts you from everything else until you can get warm. To this day, I get anxious when I am cold. I worry that I will never be warm again, as was true for two years. It's a survival mechanism. It's trauma. I used to love winter and being a little bit cold made me excited and energetic. Now it scares me.

The remainder of the semester was a combination of exciting improvements in my playing, stress from everything I needed to do for uni, worrying about money, trying not to be cold, and internal turmoil — I was still constantly trying to convince the ED voice that I should eat more — hunger and exhaustion from doing too much with not enough fuel. I tried to convince myself that this was exciting; I was living my best life and everything would be ok when I finished uni. I would get to Europe eventually and work as a freelance musician, travelling around the world with a chamber orchestra or smaller chamber group.

I made one clever choice, which was to ask Ann and John if they could drive me to uni for my recital. For the first time I didn't have the 9 am slot — I had the 9.30, which suited me perfectly. I wouldn't need to get up before my usual 7 am, but I would still be finished nice and early before I crashed from lack of sleep and the exertion of a stressful day. It would be very cold so early in the morning though, and I didn't want my hands to get numb on the walk. I also didn't want to tire myself out. I could push through in other circumstances, but I wanted to be able to concentrate and give my best performance — though not so much that I could convince myself to eat a half-decent breakfast. Ann and John said yes, because they're lovely, and we cranked the car's heater on the short drive.

I don't remember much of the actual recital except that it went generally well, felt like a marathon and I was relieved when it was over. John needed his car afterwards so Ann, Harriet and I walked home together afterwards, to celebrate. Myf and Paul, another friend from MONA, were coming over later too. I was happy but exhausted and starving. As we walked up the hill, I worried about what I would eat and when. I haggled with the ED voice, trying to compromise on what time I could eat; and if I was allowed to eat extra since I had used a lot of energy performing and stressing, or if it would make me gain weight. I didn't know how long everyone would stay at our place, as there was no concrete plan. Would I need to feed them? Would we go out for lunch? Eating out meant spending more money, which I didn't want to do. But I also didn't want to serve them my food. If I did that, I would need to spend money buying more, and find the time and energy to go to the shops again.

I had been saving a bottle of champagne for the occasion — work had given it to me; I forget why. I was starting to fear the calories in alcohol again though, so I didn't allow myself to have more than a small glass. It went straight to my head since I hadn't eaten for a few hours. We had fun, but I was mentally and physically exhausted. I struggled to concentrate on the conversation and my laughter was forced — laughing actually uses a lot of energy, but I never realised until I had little to spare.

I continued to worry about whether I would need to put out food for my friends, and what they would want to eat. I really just wanted to eat my usual lunch, which was mostly vegetables — they filled my stomach but were low in calories. But I didn't want to share my precious vegetables with everyone — which made me feel greedy and selfish for not wanting to share — nor did I think they would want to eat my weird lunch anyway. If I made something else for them but ate my normal lunch, it may be awkward and I was hyper-aware of others possibly judging what I was eating, especially Myf. All this was spinning around my light-headed head as I pretended to happily celebrate finishing uni.

At some point, Ann, a natural entertainer, disappeared into the kitchen for a while. I guessed what she was doing and went to help. She had made a few dishes using only a few things from the fridge that were mine. The rest was food she and John had bought and leftovers from work. I was relieved, but also felt bad that she was using her food to entertain my guests. But mostly I was relieved, such was my fear of spending money. I often wondered if Ann had an inkling that I felt anxious spending money. Maybe she thought I was just poor, as I was a student, only working about eight hours a week. It wouldn't be an unreasonable conclusion, given how little I spent and the fact that other students sometimes had zero dollars to their name. Whatever her reasoning, Ann saved the day again with her usual ease and calm. Everyone had fun, except me; I was exhausted, stressed and hungry, but incredibly grateful to Ann.

Later in the afternoon, we heard a knock at the door. I answered it to find a woman holding a huge flower arrangement.
"For Hannah," she said aggressively, as she shoved them at me.
"Oh? I didn't order… Who sent these?" I was confused.
"I dunno, read the card," she replied grumpily, before turning around and stomping away.
After closing the door, I turned to find Ann standing a few feet away, her mouth open in shock.
"She was rude, right? That wasn't just me?" I asked, still stunned by the woman's abruptness.
"Oh my gosh, what was her problem?" Ann exclaimed.
I found the card, which was from Mum and Dad, congratulating me on my recital and finishing Honours. I pretended to be happy in front of my friends, but inside I was attempting to sort through my guilt for how much they must have spent on the flowers; gratitude; guilt for not talking to them; guilt for being angry; anger that they had tried to buy back my love; sadness that I

couldn't be happy to receive their gift and congratulations; sadness that we couldn't have a better relationship…

Hobart Post Uni

After my recital, I accepted all the work I was offered during Dark MoFo. I always put my hand up for extra hours and shifts, even when I was cold, hungry and tired. I maintained a lingering worry that I would stop being given shifts and become destitute, or reliant on Mum and Dad. The ED voice used this fear to push me to work as hard as I could — to continue clearing plates even though my legs threatened to give way; to pretend I didn't mind skipping my meal break if we were busy. If others could work long hours then I could too, even though I was eating much less.

I tried to see as much of the festival as I could when I wasn't working. As a MONA employee, I had free entry into some shows and events — the thought of paying for anything was too stressful to even consider. There were a lot of things I wanted to see but never did, because I was exhausted after work. Aside from being worn out, it was late June, so Hobart was very cold, and I just wanted to be home in my pyjamas.

I went to the Winter Feast one night after work, with Ann and John. The best restaurants and catering companies from around Tasmania served food and drink from small market stalls in a huge shed near the jetty. There were long rows of tables down the centre and the walls and ceiling were decorated with red lights and pagan figures. I assumed there would be lots of free tasting samples on offer, from which I could form a semi-decent dinner. Unfortunately, the few samples I found were either meagre or had a small fee attached. Most stalls didn't offer any. The food also was more expensive than I had expected. I didn't feel comfortable spending more than ten dollars, but proper meals started at 20. In the end, I bought a few skewers of satay chicken for five dollars. It was delicious but small, so I was still very hungry afterwards. I also worried that I had consumed more calories than I usually would at dinner, as I knew the sauce contained peanuts and oil, both of which were fear foods due to their nutritional density. I had possibly eaten "too much" but was still hungry, cold and exhausted. It wasn't at all what I had hoped and I was relieved to go home.

Another night after work, Ann and John's friends, Lorna and Toby, came over for dinner.
"How was work?" Lorna asked, making small talk.
"Crazy. I'm knackered," I replied.
There hadn't been time for me to eat lunch, so the ED voice praised me while my body struggled to remain vertical.
"Must be busy with MoFo on hey?" Lorna empathised.

"I just feel like I'm walking into a war zone every time I go to work; I'm so stressed about everything and it's chaos," I said, in a rare moment of complete, unfiltered honesty, caused by my exhaustion.
Lorna was shocked. "Work shouldn't be like that. That's not ok!"
Her words hit home. I shouldn't feel stressed every time I went to work; it wasn't healthy.

My plan for the rest of the year was to continue learning from Peter — improving my playing and preparing for a postponed trip to Europe the following year, when I would have somehow recovered — and work a few extra shifts at MONA, as my Centrelink[19] payments stopped when I finished uni. It didn't take long for me to start wishing I was back at uni, instead of serving food and clearing plates in a seemingly endless and pointless cycle. The ED voice loved the extra exercise and lack of food though. After about a month, my shifts were suddenly reduced to only one per week. When this happened two or three weeks in a row, I worried it would continue. I wondered if I had offended the person who made the roster, if she thought I wasn't a good worker, or if she had simply decided she didn't like me. I didn't feel I could ask her outright though, so instead I put in extra effort, pretending I was overjoyed to be at work, made sure I was always on the ball and was especially nice to her. I continued to be rostered for only one or two shifts a week. To avoid dipping into my savings, I would need to start earning more than $100 a week.

In my last semester, someone told me that working in the music library at uni was a good job and paid more than MONA. At the time, though it sounded great, I chose not to apply to work there. It would have been much more convenient — I could walk there from home instead of being a slave to Hobart's sketchy bus service — relaxed and relevant to my studies. However, working at MONA allowed me to burn more energy, as I power walked around for six hours and often didn't get to eat lunch. But when my shifts there were reduced, I handed in my resume at the library. Luckily, they were looking for someone to fill a few shifts, so I started working there a week or two later. It was only one five-hour shift and two annoyingly short lunch covers, but it was better than nothing, and I hoped my hours would increase.

Overall I enjoyed working in the library. Most of the people there were nice, as they were students and staff. When I wasn't checking books in or out, I could read or chat with friends who happened to be there. I didn't mind

---

[19] In Australia, some students are eligible for fortnightly payments from the government, to help cover living costs.

checking books out; most people were polite, it didn't take long, and I got to look at interesting titles. Checking them in was even better, because I didn't have to talk to anyone. The lunch covers were short and sweet, but annoying because they forced me to break from my meal timetable and eat later — I couldn't allow myself to eat earlier. The long shift had its pros and cons. I had to get up earlier than usual and walk there in the cold Hobart morning but, as it was early, there was rarely anyone there for the first two hours. Because I didn't allow myself to eat breakfast before 9 am, I brought it with me and ate behind the desk or in the little back room, when no one was around. However, If there was a lot to do, or people were in the library earlier than usual, I wouldn't have time to finish my breakfast; sometimes I didn't get to eat anything. I felt lightheaded, irritable and tired on those days, but the ED voice congratulated me for my hard work and willpower.

Later in the year, I picked up two hours of violin teaching at a music studio. My weekly shift started about an hour after one of my lunch covers at the library. In some ways, this worked well, as the studio was on my way home. However, I had to fit in eating lunch between my shift at the library and teaching. For most people, this wouldn't be an issue; they would just eat while walking to the studio. But I was still avoiding bringing food out with me where possible, even though I had started using a handbag, in which I could store food. After my shift at the library, I would power walk to Woolworths, get some canned vegetables and a small container of cottage cheese, use the public toilet — I had to go the toilet directly before eating, no exceptions — then eat. Being a slow eater, this always felt rushed. I planned my movements in advance, but there was no room for delays — they were timed to the minute.

Not long after I finished uni, Christie moved to Brisbane to be with her boyfriend. I put an ad on Gumtree, advertising our spare room, and we interviewed a few people. The person who "won" — as he put it — the position of housemate, was a self-described bogan from Taree in NSW. Callum is actually very intelligent and was coming to Hobart to do his PhD in Geology. He had spent the previous two and half years travelling around Asia on a motorbike and had lots of stories to tell. Callum was always himself, whether happy, tired, or expressing a controversial opinion. I was more guarded than usual when I spoke to him, fearing he may make fun of me for something I said, but I came to learn that I didn't need to be. I quite enjoyed talking to Callum because we could talk about all sorts of things; he often had interesting points of view and asked unexpected and thought-provoking questions.

One night when we were chatting, Callum suddenly frowned and stared at me. "What?" I asked, worried I had blown my cover and revealed just how dorky and awkward I was.
"Are you Autistic?" He asked.
Oh gosh, did he think I was weird? What had I said? I could feel myself blushing. I decided to feign nonchalance.
"You know, I've sometimes wondered,"I laughed. "But I don't think I am, because I feel empathy — a lot — and Autistic people don't. I don't know how they can not feel it though. Weird."

I mentioned the conversation to Ann and John later because we sometimes affectionately shared funny Callum stories. Ann looked thoughtful for a few seconds.
"Autistic people can't look others in the eyes either, and you do," she said. That made me think.
"Really? I never look people in the eye." Looking into people's eyes had always made me feel uncomfortable.
"Yeah you do, you're looking in my eyes right now," James laughed uncertainly.
"No, I'm looking at your nose," I replied. "Sometimes I look at your eyebrows and your mouth…"
Didn't everyone? I thought people only looked into the eyes of the person they loved. Authors write about it — "she looked into his eyes and felt her heart swell…" I did a few online 'Am I Autistic' tests online, but was always borderline, so I assumed I wasn't. Like a good millennial, I also had a healthy scepticism of online tests.

A few weeks after my recital I got my haircut. I had been wanting to for a while but hadn't had time in the lead-up to my recital. I went to a place I had noticed earlier in the year, which advertised $30 haircuts. I had been cutting my fringe myself since I moved to Hobart and it had become a bit untidy — Mum used to cut it when I lived in Perth, even after I moved out. I hoped the hairdresser could tidy that up and style the rest of my hair a bit. It was the longest it had ever been and I had been plaiting it or wearing it in a bun because I didn't know what else to do with it. I assumed the hairdresser was average, since she was charging so little, but I was stunned when she cut my fringe while it was still wet! Rooky mistake. She didn't do a much better job with the rest of my hair. It was one of the worst haircuts I have ever had. I was so self-conscious that I tied it up as soon as I left.

I had been thinking about shaving my head since high school and the terrible haircut made me consider it again. Finally I decided to shave my head to raise money for eating disorder research. I looked into different treatment centres and research being conducted around the world but was disappointed by the vacuum. Similarly, I couldn't find anything helpful about The Butterfly Foundation's work. From what I had seen, all they did was cite the statistics of people with eating disorders on their website, sell fundraising jewellery at Sportsgirl, and make advertising material featuring attractive, slim, smiling young people who were implied to have recovered from an eating disorder.

I decided to look into the ANGI[20] study, for which I had given blood earlier in the year. It was being conducted at King's College, London, and they were accepting monetary donations. Alanna had told me about a book called '8 Steps to Recovery from an Eating Disorder,' by Carolyn Costin, who had recovered from AN herself, and now ran an inpatient clinic in Monte Nido. I decided to donate the majority of the money I raised to the ANGI study and use the remainder to buy a copy of Carolyn Costin's book for any of the inpatient clinics in Australia who would accept it, for the patients, nurses and clinicians to read. If treatment in other clinics was as bad as it was in Heathgrove then this book would be needed. I considered using the money I raised to buy myself a copy of the book — I wanted to read it but couldn't bring myself to pay it — but I felt it would be dishonest to use the money for myself.

It felt good to have a purpose again and be working to help people. I set up a Go Fund Me page and made a Facebook event for the shave night — I decided on the first of September because I didn't want to have a bald head in Winter, though Spring in Hobart is still icy. Aside from raising money, I wanted to use the campaign to raise awareness and educate the public about eating disorders. I asked some friends from Heathgrove to write about their experiences, so I could post them on the event page. I also wrote my story and shared it anonymously:

Ever since I learnt what anorexia is, when I was ten years old, I could understand why someone would starve themselves to be thinner. Even though I thought something like that would never happen to me, another part of me always knew I would one day have anorexia.

---

[20] The Anorexia Nervosa Genetics Initiative aims to identify the genes that predispose people to AN. Aside from helping develop more effective treatment methods, this information will enable future generations to find out if they are predisposed to the illness, so they can take preventative measures if they choose.

I've always been a perfectionist, eager to please, a high achiever, and scared to get in trouble, and for most of my life that made people like me. Teachers said I was a good student and Mum and Dad were proud, so I kept doing what I was doing. I had a bit of a hard time fitting in at school in my teens. Looking back I possibly had more friends than I realised, but I felt like a bit of a dork, socially awkward and not all that interesting to be around.

I started wanting to lose weight when I was about 15, though at the time I was already underweight compared to the general population; always have been. At first, I only cut out unhealthy food like chips and chocolate. Mum and Dad noticed, and I lost a bit of weight, but it was probably nothing unusual for a girl my age.

When I was 16 I started restricting more, not only cutting out junk food but also generally not eating enough. I think it was at this point that I started exercising regularly. I'd never been that active before — a bit of a dweeby bookworm actually — but I started going for walks every day and doing sit-ups, push-ups and squats in my room in secret. This phase only lasted one school term. I remember Mum yelling at me sometime in the holidays and scaring me into eating a proper amount. She also, in her outburst, told me that not everything I ate would turn to fat on my body — something I'd somehow got into my head. For the rest of that year, things were ok. I started eating more, gained a bit of weight and was happy.

I started restricting again the next year, early on in year 12. First I cut out fats because fats are bad, right? That's what the people on tv say. I thought that when people told me it was ok to have a bit of fat in my diet, that was just because no one wanted to stop eating delicious fatty foods. So I cut out as much as I could. The only proper meal I had was dinner because Mum and Dad made it and I couldn't control what went in, not that I didn't try. Throughout that year I gradually ate less and less and exercised more and more. I did literally hundreds of sit-ups every day, and about a hundred push-ups and squats. I started going jogging in the afternoon, and then switched to the morning, just in case it was too dark when I got home in the afternoon. On days when it was raining, I fretted that I would put on weight from missing the exercise and would usually make myself go anyway. Sometimes Mum managed to stop me.

Mum and Dad and my Doctor knew something was wrong and kept trying to make me eat more, as they saw the number on the scales getting lower and lower. They would tell me off when I lost weight and asked why I couldn't just eat more. Mum lost it with me a few times, but I was terrified to eat more than what I'd decided was acceptable.

I felt the cold so much that year but refused to wear long pants to school. Mum and Dad made me wear tights, but I usually took them off as soon as I could. Someone had told me the year before that you use up more energy if you're cold, as your body tries to stay warm. I tried to keep my jumper off as much as I could too and used the heater at home as little as possible. I wondered if I had anorexia, but I still didn't think anything like that would ever happen to me, so I thought nothing was very wrong, and I should be able to deal with it. If I had anorexia then I would do something about it because that was bad, but while I didn't, I should stop feeling so sorry for myself. Other people were as skinny, or skinnier than me — though there can't have been many — and I should be able to be that skinny too. I'd always seen my thinness as an achievement, even when I was much younger because everyone wants to be skinny, right?

I got steadily worse throughout that year, restricting more and more, exercising more and more, and losing more and more weight. I dreaded going to the Doctor, because I knew I'd either have put on weight, and would feel like a failure, or would have lost weight, and been told off, even though I would be happy inside at another "achievement".

My Mum thought I would go back to eating normally when I finished school because I wouldn't be so stressed, but I didn't. I went on leavers with my friends but I was too scared to drink alcohol because of the calories. I knew I shouldn't go for a run on Christmas Day, so I exercised as much as I could in my room and worried the whole day about putting on weight.

Things kept going the same way the next year. I took a year off to have a break from study, and hopefully a year of fun, but my routine and rules for myself were too rigid for that to happen. Every day was a working day. It started with exercises in my room and then a run, even though I hadn't yet eaten and really didn't have much in the way of energy stores in my body. Then I had a carefully measured-out breakfast, free from any fat. The rest of the day was filled with exercises in my room every hour or so, tiny snacks, arguments about how much I should eat and whether or not I was hungry — inside my head and with Mum and Dad — worry about what I had eaten, hunger and tiredness. But I couldn't sit down. Not unless I was reading, and even then only for a short period of time. I had to stand as much as possible because that would burn more calories.

(BMI)

When my BMI dropped below 15 my Doctor told me I had to go into hospital. I played the "You can't force because I'm 18" card, having turned 18 about a week before, but apparently, by law, she could. I went onto the waiting list for the mental health ward in a hospital and a bit over a week later, was admitted.

I was so proud to need to go to hospital. It was such an achievement to have lost so much weight that I was in the danger zone and needed hospitalisation. I also thought it would be a good test of who my true friends were, to see who visited me. I was still worried that people didn't really like me very much and might not care. I thought others would be proud of me too, for having lost so much weight that I needed to be hospitalised. That's how messed up my thinking was.

I should probably explain here what had been going on in my head for the past year or so. I don't know when it happened, and it was probably so gradual that I didn't notice until it was pointed out to me, but a little voice had emerged in my head which told me I wasn't skinny enough, that I should exercise more, eat less, that I was lazy, that I lacked self-control etc. This voice grew stronger the more I followed its instructions. Yes, I sound like I have schizophrenia. For anyone who read Animorphs or watched Stargate SG-1, think of having an urk in your head, or a Goa'uld, and trying to fight it. That's what having an eating disorder is like. If I disobeyed that voice I would feel so incredibly guilty that I worried myself into an anxious mess, often close to tears, or would find some way of righting my "wrong". I used to stand at the kitchen bench at home, arguing inside my head with the voice about whether or not I should eat, or what I should eat. These arguments were never ending and I could never win. I fought with logic, but somehow I was still always wrong, and I accepted that.

Anyway, hospital. We were weighed every morning at about 7 am in our underwear, to prevent us from hiding weights in our clothes. After the first day or so, I got up around 6.30 am to get some secret exercise in. I had to be careful I wasn't caught by the night nurse doing her rounds, or the nurse who came to fetch me to be weighed. After being weighed there was a bit of time to get dressed and ready for the day. We all ate breakfast together, with one or two nurses at our table to watch us. We could choose what we ate within certain guidelines. We had to have some sort of bread or cereal, fruit, protein and milk or yoghurt. And we had to have butter or margarine and some sort of spread on the bread. We were given half an hour to eat and at the end of that time, the nurses would write down what each person had left on their plate.

This was the same for all of our meals, with a shorter time limit for snacks. After main meals, we had to go into the lounge room for half an hour of rest. No one was allowed to go to their room first. This was to stop purging and those of us who felt compelled to exercise straight after each meal, from doing so. After breakfast and dinner, we were allowed to have a hot drink. Only two per day. This restriction was for people who drank tea and coffee for the flavour and short-term fullness without the calories. This didn't bother me because I was actually a bit scared of hot drinks — I needed to stay cold to burn up energy! The rest of the day was taken up with two 1 1/2 hr group therapy sessions, meals, snacks, rest time and lots and lots of free time. Each day was about the same, which different types of group therapy on different days.

Hospital wasn't all bad. The people I met there are all lovely, beautiful, kind, amazing humans and I'm still in touch with a lot of them. They're just great people to be friends with. It was nice to be surrounded by such wonderful people all the time and I don't know how I would have coped with everything if it wasn't for their support and understanding. We understood what each other was going through in a way the nurses and doctors and psychs never would. And just knowing that everyone else was going through the same things — having to gain weight, eating scary food, struggling with that voice in their head, feeling fat — was a big help. We were all in the same boat.

That brings me to the horrible side of hospital. I suppose it's a bit like getting old. When we're babies and toddlers we can do more and more each day; stand up, walk, make new sounds, and slowly become more independent. When people get old they are able to do less and less each day. Joints hurt more, they get weary faster and slowly lose their independence. When I was losing weight part of it was exciting, as I saw myself getting thinner, saw more and more of my ribs, and watched my hip bones protrude beneath my belly. While putting on weight I had less to be proud of each day. I remember the disgust I felt the first time I saw my tummy roll when I bent over and when I saw that the tops of my thighs touched when I stood with my legs together. The strict rules of the hospital made it almost impossible to obey the voice in my head, but that didn't stop the guilt. And we had so much spare time during which to dwell on how much we'd eaten that day, how little exercise we'd done, how much weight we'd gained and just generally get bored. I found some of the group therapy sessions helpful but it was nowhere near enough. Some made me aware of underlying thoughts or gave me the opportunity to talk about how I was feeling, but that was the extent of it. I was never given tools with which to fight all the abuse the voice threw at me.

I was set free after 9 weeks and one day. During my stay, I'd had some days out with my family and a few nights at home, but being let loose and given control of all of my meals was daunting. I'd already decided before I left hospital that I would lose a few kilos and then start eating normally. Mum and Dad noticed this pretty quickly and so began the next few years of weight fluctuation.

Since leaving hospital my weight has gone up and down drastically, with Mum and Dad sometimes controlling some of my meals, sometimes all of them, giving me back a bit of control, taking it back... I've been to different psychologists and psychiatrists, tried different treatment methods, been so depressed I didn't want to live, and didn't see any hope of being happy again. I missed being a kid and not knowing what a calorie is, eating biscuits when Mum and Dad went out, running around just because I wanted to, not to burn up energy.

It's been about 5 years since I got out of hospital and I'm still not fully recovered. I still have that voice in my head and, while I'm slowly learning to disobey it and find other things to strive for, it is incredibly persuasive and uses all of my intelligence against me. Having said that, my thoughts are a lot healthier than they were. I remember, a few years ago, reading back over the diary I kept in hospital and being shocked at some of the things I truly believed. I wish I could remember what they were now, but in some ways, it's probably good that I don't, in case I start believing them again.

Everyone knows the basics of anorexia: You eat less, exercise more and lose weight. Some die, some recover. But what people don't know is everything that goes with it. Because I had anorexia my parents will never completely trust me to look after myself. They will always second-guess me if I say I'm not hungry or don't finish everything on my plate. We've said and done and felt things during the past 7 years that cannot be unsaid or undone or unfelt. I think our relationship will always be a bit complicated and I'm sitting here with tears in my eyes thinking about it. And the horrible unfairness is that none of us did anything wrong to deserve this. We were all trying to do the right thing. I thought it would please other people if I lost weight and thought I was working hard towards a worthwhile goal. Mum and Dad were trying to help me when they told me to eat and made me sit at the table, sobbing, until I'd finished the food in front of me. I hated them for it. The voice in my head made me feel horrible. They tried to act strong and I hated that they were able to sit there and watch me fall to pieces. Then later I would hear Mum bawling her eyes out and I felt guilty for what I was putting them through. And at the same time hated her for thinking she had it tough while she was making my life hell.

It literally takes over your life. Food and exercise and calories were always on my mind. I was always tallying up how many calories I'd had that day, how much fat, how much energy I'd burned from exercise, and how many hours I'd spent sitting. I always stopped to look at cakes in cafes because my body craved the calories and fat, yet I was terrified to have more than a bite. I compared myself to everyone, always checking that I was thinner than anyone I met. I couldn't concentrate properly because, apart from being preoccupied with food, exercise and calories, my brain wasn't getting enough energy to function properly. I couldn't put energy into the things I loved because I literally didn't have that energy.

Social situations became hard because my main goal every day was to burn up as much energy as possible — I used to think it would be wonderful to be a personal trainer, so that really would be all I'd have to focus on, and no one would think it odd, because that would be my job! If someone suggested watching a movie I'd immediately start thinking of reasons why we shouldn't, or couldn't, watch a movie. Too much sitting and doing nothing would make me fat! At the very least I'd make sure I was drawing or moving while we watched, to keep my little voice from berating me too much. And then I'd eat less later and do extra exercise when I got home.

I could go on, but there are just so many areas of my life that were affected by anorexia and, to be honest, I've probably forgotten a lot of them. But I know it was on my mind all the time, even when I was asleep. I was always scheming, looking up low calories recipes, checking the number of calories and fat in a food, exercising, working out when I could exercise next, arguing with the voice about what I would eat, or if I could eat, working out how to hide food from Mum and Dad, thinking up excuses for eating less, working out how to eat a meal away from them, thinking of ways to make dinner less fatty — even though we ate very healthy — the list goes on! You don't get holidays or weekends or even nights off from anorexia.

I remember one day, not long before I went to hospital, Mum asked me if I wanted to get better, or if I would just keep losing weight until I died. I had thought about this a lot. I had decided that I would get better when I'd lost enough weight; when it was dangerously low. That would be enough of an achievement and I would start eating what I wanted again. Of course I didn't realise that things already were serious... But I had also decided that I wasn't going to starve to death. That was the healthy part of me, because the sick part, that little voice in my head, told me that dying from anorexia would be the ultimate hero's death. I understood what the warriors in movies were talking about when they said they wanted to die on the battlefield, fighting for what they believed in. That's what I thought starving myself to death was — dying as a hero.

Since treatment for Eating Disorders is long, horrible and doesn't have a high success rate, I believe the best treatments are prevention and early intervention. Studies have shown that the longer a person is sick, the harder it is for them to recover. Their disordered thinking patterns become more ingrained and, therefore, harder to change. Thinking back to my own Health lessons in high school, the only time a teacher spoke about eating disorders was to say "It's better to eat too much than nothing." This was said while we were learning about healthy eating. I was in year eight and knew very little about AN. I assumed the Health curriculum hadn't changed much since I was at school.

As part of my campaign to raise awareness, I emailed the person who seemed to be in charge of the high school Health curriculum in Western Australia — the curriculum differs between states, so I would need to contact them all individually. I downloaded some PDF brochures from an English eating disorder charity's website, which contained statistics, warning signs, suggestions for how to help someone who was suffering from an ED, and other helpful information. I thought they would be good resources for the education department to pass on to schools. The man I emailed replied, saying they were happy with their current Health curriculum but that, if I wanted, I could contact schools directly, as they may choose to pass the information on to their students. I googled how many high schools there are in WA and, though I did consider calling them all, eventually decided against it. I replied to the man at the education department, who clearly felt he knew more about eating disorders than me, and asked if I could send him the documents I had downloaded, to pass on to schools. He said to "send them through," and I did so, with little hope that they would ever venture out of his Downloads folder.

Around this time, a friend from uni asked if I wanted to tour China for about a month at the end of the year, as part of a string quartet, accompanying singers performing Broadway songs. Yeah I did! The pay wasn't great, but flights between Melbourne and China, accommodation and transport in China, and some food, was included. It was a free trip to China; I didn't really care how much they were paying as long as I didn't make a loss. I still had the small problem, however, of my passport being in Perth. I accepted the job, hoping I would find a way to get hold of my passport in the next few months.

Luckily, Dad messaged soon after to say he had work in the Eastern states and could easily come visit me, if I wanted to see him. We had been lucky that,

since I moved to Hobart, Dad had run a few training programs in Launceston, Melbourne, Sydney and New Zealand, and usually took advantage of the proximity by visiting me. I still hadn't spoken to Mum and Dad since Mum had told me I couldn't go to Europe, but if Dad came to Hobart, he could bring my passport. My anger and hurt were also starting to fade and I had been thinking about breaking my radio silence. I was unsure how they would feel about me going to China, but hoped they would view one month of travel in a group more favourably than a few months solo in Europe. When I called Dad I decided to tell him I was going to China, instead of asking permission. He sounded a bit worried, but also hesitantly excited. "It would have been nice if you had replied to our messages though, instead of calling because you wanted your passport," Dad said.
"I was so angry about Europe Dad… Too angry to talk to you…" My embarrassment at trying to explain my anger made it sound like a weak excuse.

(Food)

I was apprehensive about eating with Dad while he was there. He was staying on our couch, so he would see all or most of my meals. I started planning how I could fool him into thinking I was eating more than I was as soon as I knew he was coming. My breakfasts consisted mostly of vegetables, with a bit of protein. Eating more than my allowed calorie limit was terrifying so I needed to make a breakfast that appeared to be more substantial, but wasn't. I told Dad I would make a surprise breakfast for both of us on his first morning, so I could cook without him seeing. I had already planned what I would make and steamed and mashed some pumpkin before he arrived in Hobart. In the morning, I shaped the pumpkin into four bread-sized rectangles, toasted them under the grill and served them with scrambled eggs on top. When I served Dad, I told him I had mixed the pumpkin with almond meal and eggs, in an attempt to make bread. We laughed at how it hadn't really worked and the difficulties of being intolerant to gluten. It seemed I had successfully deceived him. I was still hungry though, because I hadn't eaten as much volume, in the form of vegetables, as I usually did. But I was used to pretending to be happy and energetic when I was anything but. I would just have to keep up the facade until our next meal, which would hopefully be more filling but equally low in calories.

In the first week of the fundraiser, a very generous friend donated $500, with the comment, "You need to raise your target Hannah!" I was astounded, and so incredibly grateful for her generosity. When I used to raise money for Jump Rope for Heart, before internet banking existed for the public, people would usually donate a gold coin, or a five or ten-dollar note if they were generous. Now, people were happily donating $50 and $100. Some friends and family knew I had AN, but others just thought it was a good cause. Or maybe they were impressed that I was shaving my head. One friend suggested I "just get it cut short like it used to be, don't completely shave it." But that wasn't the point. If I just got a pixie cut I wouldn't be getting out of my comfort zone for a good cause. I was also getting quite excited about shaving my head. I was curious to see how I looked.

On the night of September 1, I invited my close friends over for a head-shaving party. My idea was that, if they donated, they could chop some hair off. True to form, I had been worrying about what to feed everyone, however, I got lucky. I had worked at a big function at MONA a few nights before and, as usual, there were hundreds of dollars of cheese left over from the huge grazing boards, as well as lots of fancy cakes. Everyone who worked that night got to take home a few boxes of cheese and cake, so I used my bounty to put on a good spread for my friends.

I had a great night, and I think everyone else did too. I always say it was the most enjoyable haircut I ever had. We sat around eating cheese and cake — though I kept track of how much I was eating, only having very small pieces of cheese — chatting and occasionally chopping off some hair. Everyone, except Ann and I, was hesitant to cut it at first and flinched at the sound of the scissors severing the hair, but most of them got used to it eventually. As I didn't have much control over where people were cutting, and often couldn't even see what they were doing, they eventually let loose and had fun. I went through a range of hideous hairstyles, including a mullet, rat tail and balding man with a combover. Ann did the final shave with a disposable razor and John' shaving cream, and she went at it with gusto. She was really having fun. By the end of the night, we had raised $3000 and a few more donations trickled in over the next few days. I was, and still am, amazed and indescribably grateful to everyone who donated.

Sometime in the second half of that year, I happened to read an article written about an interview with Evanna Lynch, who acted the part of Luna Lovegood in the Harry Potter movies. I hadn't known that she had been a huge fan of the book series before she auditioned and was absolutely starstruck to be around Daniel, Emma, Rupert and the other actors. I told Ann my new trivia when we were both in the kitchen later that day, as she shares my love for Harry Potter. "Yeah, I read she used to have anorexia. Apparently the books helped her recover. I think she wrote to Rowling while she was sick," Ann said.

I tried to keep my face expressionless and feign only mild interest. I told as few people as possible that I had AN because I didn't want them to treat me differently, so I didn't want my reaction to this new information to expose my secret.

I excitedly googled "Evanna Lynch anorexia" and read a lot of conflicting articles. Some claimed Jo told Evanna she could have the part of Luna in the movies if she recovered; others said she had written to Jo while she was in hospital, and then auditioned after she recovered. I have since read Evanna's book[21] and know what actually happened. I was hoping to find a video, article or interview transcript with Evanna, in which she explained her experience with AN in detail, including how she recovered. Unfortunately I did not. I did, however, find a video of her giving a speech at a college in America. She didn't speak about her experience with AN as much as I had hoped but, near the end, she summed up humanity's actions with one universal and undeniable truth:
"There are only two fears which prevent us from reaching our goals... Firstly the fear that we're not enough, not good enough, ie. the fear of failing; and secondly, the fear that we won't be loved."
She had hit the nail on the head. I was scared to eat more because I feared people wouldn't love me in a bigger body, and that that would prevent me from succeeding in life. Given that diet culture is everywhere, it's no surprise I had come to believe that, especially as I hadn't felt that I fit in with my peers since I was about ten. Even at university, I felt I was an oddball, on the outer, and that I needed to keep up an act to avoid people discovering that I was actually a loser. It was a lightbulb moment, but unfortunately not enough to make me overcome my fear of gaining weight.

I spoke to Alanna about Evanna's speech and said I felt it would be helpful to know how she had recovered. The only people I knew who had recovered had either had very different triggers and treatment experiences to me, or didn't want to talk about it, which I respected. I felt, from what Evanna said in her speech, that the feelings and events that had led us both to AN were similar, and that I might benefit from learning more of her story. I decided to write to her. After a bit of googling, I found a postal address for her. I wrote a short-ish letter on some Harry Potter writing paper I had been given when I was nine, briefly telling her my story and why I wanted to talk to her. I posted it full of

---

[21] The Opposite of Butterfly Hunting. I highly recommend this book. I identified with it so strongly and, in my opinion, Evanna does an incredible job of articulating her feelings and thoughts. It is the best book I have read, so far, about anorexia nervosa.

hope. It was returned to our address later that year with a "recipient no longer resides here" stamp on the envelope.

Ann, John and I all enjoyed cooking, and Ann and I especially, liked making up our own fusion meals. We started cooking dinner together quite often, unless they had other plans for the night or just wanted to do their own thing. Sometimes Ann would find a recipe during the day and buy the ingredients to recreate it. On other nights we would look at what we had in the fridge and throw around ideas. We each had our own shelf in the fridge, to keep our food separate, but when we cooked together, we shared. While I loved cooking together, and ate much more interesting and nourishing food when we did, it also put me on edge. As spending money caused anxiety for me, and I had to plan my trips to the shop around everything else in my busy days, I tried to make my food last as long as possible. I bought almost the same vegetables every week and rationed everything out carefully so they would last the week. However, cooking together meant I couldn't necessarily stick to my strict plan of food usage — unless I divulged my odd ways and anxiety to Ann and John, which I didn't want to do. I usually had varying amounts of butterfly activity in my tummy during most of the cooking process, worrying that Ann may ask to use something from my shelf that I was planning to use the following day, or that I considered expensive. They rarely did. We mostly used food from their shelf. Again, I wonder if they assumed I didn't have much money, even though I was no longer a student, and wanted to share their food to look after me. Maybe they thought I was thin because I couldn't afford more food. Maybe they didn't even think about whose food we were using, or didn't want to use mine because it was boring compared to theirs. Either way, I'm very grateful for their generosity and, overall, we had a lot of fun cooking together and chatting.

For the remainder of the year, I worked at the library, MONA and the teaching studio. I continued practising in the morning until 9 am, when I allowed myself a 30-minute breakfast break, then practised again until 12.30 pm, unless I had work or a lesson. I was gradually eating less, partly from fear and strict food rules; partly because work often clashed with my self-imposed eating timetable. I know I'm not the first person to have an odd work schedule. If I had been flexible I could have easily found time to eat. But the ED voice didn't compromise. If I had a choice between eating early, eating very late, or not at all, I would choose option two or three.

Violin lessons were an added complication. Peter fitted teaching around meetings, taking one of his children — sorry, dogs — to the vet, walking the dogs, cooking for the dogs, and his own practice, so I agreed to whatever time he offered unless I had work. My lessons often clashed with my timetabled eating times, so I always planned out my days in advance. Any rational person who was offered a 1 pm lesson would have eaten beforehand, then maybe again afterwards. Or maybe they wouldn't get tired if they had a late lunch every so often, because they were eating an adequate amount of food the rest of the time. It was because I wasn't eating enough that I planned my meal times in advance, ensuring they were evenly spaced throughout the day, and I tried to eat directly before anything that required energy. I didn't want to eat lunch before my lessons though, because I wanted to eat when I got home, as a reward. This meant having a very late lunch and being hungry, tired and lightheaded throughout the lesson, making it almost impossible to concentrate. I was struggling to stay upright, let alone remember notes or take on new information and advice.

In my sessions with Alanna, we talked in circles about Mum and Dad's supervision, fitting in food around work, increasing my food slowly, and my fear of gaining weight. Sometimes I felt I could eat more, that maybe I would feel ok in a slightly bigger body if I gained the weight slowly, but I was too scared to spend money on the extra food. I didn't even allow myself to buy yoghurt, one of my favourite foods, because it was cheaper, though much more time-consuming, to make it myself in a saucepan and thermos. I couldn't bring myself to spend the extra three dollars on a litre of yoghurt!

I hated working at MONA, though only because it was exhausting, stressful and repetitive. The people I worked with were mostly lovely, but hospitality is not for me, especially when my body is starving. I was counting down the days until I left for the China tour, where I would get to explore a new country and perform great music. I also hoped the change of routine would force me to change my eating habits, allowing me to eat more. I was aware that I had had the same hope the previous year when I went to the USA, but this time there wouldn't be corn syrup in everything, so I wouldn't get constipated and lose my appetite. At some point, the Broadway tour was cancelled, but the same company invited me to play in the pit for a production of The Marriage of Figaro instead, which was also touring China, around the same time of year. I happily agreed.

China

I flew to Melbourne first, for a week of rehearsals, after which we all flew to China. I had been looking forward to being more free with my money in Melbourne. I also decided it was a good time to start eating rice again — there would be lots of rice in China. Unfortunately, there weren't many food places near our rehearsal venue, and the few options were trendy cafes, with trendy food prices. I resorted to bringing supermarket sushi with me each day and looked longingly at everyone else' gourmet wraps and interesting smoothies. At least I was eating rice though!

I already knew a few people from Perth and Hobart in the orchestra, but I got to know everyone else during the week. I was surprised at how friendly everyone was, and that I was able to chat to almost everyone without feeling as awkward or anxious as usual. One person in particular, Abi, was very friendly and introduced herself to each person almost as soon as they walked into the rehearsal room on the first day. It was so easy talking to Abi. She was always kind, friendly, non-judgemental, and had all sorts of interesting stories and questions. Later, while on tour, my roommate Erin and I joked about "Abi questions," because they were so strange, obscure, interesting; questions that I had never been asked before, and had never thought to ask anyone else. Abi got on with everyone, so I was happily surprised when she seemed to want to hang around with me more than others.

I had a wonderful time in China. It had never been on my travel bucket list, but I have never regretted going — and, since 2020, I never miss an opportunity to tell people I have been to Wuhan! Some things were so different and strange we just laughed. I loved spending time with the others on the tour, staying in nice hotels, having interesting conversations, and exploring each new town. Most of our performances were in small towns — small by China's standards anyway — where the locals rarely saw white people, so everything was more traditional than in Shanghai, Beijing and the other, bigger cities, that attracted more tourists.

One of my favourite times of the day was breakfast. The Chinese traditional buffet breakfast is right up my alley. It differed between hotels but there was always fried rice, a variety of cooked vegetables, noodles, broth, eggs cooked a few different ways, tropical fruit, dumplings and Asian baked goods. There was probably meat too, but I wasn't interested in it, so I took no notice. At the beginning of the tour, I included a small serving of fried rice in my breakfast, but I quickly reduced this until I wasn't having any rice at all. So much for my resolution to face my fear of carbohydrates and get back on the road to recovery. There were so many other things I wanted to try, and cutting out the calories in the rice allowed me to eat the calories in more interesting food. I gravitated more and more to the vegetables though, because they're so low in calories that I could eat a lot without feeling guilty. I usually had a few platefuls of food for breakfast and was rarely hungry at lunch, because my body was still digesting. Sometimes others marvelled at how much I ate while remaining so thin. I found it amusing how little people understood about nutrition.

I had felt self-conscious eating with others — particularly those I didn't know well, or who were very pretty or thin — since I moved out of home and, though I was eating mostly vegetables, I worried that others on the tour would think I was greedy for eating so much. I tried to limit myself to only two platefuls of breakfast, instead of three or four, but I couldn't stick to it. Because I knew I wasn't consuming many calories, I wasn't worried about gaining weight. I worried people would judge me, but my desire for food was stronger, so long as it was low-calorie food. I would never have allowed myself to eat three plates of rice or eggs — the guilt and self-hatred would have been too high — but after so many years of restricting and worrying about money, it felt wasteful not to eat this never-ending supply of delicious, free food. I wondered if this need, to take advantage of any food freely available, was common for people who had denied their bodies adequate nutrition for an extended period of time. Turns out it is, but people rarely talk about it.

(Exercise)

As the tour progressed I began to pay more attention to how much exercise I was doing, even though we were doing a decent amount of walking as we explored each town. One night, a friend suggested we go check out the hotel gym. I have always found gyms interesting and exciting, with all the strange equipment designed to exercise specific muscles. For a few days I used the exercise bike, just for fun and to pass the time. However, when I considered taking a break from cycling the next day, I felt guilty. I started going to the gym every morning to ride on the bike for about 20 minutes. One day, Abi and two other friends on the tour asked if I wanted to do yoga with them in the gym the next morning. I thought it might be fun, but also wanted to make sure I burned as many calories as I usually would on the bike. I predicted that a self-directed yoga class would mostly consist of talking and relaxed stretching than anything physically demanding. I declined, choosing the safe, well-trodden path of ED-approved exercise over time with friends. I made up an excuse about wanting to sleep in, then was careful to make sure they didn't see me at the gym the next morning when I went to the room with the bikes.

We travelled to a new town every three to five days. Sometimes this was an hour's drive on the bus; on other days it was a full day of travel on bullet trains, buses and planes. It was hard to find decent food for lunch on these days, as most shops at the train stations only sold chips, lollies and my other fear foods. I always scoured the kiosks hopefully, but never found anything I could eat without guilt. After a few trips, I learnt to bring an apple or two with me. I told myself I didn't need to eat much, since we were sitting down for most of the day. Even eating an apple gave the ED voice cause to berate me for my greed. I had read enough articles about exercise and weight loss to know that sitting down still requires energy, however, I worried that anything I ate would be turned into belly fat because I wasn't getting my heart rate up. I was usually hangry by the time we had reached the next hotel and had to work hard to stop myself from snapping at others or being anything less than polite and helpful. I was always impatient while we searched for a place to have dinner. My body was screaming at me for food.

Overall I had a great time in China and I didn't want it to end. My eating gradually worsened, but I loved exploring a new country with (mostly) lovely people. I had an appointment with Beth when I got back and discovered I had lost a few kilos. I was genuinely shocked. I knew I had been mainly eating vegetables, but overall, my energy had been better than before I left Hobart — I had actually wondered if there were more calories in those seemingly innocent vegetables than I thought after all. I had worried that I may have gained weight.

I stayed in Hobart for another few weeks before moving back to Perth. I was looking forward to going home, so I could stop working in hospitality and would no longer need to be completely self-sufficient. While I was scared Mum and Dad would take control of my meals again or, at the very least, watch everything I ate and comment when it wasn't enough, I was looking forward to not worrying about paying for food, rent and bills.

I was sad to leave my friends though. I had a party the night before I left, so I could say goodbye to everyone. It was a fun night and I was pleasantly surprised at how many people came. I was very hungry though. I decided to set out plates of finger food around the house, but I was scared to spend too much money. I ended up getting creative with the food I had left in the fridge and pantry, and various leftovers I had taken home from work. I made a few different sweet slices and put out some cheese, but it was all energy-dense, which scared me. I had hoped others would bring carrot sticks or a simple salad, with which I could fill my stomach. But, as over half my friends were students or just out of uni, most people brought chips, chocolate or nothing. I don't blame them at all — I was probably the only one who wanted to eat vegetables anyway. I didn't eat very much and felt guilty for what I did.

Perth

I housesat for six weeks from the day after I got back to Perth, which was a relief. I knew Mum and Dad wanted me to stay with them since I hadn't been home for almost a year, and also so they could watch what I ate, so I felt a bit guilty. But I had been worried about living at home again because I would have to hide my increasingly disordered eating habits — changing them would be terrifying. I was glad to put that off and have some time to myself, to be as disordered as I liked and bask in the ED voice's praise.

(Food and exercise)

I loved housesitting and so did the eating disorder. I could buy fat and sugar-free yoghurt, since Mum and Dad weren't there to see, and eat it with much less guilt than regular yoghurt caused. Then I took it one step further and mixed it with cold mashed pumpkin, so I could eat more volume with hardly any extra calories. There was a pool at the house, so I made the most of it. I have loved swimming since I was young, but the ED voice quickly converted swimming from a relaxing hobby to mandatory exercise. Every morning, before breakfast and violin practice, I had to swim laps for 20 minutes. After a week or two, I started doing workouts before the swim. Just short, 15-minute classes I found on YouTube, but they were intense workouts and hated them. It didn't take long for my limbs to become so weak they shook, but I knew that if I exercised half-heartedly, the resulting guilt would be far worse and long-lasting than muscle pain and fatigue. Fifteen minutes of fighting exhaustion was better than a day of hating myself.

I had planned to be freer with my spending when I got back to Perth, as I wouldn't be paying rent or bills. I didn't have any work booked yet but I assumed I would start playing with SO again when the 2016 season started. Unfortunately, my car broke down while I was housesitting and it needed a new engine, which cost over $5000. Spending such a large sum, especially on something I didn't care about and wished I didn't need, changed my mind about allowing myself to spend more.

At the end of January, when my friends came back from holiday, I moved back to Mum and Dad's. Luckily, my fear that Mum and Dad would start Maudsley again once I was living with them, did not become a reality. They did watch what I was eating though, while pretending not to. As on previous visits home, I ate away from the house as much as possible, often arranging my days to make sure I would be out of the house for morning tea, lunch and afternoon tea, if possible. If I had no excuse to go out, I tried to eat lunch at a different time to them and took morning and afternoon snacks to my room to "eat" — so I could hide the food somewhere to dispose of later.

I hated deceiving Mum and Dad, but my fear of gaining weight was greater than my dislike for deception. I yearned for them to feel they could trust me, so we could have a healthy relationship again. I attempted to achieve this using more deception, making myself meals that looked like they had a good balance of carbohydrates, protein and oil, but didn't. I planned these meals in advance and experimented with the presentation, attempting to make it look as though there was more rice than there actually was. These meals were usually some variation of vegetables, spinach leaves, rice and homemade hummus. I hoped that, if I combined everything, they wouldn't be able to see how much, (or little), rice I had used. I also told them I made the hummus with olive oil and tahini when, in truth, I used minimal tahini and omitted the olive oil completely. I was essentially eating a lot of spinach and vegetables, a small amount of rice, and some blended chickpeas.

(Exercise)

I was stressed knowing I wouldn't be able to continue my morning exercise. Mum and Dad would be able to hear me jumping around and puffing from their bedroom and would definitely stop me. I might be able to get away with going for a walk each day — they would never allow me to go for a run — but Mum would assume I was exercising to burn calories, not for enjoyment, and would probably time my walks. I didn't feel a walk was strenuous enough anyway, compared to the pilates, cardio and swimming I had been doing. I made myself a routine of the most intense weight-bearing yoga poses I could find. If I held the pose or only moved my legs in the air, I could exercise almost silently. I only did this for about 15 minutes each day, but I still dreaded and hated it, because I was doing it to appease the ED, not for enjoyment or health. I also worried, every morning, that Mum and Dad would hear me. However, I had planned an excuse — if they caught me in the act, I would tell them I was doing some yoga stretching — I kind of was anyway.

I was happy to escape Mum and Dad again, not long after I finished housesitting. This time I went to Brisbane for a season with the Australian Youth Orchestra, (AYO). It was a relief to be away from their watchful eyes again, but every day I had to find a way to do my morning exercise without my roommate seeing. I tried to do it while she was in the shower, but she usually took less than 15 minutes. On other days I did it on the balcony, hoping neither she nor the other girl with whom we were sharing the apartment, would come out of their room and see me. Unfortunately, they did.

I told them I was doing yoga and they seemed to believe me, though maybe wondered why I was doing it on the balcony instead of inside. Or maybe they thought it was perfectly normal and didn't think anything of it.

AYO was mostly enjoyable, though I found it hard to be surrounded by so many people because I constantly compared myself to anyone who was thin. I knew I had body dysmorphia, but didn't know *how* wrong my perception was — because of the dysmorphia. I would also zoom in on one area of a person's body, for example, theirs arms. I might think their arms were thinner than mine, and maybe they were, but the person was also shorter than me. But how much shorter? If I were to enlarge them until we were the same height, would our arms have the same diameter? And what if their arms were smaller than mine, but they had bigger legs? Their arms were still smaller than mine though. I should be able to be the smallest person in the room; I just needed to work harder.

Sometime between finishing housesitting and going to Brisbane, a friend called to ask if I wanted to take over his violin teaching job at a nearby school. He was going back to uni that year, so wouldn't be able to continue teaching. I hated teaching but figured it would be good to have some income on the weeks I wasn't playing with SO, so I took him up on his offer.

(Exercise)

It was only a day and a half of teaching, which suited me. Unfortunately, some of the students had to have their lesson before school, so I had to get up earlier than usual to get there on time. I preferred to exercise before I left home so I wouldn't need to worry about finding the time and energy later in the day, but on some days, if Mum and Dad were already up, I worried they would hear me and make me stop. I couldn't skip a day though, so I had to be creative. There were many days that I exercised in the bathroom at school — each teaching room had its own bathroom, which I could lock, so there was no danger of anyone walking in. I worried that doing the 'mountain climber' would make me sweat in my teaching clothes, but I was more worried about gaining weight. One day when, for some reason, I couldn't exercise incognito at school, I drove to a nearby park after teaching and did my exercises there. I told myself it wasn't really a strange thing to do, as runners often stop to stretch and do push-ups and squats in parks — just not in tights and a dress. I tried to find a secluded area, but some people walked past. I kept my head down, telling myself I would probably never see them again, so what they thought didn't matter.

I contacted SO when I got back to Perth, to let them know I was available for casual work again. The orchestra manager said that, as I had been away for a few years, and there had been some changes in the orchestra — a new conductor and concertmaster — I would need to re-audition. Everyone I spoke to said it was very strange that I was asked to re-audition, but I didn't feel that I could question their decision. I would just do another audition. There was one coming up in a few months.

I considered having a lesson with Dorothy — my high school violin teacher — or someone in SO, to help me with the excerpts, but I was anxious about spending money to pay them for their time and thought I should be able to prepare without a teacher, now that I had finished uni. I was a bit nervous about the audition, but no more than any other performance. I thought I played quite well and only made a few small mistakes. After everyone had auditioned the panel asked to speak to us individually. I was confused, as this hadn't happened when I auditioned six years earlier. In a nutshell, they said my playing was very organised and the notes were accurate, but I didn't play loud enough. I was confused as to whether I had passed the audition or not. It wouldn't be hard for me to play louder — that's an easy fix — so maybe they were giving me feedback for when I played with them next? No. They said to apply again next time they held auditions, and maybe have a lesson with one of them, so they could help me prepare.

I didn't know how to feel. I had thought I would pass; after all I passed the audition when I was 17 and surely my playing had improved since then. Mum and Dad's voices oozed sympathy when I told them, which annoyed me. Mum said that maybe I should have had a lesson with Dorothy, so she could help me bring out the musicality. She also said the musical expression had disappeared from my playing when I got sick. The unspoken implication was that I should recover and then I would be able to pass the audition. I didn't want to hear it. I had planned to work with SO for a bit in Perth, while I worked out what I wanted to do next violin-wise. I had hoped the income would help me feel better about spending money. Unfortunately not.

I started seeing Adelle again — the psychologist I had seen at CCI. Unfortunately, as with Alanna, our conversations went in circles. I was terrified of making even small changes to my eating and there was nothing she could say to convince me. I didn't want to feel guilty for eating and I didn't want to put on weight. I knew I would probably be a much better violinist if my brain was nourished, but the ED voice told me I could be a better violinist in my current state if I just worked harder. We also spoke about Europe. I wanted to go later that year, to audition for some orchestras and have lessons, before touring Europe and China with AYO. Adelle wanted me to see Mum and Dad's point of view, but I already did; I just disagreed with it. Maybe I would get sick in Europe, in which case I would admit I was wrong. But maybe being away would help me recover.

One day, when I was practising at home, Mum came in and said she had made me lunch. She wasn't asking if I wanted some of whatever she had made, or letting me know I could help myself later when I chose to have lunch. Her tone of voice implied that she had done something nice for me, but I knew it was an act — she had done this to force me to eat a proper meal. My stomach tightened as I wondered what terrifying energy-dense concoction she had cooked up. I played dumb.
"Oh, I'm not hungry yet. I'm still practising."
"It'll go cold if you don't eat it now." Again, in her no-nonsense voice, thinly veiled by false cheer.
For anyone who didn't have my medical history, it would have been perfectly understandable for them to decline, but I knew Mum wouldn't back down. Things would turn nasty and Mum scared me when she was angry. I reluctantly agreed, and anxiously followed her to the kitchen.

Mum had made an Indian rice dish and pretended to be excited about the spices in it and homemade paneer she had made. She had already dished me up a big bowl. I can't remember what her excuse was for not having any herself. Since she wasn't eating with me, I decided I would eat as slowly as possible, until she had finished washing the dishes, then find somewhere to dispose of the rest when she was out of the room. I soon realised Mum had predicted this and was deliberately keeping herself busy in the kitchen until I finished eating. I was furious with her for forcing me to eat so much rice, which she knew was one of my fear foods. I felt that she was doing it out of malice, though the reasonable part of me knew it was out of desperation. That didn't stop me from being terrified of putting on weight though. I don't know why Mum decided to make me lunch that day. Luckily she didn't do it again.

Mum and Dad brought up the clinic in America again, and again I resisted. I still didn't want to "waste" a month or more of my life when I needed to go to Europe to start living my life. At some point I realised that, while they definitely didn't want me to go, they wouldn't actually stop me from going to Europe. So I started applying for auditions, looking at airfares and planning my route. I only half believed I would go, even as I entered my debit card details into the airline booking screen. I still thought they would stop me. It was scary, organising the trip on my own without their input or support. It felt wrong because I knew they didn't approve.

A month before I was due to leave for Europe, I went to Fairbridge Festival with Lucy and her fiancé, Kieran. I had been to the festival almost every year with my family since I was nine until I went to Hobart. It was one of my favourite weekends of the year and I had really missed it. I had planned to use some money I had been given for Christmas, to buy my meals while I was there, instead of bringing food with me. I knew I would struggle to spend the money, so I had set this money aside, and compartmentalised it in my head as being separate from my savings and therefore ok to spend. However, I was finishing another housesit the day before the festival and still had quite a bit of food left — mostly vegetables. I decided to cook up a big batch of curry, freeze it in separate containers, and take them to Fairbridge to eat over the weekend.

The ED voice congratulated me for saving money, but it was annoying having to go back to the tent to fetch my meals, especially because walking there and back made me even more tired than I already was. The ED voice congratulated me on the extra exercise though. I eyed the food trucks longingly. They have decent food there; not just junk food, but curries, salads and sushi too. However, after deciding not to spend the Christmas money, I couldn't talk myself back into it. I allowed myself to buy small, cheap things, like coffee or ice cream — I made a deal with the ED voice that, if I restricted at lunch I would be allowed an ice cream — but nothing that cost more than four or five dollars.

On the last day, it bucketed with rain and the temperature plummeted. It was so wet that some venues had to cancel performances because water had pooled around the electrical equipment. I was cold and very tired, after a weekend of eating mainly vegetables, walking around and standing up to watch concerts — I wouldn't let myself sit down, for fear of not burning enough calories and gaining weight. I had a 20-dollar note in my wallet, but couldn't bring myself to break it — in hindsight, that was my undiagnosed OCD at play. Aside from the 20 dollars, I only had a two-dollar coin. I went to the Hare Krishna food truck and asked the man serving if it was possible to buy two dollars worth of the ten-dollar curry plate. I said I only had two dollars left, but I said it with a smile on my face, as though I wasn't worried about it; just another carefree hippy. I didn't want him to feel sorry for me or think I was poor. I hoped he would assume I had spent all my money for the weekend. He kindly filled the plate with curry. I don't know if he noticed how thin I was, if he would have done the same for anyone in the Hare Krishna spirit, or if they had a surplus of food that would have been thrown out anyway. Whatever the reason, I was, and still am, very grateful for the hot meal. While I was eating, I worried about how much oil had been used and if I would put on weight.

About a week before I flew out, Dad brought up the subject of travel insurance. He was worried I wouldn't be covered if I needed treatment for complications caused by AN while I was away. It was definitely a pre-existing condition. He found another insurance company that might cover me, but it was three to four times the price of the insurance I had already booked. I wasn't keen on paying more and didn't think I would need it anyway — Europe was going to help me recover; that was the plan. There was also a catch: the insurance company Dad had found told him I wouldn't be covered unless a medical doctor agreed, in writing, that it was safe for me to go. I asked Krish, who gently replied that he didn't feel comfortable doing that.
"What does that tell you?" Dad asked when I told him.
"That he doesn't think it's safe for me to go," I replied, dejected.
"And what does that tell you?" Dad prompted.

The day I was due to fly out, the house felt very tense. Mum hardly spoke to me. She was probably doing her best not to fall apart. In the afternoon, while I was packing, she came into my room and sat on my bed.
"So what city are you flying into?" she asked quietly. She hadn't asked until that moment, probably because she didn't want to think about it. I hadn't spoken much about my travel plans because I was scared to bring them up, in case it caused an argument.
"Stockholm," I replied carefully. Was she about to snatch my passport away so I couldn't leave the country?
"And where are you going after that?" I think she was genuinely trying to take an interest, not checking up on me. I started to cry, because I had wanted to have nice conversations like this while I was planning, and to be excited together.
"Why didn't you ask me this before?" I asked, through my tears. I don't think she understood what I was getting at.

I was going to be away for my birthday, so we had an early birthday dinner of sorts at Adam and Avril's house, before going to the airport for my late-night flight. Gran and Grandad came too. It should have been exciting, celebrating my birthday before an overseas adventure, but it felt strained. Or maybe I was imagining it. Either way, I was stressed all night. I was still questioning if I was doing the right thing as I stepped onto the plane.

Europe

I landed in Stockholm a few days before my audition, to give myself time to adjust to the time zone and practise. I was staying in a hostel — partly because that's what I always do when I travel and I like it, and partly to save money — so I couldn't practise there. The person I had been emailing at the Swedish Radio Symphony Orchestra had kindly arranged for me to practise in the percussionists' store room. The building where they rehearsed, and where auditions would be held, was about a 30-minute walk from my hostel.

(Food)

I didn't want to eat breakfast at the hostel, and then tire myself out walking; I wouldn't have any energy left to concentrate while I practised. Planning ahead as always, I had bought a small, single-serve tub of yoghurt the day before, which I could take with me and eat at 9 am after I had done some practice — I could eat breakfast later again, since Mum and Dad weren't watching. I had to stop my morning exercise, since I would be staying in dorms for most of my trip, but reasoned that I would be walking a lot, as I had in Hobart, so I felt ok about it. I would have preferred to have a big serving of vegetables at breakfast, to fill me up, but that was too much of a hassle. I didn't have a plastic container and didn't want to buy one or carry it with me. I told myself I should be able to survive on the small yoghurt anyway; it had the same number of calories, just without the volume of vegetables. I should be able to ignore the hunger. I forced myself to practise for four hours as planned, but my concentration was terrible. I shouldn't have been surprised. My concentration during practice had been terrible for almost two years. Being in a new country wasn't going to change that.

My reward for struggling through the long, (and largely ineffective), practice session, was lunch and exploring. I searched for somewhere to buy a lunch that was cheap, low in calories and hopefully high in vegetable content, then let myself be a tourist for the afternoon.

On the day of the audition I was, unsurprisingly, tired, but still couldn't convince the ED voice to allow me a decent breakfast. Luckily, mine was the second audition, so it was over quickly. I was relieved to get it over with early, instead of tiring myself out practising all day. I wasn't too nervous, but didn't give an amazing performance. I was too tired to put everything into it or concentrate properly. ED berated me for not having the willpower to push through the brain fog and physical exhaustion. This was important. Why couldn't I make more of an effort? I didn't get past the first round, but I didn't mind. I had more auditions and I had enjoyed the process.

After another audition in Norköping, which was similarly unsuccessful, I flew to Berlin. I didn't have an audition there, but had about two weeks to kill until the next one. Berlin was kind of on the way to Austria and it was on my travel bucket list, as was seeing the Berlin Philharmonic. I could catch up with friends from Australia who were studying there, and I had organised to explore Berlin with Matt, a friend from Hobart, who was living in the South of Germany.

It was a long travel day. I took a bus from Norköping back to Stockholm, another bus from the Stockholm bus terminal to the airport, flew to Brussels, and wandered around the airport for two or three hours before flying to Berlin, where I got a bus to somewhere near my hostel and walked the rest of the way. I had breakfast before I left my Airbnb in Norköping, and hoped that short flights in Europe wouldn't be as stingy as in Australia, and would feed us. They did not. Food was available for purchase, but I wasn't going to pay the exorbitant prices. I decided to wait until we landed in Brussels.

When I tried to buy something in the airport I was told they didn't accept Swedish Kroner and that I would need to go to the currency exchange desk or pay with my travel card. Not wanting to waste my Swedish cash, I found the exchange desk, however, the man there said he could only exchange notes. This was fine; I had notes, but I also had a lot of coins, which were now worth nothing unless I went back to Sweden, which wouldn't be happening anytime soon. Feeling that I had wasted about 20 dollars Australian, I felt guilty for even considering spending anything on food. But I was starving and exhausted; I needed fuel. As I was in an airport, everything was expensive. The only food I felt was within my penny-pinching budget was junk food, which was all high in calories and therefore only something I could look at longingly. I continued to walk around the airport, looking at all the food places, hoping I would find a bargain. I did not. I hoped I would be fed on the plane. I was not. They didn't even try to sell us food; there was no time. It was one of those shaky, straight up and down, 50-minute flights.

I had trouble finding the correct bus stop at Berlin airport. Nat, a friend who was studying there, had told me it was easy to find, really obvious. Not to me. Eventually, I found a local who was able to point me in the right direction. I missed the stop where I should have disembarked to change buses — again, Nat had told me it would be obvious, but it wasn't to me. I got off the bus a few stops later, having realised I must have missed my stop. Another traveller waiting under the bus shelter was kind enough to look up the route to my hostel on his phone and give me walking directions — which I only half understood. I walked for about half an hour, with my suitcase, violin and hand luggage, until I found the hostel — with more directions along the way from helpful locals. I was exhausted and ravenous. I hadn't eaten since breakfast and had had a long, stressful day, navigating the public transport in Sweden and Berlin.

Matt was already in the dorm when I finally arrived. We hadn't seen each other for about six months and, to be honest, we hadn't even been close when I was in Hobart. I felt I should make small talk for a while and catch up. But I couldn't think of anything to say after "How've you been?" I was too worn out. I wracked my brain for something else to say, but nothing came.
"Do you want to go find dinner?" I heard myself asking. I was worried he would feel the question was abrupt, but Matt didn't seem ruffled
"Sounds good," he replied. Maybe he was hungry too.

Usually, I check out all the food options, so I can make an informed decision and know I'm getting the best value for money. However, my hunger was so extreme and all-consuming that I was incapable of concentrating on anything else. I also felt incredibly weak. I had been hungry since not long after I ate breakfast, with continued hopes of food throughout the day, which had all been dashed. We didn't look around for long before deciding on an Indian restaurant. It looked nice, but the prices were higher than I wanted to pay. I didn't want to say that to Matt though, in case he thought I was some strange type of scrooge.
"Do you want to share one curry between us?" I asked, desperately trying to decrease my dinner bill. "Our family always shares when we get Indian. The serves are usually enough for two."
Matt seemed happy to go along with this — he seemed relaxed about most things — and ordered himself some naan as well. I had succeeded in halving the cost of my dinner.

When the eggplant curry came out — I had suggested a vegetable dish because it would be lower in calories than something with meat or lentils — I was worried. The serve wasn't nearly as big as I had expected. Even I could see it was only enough for one person. Usually, I have as little rice as possible while loading up on vegetables, but there wasn't enough curry for me to do that. I ate more rice than the ED voice wanted me to and felt ashamed for giving in to my hunger. I told myself it wouldn't make me gain weight, since I hadn't eaten lunch, but I couldn't know for sure, so it didn't ease the guilt. I was still hungry afterwards, but Matt was full, having eaten more rice and a whole naan, so I felt I would appear greedy if I suggested dessert. I knew it was illogical for me to consider dessert after feeling guilty for eating rice. I think Mum and Dad's insistence on me finishing my rice while we were doing Maudsley caused a knee-jerk reaction in me, making me perceive rice as the enemy; one of my biggest fear foods.

The rest of my time in Berlin was great, though my worries about food and spending money remained. Luckily there was a lot of reasonably priced food there, so the cost didn't worry me too much. We did a lot of walking as we explored the city, which the ED voice loved.

Vienna was similar, though I was starting to feel more tired and hungry. I kept telling myself to make the most of my time there though — to go out at night and see a free performance by the Vienna Philharmonic; stay out late to see a friend from Perth; walk around all of Schöbrunn even though I was lightheaded and unable to appreciate the beauty because of my fatigue... It was also in Vienna that I decided gelato was an acceptable substitute for carbohydrates at lunch. This continued until I left Italy.

I took a train from Vienna to Klagenfurt, where I had another audition and a lesson with a teacher there, who had been recommended by some friends. Luckily I was renting a room in a share house with friends of a friend, so I could practise there and didn't need to lock up my valuables. Practising continued to be a struggle, and I relied on my willpower to persevere. I practised an hour or two before breakfast, which was rarely filling, then did another two to three hours before a similarly unsatisfying lunch. In the afternoon I had fun exploring the city.

The first round of auditions was in the morning; the second round would be in the afternoon. I was glad I wouldn't need to spend the day stressing and practising and could perform while I was still reasonably fresh. A friend from Perth, who was studying in Klagenfurt, had told me about a sushi train buffet that only cost ten Euro, at which I planned to have a celebratory lunch after the audition — unless I got through to the second round. It would be a long day if I passed the first round, and at least half of me didn't really want to. I just wanted to play and then have the afternoon off. That's how I felt about most of the auditions I did in Europe. I wasn't really invested in any of them, since I was doing so many. It was more for the experience and an excuse to go to Europe. I didn't really know what I was aiming for, as much as I tried to convince myself that I was putting everything into violin.

(Food)

On the day of the audition, I had a small tub of yoghurt for breakfast — I couldn't have a bigger breakfast because I needed to save my calories for lunch at the sushi train — so it's no surprise that I felt lightheaded all morning. Adrenaline gave me a small boost when it was my turn to audition, but left me drained afterwards. As in Sweden, I couldn't put as much energy and emotion as I wanted into my playing. I gave it my all, but my all wasn't much. It was an average performance.

Afterwards, I waited in the cafeteria with the other violinists who had already auditioned. I was exhausted and my stomach felt like an empty cave, but I didn't want to spend my money on the unappetising food they served. I would probably need to buy my lunch there if I got through to the next round but, if that happened, I would wait until closer to the audition time, so I would still have some food in my belly when it was my turn to play. When the panel had their lunch break, a list was pinned to the notice board, displaying the names of those chosen to progress to the second round. Part of me remained hopeful, but I knew it was very unlikely the panel had been impressed by my playing. Unsurprisingly, my name wasn't on the list. I didn't mind.

After being hungry all morning, my body had finally given up on me and turned off my hunger cues. I didn't feel that I deserved a nice lunch anyway, since I hadn't had the willpower to concentrate and give a better performance. I suddenly decided ten Euro was too much to spend on lunch anyway. I had only been spending a few Euro on meals since I got to Austria, as I had been buying from the supermarket instead of restaurants and cafes. Increasing my budget, even for only one meal, felt reckless and greedy.

My next stop was Venice, which was the city I had been looking forward to the most. I had spent a day in Venice on my school's music tour and had been completely enchanted, but a day wasn't enough. I stayed in a cheap hostel on the mainland because I couldn't justify paying over 50 dollars a night to stay in Venice. My room was a four-person tent with two bunk beds. There was room to stand though and there were power boards, so I was happy, especially for ten dollars a night. There was a shuttle bus that drove to and from the bus depot in Venice every hour or so but, after the first day, I learnt that the local public transport bus was cheaper and more regular.

(Food rules)

Before I left Australia I had developed a rule that prevented me from eating breakfast until I had drunk three glasses of water. Sometimes this was in the form of tea, depending on the weather. I had found a way to stick to this rule throughout the trip and decided I would continue to do so unless it was absolutely impossible. As I didn't let myself eat until 9 am, the water helped stave off the hunger. I wanted to get to Venice as soon as possible though, to make the most of my time there, instead of waiting to eat at the hostel before getting the bus in. I bought a single-serve tub of yoghurt — within the allowed calorie limit — and a Litre bottle of diet soft drink from the little shop at the hostel and took both with me on the bus. I drank the soft drink to fulfil my drinking rule, then ate the yoghurt when the clock allowed.

I hadn't expected to be charged one Euro fifty every time I needed to use a public toilet. Most people probably made use of the toilets in restaurants when they had meals, which I had planned to do. I soon found this to be a problem though, as all the eating places I could find — with the exception of fast food joints, at which I was definitely not going to eat — were expensive. Preying on tourists; fair enough. On my first day, I managed to sneak into the toilet in a restaurant and a Mcdonald's, without buying anything, but I didn't want to have to keep sneaking around. I was nervous I would get caught. For the remainder of my stay in Venice, I timetabled my days so I could use the free toilets provided by the galleries with an admission fee just before my next meal.

(Food)

On the first day, I bought my lunch at a cicchetti restaurant, as I wanted to try something distinctly Venetian, and it sounded yummy but not too scary. It was more expensive than I expected though, so from then on I was on the hunt for cheaper food. I found a supermarket later that day — the only one I found in all of Venice — and visited it twice a day for the remainder of my time there, to buy lunch and dinner. I would buy one or two tins of vegetables and some form of lean protein, to mix with them. I had a stash of salt and pepper sachets in my bag, which I had taken from a cafe at some point, which I sprinkled into the tin to add flavour. After I had eaten my veggies, I usually treated myself to a scoop of gelato, continuing my new rule of substituting it for carbohydrates.

After four days in Venice, I took a bus to Florence, where I stayed for almost a week with Kelly, a friend from high school. Kelly planned to stay there for about a year, to learn Italian and have singing lessons from a teacher who lived there. Though she would have a year or more to see the sights, Kelly was keen to see as much as possible in that first week, before her days were filled with language classes and homework. I was too but balked at the entry fee to some of the galleries and old buildings. I was constantly suggesting we take the cheaper options, or trying to find excuses as to why we shouldn't go to another gallery — spending ten Euro on one entry ticket was as much anxiety as I could handle each day — all the while trying not to sound argumentative or bossy. I'm not sure if Kelly thought I was acting oddly. Maybe she just thought I was on a tight budget.

Florence had its first-ever Pride parade while we were there and we were excited to march. There were a few small floats, some people with percussion instruments, and others danced in matching costumes, but most of us just walked. There were a lot of bright clothes and rainbow flags and everyone was happy and friendly. The parade travelled from the outskirts of the city to the centre, circled around the Duomo,[22] and then continued to wherever they were holding the afterparty. Kelly and I hadn't decided yet if we would stay for the afterparty, but we both wanted to walk there with the crowd. I had been tired on and off in Florence — partly from the stress of solo travel, broken sleep and busy days; and partly, (mostly?) from not eating enough — and was feeling particularly tired that day. But I still wanted to march. Unfortunately, by the time we got to the Duomo, I was very tired and felt overwhelmed at the thought of walking all the way to the after party, and then back to our apartment. Usually, I can force myself to keep walking, even when I'm tired and lightheaded, as long as I don't also have to concentrate, talk or carry anything heavy. But that day I was completely knackered and eventually made the decision to stop. Kelly was excited about the parade and wanted to keep walking, so she did, while I returned to the apartment.

At the end of my week in Florence, I took a sleeper train to Paris, where Aunty Diana, Uncle Paul and my cousin Kath, met me. They were on holiday in France and I was joining them for a week. First up was four days in Euro Disney. I was worried things may be awkward, as I hadn't seen Paul and Diana since I was about six and, though Kath had come to Perth just before I moved to Hobart, we didn't know each other well. I was also worried about the price of food in Euro Disney. I assumed it would be much the same as in Disneyland, which was at at least five times as much as I had been spending on the trip so far. The thought of buying expensive meals for four days gave

---

[22] At the time, I assumed the Duomo was on the parade route because it's such a famous landmark. It took me six years to realise it may have been chosen because it is a *Catholic* landmark.

me butterflies. Luckily awkwardness wasn't a problem. They were all eager to help me feel at home and we were usually all together, so there were never any awkward silences.

Kath had emailed me a few weeks earlier to ask what I usually ate for breakfast and what my food intolerances were, so they could make sure they had food in the house that I could eat. I was embarrassed about my odd eating habits and also didn't want them paying for my food, so I briefly told her that I usually have scrambled eggs and vegetables, but that I could pick some up when I got there. When we went to the supermarket, Diana told me to put my food through with theirs, and wouldn't take the cash I offered for my share. I didn't think it was right for them to pay for my food, but I was immensely grateful.

Exploring Euro Disney with Paul, Diana and Kath was very relaxing. Contrary to my visit to Disneyland, during which I had rushed around trying to go on all the rides Avril had recommended, they took their time. They go every year and stay for about a week, so there was no need to rush for fear of missing rides. When we had lunch on the first day I tried to give Diana money, but again she said not to worry. I wondered if maybe we would take turns to buy meals.
"Will I get this one then?" I asked when we had dinner that night, doing my best to sound casual.
"Oh no no no," Paul and Diana replied, before quickly changing the subject.
"Oh... thanks," I said self-consciously.
I continued offering to pay for the next few meals until I felt it would be awkward to continue. I was secretly glad because I couldn't even imagine how anxious I would feel paying those prices. Near the end of my time in France, I told them I would make us dinner that night, which they finally accepted. They seemed to enjoy it, so I felt a bit better about accepting their generosity. However, I knew what I had given them was small in comparison.

(Food)

Paul, Diana and Kath didn't have breakfast at home in the morning because, as Paul and Diana are special Disney members, we got to jump the queue through a secret door, which led to a room with free tea, coffee and pastries. While they ate a big, delicious breakfast, I drank coffee and looked at the food longingly, wishing wheat didn't give me awful tummy aches. Because they ate a big breakfast later in the morning, they usually weren't hungry again until dinner. I didn't realise this until the third day. I kept expecting someone to suggest we have lunch, but they never did. As I was only eating an egg with vegetables for breakfast — or sometimes no egg, just vegetables — I was always exhausted and starving by dinner time. The ED voice thought skipping lunch was great, but I had to work hard to pretend I was having fun, make conversation and remain vertical. At least I didn't feel guilty for having a big dinner and sometimes dessert.

From France, I went to London, where Josie, a friend from Perth who was studying there, kindly let me stay in her room while she was on holiday in Ireland. She had two housemates; Lexi, who was only there the first night, and Shannon, who was surprisingly easy to talk to. Shannon and I both liked to keep to ourselves, which helped. As when I was in Austria and Sweden, I practised in the morning and then explored in the afternoon. I went to shows on West End most nights, so I was always grateful to climb into bed after long, full days. I continued to make myself practise, while drinking a few cups of tea, until I had breakfast at 9 am. This was getting harder and harder, especially with the late nights. As breakfast was my long-awaited reward after practising, I liked to be completely relaxed while I cooked and ate, which could only happen if I was by myself. One morning I kept practising past 9 am, waiting for Shannon to leave for work.
"Are you working today?" I finally asked, when I went to the kitchen to make yet another cup of tea.
"No, I've got the day off," she replied happily. "I'm going to stay home and work on my novel."
Completely within her rights, but I felt anxious cooking and eating in front of her.

Part of the reason I went to London was because I had an audition in Norwich, for a chamber orchestra that traveled throughout Europe. I love touring and chamber music, so I was more excited about this audition than the others. Shannon helped me work out how to get to Norwich by train and how to buy the ticket. I balked at the price, but there was no cheaper option. I told myself it was for violin, not a fun tourist thing, in an attempt to justify the cost.

The audition was in a church about a kilometre from the train station. The chamber orchestra had a concert there that night, so they held auditions after their sound check. I packed myself a small snack to eat while I was warming up, but it didn't fill me up or give me much energy. I looked longingly at some boxes of fruit juice that had been stored in the warm-up room, but I knew they contained added sugar. I would feel guilty if I drank one. I was already feeling tired and weak when it was my turn to play. They had asked me to prepare the first movement of a Mozart Concerto and the Adagio from Bach's G Minor Sonata. I was relatively happy with my performance of the Mozart, though

some sections weren't as clean as they could have been. My mind went blank about 20 seconds into the Bach, which I was performing from memory. I had no idea what the next note was, or the next phrase. I couldn't even jump ahead to a later section; the rest of the piece eluded me.
"That's ok, we've heard enough anyway. Thank you," one of the panellists said, after watching me flounder for about five seconds. He spoke kindly and without any negativity about my playing. A week or so later, the orchestra manager emailed to say my audition was unsuccessful. The panel said I played well but didn't make a big enough sound.

From London, I went to Manchester for about a week, to visit Linda, another uni friend from Perth. She was doing her Masters at the Royal Northern College of Music and absolutely loving it. I arrived in the evening and Linda met me at the bus station.
"Do you want to go out for dinner before we go back to mine?" She asked. "I don't have much food in the house at the moment."
I hadn't asked her what she wanted to do food-wise during the week, but I assumed we would do a mixture of eating out and cooking at her house.
"Sounds good," I agreed. I would have preferred not to spend money eating out, but the ED voice had ordered me to skip lunch, since I would be sitting on the bus for five hours, so I was ravenous and light headed. I figured Linda would know somewhere cheap to eat.
"I mostly eat out," Linda said, as she led us to a new burger house she wanted to try. "I don't have time to cook, with uni and everything."

The thought of buying most of my meals out made me anxious, but I told myself it would probably be ok. I had seen a lot of cheap takeaway places in London and assumed Manchester would be similar. However, I soon learned that Linda didn't go to the cheaper places; she went to nice places. I was stressed as I looked at the menu that night. Everything was ten pounds or more.
"Do you want to share a meal?" I asked. "They'll probably be huge."
"Good idea," Linda happily agreed.
Unfortunately, it was not big. As we were in a burger house, half the meal was bread, which Linda could eat, but I couldn't. I'm always happy to cut out the carbohydrate if there is enough volume from vegetables, but there wasn't. I was still very hungry and tired after eating, but didn't know what else I could buy that wouldn't cost too more than a few pounds. If I was by myself I would have searched until I found something that was cheap and filling but not too high in calories — a difficult quest, but sometimes I succeeded — but I wasn't by myself. I pretended I was full and happy when we had finished eating and left for Linda's house.

Overall, I had a lot of fun in Manchester. Linda and I had some great chats and I found I could almost relax and be myself around her, which is rare for me. We found it easy to plan our days and coordinate her rehearsals and gigs with my practice and hanging out together. I was repeatedly surprised at how easy it was. But it was also very tiring. I still made myself drink about a Litre of water before I ate breakfast — in the form of hot tea, as the weather was still cool — and couldn't eat until after 9 am. When Linda had rehearsals in the morning I practised before breakfast, which helped me feel like I had accomplished something and hadn't wasted a day. If she had a free morning, we went out to do touristy things, which meant I missed practising. We were also keen to make the most of the day and left the house by 8 or 9 am. I couldn't let myself eat breakfast before we left, so I went without breakfast. Sometimes Linda did too, but she would buy herself something to eat while we were out, which I was too scared to do. I felt increasingly hangry, tired and lightheaded as the morning progressed, doing my best to pretend I was having fun until we had lunch.

At every meal, I tried to find excuses to reduce the cost. I tried to explain to Linda that I couldn't spend too much on food, but tried to act casual, as though I was any other 20-something trying to see Europe on a budget. I couldn't understand why I felt so anxious spending money anyway, let alone put it into words. I was scared Linda would think I was a Scrooge if I asked to cook at home all the time. And I didn't want to make her miss out on nice meals just because of my illogical anxieties. I always suggested we share meals, but remained hungry when all the food was gone. Sometimes Linda was too, but would buy herself something else to eat later. Though I had a great week and loved getting to know Linda better, I was on alert most of the time, worried about where she would suggest we eat and if I would be hungry afterwards. It's interesting though because, at the time, it felt like a relaxing week; a good break after practising hard and burning the candle at both ends for so long. But I was tired and stressed for at least half of my waking hours that week. Maybe I had become so accustomed to feeling that way and, since there were also a lot of fun times, and I had finished my last audition, the week felt carefree in comparison.

Tour

After a wonderful week, I took a bus back to London and stayed the night at Josie's again. The next morning we took a train together to Ede, in The Netherlands, where we would start rehearsals for the AYO tour. We were both keen to settle ourselves in the buffet car listed in the booking information, as the journey was five or six hours. Because I planned to spend most of the day eating and would be mainly sitting, I didn't have breakfast before leaving Josie's house. I was hungry and tired from the previous day's travel and a late night, but was also looking forward to the free food.

"Are you sure it's free food in the buffet car?" I asked Josie that morning, as we walked through the train station in London. "My train to Paris was meant to have a buffet car but it was just a small restaurant that sold overpriced food."
"Hmmm hard to know. Might be a European thing," she replied.
I decided to check, and I'm glad I did. The lady at the information desk confirmed that it was not, as we had hoped, a carriage full of free food, but instead a place where we could buy food. Since I had told myself I wouldn't need to spend any money on food that day, it was very hard for me to convince myself to do so, especially as the train ticket had been quite expensive. I bought something small, partly to save money and also because I was scared to eat "too much" since I wouldn't be getting much exercise that day. I bought myself a salad and an apple, which was nowhere near enough for breakfast and lunch.

Navigating the trains wasn't as straightforward as I had hoped. We also had to buy an extra 15-Euro ticket, for the train from Amsterdam to Ede. We walked from Ede station to Akoesticum, where we would be rehearsing and living for the next week. It was only a short walk but, after a stressful day with hardly any food, every step was an effort, especially as I was carrying my luggage and violin. I was trying to hold a conversation with Josie and had to work hard to hide my hangry mood. I just wanted to get to our room and lie down.

When we got to Akoesticum, a friendly woman greeted us in the entrance hall, gave us our room keys, information packs and pointed us towards the elevator. Being polite to her tried my patience, but we were almost there — soon I would be able to lie down! The elevator went to the second floor, but ours was one of a few rooms on the third floor, which was up a short flight of stairs. When I discovered I would need to carry my things up the stairs I nearly cried. I didn't know if I had enough strength left in my arms to lift my suitcase. Somehow I did, but I felt like a rag doll when I got to the top. We had arrived.

I had had a great time travelling for the past two months and was proud that I had successfully navigated, mostly solo, around Europe. However, I was relieved that I would be looked after by a team of proper adults for the next month. No more hostel dorms where I had to make sure my violin and passport were safe; no more stressing about missing my bus or train to the next city. I could hang out with people I already knew, who spoke English, about half of my meals would be provided and others would take care of travel arrangements.

(Food rules and food)

I was looking forward to meals at Akoesticum. We had been told the chef took great pride in serving good quality food made from locally-sourced produce, and catering to a variety of dietary needs. The dining room was set up for buffet service, so I assumed breakfast would offer lots of cooked spinach, fried tomatoes and fruit, as well as the more energy-dense, scarier eggs, bacon, sausages and bread. Unfortunately, there were no vegetables and the only fruit on offer were apples and bananas. By this stage, I was wary of fruit because I wasn't sure of the calorie count. I had googled it many times but, to be accurate I needed to weigh the fruit and that was hard when I wasn't at home. Even at home, I made sure I only used the scales when Mum and Dad weren't in the room because I knew they would know what I was up to. I didn't know what to do. I longed for scrambled eggs and sausages but, even though they're mainly protein, I couldn't convince myself to eat more than a tablespoon or two of eggs. Most days I ended up having an apple, which worried me, and the whites of a few boiled eggs. There was a big bowl filled with sachets of Nutella and other chocolate spreads, and I often spread these onto some of my egg whites. I didn't allow myself to have more than half a sachet a day, but I still felt guilty. My friends noticed my breakfasts were strange, but once I listed my food intolerances, they didn't question me any further.

I did my best to drink a Litre of water before eating, but it was harder when we had breakfast in a big group. After a few days of problem solving, I decided to make four cups of herbal tea and carry them to my table on a plate. There, I drank them as quickly as I could, went to the toilet, and then ate breakfast. I worried the AYO staff would see me carrying the teacups and think I was being silly, or taking advantage of the free tea. Luckily that never happened; I would have felt so ashamed and embarrassed because I knew we were representing AYO and Australia. It made breakfast time stressful, because I had to get through the tea before I could eat, and I had a constant fear, whenever I was at a buffet or sharing food with others, that they would run out of one of my few safe foods.

My fear was heightened at lunch when they served soup, bread and salad. As I couldn't eat the bread and the soup was mostly vegetables and water — which the ED voice loved — I had to eat a lot to feel somewhat full. I always worried they would run out of soup before I'd had enough to fill my belly. I had at least two plates of salad too, feeling guilty if I put more than the smallest taste of cheese onto my plate.

(Exercise)

On most days we rehearsed for about five hours, so we usually had either an evening, morning or afternoon free. I always made sure I went for a walk in the forest beside the Akoesticum property, or into town. As I was walking much less than I had been the previous two months, and was spending a lot of time sitting in rehearsals, I was worried I would put on weight. There were a few days when we were in rehearsals all day and after dinner, so I got up early to go for a walk. I wanted to power walk for at least an hour, as I had been walking an average of a few hours a day before AYO and would be sitting for the rest of the day. Some mornings I couldn't fit that in though, because I also wanted to make sure I got enough sleep — sometimes I made somewhat smart decisions about my health. One day I attempted to go for a half-hour run instead of walking, because others in the orchestra had been talking about enjoying their morning or evening runs. However, I wasn't in the habit of running and didn't have that sort of fitness. When I gave into my tiredness and breathlessness I was disgusted with myself. Others in the orchestra were going for hour-long runs, so I should be able to run for at least half as long. Instead of running, I power-walked, but that didn't feel like enough of a workout to make up for a day of sitting. As no one else was around, I checked the time and did some mountain climbers, push-ups and sits-ups for ten minutes, right there on the forest track. I jumped up when I heard a noise and saw a man walking towards me with his dog. I walked past him, hoping he hadn't seen me on the ground, and was grateful I had managed to fit in ten minutes before he interrupted.

As on previous music camps, being with people around my age all day meant I was constantly comparing myself to them. There were a few girls in particular, who I was always looking at, trying to work out if they really were thinner than me, or if my body dysmorphia was playing tricks on me. Every time I looked though, I couldn't find any part of their bodies that was bigger than mine. They had flat stomachs, their arms were thinner, were their legs bigger? How could they be so thin if their eating wasn't disordered? Or were they? To this day, I scrutinise the photos these women post on social media, trying to find a part of their body that is bigger than mine, and looking for signs that they may also be restricting their food intake.

I longed to ask my friends if these other girls were thinner than me, but no one on the tour knew I had AN and I wanted to keep it that way. One evening, Josie told me she had overheard the two girls sitting behind her on the bus talking about me. They were commenting on how thin I was and one suggested I might be anorexic. I don't know if they were speaking negatively, but Josie is incredibly loyal and decided they needed to be set straight. "She's not anorexic; actually she eats a lot," she told them.
I am still so incredibly grateful to Josie for her bravery and loyalty. However, I also felt bad for not being honest with her. I felt that, in a twisted sense, I had unintentionally made a fool of her, because the girls had been correct. I also felt proud though, that I had succeeded in making myself so small that people were talking about it.

(Exercise)

When we left Akoesticum to embark on our tour of Europe, China and Australia, we stayed in hotels, which meant I usually had access to a gym. It didn't take long for me to incorporate a trip to the gym into my morning routine. I would go as soon as I got up, cycle for about 20 minutes, have a shower, and then go down to breakfast. I dreaded seeing another AYO person in the gym, in case they thought I was anorexic or obsessed with exercise — yes, I absolutely see the irony in that — but a potentially awkward encounter was preferable to missing out on exercise. Once it was part of my routine, I knew I would feel guilty, fat and lazy all day if I skipped it. On some of the travel days we needed to check out of the hotel around 6 am or earlier. Like most people, I don't love getting up early, but it's even harder when you're malnourished. However, on these days, I made myself get up about half an hour earlier than I would have otherwise needed, so I could fit in 20 minutes on the bike. In some hotels, the gym didn't open until 7 or 8 am, but I always planned ahead. I would either do an extra session on the bike the night before or head to the gym as soon as we reached our next hotel, no matter how tired or hungry I was.

Touring is tiring for most people. Navigating foreign cities can be stressful, especially if you don't speak the language. Rehearsing and performing uses a lot of energy, and being around others can be draining. Sometimes meals are rushed, or there isn't time to eat at all. Sometimes you don't feel like eating the food served, because it's different to what you normally eat. However, most people who eat and rest intuitively manage to tour without feeling hungry and exhausted for most of their waking hours. They don't regularly feel lightheaded, or wonder if their legs will give way when they stand up. It didn't take long for me to feel this way. During most concerts, I struggled to focus because my head was spinning. I experienced this so often that I came to expect it. It became the norm. By the second half of the tour, I was so exhausted that I hated standing up during applause or walking offstage after concerts. I dreaded it. And the Europeans love to applaud. We usually performed two or three encores, standing up and sitting down a few times between each.

While I was in London, I recorded an audition for Southside Sinfonia, a chamber orchestra in London. They would be holding second-round live auditions in Sydney a few days after the tour finished. Luckily, the tour ended in Sydney, so I had arranged to stay with Vic, a school friend who lived there, until the day after the auditions, in case I got through to the second round. While we were in Ede, I received an email "regretfully" informing me that I wouldn't be progressing to the second round. Part of me wasn't too disheartened, because I hadn't put everything into the audition — I hadn't put my all into any of the auditions, because I didn't have the energy. But part of me was disappointed because it was the last audition result from the whole trip and it was a no. I hadn't minded too much when I didn't pass the other auditions, because there were always more. But there wasn't another anymore. This was the last one.

I think that's why I bawled my eyes out when I said goodbye to everyone the morning after our final concert. Luckily I could cry in the privacy of our hotel room. I sobbed harder than I had sobbed in a very long time. I had been looking forward to this trip and the tour for so long. I had truly hoped being away from home would help me start to recover from AN. And part of me had dared to hope it would lead to a job or another exciting opportunity. But none of that had happened, and now this amazing trip was almost at an end. For a moment I wondered if I would have been successful in any of the auditions, had I been well, but the ED voice admonished me; I only had myself to blame. I should have worked harder and not given into my tiredness, regardless of how malnourished I was. How could I expect to succeed with such weak willpower? I would have to go back to living with Mum and Dad, hiding my disordered eating habits, and teaching, which was tiring and depressing.

Post Europe

Living with Mum and Dad again, after being away for three months, was even harder than it had been before I left. The ED part of me felt trapped, so I was anxious and scared. Mum and Dad had noticed that I had lost weight while I was away and were watching me even more closely than before. I knew it was only because they cared and desperately wanted me to be well, but it didn't make the attention any less terrifying for me. Luckily, Lucy and Kieran had asked me to dog-sit for them while they went on holiday. They left about two weeks after I got back, but said I could come stay with them a few days earlier if I wanted. I felt awkward being in their space and eating with them — did they really want me there? Should I give them more space? — but it was better than being at home.

Living alone again and dog-sitting was great. I could eat what I wanted and exercise without worrying about anyone watching. It was cold though, even though it was early Spring. Everyone in Perth was commenting on how long it was taking to warm up after winter that year, but I felt it acutely, having very little body fat. I dreaded going outside to walk the dog because I had to leave the heater.

Lucy and Kieran asked if I wanted to continue living with them after they got back, but I felt they were only saying that to be nice — surely they didn't want me around third-wheeling. Also, I didn't want to pay rent. My only work was six hours of teaching per week, and the odd gig. Luckily, a friend's friend, Nate, was away working in Hobart for a few weeks and his house was empty. Nate's sister had been stopping by every few days to feed his fish, but he said he didn't mind me housesitting. It felt odd staying in the house of someone I had never met. I felt he was only letting me stay there to be nice, not because he actually needed a house sitter. Would he have preferred that I wasn't there at all? But my desperation to live anywhere other than with Mum and Dad helped me to ignore these worries. I thanked my friend and moved to Nate's the day after Lucy and Kieran got home.

Nate's house was in a great location, but it was very cold. Hardly any sunlight found its way to the windows. Even with the heater up as high as it would go, I was so cold my muscles were always tense. There is no part of me that is complaining about this, neither now, nor at the time. Nate was incredibly generous to allow me, a stranger, to stay in his house.

(Food and exercise)

I discovered the cheap fruit and vegetables at Spudshed while I was housesitting for Kieran and Lucy. I was mostly avoiding carbohydrates by this point, and couldn't convince myself to buy protein. Instead, I ate the tinned beans, eggs and low fat tuna I found in the fridges and pantries of the people for whom I housesat. As Nate had known he would be away for a few months, he had given away any perishables in his fridge before he left. His pantry mostly contained food to which I was intolerant and fear foods — no beans, eggs or tuna. During the month I stayed there, I hardly ate any protein, except when I went to Mum and Dad's, or Lucy and Kieran's, for dinner. I had become even more strict with my spending, since being in Europe had used a decent chunk of my savings and I didn't have a lot of work. I spent about ten dollars a week on my groceries, which included a two-dollar five-kilo bag of carrots. Small wonder I was always freezing in that house. My body only had its own muscle to burn to keep me warm. I wasn't giving it anything.

Every morning, as soon as I got up, I did 30 minutes of exercise. I had saved a variety of exercise videos on YouTube — Pilates, HIIT, cardio etc. — and copied the instructor. After that, I had a shower and practised — I was preparing a program to audition for a postgraduate course at RNCM, where Linda was studying in Manchester — while drinking a few cups of tea. Breakfast was still at 9 am, followed by more practice until 12.30 pm. Nate had an exercise bike in the lounge room, and one day I decided to try it. After a few days, cycling before lunch became compulsory. If I skipped it the ED voice would pile on the guilt until I had either restricted more than normal at my next meal, or cycled later in the day. One perk of the cycling was that it warmed me up for a little while.

While I was at Nate's I applied for a position at the SO sales call centre. It was a three-month casual position and I would be calling past concert-goers and subscribers to ask if they wanted to subscribe the following year or renew their existing subscription. Some friends had worked there the year before and said it was an ok job. It was by no means my dream job, but it was in music and it was steady. And, as I was still applying for other jobs and courses overseas, I hoped it would just be something to tide me over until I found a full-time job performing.

I was offered a position, with about six others. Most of us got on quite well. The weekday shifts were from 4 pm to 8 pm, which was an annoying time for eating dinner and getting home using public transport. While I was at Nate's it was an easy bus ride but, unfortunately, he returned home a week after I started the job. We were allowed to take a quick break from calling to eat dinner, but after the first few shifts, most of us just had bites of food between calls. Though we sat down to make the calls, I found it mentally draining, talking to people and cold calling for most of the shift. I surprised myself and everyone else when I was the highest seller almost every week, even breaking new records. Most of the time I wasn't really trying very hard. We were paid a commission for sales, but I was too tired to put in much effort, even for the promise of extra money. Maybe it was because I wasn't pushy that I convinced people to subscribe. I still don't know.

(Food)

I had spoken to Kieran and Lucy about Nate coming home and where I would live. They kept offering me their spare room and, even though I didn't believe they actually wanted me to stay there, I eventually took them up on their offer. My eating was far too disordered to go back to living with Mum and Dad. My meals consisted almost entirely vegetables by this stage, with maybe a small amount of sauce, peanut paste or cheese; protein was a garnish if it was there at all. I lived with Lucy and Kieran on and off for the next year, housesitting whenever I could. I paid rent, but not very much, which also covered my share of bills and bits and bobs in the fridge and pantry, like condiments and spices — very generous of them. Though they maintained that they liked having me there, I never believed them. When I housesat, I didn't have to worry about bothering them. It also meant that my eating and exercise could be as disordered as the ED voice wanted, without needing to worry about what Kieran and Lucy would think.

Auditions and Work

My submission to RNCM needed to include 30 minutes of unedited footage from a recent performance, preferably with piano accompaniment. This meant that, unfortunately, I couldn't make a few recordings at home when I was feeling relatively energised. I decided to play the third movement of Tchaikovsky's violin concerto and a Bach Sonata. I spoke to someone at a church near Mum and Dad's house, who said I could use it for free if I wasn't profiting from the performance, and if members of the congregation could attend. That was fine by me. I just wanted to record my performance with as little cost or stress as possible. I invited family, some friends and previous violin teachers.

I asked Heidi, who has been my accompanist since I was eight years old, if she could accompany the Tchaikovsky. She was happy to, and said she would play for free, as a thank you for being such a good dog, chicken and house-sitter — I had looked after her family's house and animals a few times by this point. Heidi suggested I stay with her and her partner Ellen in their house down South, so we could rehearse using the piano they had there; she much prefers that piano and the acoustics of the house. Heidi and Ellen said I could stay on in their house after they went back to Perth, to have a little practice retreat — another thank you for housesitting, though I maintain that it was completely unnecessary, because I loved looking after their home.

I was apprehensive about staying with them — would it be awkward living together? What would they think about what I ate? Would I be able to exercise? So I made plans. I decided I would have to wait and see what happened with the awkwardness; maybe it would be ok. They're both lovely people and there would be three of us, which is easier than one-on-one. I would just let them take the lead. And I would only be there with them for two or three days.

(Food and exercise)

When it came to making my food look normal, breakfast was my main worry. Most people have toast, cereal or some sort of yoghurt concoction, but I am intolerant to most breads and cereals. The only ones I can have are very expensive, and far too high in calories, for me to consider. I can eat yoghurt and love it, but I never allowed myself more than a few spoonfuls at a time. I couldn't eat my usual breakfast with them though; Lucy and Kieran had come to accept my strange breakfasts but I didn't want to create any unnecessary awkwardness with Heidi and Ellen or make them think I was restricting my food — Mum had told Heidi I had AN when I went into hospital in 2010, and she had visited a few times with her children. My solution was to make fake bread, using my food intolerances as an excuse for its odd ingredients. The only ingredients were chopped cabbage and egg whites, but I told Heidi and Ellen that they contained mostly rice flour and egg, with a bit of cabbage for moisture. I got the feeling they didn't believe me, but neither of them said anything, so I sat there eating, feeling awkward, and tried to keep the conversation on anything but my food.

Heidi had mentioned there were a few bedrooms at the house, and that I would have my own, so that solved the exercise problem. As long as I got up before they did, I could exercise without them knowing. I had to change my exercise routine a bit — I worried they would be able to hear me if I did any jumping or running — and just hoped they wouldn't hear me moving around or puffing.

Though I found it much easier to navigate cohabitation with Heidi and Ellen than I expected, I breathed a sigh of relief when they left to go back to Perth. I felt I had only just succeeded in appearing normal and, even then, it had been a huge effort. I wouldn't have been able to keep it up for much longer. I had brought food with me from Perth, as there were only one or two small shops near their house and I hadn't known what Heidi and Ellen's plan was food-wise. I didn't want to bring too much though, because I worried they would think it odd for me to bring so many vegetables. We ended up cooking together at every meal and had mostly used their food. At the time I wondered if this was deliberate; if they were worried about my eating, or how much food I could afford. Whatever the reason, it meant I had a decent amount of vegetables left for the rest of my time there. Only a day later, I realised I had already used a large portion of what I had left, and would need to ration myself carefully for the next few days. I considered driving to the closest shop but was worried for two reasons: the price of food would be much higher there than at the Spudshed, and it was about a 30 kilometre round trip to the supermarket. As petrol isn't cheap, I was always very aware of how far I was driving. I also made sure I filled up my tank on the cheapest day. The drive to and from the holiday house would use about a tank of petrol but I reasoned that, as I would be away from Lucy and Kieran's for the week and therefore wouldn't pay rent — they were very generous like that — the cost balanced out. I would fill up a day or two after I got back to Perth, on the cheap day. I had it all worked out almost to the litre. If I drove to the shop and back I may not have enough petrol to get home without filling up, which would mean paying a higher rate per litre. I could have just put in a small amount and filled up the rest on the cheap day, but I found getting petrol stressful and tiring and did it as rarely as possible, so if I could avoid an extra trip I would.

(Food and exercise)

Because I couldn't bring myself to spend five dollars on petrol, I divided the food I had left into little piles in the fridge — one pile per meal — so I wouldn't run out. I was more tired than usual, and it was even more of a struggle to focus while I was practising. I was annoyed at myself for not making the most of my practice time while I had this beautiful home to myself. I did my best; I tried to convince myself that I was feeling fine and enjoying myself. I told myself that I wanted to go for a walk to explore the area, even though I had to force myself to continue walking forwards until I had been walking for the amount of time ED and I had agreed upon before I allowed myself to turn back.

On my last day, I was exhausted even before I packed up my things, cleaned the house and washed my sheets, in preparation for leaving. I was lightheaded and my legs felt weak. I was dreading the drive home, but somehow I made it. I had to stop at the Spudshed on the way too, otherwise, I wouldn't have anything to cook. Lucy and Kieran would have been happy for me to eat with them, but they had already done so much for me. And their meals were full of fear foods. I bought my groceries before I went home because I was worried that, if I went home first, I wouldn't be able to drag myself out again.

I wanted my concert to be on a Sunday because we went to Mum and Dad's for dinner on Sundays and they live near the church I had booked. I didn't want to use extra petrol driving there twice in one week. Mum, Dad, Gran, Grandad, two family friends, Adam and his girlfriend Avril, came. Adam had agreed to take care of recording the video and audio.

I always ate less during the day on Sundays, because I knew I would eat more at dinner, in an attempt to pretend to Mum and Dad that I wasn't restricting. Though I wanted to hold the concert on a Sunday to save my petrol money, I also wanted to give a good performance, which required energy and concentration. This would be a huge effort for me on any day, let alone a day when I was eating even less than normal. As usual, I planned in advance as much as I could and told myself to power through. I made my usual Sunday food restrictions and hoped adrenaline would get me through. It did — just. I was knackered afterwards and had quite a few memory slips during the Bach — my head felt completely empty. But I made it through.

Earlier in the next year I applied to work with the West Australian Youth Orchestra, (WAYO), of which I had been a member when I was at school. I knew that a friend who had been working for them was moving to Melbourne, so I assumed there would be a vacant position. I figured that, though I didn't want to work in music operations long term, it was a job in music with nice people, and it was regular work. They offered me a job and I started working five-hour shifts on most Saturday mornings. We set up the chairs and music stands for the orchestras, recorded attendance, set up and packed away morning tea, monitored the kids, packed up the chairs and locked up the music and other bits and pieces at the end of rehearsal.

(Food and exercise)

We started at 7.30 am, which meant getting up at 6 am. I hate early mornings, but I can make myself get up if I need to. There were two main problems with the early start though: breakfast and morning exercise. I couldn't allow myself to eat before I started work; it was far too early. I would be hungry again by mid-morning and didn't allow myself to eat lunch until 1 pm. It was better to eat breakfast later, then I wouldn't have to wait so long until lunch. Walking around carrying chairs and music stands with no food in me became harder and harder. I also had to hold a conversation with Lisa, the friend with whom I was working. She's lovely, but chatting and pretending to be happy was an extra strain on my already struggling brain. Once we had set up the orchestra I had to find time to eat too, which wasn't always easy. Sometimes I was asked to do extra jobs during the time I had planned to eat. I experimented with different breakfasts, to see which were the easiest to eat while working, and kept me full. At home, I usually had microwaved cabbage and carrot, curry powder and salt for taste, and maybe a tiny amount of peanut paste. For the first few weeks at WAYO I made a cabbage smoothie — by smoothie, I mean blended cabbage and water — with some sugar-free cordial for taste. I wondered what Lisa thought as I drank it. I deliberately brought it in a white container, so she wouldn't be able to see the strange colour and consistency.

I spent a lot of time thinking about how to fit in my exercise on these mornings. I considered doing it when I got home after work, before I ate lunch, but knew I would probably be exhausted by then and didn't want it weighing on my mind all morning. Sometimes I had to go straight to a gig or something else after my shift and didn't want to risk missing a day of exercise because I had run out of time. I decided to skip my exercise on Saturdays and increase it from 30 to 35 minutes on the other days. The extra five minutes would accumulate to cover the half hour I missed on Saturdays. Although I had to get up early, it was nice to have a day when I didn't have to exercise.

I continued my exercise, practise, breakfast, practise routine every morning, unless I had something at the same time that I couldn't miss, such as WAYO, teaching or a rehearsal. I continued to apply for jobs and training programs, but my auditions were always half-hearted. I didn't have the energy to concentrate or play with expression, and I was scared to spend money on violin lessons, for a teacher to help me prepare. I always told myself there would be more opportunities, so it didn't matter if I wasn't successful. I was seriously doubting myself though. Was I actually good enough? Did I have what it took to be professional? Friends who had played at the same level as me when we were teenagers were winning jobs, getting accepted into amazing training programs or getting offered more gigs in Perth. The healthy part of me, at this point very quiet, reminded me that I was giving myself a huge handicap by not feeding my brain and body, but eating more was truly terrifying. I would rather struggle through each day, feeling tired, lightheaded and hungry, than hate myself for being lazy and greedy. Clinicians and people who had recovered told me I would become used to a bigger body and the extra energy and freedom would be worth it. They said the ED voice was lying when it told me I would never be happy if I put on weight, and that I wouldn't know until I tried it. But I had. I had been at a healthy weight when I left hospital and at an even higher weight when we did Maudsley, and I hated myself so much it hurt. It was horrible; worse than constant hunger and exhaustion.

It was around this time that I read an article about Ed Le Brocq's[23] (nee Ayres) time teaching at the Afghanistan National Institute of Music, (ANIM), his gender transition, and his new book, Danger Music. I was intrigued and googled ANIM after reading the article. I was inspired by the school's work, bringing music back into people's lives after Taliban rule. For fun, I looked at the jobs page and saw that they were looking for a violin teacher — what a coincidence. I sent them my resume and a cover letter. I didn't love teaching, but this job would be much more meaningful than teaching upper-middle-class kids who rarely practised, as I currently did.

A few days later, I received a reply informing me that I had been shortlisted, and asking if I was able to use Skype for an interview with the school's director and the flute teacher. I was excited. Maybe I would be offered the job. Maybe being in a completely foreign environment, busy with full-time work, would help me break my strict routine. The interview seemed to go well. It

---

[23] Ed is a presenter on ABC radio. While I was in Hobart, I bought Mum his first book, Cadence, for her birthday. We both loved Ed; Mum used to listen to his breakfast radio show if she happened to be driving while it was on.

sounded like a big workload, but everyone else was coping and enjoying it, so why shouldn't I? (other than the fact that my body was starving). I wondered why they were telling me about the high walls around the school and the armed security guard though. I already knew Afghanistan was dangerous; describing their tight security didn't alleviate my worry, it increased it, because it meant that security was necessary.

Again, it only took them a few days to email, offering me the job. I was excited, but also knew it was a huge decision. I would need to organise a working visa, accommodation and flights, and make new friends there, not to mention tell my family my travel plans! The director recommended I speak to their previous violin teacher, who had taught there at the same time as Ed, so she could give me a better idea of what to expect. I also spoke to a school friend's Aunt and Uncle, who lived in Kabul on and off, while doing volunteer work. They provided a western perspective of life in Kabul and were very honest about the dangers, particularly for a young, white girl. They mentioned an explosive that had been deliberately detonated during an ANIM concert, which left the director partially deaf in one ear. He had failed to mention that. I was leaning towards accepting the job, but still had doubts.

Eventually, I spoke to Dad, who was understandably worried. Aside from the obvious dangers of moving to a war zone in a developing country, I had proven myself to be incapable of making healthy decisions around food, exercise and my general safety on countless occasions. What if I made myself so sick that I collapsed? How did their hospitals compare to Australia's?

Aside from considering moving to a war zone, my year continued much the same, with my eating and exercise becoming less and more, respectively. Surprisingly, I passed the first round of auditions for the Sydney Symphony Orchestra Fellowship, which would start at the beginning of 2018. I thought my recorded audition had been average at best, but the panel must have disagreed. I would need to fly to Sydney to perform live for the second round. I balked at the cost of flights, however, AYO was flying me to Melbourne shortly after the audition for a paid tour, so half of my airfares would be covered. The rest I paid for using the frequent flyer points I had accumulated during my travels the year before. Again, I didn't put everything into the audition. I didn't really want to be an orchestral musician but, as most of my travel costs were covered, and I could stay with Vic in Sydney, there wasn't much to lose by trying. I was scared to spend the extra money to really give it my best shot, even though I knew that not giving it my all reduced my chances of success. Even paying for train rides and a rehearsal with the accompanist in Sydney gave me uncomfortable butterflies.

Vic did her best to be a good host and make me comfortable, and I did my best to appear normal and easygoing. However, my routine was so rigid, and I was so scared of change, that I made things hard and awkward for both of us. There was no way I could skip my morning exercise, which was becoming more and more intense. Vic lived in a studio apartment, so I had to do it in front of her, while she was getting ready for work. I told her I enjoyed it, that it woke me up, but I could see she knew there was something else going on. She knew I was still struggling with AN and guessed that the exercise was related, but didn't know what to say.

There was also the ever-present problem of money and food. Vic bought most of her food out but was happy for me to cook at her place. She was at work for two of the three days I was there, so I could cook and eat by myself. She wanted to go out for dinner, but spending that much money on a meal, when I could cook myself for a fraction of the price, filled my head with quarrelling voices. We went out for dinner the night I arrived and I chose the cheapest option. When my meal arrived, I regretted it. It wasn't what I had hoped and I knew I would have preferred the other dish I had been considering, which cost two dollars more. While I was deciding what to order, I hadn't been able to convince myself to spend the extra two dollars. Now that I was eating however, I felt it would have been a better use of my money to spend the extra two dollars on a meal I would like, than slightly less for one I wasn't really enjoying.

(Food)

The following night, the night before my audition, the ED voice wouldn't allow me to buy dinner out for the second night in a row, so I made myself some stir-fried vegetables and brought them with me in a container to the shopping centre, where Vic bought dinner in the food court. I had planned to buy myself something small to have with my almost zero-calorie dinner, but everything was either too expensive or too scary.
"You know that's basically just vegetables? There's no protein or carbohydrate or anything to give you energy," Vic said as we ate our meals.
"Yeah," I replied self-consciously, wondering why she was pointing out the obvious.
"Oh," she said, realising, possibly for the first time, that it was deliberate.

I considered skipping my exercise on the morning of the audition but decided it was better to just do it, so I wouldn't feel guilty or have to worry about exercising later in the day. I was already exhausted when I arrived at the Sydney Opera House, where auditions would be held. The orchestra manager took me to a warm-up room and told me there was a chance I would be called back for a second audition that afternoon if the panel felt they needed to hear anyone again.

I had brought breakfast with me, but couldn't allow myself to eat it until 9 am. My audition was meant to be around 10 am, however the panel were running very late, so I wasn't called in until after 11 am. I was exhausted from taking the train in, power-walking for 20 minutes in the cold from the station, practising and warming up, and using up a lot of nervous energy. I didn't play well at all. It was probably the most nervous I have ever felt during a performance. I had felt comfortable playing with the accompanist during our rehearsal the previous day. She was wonderful and fitting my part with hers was almost effortless. I would have enjoyed our rehearsal had I not been feeling lightheaded. But that wasn't the case in the audition. I was playing so carefully and timidly that she had trouble following me at times. I came out of the audition feeling relieved it was over, but also downhearted and frustrated with myself. Maybe I would be called back in the afternoon and would have a chance to give a better performance, but I didn't hold much hope.

I had promised myself an ice cream after the audition but, as on countless previous occasions, I broke my promise because I was scared of the calories and the price. Instead, I walked around the jetties, looking longingly at the different ice cream flavours and trying to convince the ED voice to let me buy one. I met Vic and her work friends for lunch while waiting to hear if I would be asked back for a second audition. I didn't buy myself anything to eat for lunch though. Partly because I couldn't find anything that was cheap and low in calories, with lots of vegetables, and partly because I wanted to eat as close to when I played as possible, if I got a callback, so I would have energy. I tried to give Vic, who could see how pale and exhausted I was, a believable explanation as to why I didn't want to eat, but I think she knew I wasn't being truthful.

During lunch, the manager called to say the panel didn't feel the need to hear anyone again. I didn't know if this would help or hinder my chances of being accepted. However, I was relieved I wouldn't need to play again. I didn't think I would be able to muster the energy. I'm not exaggerating when I say I had never felt so exhausted. I went back to Vic's, a journey that seemed to take forever, as I felt weak, lightheaded and was absolutely famished. But I was also angry at myself for not playing better in the audition. I made myself do extra exercise as my lunch cooked — partly as punishment, partly to let out my anger and partly because, if I couldn't be good at violin, then I would need to be thinner.

I flew to Melbourne two days after the audition. Abi[24] picked me up from the airport and I stayed with her for a week. She was living with her grandmother, partly as a carer, and partly to have some independence from her parents. I had been apprehensive about living with her grandmother, worried that it would be awkward, but Abi assured me that she spent most of her days reading biblical books and preferred to be left alone. I was also relieved to find that I would have my own bedroom, so I wouldn't need to worry about anyone seeing me exercise.

I had a great week with Abi. Being with her was as effortless as it had been in China but, similar to my time in Manchester, I was always worried about my next meal. We cooked at home most of the time, so it wasn't too expensive, but I always worried I would still be hungry after a meal. If I was at home I could nibble on a piece of chocolate or eat more vegetables, but I felt awkward doing that with others around. Luckily, Abi knew about the AN but never commented on my disordered eating.

One day we decided to go busking, then spend our earnings on a nice lunch at the food court nearby. Unfortunately, it was a cold, rainy day, and we only made about nine dollars in total. We had planned to busk for at least two hours, but it was so cold my fingers were going numb and I was chilled to the bone. Abi was also keen to get inside, so we stopped after about an hour. I hadn't mentally prepared myself to spend my own money on lunch, only the busking money. Just thinking about parting with my money made my head spin and gave me nervous butterflies. The cheapest meal option at the Indian food kiosk Abi had recommended, was a large meal for one, and cost more than our meagre earnings. I suggested we share it and Abi happily agreed. The curry hardly made a dent in my empty belly and I was still tired and cold afterwards. I had even broken my rule and eaten some rice, but I was still consumed by a gnawing, all-consuming hunger. Guilt too, for eating the rice.

Cold was the theme of that week — Melbourne had an especially cold winter that year. Luckily the house was warm. Abi's grandmother had central heating because, in Abi's words, "She's old, you know.." One of the few times I was warm enough outside was when we walked up a big hill in some beautiful bushland nearby. The ED was excited about the exercise, but my legs were weak and visibly shaking for about half an hour afterwards. I warmed up though!

---

[24] My friend from the China tour.

Abi went to Queensland to visit her boyfriend about a week before my tour started, so I needed somewhere to stay until then. I asked Kate, one of my oldest friends, who now lived in Melbourne, if I could crash on her couch. She was in Europe with her boyfriend, Lachlan, but they were happy for me to stay in their room and their housemates didn't mind. In many ways, this was preferable to a couch, mostly because it meant I could exercise in private. Luckily their housemates were really lovely and welcoming and weren't home very much during the week. Even though they didn't seem to mind me being there, I was much less anxious when no one else was around — pretending to be normal and holding a conversation was stressful and exhausting and I still worried that they didn't really want me around.

I had been in contact with Jen, who used to teach violin at ANIM and she kindly agreed to Skype with me while I was at Kate's. She was very positive about the job at ANIM while admitting it was a big workload and sometimes the conditions were challenging. She said it didn't take long to get used to living in Kabul. Yes, there were lots of power blackouts, dodgy internet, bomb scares and gunfire, but it became the norm. She suggested I speak to Ed though, and gave me his number. I won't deny that I was quite excited to speak to a minor celebrity.

I spoke to Ed a few nights later and he painted a very different picture of the school. He spoke seriously about the dangers of Kabul and agreed with me about the high walls and security guard at ANIM — it was worrying that that level of security was needed.
"You have to remember the culture there is different too. Some of the older students are around twenty. A few of them made advances on me while I was there. At the time I identified as a lesbian and I was a decent bit older than them, so I had an excuse to say no, to turn them down. But you sound younger. You might find it harder…" Ed trailed off uncertainly.
"But don't they know… I thought the school would be more forward-thinking. Aren't there rules?" I struggled to articulate my question.
"Ummm well, it happened to me. Things may have changed," he said uncertainly. "Have you sorted your visa and accommodation?"
"No," I replied, overwhelmed at the thought of everything I needed to organise. "I haven't accepted the position yet. I wanted to find out more about the job and living in Kabul."
Ed seemed relieved. We talked a little more but I didn't want to take up his time.
"So I would say.. no.." were Ed's parting words of advice, before we said goodbye. I was shocked. I thought he would still encourage me to go, that the good outweighed the bad. He had spoken positively about his time there in the

article I read. But maybe things in Kabul had become more dangerous. Maybe he felt I would be more vulnerable there, as I was younger. Maybe he had been happy to put himself in possible danger but didn't want to encourage someone else to do the same. Whatever his reason, it tipped the scales back to somewhere near the middle — indecision about whether or not I should accept the job.

Coincidentally, the Melbourne Symphony Orchestra were holding auditions for casual violin work about five days after I moved to Kate and Lachlan's room. I had emailed them about auditioning before I left Perth and the audition date worked well with my plans, so I applied. I only had five days to learn the excerpts and brush up on my Mozart Concerto, so I got back into my exercise-practice-breakfast-practice routine — I had taken a break from practice while I was staying with Abi. I was finding everything increasingly exhausting, partly from the stress of being away from home and moving around, and also, of course, from a lack of nutrition. Once again, willpower got me through. After my audition, the panel said the notes were perfect, but my playing lacked musical expression and personality. How many times had I been told this now? The rejection didn't really bother me. I had a few days free now until the tour started. Time to start learning the tour music.

(Food rules, food and exercise)

Kate and Lachlan arrived home the day before I moved to the tour accommodation. They arrived in the middle of the night, so I slept on a mattress on the floor of a little alcove near the front door that night. As usual, I had been trying to think of ways to exercise without anyone seeing, as my alcove had no door. I decided to get up earlier than usual, so there was less likelihood of anyone else being up and about. My exercise was only interrupted once, as Kate and Lachlan had risen early to go to the supermarket. They were trying to be quiet, so I didn't have time to jump back into bed when I heard them. Instead, I pretended to be kneeling on the floor tidying my bedsheets, while trying not to pant audibly. Luckily they were in a rush to leave, as they were very hungry, so my exercise wasn't interrupted for very long. Because I hated it, I always wanted to get it over with as soon as possible, and interruptions only prolonged the chore. Luckily I had finished exercising by the time they got back from the shops.

Kate and Lachlan made themselves a big breakfast when they got home. The combination of odd meal times on their flights, and unappetising aeroplane food, meant it had been a while since they had eaten. As it was before 9 am, I couldn't eat yet. I would have felt odd cooking in front of them in their kitchen anyway, especially as my breakfast food was objectively odd. After they had eaten, Kate suggested a walk. Apparently, it was a weekend tradition. Jack, one of their housemates, came too. I figured we would be back in time for me to eat a late breakfast, which I would enjoy all the more, having really earned it after the walk. Unfortunately, their walk route turned out to be quite long. It was also very cold and windy, as we were walking by the water and it was winter. I kept hoping one of them would suggest we turn back. How far did they usually walk? When we came to a suburban cluster of shops, Jack suggested getting coffee to warm up. I got the impression this was part of their walk tradition too. I was grateful to get out of the elements but didn't want to pay for a coffee. I said, as casually as I could, that I didn't want anything, and sat with them, pretending to be enjoying myself, trying to warm up, trying to stop my head from spinning, trying to concentrate on the conversation and trying to muster the energy to ask Kate and Lachlan about their trip. I wanted to hear all about it, but I was too tired to hold a conversation. I just wanted to leave. Even if it meant going back outside to the cold and walking again, at least I would be heading towards home, warmth and food. Eventually, we left. By the time we got home, it was past midday. I decided to skip breakfast and call my first meal of the day lunch. The ED voice was excited about missing a whole meal and congratulated me.

Touring

Rehearsals for the tour began the next day, so I moved to the accommodation AYO had organised, in Carlton. I was, and still am, incredibly grateful that I had such a wonderful roommate. Mal is one of those rare people with whom I can just be me. Conversation flowed easily, without me needing to guess at what they meant, or worry about saying the "right thing". I was glad I could be almost at ease when I was in our apartment, since rehearsals were exhausting.

Overall, it was a lot of fun. It was a contrast of wonderful times making music and hanging out with great people; and struggling through rehearsals feeling hungry, exhausted, cold and lightheaded. The rehearsal venue was about a 20-minute walk from our accommodation, which I would usually have enjoyed. However, because of my malnourished state, it was a cold walk that used up precious energy before an exhausting rehearsal; and another cold walk on weak legs at the end of a tiring day, while hunger gnawed at my stomach, begging for food. Surprisingly, I finished the tour with net positive memories, probably because feeling hungry and tired was just a fact of life by then, and being on tour was more fun than my (also tiring but less exciting) work in Perth.

I was only back in Perth for a few weeks before I left for the next tour. I had two back-to-back from August to mid-September. The first tour was especially exciting because we were visiting a few states, finishing with performances at Ukaria, a beautiful concert venue in the Adelaide Hills. We were also performing with some well-known musicians.

(Food)

It was still very cold and I was feeling it acutely. I had decided I would buy more food out on this tour, instead of buying frozen vegetables and microwaving them in the apartment. If I ate out, the food would be more calorie-dense, but it wouldn't make me as anxious as if I made it myself, because I wouldn't know the exact amounts of the ingredients. I wasn't going to be ordering an oily curry with rice, but a vegetable curry with some protein, some oil I couldn't see in the sauce, and no rice, would be ok. However, when I got to Sydney and scoped out the restaurants near our accommodation, I couldn't convince myself to pay the prices. I returned to eating microwaved vegetables with small amounts of hummus or cottage cheese for all of my meals. I honestly enjoyed the taste of these meals and didn't mind eating the same thing on repeat, but they provided very little in the way of fuel. Every rehearsal was a test of my willpower to continue standing and concentrating, and the minutes dragged by. It was great music, and I wish I could have appreciated it, but I was chronically aware of the emptiness in my stomach and had to constantly force myself to focus on the notes. Just making myself concentrate required concentration.

One day I decided to buy my lunch from a food court near our rehearsal venue. There was an Indian kiosk with its menu and prices listed online, and I found a curry option that came without rice, at a price that didn't make me anxious. I was very excited about this treat and looked forward to it all day. When I got there, the menu was slightly different, and the option I had found online was displayed differently. What I had thought would be a main meal-sized serving of curry was actually very small — it was served in one of those round, 250mL takeaway containers. I scoured the menu over and over again for other main meal options that cost less than $10 and didn't come with rice. Any meals that were all curry — no rice — cost much more. I needed volume, without rice, with a single-digit price tag. A pipe dream. Eventually, the man who had been standing behind the bain marie waiting for me to order, who seemed to be the manager, went out the back. Another man, an employee, remained, waiting in case I, or someone else, ordered. I think he could see I was struggling with more than indecision. Maybe he saw how thin I was and guessed I either had AN, was very sick with another illness, or was poor. "What are you looking for? Can I help you?" He asked eventually.
"On your online menu there was a large curry without rice for seven dollars, but here it comes in a small container," I explained, doing my best to sound casual, not like an obsessive planner who checks menus of food court eateries online.
"I can do that for you," he said quietly, presumably so the manager wouldn't hear. He filled a large container with the curries I pointed to. When I paid, he gave me back far too much change, with a meaningful smile. I paid five dollars or less for that meal. I am eternally grateful for the kindness of this stranger.

For most of the tour, I shared apartments with two or three others. I found socialising in my down time stressful and exhausting, but I could pretend to be normal for a few weeks. Rooming with more than one other person made me feel less pressure to participate in conversations, where I might say the wrong thing. While there were some lovely people on tour, I would have preferred to have a room to myself, but I understood the tour's budget didn't stretch that far. In Hahndorf, South Australia, I shared a room with just one other girl, Alice. Unfortunately, it was a single room, with a small kitchenette and bathroom. As there was no gym at the accommodation, I had to exercise in front of Alice. I had known this before I left Perth and decided I would need to scope out my options during the tour, or when I saw the accommodation. Maybe there was a gym that wasn't mentioned on the accommodation website, or I could go to a nearby park.

(Exercise)

Alice had been on AYO tour the previous year, so we had chatted a bit, but I thought she was beautiful and fashionable, and therefore assumed she would think I was a fat, ugly loser. By the end of the tour, I was starting to realise that she is actually a wonderful person and not at all judgemental. Almost ten years after high school I still had to remind myself that not all pretty people are mean. Even so, when I read that we were rooming together, I was worried. I would have to pretend to be normal and try to be cool for a few days, with no one else in the apartment to act as a buffer. However, throughout the tour, I had some great conversations with Alice and trusted that she really is a genuinely kind and giving person, who always wants to do the right thing and avoid hurting anyone. I decided it would be best to just tell her about my morning exercise, and say I did it to strengthen my core so I would be less likely to get an injury from playing violin. Alice thought the exercise was a great idea, and congratulated me for being proactive. I felt self-conscious doing burpees, squats and all sorts of other exercises between my bed and the wall, while she lay in bed, but it was nowhere near as awkward as it could have been. I had considered going outside to exercise, but it was far too cold.

In the last week of the tour, I picked up some sort of bug — probably because my body was under so much stress — which sapped what little energy I had, and made me feel generally under the weather. When I'm getting over a cold, I find it hard to judge if I'm improving based on how I feel when I first wake up in the morning. I think most people feel tired and groggy when they've just been woken up by their alarm. So, each morning when my alarm went off, I told myself I felt weak and tired because I was still sleepy, not because I was still sick. Exercising was more of a struggle than usual, but I told myself I was probably fine — surely I was better by now — and continued. In truth, I was still sick and the exercise was fuelled by adrenaline and willpower, leaving me even more tired than usual for the rest of the day. Luckily I was only sick for a few days and had nearly recovered by the last two days, which is when our performances were.

We finished the tour at the end of August, so it was still very cold. Some of the rooms at Ukaria were heated, but others were freezing. I drank tea constantly whenever it was available, and would squeeze my hands around my mug, even after I had emptied it, trying to coax the blood back into my fingers. The outside chill crept into our accommodation unless the heater was on high, so I learnt to leave it on even when we were out. I couldn't bear to wait an hour or more for the heater to take the chill from the air, while my body silently screamed at me to find warmth. Again, I have great memories of that tour but, in truth, it was exhausting and I was usually hungry; so hungry I felt as if there was a hole where my stomach should have been. And cold.

(Food rules and food)

I was back in Perth for one night, before leaving again for the next tour. Because of the time difference and length of the flight, those of us from Perth usually had early morning flights. I got up around 5 am, did my exercise, then Kieran kindly drove me to the airport. Even though I had risen much earlier than usual, I couldn't allow myself to eat breakfast until 9 am or later. I considered the fact that, because of the time difference, eating at 7 am Perth time would be 9 am Sydney time, but the ED voice argued that I was being weak and greedy for not being able to wait until the correct time. I walked around the airport, salivating while window-shopping the overpriced, calorie-dense food being sold. I saw a friend who was also coming on the tour from a distance, eating a cooked breakfast with her mum, and wished I had the freedom to do the same.

My energy and hunger were much the same during this tour as on the previous two. I was still recovering from the busy schedule of the previous tour, though others said they felt same. The ED voice took this as proof that my exhaustion wasn't due to a lack of nutrition. It was normal to be tired; everyone else was. The venue for our final concert was absolutely freezing. It was a warehouse that had been transformed into a trendy music venue, so it probably had no insulation. I kept my jacket on for as long as I could before I had to take it off to perform. Everyone was cold, but my back and shoulder muscles were constantly tensed and my fingers were partially numb.

That night, I stayed up late chatting with friends in someone's room. Most of us had done two or three of the tours that year and were sad it was over, some of us not knowing when we would see each other again. One friend took a panorama photo of us all and when I looked at it later, I noticed how thin my legs were. What an achievement! The ED voice's congratulations gave me a warm glow in my tummy.

More Auditions and Work

Around this time, Brooke, my supervisor from the SO call centre job I had worked the previous year, messaged to ask if I would be interested in joining the team again that year. I didn't need to think about it; there was no way I wanted to do that again. However, a friend from the previous year suggested I apply for the position of supervisor, as Brooke had moved to a different role and SO were also looking for someone to replace her. Returning to the job made me feel like a failure. It was a reminder of all the auditions I hadn't passed, and that my dreams of being a successful, touring violinist, still hadn't become reality. Was I another one of those people who showed potential as a teenager, only to become an average musician as an adult? Part of me knew it was the AN holding me back, but most of me doubted that I would be good enough to perform professionally, even at a healthy weight. Feeling defeated, I applied for the supervisor position. I wouldn't have to call patrons, only input the sales data and support the callers. I figured it wouldn't be a terrible job, even though the hours were annoying and I wouldn't be working as a violinist. They offered me the job straight after my interview and asked if I could confirm my availability for the full three months. Then I told them about the job in Afghanistan.

I still hadn't made a decision and had applied for the SO job to keep my options open. The director of ANIM had emailed only a few days earlier to ask if I had come to a decision, as the students had been without a teacher for a while. Aside from the dangers of living in Kabul and the complications of organising a working visa, I also had other concerns: Mum and Dad would be terrified for me; finding a place to stay long-term, in a new country, where I didn't speak the language and knew no one, would be complicated, tiring and stressful; would I have the energy to teach full-time? How would I cope with the heat? And my two biggest concerns: would I be able to fit in 30 minutes of exercise before I went to work each day? And how would I find a time and place to exercise while in transit from Perth to Kabul, and in the first day or so? It was about 20 hours of travel and it was unlikely I would be able to exercise in the airport. Illogically, missing one or two exercise sessions was my biggest fear.

I called Dad to talk over the options after my interview with SO. They wanted me to start later that week, so I needed to decide quickly. Unsurprisingly, Mum and Dad were 100% against me going to Afghanistan, not only because of the dangers of living in Kabul, but also my health. I knew my weight was dangerously low and felt the effects during most of my waking hours — exhaustion, brain fog, cold, hunger, weak muscles — but I didn't know what to do. I was terrified to gain weight or eat even a little more, but I also felt this job was my last chance. What else could I do that was meaningful? If I wasn't performing, at least I would be teaching music, instead of working in an office. I felt even more tired and overwhelmed than usual that day, maybe because I had just moved to a friend's house to dog and cat sit for a few weeks. The fear of what would happen if I missed a day of exercise dominated my thoughts. Moving countries felt like a huge, tiring ordeal — to be fair, it is — while working at SO would be much easier. The hourly rate was about the same too. And if I stayed in Perth I could audition for the tutti violin position SO had recently advertised. That was my decision. I was sitting on my friend's front steps in the sun, talking to Dad on the phone. I just sighed and gave in. I was so tired; I didn't have the energy to move to Kabul. I felt guilty for choosing what I perceived to be the easy option, but a big part of me knew that it was for the best. Lucy and Kieran were relieved when I told them I had decided to stay. I hadn't realised they had been so worried.

It didn't take long for me to settle into the job at SO. It was more enjoyable than calling. I got on well with most of the people in the calling team and rarely had to talk to patrons. If sales were slow I could just read a book or scroll through Facebook at my desk. I read most of Danger Music, by Ed Le Brocq, while I was at work. It was also there that I googled Lindsey Stirling, a popular violinist who became famous after auditioning for America's Got Talent, and learnt that she used to have an eating disorder. I wondered if, as a musician, she may have had a similar experience to me, or would have advice on how to use music as an incentive to recover. I found an email address for her manager and emailed her, briefly outlining my experiences with AN, asking for advice and requesting that she pass my message on to Lindsey. The manager, who is also Lindsey's sister, sent a long reply a few days later, which I read at work. I'm grateful for the time she took to send such a thoughtful email, but it wasn't at all helpful. She said Lindsey's Mormon faith had helped her recover, and suggested I think about what I wanted out of life, how the eating disorder was affecting me etc. — the questions people who have never had an ED ask, thinking they will be groundbreaking and immediately cure me, but are just annoying and patronising, because I have asked myself the same things hundreds of times. No help there.

Practice, teaching, work and gigs kept me busy for the rest of the year. My morning practice routine remained the same, after which I had lunch, before catching the bus and train to work. I didn't get home until about 9 pm, so I usually read, caught up on admin or chatted to Lucy and Kieran until the ED voice allowed me to go to bed, unless I was housesitting. I was almost always exhausted and stressed but felt I should be able to keep going because everyone else was. Though I felt lazy sitting down for most of my shifts at work, I was also glad. I became aware of just how weak my legs were every time I had to stand up to speak to the team or look at someone's computer. I settled back into the same dinner and cup of tea routine as I had the previous year but, again, sometimes dinner had to be postponed if lots of sales were coming in. Even though I was hungry and lightheaded, I felt I should prioritise work, because I knew my manager would. "I'm hungry" sounds like a weak excuse to others, unless they realise that you are literally starving.

One day, I was particularly hungry when I left for work. I hoped dinner would fill me up, though that was still four hours away, according to my eating timetable. Unfortunately, dinner did nothing to curb my hunger, and my head continued spinning throughout the evening. After work, it took about an hour to get back to where I was housesitting using public transport. Throughout the journey, while I struggled to concentrate on reading, I willed the train, then the bus, to go faster. I was desperate for food and worried I would faint. When I got home, I finally had access to food, but I still couldn't allow myself to eat "too much." I ate steamed vegetables with tiny amounts of tahini and peanut paste, but my stomach still felt like a huge gaping hole. My hunger felt infinite that night. I went to bed still hungry and hoped things would be back to normal the next morning. I experienced this insatiable hunger every so often, when nothing I ate satisfied me, even briefly. It may have helped if I had eaten something remotely filling, such as a decent serving of complex carbohydrates or protein. But I didn't want to have to endure the guilt, self-loathing and hateful criticism from the ED voice that I knew would follow. So I ate extra vegetables and hoped my next meal would curb the gnawing, distracting hunger. Eventually, it would lessen, to be replaced by the worry that I had unknowingly eaten "too much."

About a month after I started supervising the calling team, I had my audition for the tutti violin position in SO. I wanted to eat breakfast just before my audition, so I would hopefully feel full, and wouldn't have wasted the precious little energy in my meal on unimportant activities, such as sitting on the train or walking to the audition venue — I could do those things on an empty stomach, with weak legs and a spinning head if necessary. As usual, my nerves and stress sapped all my energy, so I was running on empty before I had even started warming up. I played as little as possible, to conserve my energy, while still making sure I practised all the difficult sections. Having a quick rehearsal and making conversation with the pianist just before the audition, used even more energy; my tank was almost on empty.

By the time I went in to play, I was lightheaded and just wanted it to be over. The lack of energy only increased my nerves, because I knew I was more likely to make mistakes if I couldn't concentrate. I had promised myself that, if I didn't make it through to the second round — in which case I would need to stay there to do another audition in the afternoon — I would go to an Indian buffet restaurant I loved. I felt ok eating there, as long as I didn't eat any rice; only curry and a tiny amount of dahl. I knew there was oil in the curry, but I could pretend there wasn't too much because I couldn't see it and didn't know the recipe. I forced myself to concentrate on my playing as much as I could, but willpower can only achieve so much. My body had so little left to give. After I played, I waited with the other hopeful violinists, for one of the orchestra managers to come out and announce who had made it through to the next round. Not me. Again, I was mostly relieved.

A few days later, Dorothy, a previous violin teacher, messaged to ask how I had gone in the audition.

Me: Not great. I was too nervous to put any musical expression into my playing. I've applied to do a recorded audition for a BBC orchestra in London later this year, but I don't know how much longer I can keep auditioning and getting knocked back. It's emotionally exhausting.

Dorothy: I have an idea that could help you be successful in future auditions. Better to talk about it in person though. When are you free to come visit?

I was intrigued by the mystery and the promise of a job performing, so we organised a time to catch up a few days later.

A few days later, Dorothy and I sat outside drinking herbal tea while John, her husband, did something with the pool filter. I think he was deliberately keeping busy, staying out of the conversation. We talked a bit about the audition, who had been awarded the job, my work in the sales centre, and their recent holiday, before Dorothy brought up the reason I had come.
"I think I know what's stopping you from winning auditions," she said.
I had butterflies from the excitement of finally discovering Dorothy's secret.
"What's that?" I asked.

"I think it's your anorexia," she replied. "If you're not eating enough you won't have the energy to concentrate on all the notes you have to play. I think that's also why you struggle to make a bigger sound. You're too tired."
I had hoped Dorothy was going to reveal a magical secret that afternoon, or at least a musical one. I felt hopeless. And embarrassed. Talking about my eating disorder was always awkward.
"I think you're right. I've thought that for a long time. Mum says it too. It's so hard to concentrate…" I didn't know how to put my conflicting and confusing thoughts and emotions into words.
"Then why don't you eat more?"
I tried to explain that I had tried to use violin as an incentive to eat more, but that it wasn't enough. I didn't want to hate myself at a higher weight, and kept telling myself I should be able to succeed in music, even in a malnourished body; I just needed to work harder. Listening to me speak, I think Dorothy began to understand the warped thinking caused by AN. She asked some more questions and I tried to explain, but I still felt embarrassed. I didn't want to brush her off though, or make her think I didn't trust her. I could see how much she cared; she was blinking back tears.

"How about we make a deal," Dorothy suggested. "I'll teach you for free and help you prepare for your audition. But you have to take steps towards recovery."
I was blown away by her kindness, but also worried about my side of the deal. "What steps?" I asked.
"We can work that out later. You have a think about that."
I was stuck on the free lessons too. It was far too generous, but Dorothy insisted she wanted to. I wanted to have lessons again too. In the end, I agreed, though I still felt guilty for accepting free lessons. I should be paying her. I decided I would bring her a gift each lesson; homemade biscuits or something. I left their house soon afterwards, as I had to teach my own students.

Until that conversation, I had almost convinced myself that I was mostly happy in this half-life; that I would never recover, but could be semi-recovered and get the best of both worlds — be thin, but just well enough to be able to do what I needed to get by. In hindsight, it was naive of me to even consider myself to be semi-recovered. My eating was the worst it had ever been and my weight was lower than when I was admitted to Heathgrove. But the conversation with Dorothy made me consider recovery again; made me wonder if it was possible and worth it. Maybe I was actually good enough at violin to have a job performing; Dorothy thought I was. Teaching my own students that afternoon was more of a struggle than usual. Standing and concentrating for that long was exhausting at the best of times. However, that day I was also trying to hold myself together emotionally and my head was whirling with thoughts. I had planned to go to a friend's graduation recital after teaching, but I messaged her to apologise. I needed to go home, be by myself, and think. Luckily, she was very understanding.

Dorothy suggested I bring the music for the BBC orchestra audition to my lesson the following week. I started to hope I might actually get the job. Near the beginning of our first lesson, Dorothy started helping me "get your sound back," as she put it. It was exhausting. She wanted me to use more bow all the time and demanded much more musical expression than I was used to giving. She always set aside two hours to teach me, before her first student arrived. It was incredibly generous, but also left me completely wiped out.

After my lessons with Dorothy, I taught for about two hours at a friend's home studio, during which I exercised all of my willpower to remain vertical. For someone as naturally impatient as me, refraining from snapping is difficult at the best of times. I didn't realise quite how much mental energy patience requires until I started teaching small children with my malnourished body and brain.

After the second or third lesson, Dorothy asked what steps I had taken towards recovery. I hadn't had the mental space to make any concrete plans yet, as much as I genuinely wanted to.
"I haven't worked that out yet…" I tried to explain, self-consciously. I knew it sounded weak.
Dorothy's face immediately became serious. "If you don't hold up your end, the deal's off."
"I know, I just don't know what I should be doing…" I scrambled to explain.
"I want you to get yourself a book and, each day, write down what you're going to eat and how much weight you'll put on each week. Maybe a kilo? Then you can show me when you come here."
It was too much. Too fast. I couldn't put on weight yet. Maybe eat a tiny bit more, but I wasn't ready to actually gain weight yet.
"I-I-I can't, sorry. That's too much. I can't do that. We can stop lessons.." I think she saw that I was genuinely terrified. I was trying not to cry.
Her face softened, and so did her tone of voice. "Ok, how about you start by writing your practice goals and reasons to recover every day. Writing it down might help."
I started the notebook the next day. I listed my practice goals, reasons to recover and anything I did that day that would help me work towards

recovery, such as meditation. I also chose a recovery quote that felt relevant, to copy into the book.

Around this time, I went to my friends' housewarming party. I had a terrible tummy ache for most of the night because I had restricted food more than usual during the day, in anticipation of a higher-calorie dinner at the party. Morgana, one of the hosts, kindly let me lie down on their[25] bedroom floor whenever I needed, to ease the pain. They're a very understanding person, but also knew about my AN and gut problems. That night, during the windows of time between lying on Morgana's floor, I had two life-changing conversations.

One was with Morgana. We had been talking on and off for a few months about them getting an Autism diagnosis. They had been researching it for a while and speaking to different psychologists. One had told them they couldn't have it because they were clever and able to succeed at university, so Morgana stopped seeing her. I didn't know much about Autism, so I didn't know if the psychologist was correct. Morgana had decided to fly to Brisbane to be assessed by Tony Attwood. I had sometimes wondered if I was Autistic, ever since my conversation with Callum in Hobart. I'm a perfectionist, have OCD tendencies, feel awkward socially and sometimes friends had joked that I might be Autistic. When I mentioned this to Morgana, they were interested and encouraging.
"But I can't be, because I feel empathy, a lot of empathy," I said.
"Oh, that empathy thing is a myth," Morgana started to explain, but they were called away to help in the kitchen before they could finish. I wondered what they meant, but was soon distracted by my pain and other friends at the party.

The other conversation was with Gilbert.
"How's it going?" He asked, with a tipsy slur.
"Oh I'm exhausted," I replied. "How've you been?"
"Why are you tired?" He asked.
"I haven't had a proper sleep in months. I keep waking up during the night."
"Why?" he asked.
"I wake up absolutely busting. I must have a tiny bladder," I joked.
"You've gotta go to the dunny before you go to bed. Don't you know that?"
"Duh, I go just before I go to bed. And I don't drink anything after 9 o'clock, but I still need to go during the night. And it's not just once. It's a few times."
"That's not normal.," he said seriously. "That means there's something wrong with your kidneys. Have you been to the doctor? You should be able to sleep through the night without needing to go to the toilet…"

---

[25] Just FYI, yes I am deliberately using they/them pronouns for Morgana.

Gilbert continued his lecture, telling me, with no subtly, that I was making myself very sick by starving myself, and that it was very serious. Gilbert was almost a qualified nurse at this point, so he knew what he was talking about. I was grateful that he cared enough to tell me the truth, even at the risk of angering me. I wasn't angry though, not at all.

"I don't know what to do," I said, feeling helpless. "I don't know how to convince myself to eat more. I'll feel so guilty and I'll hate myself. I keep telling myself that I can work hard at other things, not just being thin. Like music, but it's not enough... I feel I should be able to be good at music *and* be thin, if I just work harder..."

"It's not that though. Even without music or being clever, or any of that. You're worthy as a person, even if you couldn't play violin. You're a good person."

That had never occurred to me.[26]

---

[26] Dad would like me to point out that a lot of people had told me I was a good person, worthy of love, but it had never hit home as it did that night.

Siobhan

Dad and I had sat down to discuss my physical and mental health a few times since I got back from Hobart. Each time, I lied about the strength of the ED voice and my food intake. However, I spoke truthfully when I said I wanted to recover; I just didn't know how. In every recovery story I read, people had a strong incentive to recover — going to university, having the energy to enjoy a hobby, or getting their life back. But I had been to university, I was still playing violin a lot — I hadn't won a job yet, but the ED voice told me I just needed to work harder — and I saw my friends regularly — though I often found it stressful and exhausting.

Others also spoke about how hard it was for them to make themselves eat — every bite was a challenge — so they felt proud when they ate a fear food. I loved eating though, I just hated myself afterwards. I would enjoy eating a fear food, so there would be nothing to feel proud of, just guilt during and afterwards. And the ED voice told me that, as others had been sick for longer than me, I didn't deserve to recover yet. I needed to prove I could starve myself for longer.

Dad suggested I talk to a lived experience support worker, Siobhan, who he and Mum had met through their work with an eating disorders charity. Dad had already spoken to her and she had agreed to meet me and talk about working together towards my recovery. Siobhan had had AN and Bulimia for a long time but had recovered in the last few years. Dad had asked me twice before if I would consider working with Siobhan, but I worried that she would force me to eat more. Mum had been doing something in the kitchen while Dad and I talked — I assumed this was deliberate; that she knew she would get emotional and the talk may turn into an argument if she was involved — but at this point, she stepped in to say that Siobhan was one of the kindest, and most caring people she had ever met. Maybe she wouldn't be a force-feeder. Maybe she would listen and understand. I agreed to at least consider meeting her.

I didn't think Siobhan would be able to help me — no one had so far — but a few days later, I decided I might as well call her. I had had a productive morning, ticking things off my to-do list, and I was on a roll, so I called while I was waiting for the train to go to work. I was anxious about speaking to someone I hadn't met before, but she made me feel more at ease than most people. We organised to meet about a week later, just before I started work for the day. She suggested meeting at the art gallery because she was doing some work nearby and it wasn't too far from the SO office. I was comfortable with that because it meant I wouldn't need to spend money buying food or drink at a cafe. Unfortunately, when we met, she suggested we go into the cafe attached to the gallery. I agreed because I couldn't think of an excuse not to. I managed to avoid buying a drink though, saying I didn't feel like anything. We had a good talk and Siobhan was very understanding. I felt fat and ugly beside her and assumed she would think I was too. She was so elegant and beautiful. I was awkward and sweaty. I came away feeling hopeful about recovery though, as I had after speaking to Dorothy.

I had watched To The Bone earlier that year and, though I know a lot of people think it glamourises eating disorders, I think they did a great job. The treatment centre Ellen goes to is unrealistic, as is the existence of a psychiatrist who shows compassion, but I was surprised and impressed that the movie showed the lesser-known ramifications of eating disorders. Things most people wouldn't think about, such as memorising the number of calories in everything you eat, losing libido, making yourself cold to burn extra calories, the morbid jokes amongst patients, the strong friendships formed in treatment centres and the creative hiding places for uneaten food.

In an article I read about the movie, I learnt that Lily Collins and Marti Noxon had both had AN, and had drawn on their experiences when making the movie. Later, I found out that Lily had published a book, in which she spoke about her eating disorder. I tried to find a copy online, or at the library, with no success, so I posted a photo of the book cover on Facebook, asking if anyone knew where I could get a copy for free — I couldn't bring myself to part with the money to buy the book, even if it might help me recover. A high school friend, with whom I hadn't spoken since we left school, sent me a private message, saying he worked for the company that published her book and might be able to get his hands on a copy for free if there was one lying around. A few weeks later he sent me a photo of his hand holding the book and asked for my address so he could post it. I marvelled at his kindness, for reaching out after so many years without contact and for taking the time to find a copy and post it. I asked him how much postage would be — he was in London so it wouldn't be cheap — offering to transfer it to him. Even paying for postage made me anxious but I didn't want to take advantage of his kindness. Luckily he said not to worry about it, refusing to give me his bank details. I was relieved. A week or two later the book arrived.

The book was interesting but mostly disappointing. Lily talked about her eating disorder, but only briefly. Her description of her laxative abuse and secrecy made me think I should be doing "better," and she didn't share many details about how she recovered, or what made her choose recovery. What she did say was nothing I hadn't heard before. Throughout the book were relevant quotes in large font, occupying a whole page. Most were the sort of things you see shared on Instagram, with the hashtag #blessed, intended to inspire and attempting to be profound. The quote at the end of the chapter about her eating disorder was the same, but I remembered it because I had tried to find meaning in it that would help me. A day or so later, as I was driving down the ramp onto the Kwinana freeway, on my way to meet Siobhan, I understood that quote on a deeper level.

> There is a greater
> happiness to be attained:
> The happiness of enjoying
> myself to the fullest
> during the one life I have
> and accepting myself for
> who I am.

I realised just how much it applied to me. She was saying that there is an even greater happiness than the pure joy and pride I felt when I had restricted or exercised more than usual, when the number on the scale went down, or I noticed one of my bones sticking out more than it had before. That joy filled me with light and happy butterflies, but it was ultimately empty and short-lived. The greater happiness Lily spoke of could be found by living my life to the fullest, sharing real moments with loved ones, and doing the things I couldn't do because I was too tired, or too scared. And the peace I would find if I could truly accept myself as I was, accept my body at its unsuppressed weight, was deeper, more real and eternal, unlike the surface-level happiness I felt when I saw my bony, malnourished body. How wonderful would it be, to accept myself as I was? It tied in with what Gilbert had said to me at the party too, that I was worthy as I was, even without any musical or weight-loss achievements. It was a huge breakthrough. I talked to Siobhan about it and we laughed at the mundane location of my epiphany. But I didn't know how to constructively apply this new thinking to my life and eating. I knew I would still feel guilty if I ate more.

Near the end of my three months at SO, as Christmas loomed, I accepted some carolling gigs in the city. I had done these in the past, for various shopping centres and the city of Perth, so it was nothing new. The booking agency had requested a duo, so I asked my friend Rachel if she wanted to sing. We were booked for a few three-hour shifts, during which we would "rove" the area, singing in different locations around Carillon Arcade. It's usually a long three hours, but it's worth it for the money. I knew it would be tiring — in previous years we were usually a bit tired by the end, but also happy to be finished for the day — but this year I struggled from the very first carol to the last. Standing up was a constant exercise of willpower and breathing deeply to sing made my almost constant lightheadedness even worse. I checked the clock after each song, desperate for a break. My energy often comes in waves during long gigs, but that year I was at low tide for the full three hours. I hoped I would have more energy for the next gig, but it was no better. Luckily the weather was mild, however, because my starving body prioritised keeping my heart beating over regulating my body temperature, I had goosebumps. I didn't know why I was feeling so cold; Rachel was ok.

Finally, the SO contract finished, about ten days before Christmas. I was relieved and excited. I still needed to record part of my audition but, other than that, I had much more free time to relax and do fun things. Maybe I could start eating more too, little by little, since I would have more time and headspace. I would be housesitting for the next few months, in great locations, so I could be myself without worrying about annoying Lucy and Kieran. And I would allow myself to start spending more money. I had decided there was enough money in my savings account to serve as a buffer, allowing me to feel safer spending a bigger percentage of my income.

Siobhan and I agreed to meet at the University of Western Australia, (UWA), one afternoon. I had a rehearsal there in the evening and she had been in Subiaco that afternoon, so it suited us both. I had done some recording earlier that afternoon for a friend, so I was exhausted, but I hoped I would have more energy after dinner. I felt a bit awkward that we were meeting on a bench outside, instead of in a cafe. Siobhan knew that spending money made me anxious, so she was mindful to suggest meeting places that wouldn't require me to buy a drink or food. She had, however, suggested that we work towards spending small amounts of money, in addition to food challenges. Even though she understood my anxiety, I worried that she was uncomfortable outside, or wished I would get over my fear so she could have a coffee. Because of this, I apologised for the setting and said we could go to the common room and "make shitty instant coffee" if she wanted.
"It's ok, I'm not that desperate," she laughed.

"So I've been talking to various eating disorder specialists about your situation and health," she began. "Unfortunately, they've all told me the same thing. It's not safe for me to work with you until you have a medical assessment, so we know where your body's at."
"But I'm ok. I haven't had any heart problems like other people," I replied anxiously.

"And you're very lucky. But I worry that could happen any day now. And if we get an assessment, we'll know. Maybe you'll be ok. But Hannah, you're very underweight." Siobhan sounded genuinely worried.

"But I feel ok. I can still do the things I need to do." My voice, devoid of strength, betrayed me.

Siobhan raised her eyebrows and smiled ironically.

"What would they do in the assessment?" I asked.

"They'll do some blood tests, an EEG, a psychiatrist will talk to you, and they'll weigh you." Siobhan saw me stiffen. "I know, I'm sorry, but if you're healthy enough, we can start working together. We just have to check."

"So... should I go to my doctor?" I asked.

"Well, it's best to go to a hospital, because they'll have all the equipment and they'll be able to get your blood analysed faster."

My stomach clenched. The last thing I wanted to do was go to hospital. What if they made me stay? I knew my BMI was lower than what it had been when I went to Heathgrove, which meant that legally they could forcibly admit me. However, I also knew laws had changed since I was in Heathgrove; now the requirements for forced admission weren't based solely on BMI, but the medical assessment too. If my blood results were in the healthy range then maybe they couldn't make me stay. But what if they weren't?

I tried to suggest other options. "Can we do the assessment after Christmas?" It was December 21.

"I don't think we can afford to wait," Siobhan said. "Your body might give out before Christmas."

Hearing that scared me. I started to cry. I felt hopeless. And I was so, so tired. And I still had to get through rehearsal that night.

"What if my results aren't ok? I asked.

"They'll keep you in hospital until they can get you stable. Then we can start doing our work together."

"How long will I have to stay?" I wasn't worried about my health; rather, how long I would be in hospital, where I knew I wouldn't be allowed to exercise. I might be able to go one day without exercising. I could make up for it the next day...

"Well, that depends how long you body takes to recover..." Siobhan never gave me a straight answer on that one, though I asked her at least five times that evening. Surely no more than a few days, I thought.

While I was sobbing, Avril arrived for the rehearsal and, recognising the back of my head, walked towards us. I tried to wipe my tears away when I saw her, but I knew my eyes would still be red. I introduced her and Siobhan and asked how her day had been, attempting to make a normal conversation. Avril could

tell she had interrupted something delicate and wasn't sure what to do, but Siobhan did.
"I think I might take you up on that shitty coffee," she said. "Shall we go make one?"
"I need to look over this music before rehearsal," Avril said. "Enjoy your coffee."
"I don't actually want a coffee, I just thought you needed to be alone. I think Avril realised too," Siobhan said as we walked away. I had believed her coffee excuse.

We continued our conversation, about 50 metres away, around the corner. I kept asking why we couldn't wait until after Christmas. I had been looking forward to it, and enjoying a well-earned break over the summer. I had planned to start increasing my food anyway. But Siobhan seemed genuinely worried that my health might take a dive before Christmas. We just didn't know, with my weight so low.
"What do you have on for the next few days?" She asked.
"I've got to clean up the place I'm housesitting tomorrow, then move to the next house," I began.
"Oh that sounds exhausting Hannah!"
"Yeah," I sighed, "but the next house is in a really handy area. It'll be ok once I've moved. I move between houses all the time."
"Hmm I guess we could wait and go to the hospital tomorrow, once you've moved house. But we shouldn't leave it any later."
It's silly that my main worry about Siobhan's suggestion was that I would need to drive there again from where I was housesitting, which would use petrol, which cost money. There were a few hospitals very close to UWA, so it would be cheaper, petrol-wise, to go that evening.

Eventually, I agreed to go to hospital, though my reasoning wasn't completely logical. I was exhausted and the rehearsal would be starting soon. Siobhan and I had talked for longer than either of us expected, so I wouldn't have time to eat dinner beforehand. Even if I did eat, I knew it would still be a struggle to get through the rehearsal. I didn't want to use petrol driving to the hospital the next day and possibly paying for parking. Maybe, if I had dinner before they examined me, my results would look healthy enough not to need admission, even though my BMI was low. Worst case, if they did make me stay, it wouldn't be for too long. I should be out by Christmas and I could start gradually increasing my meals with Siobhan's help. In my fragile state, feeling hopeless about everything, I wondered if Siobhan and Dorothy were right, and I could recover. I worried that Siobhan was right about my life being in danger. I didn't want to have a heart attack when I had just started to believe that recovery was possible. Siobhan said there had been a lot of positive changes made to inpatient ED treatment in the last few years — most of them based on her advice — so maybe it would be better than when I was in Heathgrove seven and a half years earlier.

Most importantly, following my Lily Collins epiphany, I decided I had finally been sick long enough to "deserve" recovery. There had always been someone who had been sick longer than me, and the ED voice told me that, if they could keep it up for that long, then I should be able to as well. But I had realised that I was capable of struggling through every day and staying sick as long as others had. I had the willpower to be anorexic until I died. I wouldn't enjoy it, but I would do it. Not because I was too scared to recover. Not because I wasn't strong enough or brave enough. But because I just wouldn't allow myself; I would be constantly proving to myself that I had the strength to deny myself vital sustenance. When I realised this, it allowed me to allow myself to recover, because I didn't need to prove myself anymore. And that was one of the most powerful realisations I have had. I tried to explain it to Dad a few days later but, with his healthy brain that has never thought much about his weight, he struggled to wrap his head around my warped "logic." It took a lot of clarifying questions from him, and examples from me, for him to begin to understand.

I had never found a good enough reason to recover, because the ED voice always told me that I should be able to do <insert reason here> in my malnourished state. I should be able to improve my violin playing, even though concentration was a constant struggle, not to mention the physical aspect of standing and moving my arms. I should be able to do fun things with friends, even though it was exhausting and, therefore, not very enjoyable. If I was a more interesting/funny/attractive person I would have a loving boyfriend. If I worked hard enough to act normal, cool and clever and was stricter with my food and exercise, someone would love me. Others had used their love of sport, or study and work aspirations, as their incentive to recover, but the ED voice told me I should be able to do all of those things while I was sick.

This new way of thinking came at the problem from a different angle. I didn't need a specific reason or incentive to recover, because even the ED voice agreed that I deserved to recover — it knew as well as anyone that I could stay anorexic for the rest of my life, however long that may be. Knowing that, I could choose to recover. The example I gave Dad was someone choosing their subjects for years 11 and 12. A clever person would be encouraged to take the top two maths, physics, chemistry, English Literature and Economics.

However, if that person wanted to study something with a lower aggregate requirement, or maybe didn't want to go to university at all, they could choose easier subjects, and save themselves the extra work. Nevertheless, they would know that they could have passed the difficult subjects if they had chosen them. That's what I could do. I knew I could continue my disordered behaviours for as long as other patients I had met, but I was choosing not to. And the ED voice accepted that argument. In its eyes, I had proven myself. Checkmate.

I agreed to go to hospital, still unsure if I would be forced to stay the night. Before we left the university, Siobhan suggested we tell Avril what we were doing, so she could tell Adam, Mum and Dad. Rehearsal had started, which I felt awkward about missing, so Siobhan knocked on the door and asked to speak to Avril. I started bawling again when I saw her, so Siobhan explained what we were doing. I was crying too hard to speak. Avril gave me a big hug and started crying herself. She was wonderful. I hadn't realised until then how much she actually cared about me. In my distress I didn't notice, but Siobhan told me later that Avril looked relieved when she heard we were going to hospital. She knew I had AN, but didn't know what to do to help. Avril said she would call Adam and take care of everything. Even while standing there sobbing, feeling helpless and hopeless, I marvelled at how Avril was taking everything in her stride. She wasn't acting as the girlfriend anymore. She was part of the family and taking on family responsibilities — which she really shouldn't have had to do. I already loved and respected Avril a lot, but she rose to a whole new level in my eyes that evening.

The hospital was literally up the road from the university, so Siobhan drove us there. We joked about how, as it was almost Christmas, we may need to wait for a long time in the Emergency Department, while people with alcohol poisoning were given priority. Luckily, it was a relatively short wait. Long story short, because the results of my medical examination were so worrying, I had to stay. A psychiatrist came to talk to me after the results of my blood, heart rate and blood pressure had been analysed.
"Can I please go home tonight?" I pleaded. "I'm going to start eating more. I got a fright seeing how sick my body is and it's been a good kick up the bum."
"I'm sorry, I can't let you go home while your body is this sick," she replied, with genuine sympathy.
"I've already decided, I'm going to make appointments to see a dietician and my GP tomorrow and I'll start increasing my food. Please, I know I can do this. And Siobhan is going to help." I wasn't lying; I had every intention of doing these things.

"Look, it's your choice. We can admit you as a voluntary patient, or, if you don't agree to that, we will admit under the mental health act."
I laughed. "So I don't actually have a choice." It wasn't a question.
"Well you do, it will just change how we check you in," she replied, missing the point.
"But either way I have to stay here." I pushed my point.
"Yes, but it's your choice if you're voluntary or involuntary, so do you want to have a think about it?"
"Well it's not a choice then, is it?" Was I missing something?
"I'll leave you to talk it over," the psychiatrist said.
I turned to Siobhan. "Is she trying to fool me?"
"I don't know," she said, shaking her head, "but you don't want to be formed. If you are, you won't have any rights."
All of the doctors and nurses kept up this charade of my admission being voluntary for the entirety of my stay. I still haven't worked out why.

When I knew that I would be staying in hospital, I called Mum and Dad. It was about 11 pm by this stage and Siobhan was still with me. I told them I was ok, physically and emotionally, which I was; even though I didn't want to stay there, I felt positive about recovery and assumed I would be out in a day or two.

Siobhan left around midnight, and a nurse was assigned to guard me in case I tried to escape. She even accompanied me to the toilet and waited outside the door. I slept in the Emergency Department ward that night because there wasn't a room available on the Medical ward. During the night I wondered if I would be able to find a way to do some sit-ups and squats the next morning. Would the nurse leave me alone at all? Maybe I could do some when I went to the toilet. But she would wonder if there was something wrong if I was in there for more than a few minutes.

Governor

The hospital struggled to feed me breakfast the next morning. Not because I refused to eat, but because of my food intolerances. Luckily they took me at my word, but all they could think to give me was an apple and an orange. Amused, I wondered if they knew why I was in hospital, but the ED voice advised me to keep quiet. I hadn't done my morning exercise and I didn't know how much they would make me eat once I was taken to the Medical ward, so I should restrict while I could. I stayed in the Emergency ward until late morning, when a room became available. There, I was allowed to take a shower, though I had to sit on a plastic chair to minimise my physical exertion — very awkward and uncomfortable I can tell you! — and the nurse watched me in case I fainted or attempted to exercise.

For the rest of the day various doctors, a dietician, a psychiatrist and some administrative people came to talk to me. Some were conducting follow-up assessments, while others were telling me what to expect during my stay. I asked how long I would be there but, again, no one gave me a straight answer. A few people made a point of telling me I was a consenting patient, to which I replied: "But I'm not really, am I?"
"Oh yes, you could have refused admission."
"And you would have formed me."
"Yes, so it's good you agreed to stay."
"Well I didn't have much choice, did I?"
"Well, you could have refused."
And around it went. The only positive to being a "consenting" patient was that they couldn't tube[27] me straight away.

Mum, Dad, Adam and Siobhan visited that day too. Mum and Dad also went to the house I had been looking after, to feed the dog and pack up my things. Luckily, being very organised, I was able to give them exact directions to all of my belongings in the house. I had also done most of the cleaning in preparation for moving, so there wasn't much left to do.

Unfortunately, I wouldn't be able to look after the next house I had lined up, or not straight away anyway. I called Kieran, who was friends with the owners of the house. After explaining that I had been admitted to hospital, I apologised profusely.
"Are you ok?" he asked, obviously concerned.

---

[27] A Nasogastric (NG) tube, though which patients can be fed meal-replacement drinks. This can be done forcibly if a patient refuses food.

"Yeah I just have to stay because I failed the medical assessment. I'm feeling ok though. I'm just so sorry about the house. It's such late notice."
"It's ok, I'll sort it out," he replied calmly. "Are you sure you're ok?"
"Yeah, I'm just worried about finding someone to look after the house. I'll start asking other friends."
"Don't worry about it, I'll sort it out," he repeated. "Do you feel up to having visitors or would you prefer to rest for now?"
I was so grateful to have such wonderful and supportive friends and family.

Heidi and Ellen had asked me to housesit for them again early the next year, while they went on their annual trip to Germany. I loved staying in their home with their sweet, crazy dogs and sassy chickens. After I had been in hospital for a few days, Mum said Heidi had called her the night before. I had housesat for them a week or two earlier, while they went on a quick trip down south for the weekend. Heidi told Mum they had been shocked and worried at how frail I looked, and didn't want me living alone in their house, in case I collapsed. They thought it was better for me to live with my housemates, in case something happened.
"But now I'm going to be healthy. I can look after their place when I get out," I said happily.
"Well maybe… We don't know how long you'll be in here," Mum said, noncommittally.
"I'll be out by the time they go though. It's over a week until they leave."
"Well ummm… Well they've already found someone else."
That was a shame, but I understood. I thought it was a pity though, that they didn't know I would be medically stable soon, and well enough to house-sit for them.

I had been in hospital for over a week before I worked out that "medically stable" also referred to my weight. I would need to put on a lot of weight before I could be discharged. In hindsight, I'm not sure if they could legally keep me there against my will, once my BMI was a bit higher and my bloods, heart rate and blood pressure had normalised. However, the nurses seemed to genuinely not know if I could discharge myself, and the doctors fluctuated between vague, condescending and disciplinary when I asked. I didn't want to stay, but it wasn't too hard to accept the situation, once I had been there a few days. In some ways, it was nice to be able to rest. I was excited to recover too. Even if I had to stay in hospital longer than planned, I could get on with the exciting parts of recovery when I got out.

If I hadn't been feeling so positive, the stay would have been even worse than Heathgrove. Instead of being free to move around the ward as I pleased, so long as I wasn't moving too much, as I had in Heathgrove, I was on constant bed rest. I was only allowed to leave my bed to brush my teeth and have a shower, and even those activities had to be done while seated. I was supervised 24/7 by a nurse, to ensure I didn't collapse and abided by these rules. Mum and Dad brought in some colouring books I had been given the previous year and I read a lot of books. Siobhan brought in her copy of '8 Steps to Recovery From an Eating Disorder,' by Carolyn Costin — the book I had bought for most of the inpatient eating disorder treatment clinics around Australia, using the funds from my head shaving fundraiser — and I diligently worked through it, completing all the writing activities as I went. Mum and Dad came in every day, to keep me company, Adam came every few days, and Gran and Grandad, and lots of friends, visited weekly, to hang out and keep me in good spirits.

Unsurprisingly, I was in hospital on Christmas Day, but it wasn't as bad as it could have been. To be honest, it was probably better than it would have been if I wasn't in hospital. I had been wondering how I would navigate food on Christmas Day for about a month. I was eating so little by then that, even if I only ate Christmas dinner and dessert, I would have exceeded my daily calorie limit. I wanted to be able to eat at least one meal without stress though, so I had decided to do extra exercise on Christmas morning, to counteract dinner. I hadn't figured out how I would get away with eating hardly anything at breakfast though, which we always ate with Dad's family. I had been doing extra exercise in the week or two leading up to Christmas, to "save up" calories I could "spend" on eating on Christmas Day. I couldn't risk going into an energy surplus. So, though I was confined to my bed and in hospital, I was glad I wasn't allowed to do a long workout in the morning, restrict food even more than normal until dinner, and then fret about what I had eaten. Instead, I woke up when my body wanted, without an alarm, had a present thrown onto my bed by one of the wonderful volunteers who paraded the hospital corridors that morning, ate decent meals, had the energy to laugh, and enjoyed my family's company as they visited throughout the day. Of course, I would have preferred to be with them in a different location, enjoying delicious curries instead of hospital food. However, hospital food was better than hunger, exhaustion, anxiety, feigned happiness and guilt.

I usually didn't talk to my nurses much, preferring to read, text friends and family, write, or colour in. Most of the nurses were nice, but some were annoying or boring. The nurse who came on Christmas morning was someone I hadn't seen before and she was very chatty, even though I was holding an open book, clearly reading. In the end, I gave up on trying to read. I had started to enjoy the conversation anyway. Steph was lovely and became one of my favourite nurses. I couldn't help comparing myself to her though. She was so small and slim. Was she thinner than me? And if so, how did she achieve it, without severely restricting her food? Her facial features were everything I wished for too. She had a small, narrow nose, clear skin and a thin jaw — no chance of ever having a double chin. I assumed she would think I was ugly and disgusting, with my pimply skin and big nose. Surely she would think I was lazy, for sitting down all day on bed rest, but she was always lovely. I felt awkward eating in front of her because I worried she would think I was greedy. If she did, however, she hid it well. I know it was her job to be nice to me but, after scrutinising everything she did and said, I almost believed she didn't find me repulsive. I had to continually look for evidence though; I couldn't convince myself that someone so thin and pretty would actually want to spend time with someone like me.

Siobhan and I had spoken about the NG tube the few times we met before we went to the hospital. She was surprised I hadn't been tubed before and asked what I thought about it. As she suspected, I admitted that I wished I had been sick enough to need the tube. Some friends had been tubed multiple times and I felt I was a failure for not even needing it once. Siobhan agreed that many viewed it as a badge of honour. We joked that it was like the PhD of having anorexia; to be so good at starving yourself and refusing food that you needed the tube. The ultimate achievement. The ED voice told me I needed to be tubed at least once before I deserved to recover, but the thought of having a tube go all the way up my nose and down to my stomach[28] didn't appeal at all.

However, when I was admitted to hospital I changed my view. My disordered side still wanted me to need to be tubed, but my healthy side had become so much stronger since my epiphany, that it didn't want to award the eating disorder that satisfaction. At some point in the first few days, the dietician and doctors said I should be tubed but, as I was a "consenting" patient — I laughed, and reminded them I was not a consenting patient, and went through the pointless back and forth again until one of us changed the subject — they couldn't force me. Yet. If I didn't put on weight fast enough, they would want to tube me and, if I didn't agree, they would have me committed, at which point I would have no rights. So they could tube me anyway. I chose to wait and hope I wouldn't need it. Siobhan understood my reasoning — not wanting to feed the eating disorder — and agreed with my decision.

About a week after I was admitted, a few days after Christmas, the dietician and doctor told me they wanted to tube me, to speed up my recovery. I

---

[28] Rapid Antigen Tests are a joke compared to the NG tube!

wouldn't be consuming extra calories; rather, some of the Resource[29] I had been drinking during the day, would be pumped into me through the tube at night. I tried to understand why being fed through a tube was more beneficial, but they never actually gave me a straight answer. The best I got was that being fed around the clock was better than consuming everything during the day and fasting overnight. I could see how that might make sense for a body recovering from starvation, so I offered to be woken up during the night to drink one of the Resource drinks.

"No no, you don't want to do that," they said, pretending to care.
"Actually I do. That's why I said it. I don't want to be tubed."
I had this circular conversation with both the dietician and the doctor individually. Eventually, one of them said I could take the rest of the day to decide. If I chose not to get the tube, they would commit me and make the decision for me the following day.
"So I'll be tubed either way?"
"Well yes, but it's your decision."
"But it's not.."
"Yes, you can decide if you want to get it today."
Did they think I was a bit stupid?

Later that afternoon I told my nurse, whose name was also Hannah, that I may as well get the tube. The disordered part of me was so proud. Hannah put a tube in the freezer because apparently, they're slightly easier to manoeuvre when they're a bit cold and stiff. Adam was visiting at the time and said that, if I wanted, he would stay while she inserted it.
"Yes please," I replied.
Hannah had to guide the tube up one nostril, around a corner near the top of my nose, and then down to my throat. When the tube was at the back of my mouth, I had to sip water through a straw, as the swallowing action would suck the tube down to my stomach. Yes, it feels as awful as it sounds. The first time, I gagged when the tube touched my throat, which caused it to flick up and curl back on itself. Hannah felt terrible and apologised profusely as she pulled it out for a second attempt. Luckily, that one was successful. Later that night, Adam told me that he had felt sick, just sitting there watching. After the tube was in, I was wheeled, while sitting on my bed, to get an x-ray, to check that the tube was indeed in my stomach and not my lungs. Luckily it was. The next day, the doctor said he was glad I had decided to get the tube.
"Well, I didn't really have a choice."
"You did though, you chose to get the tube."

---

[29] Resource is one of the many brands of high-calorie meal-replacement drinks used for refeeding.

Et cetera.

Though I became accustomed to the feel of the tube in my nose, it was very uncomfortable in my throat and it hurt to swallow. Swallowing food was even harder. By the next morning, it was difficult and painful to talk. On the bright side, I thought this would be a good excuse to avoid talking to the annoying nurses — if only. While I was watching Tangled one day, one of the annoying nurses came in to cover the lunch break of the nurse I had been assigned.
"What are you watching?" she asked.
"Can't talk" I mouthed, pointing at my throat.
"What? No, what are you watching?"
I tried again. "Can't talk," I whispered quietly.
"What is it, on TV?" she asked, as though I had misunderstood her question and she was being very understanding and patient with me.
I gave in. "Tangled," I whispered as loudly as I could, wincing at the pain.
"Dangled?" She misheard.
"Tangled," I repeated.
"Dragons?"
I forced a smile, assuming she would realise it was time to give up. She did not, and continued to look at me expectantly. Third time lucky, she heard me, and asked what it was about. Luckily, another nurse came to talk to her at that point.

I spoke to the nicer nurses, Siobhan and my family about my sore throat and discomfort. Every time I swallowed food, it took a huge effort to push it past the tube and down my throat. It quickly became the worst sore throat I had ever had. Siobhan told me that most people experience some pain in the first few days, but that it would get better. My nurse asked the doctor for pain medication and they begrudgingly prescribed a low dose. They gave me a spray, which I could use every few hours, and a tablet, which I took twice a day. I was on a child's dose since my weight was low. The annoying nurse who was incapable of lip reading, was very strict with the spray. At first, she wanted to spray it herself but, after a few days, I insisted on doing it myself, because she always missed and numbed my tongue or gums instead of my throat. She watched me like a hawk though, and if I missed my target — difficult when I couldn't see what I was doing — and tried again, she would snatch the bottle away, reminding me that I was only allowed one spray.

After a few days, the pain still hadn't even begun to subside. Siobhan said that, for some, it took longer. Maybe it would be a week. But a week came and went. The doctors didn't believe I was in pain, assuming I was complaining in the hope that they would remove the tube. The nurses saw me struggle to eat though, and wince every time I swallowed, even when I wasn't eating or drinking, and knew it wasn't an act. Every day the doctor said he needed to decrease my dose of pain medication, and every day I told him, in a strained whisper, how much pain I was in. A few times I cried in frustration after he left, or when I tried to eat. When I tried to eat my first meal after I was tubed, I was in so much pain and discomfort that I started quietly sobbing. My nurse saw and, understanding my distress, came over to hug and comfort me.

I was in pain the entire time I was tubed. Ignoring my reports of pain, the doctors decreased my pain medication. I learnt to use the numbing spray just before eating, as swallowing food was more painful than saliva. I asked friends from Heathgrove and Siobhan spoke to her contacts in the eating disorder community, and everyone said the pain should have worn away after a week at the most. Siobhan looked into the possibility of having a narrower tube, usually used for babies, inserted, but was told it would quickly become blocked by the Resource, which is quite thick, that they were pumping in. It was a possibility, but I would probably need to have a new tube inserted every few days. I decided it was better to deal with the pain than go through the discomfort of a regular insertion.

Most of the nurses were great, which made a huge difference to my mood and attitude. If I was assigned a nurse I got on with, I usually had a good day. If I had an annoying nurse, however, I knew I was in for a trying seven hours, and tried to make it as clear as possible that I was reading. I think some nurses got bored, just sitting there watching me, and wanted to talk. I felt for them and didn't want to be rude, but Siobhan reminded me that I was the patient and looking after me was their job. They had special training for looking after eating disorder patients and were told to respect the patient's wishes. She encouraged me to make it blatantly obvious that I wanted to read, even if I felt I was being rude. She suggested I put earphones in when I didn't want to talk. Surprisingly, even this didn't always work. Some nurses continued talking, even though I was pretending to listen to music. Eventually, I stopped responding, so they would think I couldn't hear them.

After a few weeks, I had formed a hierarchy in my head, of my favourite to least favourite nurses. There were three tiers: The top was occupied by only two nurses, who were absolute standouts. The second was populated by other nurses who were also lovely, friendly, understanding and fun, but who didn't quite have that special top-tier place in my heart. The bottom tier was where the annoying, bossy, unfriendly nurses resided. These nurses either babied me; talked about food unnecessarily — they were specifically trained not to do this — tried to psychoanalyse me; asked me about my feelings when I really didn't want to talk about it — another thing they were told not to do — or talked to me when I had earphones in, or pointedly told them I was reading a book about recovery!

There was also a dungeon, below the bottom level, for the nurses who were blacklisted in my mind. There were only two nurses down there. The first looked after me on the second or third day. She had no idea about eating disorders and treated me like a child who was a bit sad. She suggested we meditate together and stood in the doorway eyeballing me, the whole time I showered — most nurses watched me in their peripheral vision, so I wouldn't feel so uncomfortable. While I understand that it's important to watch patients while they're in the bathroom, I sometimes wonder if the people who made this rule considered the fact that most of us are incredibly insecure and self-conscious about our bodies, and therefore having someone see us naked for an extended period of time exacerbates our insecurity. This nurse told me she worked for an agency because she hadn't found a full-time job yet. I didn't need to guess at why she hadn't been offered a permanent position yet...

The second nurse, Marie, was so terrible I genuinely find it hilarious. However, if I hadn't been feeling so positive about recovery, she could have caused serious distress. Luckily Marie was my night nurse, so I didn't have to talk to her too much. When she arrived Anne, my afternoon-evening nurse, started to explain that I had AN and asked Marie if she had looked after eating disorder patients before.
"Yes," Marie said with exaggerated gravity, before turning to me to say, "You're beautiful."
I restrained from rolling my eyes.

"Have you used the Nasogastric feeding machine before?" Anne asked Marie. "You'll just need to change the feed bag during the night."
"Yes," Marie replied, attempting to hide her uncertainty behind feigned confidence as walked over to inspect the machine. She asked a few questions about how the tubes were attached and which buttons to press, acting as though this particular machine was different to those she was used to. I saw through her act and I think Anne did too, but couldn't call her out on it. Instead, she explained everything, trying to impart as much information as possible without sounding condescending. Marie interjected with "Yes, that's right," every so often, as though Anne was confirming what she already knew.

I had been reading when Marie arrived and planned to read until I went to sleep. Marie had other ideas. She asked how long I had had AN, what other treatment I had tried, and what I did for work. Most nurses asked these questions when they had their first shift with me. I grew tired of answering the same questions, but I understood that they were getting to know me. I answered Marie's questions as briefly as I could without seeming rude, then returned to reading. But she had decided that she was going to cure me that night, with her wisdom and insight.

"You know you won't be able to succeed with your music if you're starving your brain."

Oh gosh, I had never considered that. Thank you, I'm cured!

"And that would be such a shame," she continued, with a tragic half smile, "given that you're so talented."

She had never heard me play; we had only just met. I could be terrible for all she knew. I opened my book again.

"I understand how you feel, you know." She gestured to the feeding machine. Here we go. "I've got the opposite to you."

Binge Eating Disorder? But surely she wouldn't talk about it with me. Nurses and Doctors were told not to talk about their own eating habits with me.

"Binge Eating Disorder," she announced, almost proudly.

Ok, maybe she was going to talk about it.

"And I've got body dysmorphia, but the opposite way to you. When you look in the mirror, you think you're fat, don't you." It wasn't a question.

"Well, no.." I began, but she wasn't listening.

"I'm the opposite. I see myself as a size 12, but I'm actually a size 36."

Oh good, we're talking about clothing sizes now. That's not a triggering subject at all. Then she told me her BMI. I had given up on reading by this point, so at the end of her Ted Talk, I said I was tired and wanted to go to sleep.

I woke up in the early hours of the morning because Marie was shining a light in my eyes and muttering close to my head. She was trying to change the feed bag over and was not having a good time. It seemed she was unsure how to make the machine start and stop, and also struggling to disconnect and reconnect the tubes. She didn't know how to lock the clip that keeps them attached, so she was trying to use brute force. She apologised insincerely for waking me up, blaming the machine instead of her own incompetence, and I used the excuse of sleepiness for my mumbled response.

Eventually, when Marie decided that everything was reconnected and working, she returned to her chair in the doorway, while I tried to get back to sleep. Later in the night, I woke again, needing to go to the toilet, as I had fluid pumping into my stomach all night. I noticed a small milky puddle on

my sheets, where the tubes connected, and told Marie. She sighed in annoyance, and bustled over, complaining about faulty tubes.
"Oh, and we've lost some of the drink too," she complained. "I bet you're happy about that," she added to me, part conspiratorial, part disapproving.
I wasn't. It was only a tablespoon or two and I actually wanted to put on weight faster, so I could get out of hospital. I was surprised she had made that comment though. She made me wait, with my bladder painfully full, while she wrestled with the clip again. After more twisting, pulling and muttering, she was finally satisfied the connection was secure and allowed me to go to the bathroom.

The next morning, when it was nearing the end of Marie's shift, there was still some Resource left in the feed bag that connected to my NG tube. It should have finished pumping into me about an hour earlier but, as it had taken her such a long time to change the bag over and reconnect the tubes during the night, we were behind schedule. I think Marie was worried this would make her look bad and didn't want to have to tell anyone that she hadn't known how to use the machine, so she sped up the pump. They can be programmed to pump in a certain number of millilitres per minute and mine was set to deliver 400mL over eight hours.
"It's not much faster, it shouldn't matter," she said, without bothering to ask if I minded.
When there were about 15 minutes until the next nurse was due to arrive, Marie decided to stop the feed, so she could disconnect me, change the tubes and dispose of the feed bag.
"Then you can have a shower and get ready for breakfast," she said brusquely.
Marie checked the contents of the bag as she disconnected it.
"Just five mils left," she announced.
I nodded.
"That's ten calories."
I nodded again. I had already done the simple maths.
"But I'm sure you already knew that," she said, again part conspiratorial and part disciplinary.
When she left, at the end of her shift, she made a similarly encouraging but patronising comment about my recovery.

An hour or so later, I was chatting to Mel, one of my top-tier nurses; she had stopped by to say hello. I told her about Marie, hoping to amuse her with my funny story. She was horrified. When I told her that Marie had disclosed to me her experience with binge eating disorder, and told me her BMI, she almost couldn't believe it.

"Oh my gosh! I'm so sorry! You shouldn't have had to go through that. Are you ok? She should know not to say that. They're told. I'm so so sorry…"
"It's fine. I thought it was funny," I replied, still laughing. And it genuinely was, such was my positivity about recovery.
"Actually, I think I should report this. Do you mind if I do that?"
"Yeah sure, actually that's probably a good idea," I replied. "I'm fine, but I wouldn't want her to look after someone else with an eating disorder. Her words could be triggering. Is it possible to put a note on my file, so she won't be assigned to me again?"
Mel gave me a knowing smile. "Unfortunately you can't request to not have specific nurses, but we can put a note in your file so you don't get agency nurses. Last night's nurse was from an agency, so you won't get her again."
I was very happy to do that. As a rule, the agency nurses were less helpful and didn't know what they were doing or how the ward ran.

The journal I started when I was having lessons with Dorothy got a lot of use while I was in hospital. It was where I recorded my responses to the journal activities in Carolyn Costin's book. I also read through the quotes about recovery, which I had written before my admission, every morning after I meditated. I wanted to remind myself why I wanted to recover, to rewire my neural pathways. After I finished '8 Steps to Recovery From an Eating Disorder' I used the journal for all sorts of brainstorms, lists and thoughts related to recovery. I listed restaurants and cafes I wanted to try, foods to challenge, fun activities I wanted to do when I got out of hospital, meals to cook myself, a sample grocery list with approximate prices beside each item, and ideas for a daily routine. I asked Mum and Dad to print out the rest of the recovery quotes I had saved and glued one into the journal each day, to add to my collection of morning reading.

I knew I was gaining weight, but hospital protocol prevented me from seeing the number on the scale. Every morning, after going to the toilet, I would sit on a chair wearing only a hospital gown. The scales were underneath the chair and the number was displayed on a screen attached to the back, so couldn't see unless I twisted around 180 degrees. One day, when I was sitting on the chair, my nurse left the room briefly to fetch something. One of the orderlies came in. He was a friendly guy but didn't know why I was in hospital. He read the number out to me, probably trying to be helpful. I thanked him, hoping he would leave before my nurse returned, so she wouldn't know what had happened. Another morning, the night nurse left my folder open to my weight graph, while she left the room briefly. I hopped off the bed quickly and managed a peak, then ran back before anyone caught me out of bed.

I could see that I was getting bigger, but it was hard to know what was bloating, what was fluid, what was body dysmorphia and what was permanent muscle and fat. I consoled myself with the fact that I still fit into my clothes, even if they weren't as loose as they had been before my admission. Whenever I looked at myself in the mirror, I searched for visible bones, to reassure myself, but these were slowly swallowed into my growing body. In the last few weeks of my admission, I couldn't find anything that even suggested frailty, and my knees looked fat to my eyes. At least I wasn't repulsed by my reflection though, or not too much more than I had been before hospital. Not so much that I couldn't pretend to myself that I felt ok. I told myself it was probably body dysmorphia, which would diminish with time. When I got out of hospital, I could start exercising again and tone up anyway.

I often worried that the extra calories I was consuming would be turned into fat, not muscle. However, there wasn't much I could do about it, as I was on bed rest and watched constantly. A few times, if my nurse left the room briefly when I went to the toilet, I would do some squats and push-ups, but I knew ten or twenty reps every few days wouldn't make much difference. So I got creative. While I lay in bed reading, I tensed and relaxed my leg muscles. I tried to do the same with my arm muscles, but it made my book move slightly and I kept losing my place. Sometimes I lay on my front and pushed my shoulders down away from my ears, so my arms muscles had to work to hold me up. I tried kicking my legs up and down while I was in this position, but the nurse noticed and told me to stop. I also tensed my abdominal muscles while I was lying on my back reading. I didn't know how much difference it would make, but I felt I had to at least try. My reasoning was both healthy and unhealthy. I didn't want to hate the way I looked so much that I started trying to lose weight as soon as I got out of hospital. I needed to feel at least a little bit ok, otherwise I wouldn't be able to bring myself to eat enough or challenge new foods. Though of course, if I had a completely healthy mindset, I wouldn't consider restricting my food at all.

I had the NG tube for two or three weeks before the doctor and dietician decided my weight and medical results had normalised enough to remove it. I would need to drink the extra Resource drinks with my meals during the day, instead of having them pumped in at night, but I didn't mind. I actually quite liked the taste and eating extra during the day was a small price to pay for not being in constant pain and discomfort. The doctor and dietician seemed surprised that I had chosen to drink the Resource myself, confirming my suspicion that they had never believed me when I said I was in pain. My nurse and I were both excited to take it out, even though she handed me a sick bag

— apparently the feeling of having the tube pulled out causes some people to vomit. I didn't, but wouldn't have cared if I did.

Even though I was stuck in the same room for weeks, I didn't feel bored or sad very often. I didn't mind spending my time reading, colouring in, talking to my nurse — unless they were a third tier nurse — or being taken outside in a wheelchair — they were worried the exertion of walking may cause a heart attack. It didn't take long for me to notice my mood improving, which I hadn't noticed when I was in Heathgrove. Small jokes and funny stories brought me such joy; I felt happier than I had in a long time. I came to realise that feeling emotion requires energy and, when the body is in starvation mode, it doesn't waste energy on positive emotions. Anxiety and fear yes, and a few other negative emotions necessary for survival, but nothing positive.

In January, Lucy went to Japan for a holiday with some friends, while Kieran stayed in Perth. They had always visited me together and, though I had lived with them on and off for over a year, I still felt that Kieran regarded me as Lucy's friend. I had never been sure if they actually wanted me living with them, third-wheeling, and always wondered if they were only letting me stay out of kindness, Kieran especially. It was his house and I was Lucy's friend. So I was surprised when he messaged one afternoon, asking if I wanted him to pop in. I had wondered if he would continue to visit while Lucy was away. When I mentioned this to him, he merely said "Of course." It took a few visits for me to believe that he valued me as his own friend, not just Lucy's. About a year later, Kieran told me that another friend, who sometimes stayed the night at their place if she was too tired to drive home after dinner or a movie night, always worried that she was imposing by staying over.
"She thinks we don't want her here but we love having her around," he said.
I took the opportunity to verify my own worry. "I thought the same when I lived here."
Kieran was genuinely shocked. "Really? But we loved having you here. Why would you think that?"
It was good to know I was wrong, even if I didn't find out until much later.

After I had been in hospital for about a month, my medical team — they called themselves my team but I joked to Adam that a team is supposed to be supportive — decided I was ready to move to a mental health ward. At first, they said that, as my address was in the catchment area of Armadale Hospital, I would be transferred to their ward.
"No," I said, laughing, before I realised they were being serious.
"No," I repeated. "I'm not going there."

I'm usually quite passive, but I think they could see that I had absolutely made up my mind. Siobhan and I had deliberately gone to Emergency at Governor because they had a half-decent treatment program for eating disorders. I knew that, if I went to Armadale Hospital, they wouldn't be trained to look after eating disorder patients and I would go backwards.

The only other option worth considering was Heathgrove. I wasn't keen, because I hadn't found their program very helpful seven years earlier. However, I had heard that it had improved a lot since then, so I was open to giving it a go. My team said they would organise a referral to Heathgrove, so I could be placed on their waiting list. However, two weeks later, when we had our next meeting — I had a meeting every two weeks with the approximately six clinicians who made up my team, which consisted of the dietician, a few psychiatrists and one or two general medical doctors — they told me they hadn't written or sent the referral. I was flabbergasted. How hard was it? Had they just forgotten? I had noticed that none of them took notes during any of the meetings but thought that maybe, as doctors, they all had very good memories and wrote notes after the meeting. Obviously, their memories weren't as good as they thought. I was shocked they had forgotten to do something so important. Did they think my well-being was trivial? #youhadonejob. A barista forgetting a coffee order is one thing, easily remedied, but a whole team of highly paid doctors forgetting to write a referral for life-saving mental health treatment? None of them were embarrassed about this large oversight either. They remained very calm, as one of them said "No, we haven't done that. Would you like us to do that?"

A few days after the referral was finally processed, someone at Heathgrove called to talk to me about their program and asked if I could come in at some point for an interview. During our phone conversation, food allergies were mentioned.
"I've got a long list of food intolerance," I said, "but last time I was in Heathgrove, Mum and Dad brought in muffins and slices I could eat, and they're happy to do that again."
"Yes, there have been a lot of changes the last few years. We don't allow any outside food anymore, but the kitchen can provide appropriate food," she explained.
"Oh that's great, though I've got some weird intolerances, like corn and soy."
"That's fine. As long as you bring medical evidence of your allergies to the interview, like coeliac test results."
"Aaaahh my coeliac test was borderline. But I react to gluten, so there's something there my body doesn't like, we just don't know what."

I react to lots of foods, but there is no medical test to prove my experience or explain the cause. By this point, I had come to accept that my body just wasn't great at digesting them. Dad is missing some digestive enzymes and has to follow the FODMAP diet, and others on his side of the family are coeliac, so bad digestion runs in the family.

"Hmm unfortunately we will need official documentation proving your allergies or the hospital won't cater for you," she said, half suspicious, half apologetic.

We discussed different options for a while, but neither of us would budge from out position.

"What if I drink the equivalent amount of calories in the form of a Resource, if I'm intolerant to something in a meal?" I offered.

"No, that can't be a long-term solution. If patients don't start eating 100% of each meal within the first week or so, they're sent home for non-compliance." Her tone was more stern this time.

I understand that they don't have many beds, and may feel that compliant patients are more deserving of a place in the program. However, maybe if their program was more effective, they wouldn't have patients being "non-compliant," because they would be getting better. Also, "non-compliant" is an incredibly offensive term. Do we call cancer patients, for whom chemotherapy has been ineffective, non-compliant? Mum was furious when I told her, but there was nothing we could do to persuade Heathgrove. So I waited for a bed to become available in the Mental Health ward at Governor.

We waited and waited, but each day the news was the same: there were no beds. I was on the waiting list, but mental health patients who came in through the Emergency Department took precedence because I already had a bed.

"What if you discharge me, so I don't have a bed, then take me straight to Emergency?" I suggested.

The medical team laughed and mumbled "no," looking down at the table, but I had been serious.

"But why not?" I asked.

They just chuckled again, muttering incoherently.

"Are you worried I'll do a runner once I'm discharged?"

They said no, followed by some unfinished sentences intended to suggest that I wouldn't understand the complex process of hospitals. I never got a straight answer.

Eventually, the powers that be decided that, instead of waiting for a bed in the Mental Health ward, we could simulate a similar environment in the Medical ward. I would no longer be supervised 24/7 and would even be allowed to eat my meals alone, only seeing my nurse when they came to give me my medication or check my blood pressure. I would still be weighed every morning, but no one would check how much I had eaten. It was a one-week test, which I definitely would have failed if I hadn't entered the hospital with such a positive mindset. As it was, I stopped drinking one or two of the high calorie drinks, though that was mainly because I genuinely didn't like them. I liked the creamy Resource, but this was a different drink, which tasted sickly sweet, like cheap cordial. I admit I was also worried my weight would continue to rise if my energy intake remained so high. I wanted it to plateau, so my medical team would think I had reached my natural set point. I hated how I looked, and felt self-conscious of how ugly and pudgy I was, especially when friends visited or I had a slim nurse. I told myself, and hoped, that it would get better when I could exercise a bit and the body dysmorphia eventually went away.

Being a lone ranger also meant I could exercise as much as I wanted, as long as I stayed on hospital grounds, and practise violin again, as long as it didn't bother the other patients. I didn't go overboard though. If my weight dropped my medical team would make me stay in hospital even longer. I allowed myself one 20 to 30-minute walk each day. However, it only took a day or two for me to start feeling anxious about the walk. I knew that, if I didn't go, I would feel guilty. I quickly designed myself a new daily routine: After breakfast, I practised for an hour or two, then went for my walk. The walk was often on my mind while I practised, and sometimes I stopped practising earlier than planned, so I could go for the walk and check it off the list in my mind.

Continuing Recovery

Finally, after passing my one-week test, I was allowed to go home. The silly thing was that the doctor who had to sign off on my release was MIA, so my nurse and I sat around twiddling our thumbs until he answered his pager. Mum left the house to come pick me up as soon as I called her; we had known I would probably be discharged that day. I wasn't sure how she felt. I assumed she would be worried about me going back to my old habits once I was out of hospital, but I think she also truly believed that I was in a much healthier state of mind. She seemed tense though — she wasn't very talkative — but I didn't want to ask if anything was wrong, in case there was and she started yelling at me.

Sara, a family friend, had kindly offered that I could live in her vacant rental for free until she found a new tenant. Sara lived in another house, so I would have the place to myself. It was incredibly generous of her and I will always be grateful. I think she guessed that I would want my own space while I was still emotionally raw from hospital. I had thought that Mum and Dad would want me to stay with them for at least a day or two after I was discharged, so they could watch what I was eating and make sure I didn't immediately relapse. However, Mum assumed I would be moving to Sara's that night, so I started packing when we got home. I was glad to be leaving straight away. While I didn't want to lose weight, I did want to start my morning exercise again ASAP, which I wouldn't be able to do at home.

Mum told me she would be leaving to go to yoga an hour or so after we got home, for which I was grateful. I would need laundry powder at Sara's house and I couldn't bring myself to buy my own. I had never had to buy laundry powder before — there was always a communal box in my share houses — and I couldn't talk the anxiously frugal part of me into starting. After Mum left I tipped some into a ziplock bag to take with me. I felt guilty stealing from them, especially after everything they had done for me since I was admitted to hospital, but told myself it was only a small amount and that they would understand.

I stopped off at the Spudshed on my way to Sara's and actually had fun buying food. I stuck to the grocery list I had made in hospital and didn't even look at the nutritional information when I was deciding which yoghurt to buy; I just chose the flavour that sounded the most interesting. I was genuinely proud of myself for overriding the ED voice's wishes. It was tiring and stressful finding the house, moving my suitcase, groceries and violin in, and unpacking, but I made sure I ate the dinner and supper I had planned. I didn't feel any guilt while I ate or afterwards.

SO held casual violin auditions about a week after I got out of hospital, so I had applied while I was in hospital. Generally, orchestral excerpts are sent out two to three weeks before the audition, so I received them while I was in hospital. I started practising the excerpts and my Mozart concerto when my supervision was lifted and hoped I would be discharged before the audition. Luckily I was, and I got straight back into practising about four hours a day. I didn't practise before breakfast though, as I had before hospital. Instead, I meditated, read through my recovery notebook, and read a book until I was hungry. I also organised to have a lesson with Dorothy a day or two after I was discharged, so she could help me prepare for the audition.

When I played for her she was so ecstatic and overjoyed.
"You've got your sound back, Hannah! It's back!"
"I just didn't have the energy before, to move.." I tried to explain, but I was embarrassed to talk about AN, even though she knew about it and had come to visit me in hospital. Aside from the embarrassment, it was an exciting lesson and I left with my heart singing.

I had made a lot of plans while I was in hospital, to give myself the best chance at recovery. I was going to cook with Mum, so I could practise making proper food for myself, with someone there to make sure I didn't skimp on oil or other fear foods. I made an appointment to see Krish before I left the hospital and he wanted to see me weekly for a while, and for me to get a blood test every few weeks, so he could keep an eye on my levels. I also made an appointment to see a dietician who specialised in eating disorders. I saw Krish and the dietician during my first week out of hospital, but I never got around to cooking with Mum. At first, I didn't ask her because I didn't have time, and then I felt that it had been so long since I had been discharged that it would be odd to ask. Like when you forget the name of a new acquaintance and, after a few months of avoiding addressing them by name, it's too late to ask.

Adam and Avril invited me over for dinner the week I got out of hospital, and told me they wanted to support me however they could.
"Thanks," was all I could say on repeat as they spoke. I was grateful and very touched by their care and the maturity they were demonstrating. It wasn't all warm fuzzies though.
"For us to properly support you, you need to be honest and tell us when you need help," Avril said seriously. I felt uncomfortable and looked down at the

table. "It won't help if you pretend to be ok or lie, like you did before. You need to tell us, so we can work out together how to help you, before things go too far."
I was even more appreciative of their willingness to risk awkwardness or harsh words, in order to help me.

I didn't know what to think about the SO audition. I had thought I would pass the audition two years earlier, when I got back from Hobart, but I hadn't. After that, I had done two more unsuccessful auditions for them. However, each time I had prepared by myself, without input from a teacher. I always focus on the notes and don't realise how much I need to exaggerate the dynamics, phrasing and all the other details, for them to come across to the audience. This time, Dorothy helped with that. I had also been exhausted during each audition, and therefore unable to play anywhere near my best.

I made sure I had enough to eat this time, though I was scared to have anything in addition to my meal plan. While I was warming up, I started feeling a bit lightheaded, and my concentration was waning. I had a Resource with me, but had planned to drink it after the audition. I felt it would be weak to give into my body's needs by breaking a mealtime rule. I also worried that, if I drank it earlier than planned, I would be hungry later. But I didn't want to spoil my chances of passing the audition. Though I didn't know if I would pass or not, I knew that, if I didn't, I would feel worthless, with an all-consuming, impossible sadness, and would regret ever trying to recover. I knew that I would question if I was at all worthy as a violinist if I couldn't even pass a casual audition when I was eating enough. I, (and Mum and Dorothy), had told myself for so long that the reason I wasn't succeeding with violin was that I was malnourished. This was my chance to prove that to be true; if I couldn't, I felt there was no point in trying to recover. If I couldn't be good at music then I may as well be tired but skinny again. I didn't need to be able to concentrate anywhere near as much when I worked other jobs, and I could fight through physical fatigue. This argument raged in my head while I was trying to concentrate on the music backstage. Eventually, I drank the Resource and, luckily, didn't feel too guilty. However, I knew I would if I didn't play well.

I felt the audition went quite well. I made a small mistake in one excerpt but was happy with the rest. The orchestra manager said they would send me an email that afternoon, after the panel had discussed my performance. It was nearly lunchtime when I got home — I still had semi-strict times for my meals, though this was more from a healthy frame of mind, to keep myself on track — so I started cooking almost straight away. I knew that, if SO emailed to say I hadn't passed the audition before I ate lunch, I probably wouldn't eat. The email came in not long before I had finished cooking and I almost didn't open it, in case it was bad news. But I did and it wasn't. I was so happy I jumped around the room, laughing. I hadn't been so happy in a long time. I messaged Dorothy, who called back straight away to congratulate me, and my family, to tell them the good news.

Soon after my audition, SO offered me a few weeks of work, starting in a month. I had enough other work to keep me busy until then though. I had picked up a day of violin teaching at a school from a friend, who needed someone to relieve her for the term. I also had a few hours of work most evenings, handing out flyers for Fringe shows around Northbridge. The Fringe work wasn't at all exciting, but I had seen the role advertised while I was in hospital and had applied, because I didn't have any other work lined up. Though it didn't take long for me to get bored each night, I enjoyed having the energy to walk around. I had done the same job for a different company the year before and walking around had been absolutely exhausting. I had often felt cold too, even though it was summer. I had hated every shift because it was a constant effort just to remain vertical.

Though Heathgrove had rejected me as an inpatient, Krish sent them a referral for me to attend their day program. It runs from about 10 am to 4 pm Monday, Tuesday, Thursday and Friday. The patients do group therapy and have most of their meals together at the hospital. I hoped their program would help keep me on track and that eating food prepared by someone else would help me transition to cooking normal meals for myself.

They invited me to come for an interview with the dietician and the program coordinator, to make sure I was a good fit for the program. They only accept people who are positive about recovery and willing to challenge themselves. Morally, I disagree with this stance, because it means that people who aren't ready to recover, but who are in medical danger, don't receive the treatment they need. The directors of the eating disorder program say that, as places are limited, they give preference to those who will make the most of their help; however, I think being able to boast a high recovery rate is the true driving force behind that decision. I set aside these thoughts though, because I knew I needed all the help I could get.

Most of the interview went well because I was positive about recovery and had started taking steps on my own since being discharged. However, my food sensitivities were still a problem. Because I didn't have a positive test result for coeliac disease or anything official from an immunologist, they couldn't organise alternate food options. Unfortunately, the strict policy which prohibited patients from bringing in their own food to eat also applied to the day program. I asked if they would accept a statement from my GP or parents about my food sensitivities, as I had had them before I developed AN. No; they would only accept an immunologist's report.

They made the unhelpful suggestion many times that, as my body was still adjusting to the increased volume of food, I was already experiencing stomach discomfort. Therefore, eating foods to which I was sensitive, wouldn't make much difference. Except that it would. It would add to the discomfort and make it even harder for me to eat. They artfully sidestepped this truth each time I pointed it out.

They suggested I go to an immunologist, who would help me systematically and scientifically challenge the foods I thought caused digestive problems. I had already done this under the guidance of Maisie, my previous GP, but they weren't interested in hearing this. I understood where they were coming from. I'm sure they heard all sorts of stories from other patients, as to why they couldn't eat certain foods, which were actually fear foods. However, testing my list of intolerances would take months. I would also need to wait a few months before I could begin testing — my digestive system wasn't back to normal yet, after years of not eating enough. If I started testing foods straight away, the data wouldn't be accurate. I was still getting tummy aches, bloating and constipation, as my body adjusted to my increased food intake, even though I wasn't eating foods to which I believed I was intolerant. When I pointed this out they said that, in that case, I might as well take part in the program and eat everything. I'm not sure if they were deliberately missing the point.

At this point, the meeting had gone overtime and we still hadn't covered everything on their agenda, because we had spent so much time talking about my food intolerances. They asked me to think about the "options" they had presented and let them know when I decided to do. After the meeting, I had a few more ideas for getting around the food problem. I can't remember what they were, but I emailed them to ask their opinion. They wouldn't budge, so I decided it would be best not to take part in the program. I didn't want to have stomach pains and constipation for the next two months.

A few weeks after I was discharged, Adam and Avril went to the USA for a holiday. While I was still in hospital, I had asked Adam if I could housesit for them and look after Maxwell, their cockatiel.

"Hmmm... Avril and I have spoken about this," he began. "Obviously we trust you to look after the house. You'll probably leave it cleaner than we do... But we don't want to enable the eating disorder. It's easier for you to slip back into bad habits if you're living alone."
As always, I felt awkward at the direct mention of the eating disorder.
"You may not believe this, but it's actually easier for me to eat well when I'm living alone," I replied.
"Riiiight..." He wasn't convinced. "Say some more about that."
"Well, I feel self-conscious eating around others and preparing food. When I'm living by myself I don't have to worry about what others think. Living alone will help when I'm challenging food too. I won't have to worry about housemates when I'm eating something scary and new."
"Why do you feel self-conscious eating in front of others though?" He asked.
"I just worry what they'll think; if they'll think what I'm eating is weird or too much or gross or ask me about it..." I trailed off.
I could see Adam didn't understand how I felt, but was coming to believe me nonetheless.
"Ok. As long as you honestly think it will be helpful. I don't want to enable the eating disorder." His eyes bored into me.
"Yes, absolutely!" I said happily.
After three weeks in Sara's rental, I moved to Adam and Avril's for the next three weeks. I didn't know where I would go after that. If Sara's house was still vacant I could probably move back there, but I doubted it would be empty much longer.

One morning, I was sitting on the couch in Adam and Avril's living room, scrolling through Facebook, when I saw my friend Holly's status, sharing that she was recovering from AN. She wanted to let her friends know so that, if anyone else was struggling, or had a friend or family member who was sick, they could talk to her. I had never known her well, but she had always seemed confident and popular. I sent her a private message, to tell her how much I admired her for taking the plunge into recovery, speaking out, and that I was in recovery myself. We had a good chat, which I would never have been comfortable having in real life, and shared with each other some of the things we had found helpful. Holly recommended some Instagram accounts she found inspiring and motivational. I didn't use Instagram much, except to occasionally post photos of random things I found funny or beautiful, or to scroll through my feed when I was especially bored. I didn't even understand hashtags or stories.

Holly warned me that I may find some of the photos confronting, not as thinspiration, but in their honesty. She was right. I was repulsed by some photos of people embracing — or, as I saw it, pretending to embrace — their weight-restored bodies. Some people photographed themselves smiling while showing tummy rolls, cellulite, or their thigh spread. The photos showed health, both physical and mental, but I was shocked. It's not something we often see, especially not the exuberant celebration of fat. But the more I looked at these photos, the more I came to realise that these were normal, healthy bodies. I gradually learnt just how warped my perception of a healthy body was. Some accounts shared motivational, but entirely truthful, quotes and memes about recovery, and the lies the eating disorder tells us. They were similar to the quotes I had collected from Pinterest, but it was helpful to read them regularly. They reminded me that the rules I had come to believe without question were actually rubbish. That's not to say I didn't continue to believe them, but I started to question them.

From the accounts Holly recommended, I found many more, and I probably follow 50 or more today. Holly's recommendations were all personal recovery accounts, but now I also follow professional anti-diet dieticians, psychologists and eating disorder organisations. I made myself stop following some of the personal accounts when I felt the user had started to relapse, or if they were early in their recovery journey and posted too many photos of them looking emaciated in a hospital gown with an NG tube. Those photos made me regret going into hospital and feel fat, gross and greedy for being happy to eat more. There are two personal recovery accounts that I have found particularly helpful, because both women have genuinely recovered, mentally and physically. When I started following them, they were not yet weight-restored and had a lot of fear foods, but were actively working to recover. Over the years I have followed their progress; their success, as well as their honesty about their struggles and horrible, intrusive thoughts, has inspired me to continue to challenge my own disordered thoughts and beliefs.

Not long after I got out of hospital, I started working through my list of food challenges. It was fun and I rarely felt guilty, because they were planned in advance and, most of the time, I felt positive about recovery. I wasn't ready for spontaneous food choices, but expanding my safe foods and sticking to my meal plan was a good start. I knew that, if I moved too fast, I would freak out and slingshot in the opposite direction. I had ice cream every night for supper; I also bought a scoop or two of ice cream a few times from gelaterias, which included the additional test of spending money; I ate dinner or lunch out about once a week, usually ordering curry and rice and eating all of the rice; and few gluten-free cakes. Once, when I met Siobhan, I ate a new flavour of Magnum I had been wanting to try. I also challenged myself to have meals and snacks with friends, as that caused anxiety.

About a week after I moved to Adam and Avril's, Stuart, a man for whom I had briefly dog-sat the previous year, messaged to ask if I could do so again. It would be for about three months this time, as he was going to England for work. Perfect timing; I was excited! His house is in Victoria Park, which is quite central, close to SO rehearsals and public transport, and within walking distance from an interesting cafe strip. I agreed without any second thoughts and organised to move there the night Adam and Avril returned. He had a border terrier called Bother, who was one of the sweetest dogs I have ever met.

I knew my body had become bigger while I was in hospital however, due to body dysmorphia, I didn't know how much bigger. Though they still fit, my clothes were tighter, but that changed throughout the day, and from day to day, depending on how bloated I was. While I was staying at Stuart's, I devised two approaches to test the truth of what I was seeing.

(Body checking)

I took a photo of my whole body, standing naked, and sent it to my laptop. Then, I found full-body photos of slim celebrities and models to use as a comparison. I adjusted the size of each image in a Pages document, so the length from head to toe was the same, then measured the width of both our waists, legs and arms. I knew that, in many ways, it was very disordered, to scrutinise bodies so closely, but my actions came from a healthy place. I was testing my body dysmorphia scientifically. I told a psychologist about this experiment a few years later and she thought it was a good idea. Later, I traced around my body on the computer screen, cut it out, and held it up to the screen to compare my paper cut-out with the slim celebrities. I was surprised to find that I was almost always thinner, or just as thin, as the celebrities.

I hesitated before attempting my second idea, but eventually, I plucked up the courage. I messaged a close friend and asked if she felt comfortable telling me if I was bigger or smaller than specific friends. I trusted her to be honest and not judge me for this strange request. I made it clear that I would absolutely understand if she felt uncomfortable, but she agreed. She was able to tell me how I compared to some mutual friends, but wasn't sure about people she had only met once or twice. The latter included two friends who are so slim I have often wondered if they deliberately restrict their food. I sent her some photos of these friends from their social media pages, but they were all taken at odd angles, or when the friend was wearing loose clothes, so she found it hard to judge. To this day, I still wonder about these friends. I've spent more time than is healthy, scrolling through their photos on social media, trying to find images that show their waists in fitted clothes, to no avail.

While I was in hospital, Siobhan mentioned that she was going to the International Conference for Eating Disorders (ICED) in Chicago in May. She had won a scholarship, which would pay for her registration, however she would need to cover flights and accommodation. Having recovered from AN and Bulimia herself only a few years earlier, she hadn't been well enough to work much for a long time and, therefore, didn't have a lot of savings.
"I could put on a fundraiser concert, to raise money to pay for your flights," I suggested excitedly.
"Oh, that's very kind," she laughed. "You need to focus on getting better though, not putting on concerts for me."
"This will give me something to work towards though; a purpose," I protested. "Anyway, it's the least I can do for you after you saved my life."
Again, Siobhan laughed and gave a vague response. I think she appreciated the sentiment but didn't think I would be up to it.

Once I had passed my SO audition, I started planning the concert. I decided to perform some solo Bach, so I wouldn't need to worry about rehearsing with an accompanist or forming a chamber group. I also asked some friends if they would be interested in performing, making it very clear that I could only pay them in chocolate, as all of the money raised would go to Siobhan. Luckily some friends who occasionally perform as a string quartet, and two friends who sometimes play modern and experimental percussion compositions together, were happy to perform.

It was a wonderful afternoon. Lots of friends came for the music and to support the cause. We all stayed outside chatting for at least half an hour after the concert, catching up. That night I felt happily tired and proud of what I had organised. We raised just over $1000. I joked that I should have shaved my head instead — I raised much more with less effort!

One night, when my mind was wandering, I started thinking about ED treatment and how it compared to the treatment of any physical condition. I decided to write down my thoughts, applying the treatment I had received in hospital to a broken leg.

Imagine that you have accidentally broken your leg doing an activity that you thought would be fun and help you to be happy. The obvious thing to do, when you go to hospital, is to reset the broken bone.

So the Doctors reset the bone, but only gradually — over the course of a month or more — and without any anaesthetic. You are in pain most of the time, but all the nurses do is talk to you about the pain and encourage you to express it when you feel the need.

You are finally released from hospital, but it will be at least a year until the bone has completely healed. The doctors didn't do a very good job of setting it straight, so your leg is still very weak and still causes you a lot of pain, probably more than when you were in hospital.

The doctors have recommended a few different types of painkillers, which you are finally allowed to use. Different drugs work better for some people than others and most are still in the trial process. They also have a range of side effects. Some people find little to no relief from any of the painkillers, but when they tell the professionals this, they are told to keep trying and that it will take time.

Some people's bone breaks again after being released from hospital and they have to go back, to go through the same slow and excruciating resetting process. Some people's bone breaks multiple times before they finally heal completely. For some people, the bone never fully heals and they either eventually die or live the rest of their life limping and hobbling.

Slipping

I was very strict about sticking to my meal plan, but I struggled when I was forced to change my routine and couldn't eat at my set times. When I had SO rehearsals there wasn't much time to eat during the morning break. Others managed but I'm a slow eater. I was also self-conscious about eating around others. Most of the orchestra only had a cup of tea or coffee, so it wasn't hard for the ED voice to convince me that I shouldn't need to eat either. I was sitting down for most of the day anyway, during rehearsal. I made sure I ate my snacks on the days I didn't have rehearsal, but it didn't take long for me to start feeling guilty about that too. My snacks became smaller, but I wasn't feeling tired or very hungry, so maybe my body didn't really need more. I noticed I was slipping, and wanted to turn things around, but then I worried that, after having eaten less for a month or so, my metabolism would have slowed down. If I started to eat more again, would I put on weight? The annoying thing was that no one could give me a straight answer to this. Everyone's body is different, so the only way to test it was to eat more and see what happens. But I was scared to test it, in case I gained weight. I had put on about ten kilos while I was in hospital and I needed to get used to this new, bigger body before I put on any more weight.

While I was housesitting for Stuart, Mum and Dad's neighbours asked if I could housesit for them for a month later that year. I was excited to live in the bush again, with Mum and Dad close by, but not in the same house. I also hoped to have dinner with Mum and Dad more often, to get back into the habit of normal eating. Luckily, the dates lined up with Stuart's return.

Unfortunately, during the month before I moved to the neighbours' house, my intake decreased and the rigidity of my food rules increased. The idea of eating with Mum and Dad was scary now. I had become less flexible about the types of food I allowed myself to eat, and had reduced my calorie "allowance." I knew that, if I ate with Mum and Dad, the ED voice would make me restrict during the day to make up for eating more at dinner.

(Food)

Instead, my bad habits increased. The neighbours had kindly left a big bowl of fruit for me, a hamper of food, and their mandarin tree was fruiting. For a long time, wasted food has made me feel stressed. When I'm cooking I only make as much food as I need and store any leftovers, however small, instead of throwing them away. It makes me anxious to see food thrown away and I'm torn between eating it myself and not consuming the extra calories. I had suspected for a while that this anxiety was related to the AN, but didn't know why or how. I didn't want the fruit to go to waste but also didn't have room in my meal plan to eat it. I gave some away, but also had the tendency to hoard food, for fear of running out — again this is related to the AN and my fear of spending money. I reasoned that, as fruit contains carbohydrates, even though it's high GI, I could replace the rice in my meals with fruit. Because of this food swap, I got out of the habit of eating rice and it quickly returned to being a fear food. A few months later, with a lot of planning, I managed to normalise eating rice again. Not long after that, I got out of the habit of eating it once more, and it remained a fear food.

While I was living there, my high school put on a concert to celebrate the 50-year anniversary of its specialist music program. Ex-students were invited to form a choir, which would perform at the concert. I had loved being part of the music program and was excited to sing in a choir again, with Miss C conducting. She arranged for our sound check to be at about 8 am, to allow people who worked nine to five jobs to be there, before they went to work. This caused a problem for me, in the sense that it wasn't really a problem, but the ED voice made it one. Getting to the city by 8 am meant leaving the house at about 7 am. Earlier than I would like, but not the end of the world. However, the ED voice had two problems with this:

Firstly, I would need to leave time not only to get dressed and have a shower, but also to exercise. Getting up early is even harder when I know I have to exercise. First-world problems, I know, but when the exercise is filed in my brain under 'punishment' and missing it creates a storm of anxiety and guilt, it becomes a much bigger deal than it should. I could have done it later in the day, but I knew it would be on my mind until I had done it.

Secondly, I couldn't eat breakfast before I left the house because that was earlier than my rules dictated. It was awkward timing though, as my breakfast time fell around the time when we would be finishing our sound check. I figured I might as well wait until I got home again, so I could have breakfast in comfort, watching Netflix. But that meant being up and moving around for four to five hours before I ate. However, eating earlier would mean getting up even earlier, probably feeling hungry for morning tea earlier and generally messing up my whole day because eating at different times made me anxious and made everything feel topsy-turvy. I could have brought a snack with me, but I didn't want to "ruin" breakfast — I felt that snacking beforehand would make me, and the experience of eating breakfast, impure. The ED voice won; I got up early, took the train to the city, walked to the concert hall, sang in the sound check, walked back to the train station and took the train home, all the while feeling very tired and quite lightheaded. I enjoyed my breakfast when I got home though. I had earned it.

(Exercise)

I woke every hour or so the night before the sound check, thinking my alarm had gone off. I was worried I would sleep through it, or wake up and go back to sleep, since it would still be dark. I was dreading exercising so early too. Eventually, at about 3 am, when I couldn't get back to sleep, I decided to get up and do my exercise, so I could stop worrying about it and could get up a bit later in the morning. I knew that what I was doing was extremely disordered, and I worried Mum and Dad would see my light on from their house, but I reasoned that it wasn't a terrible idea overall. I would be able to stop worrying. I watched part of Hannah Gadbsy's Nanette on Netflix, while I jogged on the spot, did squats, star jumps and whatever else was in my exercise routine at the time.

At my first appointment with Krish after I was discharged from Governor, he referred me to the Centre for Clinical Interventions, (CCI), so I could get onto their waiting list. I had asked my medical team at Governor to write a referral but that was one of many things they either forgot about or didn't bother to do. I had been to CCI eight years earlier, after my time in Heathgrove. I was on the waiting list for about seven months this time and unfortunately, by the time my name came to the top of the list, I had already slipped quite a bit.

My psych, Alex, was lovely and very encouraging in all of our sessions. She explained that CCI had developed a program that was much more structured than it had been eight years earlier. They were much more goal-focused, and if a patient wasn't making progress within the first ten sessions, they would need to either lift their game or their place would be given to the next person on the waiting list. It was unfortunate, but it made sense, as it was government-funded. I didn't think slow progress would be a problem for me though. Motivation certainly wasn't.

However, Alex wanted to move much faster than I had expected. I still didn't feel ready to gain more weight — I know it's rare for anyone recovering from AN to feel ready, but I had already gained a lot in a short period and needed time to get used to my new body. I wanted to work on body image and body dysmorphia, but Alex wanted me to gain half a kilo a week.
"I'm sorry, I just can't do that," I said. I didn't see the point in being anything other than completely honest. Lying about my fears had never helped.

"Why not?" Alex asked. She appeared confused but I didn't believe it was genuine. Surely almost all of her clients feared weight gain.
"I already put on so much weight in a short amount of time in hospital. I feel so uncomfortable and disgusting in my body and I need time to get used to it. And hopefully the body dysmorphia will start to go… I've got a constant commentary from the eating disorder voice, tell me how big and disgusting I look… I can't get any bigger. I'd freak out and want to lose it all as fast as possible. Then things would be even worse."
We had a similar conversation every session — Alex would talk about healing my brain, sitting with discomfort and riding waves of guilt after I ate, and I asked if we could just take things a bit slower. Even adding 50 calories a day scared me. Eventually, Alex met me where I was at, suggesting I eat an extra 50 calories a day for a week. I was only able to keep it up for a few days.

All of our sessions felt rushed. We spent so much time talking about what food I could add or change that there was never enough time to talk about the emotional side of things. It felt pointless to me. I could plan meals myself. I knew what made an adequate meal; I just couldn't bring myself to eat one, unless I restricted for the rest of the day. At the beginning of each session, Alex read my food logs — she had asked me to record what I ate at each meal and snack and how I felt during and afterwards. Whenever she saw that I had felt anxious or guilty after eating, she would ask why. The answer was always the same and, I felt, obvious: because I had eaten something different, or more than usual.

According to CCI's treatment model, sessions revolve around food and meal plans, until the patient has gained enough weight to start working through the triggers that led to their disordered eating. However, I felt I needed to work on the emotional side of things before I gained any more weight. I understand that's a red flag for psychologists; everyone with a restrictive eating disorder wants to wait until they feel ok about eating more before they actually eat more, which rarely happens. Our sessions became very stressful for me, especially as I was getting a lot of work with SO, and was trying to fit our sessions around rehearsals. Eventually, Alex suggested we take a break. She said that she could keep me at the top of the waiting list for up to three months; if I chose to come back within that time, I could, without having to wait. After that three months, however, if I wanted to come back to therapy, I would need to get another referral and start at the bottom of the waiting list. It was a relief to stop. At the end of the three months, I decided not to go back. By then, I definitely wasn't ready to increase my intake or put on weight anyway.

Although I was slipping food-wise, I still felt that, overall life was going well. I was getting lots of work with SO, so I spent most of my days practising alone, rehearsing with the orchestra, and performing. I felt that everything was falling into place. I didn't want to be a casual long-term — I still wanted to move overseas and find work with a chamber orchestra — but I was enjoying it for now. I got to play wonderful music with professional musicians and some great conductors. I also got to perform movie soundtracks live, while the movie played on the big screen. I was especially excited about Harry Potter — I was probably the most enthusiastic person at those concerts, including the audience.

When I worked at SO before I moved to Hobart, I often felt out of place, and there weren't many people I felt I could talk to. I was at least ten years younger than most of the orchestra, and the few who were closer to my age already had other friends. I was 18, so a year or two still felt like a big age gap, especially when I already felt socially awkward and generally uncool. Returning five years later, I assumed things would have changed; a two-year age gap meant less. Plus, I was on my way to being fully recovered and felt positive about life.

Unfortunately, that wasn't the case. I still felt that I didn't fit in and that not many people wanted to talk to me. I felt I was conspicuous for being an oddball and a loner. I don't know if that's how others perceived me, or if I was misinterpreting everyone's actions and facial expressions, but I felt very uncomfortable and anxious during breaks. There were a few people who always seemed happy to talk to me, but if they weren't playing that week, or were talking to others, I didn't know what to do. I didn't want to look like a loner though; that would make me seem even more awkward. Instead, I pretended to be busy. I would make a cup of tea, even if I didn't want one, check my phone for messages, check my emails and Facebook, scroll, and sometimes go outside, attempting to look purposeful, all the while trying to find someone I could talk to, or a group of people I may be able to join.

Lunch breaks were harder to navigate. After a few months of trying to fit in, I started sitting outside when the weather was nice. Even then I needed to look busy though, in case others walked past and wondered why I was sitting by myself. When it was cold I tried to find somewhere sheltered, but soon gave up and hoped there would be a chair available at a table of welcoming people in the break room. Sometimes Josie, my roommate from AYO tour, was playing, so we hung out together during breaks. Those weeks were much more enjoyable and relaxed.

Later that year I was asked to perform on a regional tour with SO. I was excited to travel but also worried about who I would spend time with when we had free time. I found out a week or two before the tour, that we would all have separate rooms, so I wouldn't need to worry about the awkwardness of sharing a room with someone I didn't know. Luckily, there wasn't a lot of free time outside of sound checks, concerts, walking to and from the venue, flights, and general things like showering, sleeping and eating. Eating and exploring the towns by myself wasn't as obvious as being alone at the break, because I was less likely to be seen by anyone else in the orchestra. Especially if I stayed in my room.

(Food and exercise)

The tour consisted of two short trips to Geraldton and Kalgoorlie, staying a night in each town, with a night in Perth in between. Both flights from Perth left very early, around 7 or 8 am, to give us enough time in each town. Because I had to exercise before I left — I couldn't give myself a day off — I got up around 5 am. I ate breakfast on the plane, though doing so made me anxious, because it was earlier than I usually allowed myself to eat. However, after arguing with the ED voice during the weeks leading up to the tour, it eventually agreed that I wouldn't have any other opportunity to eat before our rehearsal at the performance venue. I still felt guilty and disgusting though, especially as there were hardly any vegetables in the aeroplane meal. I allowed myself to eat the scrambled eggs but still felt hungry due to a lack of volume from vegetables. I guiltily picked at the sausage, while the ED voice yelled at me to stop, as I was exceeding my breakfast calorie limit. Eventually, my hunger gave into the ED voice; I put my knife and fork down and closed the food box, but I felt guilty for the rest of the day. And I was still hungry.

Partway through that year, a friend offered me a job teaching violin at a school where she taught classroom music. It was only a few hours a week, but it would increase the following year. I also did some short-term relief teaching for friends at various schools, when they went on holiday. At the end of the year I bought, and took over running, a small business from a friend. The company organises string musicians to perform at functions, weddings and private parties. I had worked for this friend for about a year and a half and, when she said she would be moving to Melbourne, I asked if I could buy the business. She agreed and we started working out the legalities, which was a lot of paperwork. She also talked me through how she ran everything. It was a very busy and stressful few months, but I knew it would calm down when we had sorted everything out, and I got used to how things worked. I decided it was worth it in the long run. Aside from the admin, I also performed at most of the gigs we booked. Sometimes I worked at WAYO in the morning, had a gig in the afternoon, then performed with SO at night. It was tiring and stressful, but I managed. I was glad I was in better health than I had been the previous year.

I settled into my new semi-recovered life for the remainder of that year and the next. I housesat almost continuously, only staying with Kieran and Lucy twice, for a few days between houses. I'm still amazed I managed to line up the housesits back to back. I had joined a few housesitting groups on Facebook, which I anxiously checked a few times a day, had an advertisement on Gumtree, and became known to friends, family and their friends, as someone who was trustworthy, clean and keen to housesit. It was stressful never being able to settle and having to regularly pack up my things and move. I had to be very organised, especially if I had to move house on a day that was already filled with work and gigs. The sits ranged in length from two days to two months, so I lived in an average of 20 houses each year. I lived out of one suitcase and kept my non-perishable food — tea, coffee, chocolate, spices etc. — in a big plastic box, which travelled with me. I tried not to bring too many perishables when I moved house, because it was more to carry and took time to pack and unpack, so I tried to time my shopping accordingly. Sometimes it was unavoidable. I knew, at the time, that most people probably just leave their food at the previous house, instead of bringing it with them, but I didn't want to spend money buying more food than I had to. Sometimes I didn't have time to go to the shops anyway. Constantly moving added stress to my life, and people often asked if I enjoyed it, but for me, the pros outweighed the cons. I got to live by myself and didn't have to pay any rent or bills. SO work was unpredictable, as I was a casual employee, so I was glad I didn't need to worry about paying rent.

Sick

One night I woke up feeling very nauseous, with things moving around and gurgling in my stomach. Luckily I got to the toilet in time to vomit. A lot came out too. I still felt queasy, but nothing else was forthcoming, so I washed my face and mouth and went back to bed. An hour or so later I woke up again, needing to vomit. I was up and down for the rest of the night, with diarrhoea and vomiting. I still felt very weak and quite queasy by the time the sun was up. I didn't feel like I had a bug, just that I was feeling the after-effects of emptying my insides. I guessed it was food poisoning, and my had body needed to get everything out. I hadn't eaten anything out of the ordinary though, and no meat, so I assumed I had just been unlucky.

As I had decided I wasn't sick, I felt I should still do my morning exercise. Surely I would be feeling better in a few hours. I felt so weak though, and I had SO that day, so I didn't want to make myself even more tired. I sat on the bed for a while, internally arguing with the ED voice. Eventually, I decided not to do my exercise, though I felt very guilty. I told myself that, if I was feeling better when I got home, I would do it then, though I hated leaving it to the end of the day.

I considered not going to work, but I didn't want to lose the income. Surely I would feel better in an hour or two anyway. I was still feeling nauseous after I showered and worried that eating breakfast would make me vomit again. I decided to wait until lunch, or maybe I would feel up to eating when I got to work. I didn't. And I still felt weak from a lack of both sleep and food.

However, as I was there, I didn't feel I could back out of playing. Maybe once I was onstage I would start to feel better. Maybe it was placebo. It was not. We were giving a short concert that morning, which was good and bad. It meant I needed to be alert and dressed up, but also meant an earlier finish for the morning. Throughout the performance, I wondered if I was about to faint. My legs shook every time we stood up to welcome the conductor onstage or accept the audience's applause. I was also worried that, in my exhaustion, I would lose concentration and make a mistake that would detract from the performance. I was relieved when it was over. However, I still had to get through the afternoon rehearsal.

I picked at my lunch slowly. I was famished, but my tummy still felt delicate. I worried that eating too much would make the nausea worse, or that my body would reject the food. I didn't want to vomit again, especially not at work. Unsurprisingly, the afternoon rehearsal was a struggle and I was relieved that it finished early. The train ride home seemed to take longer than usual. I gave up trying to read my book and just sat, slumped forward. The other passengers probably thought I was on drugs or drunk — not uncommon on the Armadale line. I felt weak all afternoon and evening, so I rested and drank electrolytes. The next morning, I felt slightly better and the nausea had gone. The ED voice easily convinced me that I was well enough to exercise. I was shaky and exhausted afterwards, but it was nothing a bit of willpower couldn't deal with. At least I wouldn't feel guilty.

A few weeks later, I woke up during the night again, needing to vomit. It was the same as before; I was up and down all night with diarrhoea and vomiting, but once my body had expelled everything, I felt much better. Still queasy and weak, but I knew I would be back to normal soon. I had SO again that day, but luckily rehearsal wasn't until the afternoon, so I had the morning to rest and eat when I felt up to it.

I didn't understand why this had happened twice now. If it had been a bug, surely I would have been sick for longer, and it was unlikely I had caught the same thing twice. Food poisoning was an unlikely explanation too; I hadn't eaten any meat, or anything out of the ordinary. A woman at SO said she had heard about a bacteria that gave people gastro symptoms, then stayed dormant in their system for a few weeks or months, before striking again. I googled it, but couldn't find any information, so I wondered if it was just a rumour.

It occurred to me that the sickness may have been brought on by stress. Worrying about my recitals had given me constipation in Hobart and mental health often affects physical health, particularly digestion. One of Mum's friends had told her that, when she was teaching at a particularly rough school, which she found very stressful, she had to keep a bucket on the passenger seat in her car, because she sometimes vomited while driving to school in the morning.

I had felt more anxious than usual about being at SO that week. I hadn't been rostered on for a few weeks and I often felt nervous going back after a break. I worried about getting back into the swing of things and trying to fit in with everyone. Whenever I thought about work, I questioned if I was good enough to be performing with a professional orchestra. I worried someone would eventually discover that I wasn't and that I was far too immature to have an adult job. When I considered this, I realised that I had been trying to convince myself that I was happy at SO. Most of the time I was, but I was feeling more and more out of place, worrying what others thought about what I wore and said and did. I became aware that, even when I was alone at home, I wondered what my colleagues would think of whatever I was doing, whether it was going for a walk, dancing as I got dressed, cooking, exercising… For the next week or so, I was very aware of how often I had these thoughts; it was almost constant. I made a conscious effort to stop myself, or bring myself back to the present, whenever I started ruminating. I worried that, if I didn't, my stress would build up again until I had another late-night vomiting session. Luckily, I didn't vomit again.

Back to Uni

In May, I started thinking seriously about doing postgraduate research; either a Master's or a Doctorate. I had considered it many times since I got back from Hobart, but always decided against it, for various reasons. This time though, possibly because I discussed it with more musicians, I didn't change my mind; instead, I refined my research topic. I spoke to a few people at different universities and decided to go to the University of Western Australia, (UWA), where Ellen — the same Ellen for whom I had housesat many times — would be my primary supervisor. I wrote up my research proposal, auditioned, answered the panel's questions about my intended research topic, and was accepted to do a Masters. I had hoped to go straight to doing a PhD but, as I hadn't written a thesis for Honours, they felt it would be better to start with a Master's. The Master's is only one year at UWA, so it wouldn't be too long before I could continue on to do a PhD.

I officially started the Masters in September and absolutely loved it. I got into a good routine of practising for three to four hours before lunch, then researching afterwards. I was hungry for knowledge and was excited to be learning about something I had been interested in for so long. Everyone at the university constantly surprised me with how helpful and organised they were. I felt positive about the future again. I hoped that, after completing the PhD, I could work at a university, doing a mixture of teaching and research, while also performing as a freelance violinist.

I decided to accept less work with SO while I was studying, so I could focus on preparing my recital repertoire and writing a really good thesis. I had hoped to receive a scholarship, which would cover my living expenses, so I wouldn't need to worry about working too much. However, as I didn't receive first-class Honours, I had no chance. I would still need to work but, as I wasn't paying rent, I wouldn't need to do too much. I hoped that, if I wrote a good thesis, I would get a scholarship for the PhD.

About two weeks after I started the Master's, Lucy messaged to say that she needed to talk to me about something. It sounded serious and my first thought was that there was a problem with Kieran. I dismissed the thought almost immediately though. He's a lovely person and would never hurt her. Lucy seemed to want to see me as soon as possible, so she came over a few days later. Before she arrived, I decided to let her bring up whatever she wanted to talk about when she was ready. I never know how to bring up sensitive topics anyway; I just make it awkward.

"So I need to talk to you about something," Lucy said, only a minute or two after she arrived.
"Yes, are you ok?" I asked.
"Yeah... Kieran and I have separated. Because I'm gay."

"Oh." Actually, in a way that kind of made sense. "How are you feeling?"
"Yeah, mostly ok. It's... it's a relief." She had visibly relaxed since she told me. "Now I just have to tell everyone."
"How are things with Kieran? How is Kieran?"
"Well, Kieran's sad, obviously. I'm sad. It's..." There were too many feelings to put into words.
"Where are you living?" I asked.
"Oh, still with Kieran. It's fine." I wasn't surprised. I guessed Kieran would be nothing but supportive. "I need to find somewhere to rent soon though. And move all my things." She looked exhausted just thinking about it.
We talked more about how she had come to realise she was gay and why she hadn't worked it out earlier in life. It seems strange to say we had a lovely afternoon. There was no awkwardness. If anything, I felt more comfortable with her than usual, and her being gay made sense almost as soon as she told me. At the same time, it felt like a big change, because we had been friends for over 18 years.

That night I started thinking about something I usually pushed out of my mind, whenever it entered my thoughts. Since I was about 11 I had wondered if I was gay. I thought some of the girls at school, and in magazines and movies, were beautiful, and often didn't want to stop looking at them. But I didn't want to be gay. This was the early 2000s and, although my parents are as un-homophobic as they come, I knew society wasn't. People at school said "that's gay" about things they didn't like, and often told gay jokes. I knew that being gay would make life harder in all sorts of ways, not least discrimination. And I wanted to have children — I was vaguely aware of sperm donors and IVF, but never considered it for myself, because I didn't want to be gay anyway. I told myself that I was just aware of girls' beauty. I heard other girls talk about women they thought were pretty, especially celebrities, so it must be normal. I almost convinced myself.

In late primary school, I already thought I was too ugly and disgusting and weird for any of the girls I found attractive to feel the same way about me. I thought that, if I was gay, only the girls I found unattractive would like me. I felt that, since I was already a gross person, being gay would amplify that, whereas, if I was straight, I would eventually work out how to be normal and beautiful. I simultaneously knew that this was illogical, but my self-loathing and society's homophobia had warped my thinking. I continued to have these thoughts throughout high school and university. The belief that I was gross worsened in high school, and my desire to be thinner was, in part, caused by my fear of being gay. The media often portrays lesbians as "butch dykes," and marvels at celebrities such as Portia de Rossi for being beautiful *and* a lesbian. Logically, and from experience, I knew that lesbians come in as many shapes and sizes as straight women. But, because I already had such a low opinion of myself, I assumed the worst; being a lesbian meant I would become bigger, butch and masculine, while I longed to be effortlessly thin and feminine. By the time society had progressed enough that I was beginning to think it would be ok to be gay or bisexual — I didn't learn about bisexuality until I was 16 — I had almost convinced myself that I was straight and just appreciated feminine beauty.

However, after hearing Lucy talk about how she had convinced herself that she was bisexual, not gay, for so many years, I questioned myself again. This time I didn't mind if I was; I just wanted to know either way. A few weeks later, I told Lucy I had been questioning my own sexuality for a while, and she said she had always wondered. We spoke about it on and off for the next few months. She sent me articles to read and relayed helpful things people had encouraged her to think about. Eventually, I decided I was probably bisexual. I wasn't sure, but I was open to the possibility. However, I decided not to tell anyone else until I knew for certain. That included my family. I felt it would be too final to tell them; that I wouldn't be able to change my mind after I had spoken the words.

Christmas that year was a bit of a disappointment. I was still in the phase of looking forward to Christmas, only to be disappointed because it wasn't as magical as it had been when I was younger. This year was especially bad though. My lack of sleep may have contributed — I had performed at midnight mass the night before — but the main cause was my presents from Mum and Dad. This is not a "last year, last year I had thirty-seven"[30] spoilt brat complaint. Rather, I felt that the presents they gave me reinforced a truth I had been trying to ignore: they didn't really know me, still thought my thinking was disordered, and wanted to change the aspects of me they labelled "sick" or "anorexic."

Mum had asked me to write her a Christmas list, so I had, but she hadn't bought anything on the list. I felt she had given me things she wanted me to want, not things I actually wanted. I felt she wanted to change me, a suspicion

---

[30] Yes, that was a Dudley Dursley quote.

I had been trying to ignore for years. But this forced me to face the fact that she and Dad didn't really know me, or didn't *want* to know some parts of me.

Mum and Dad knew the part of me that was scared to spend money was influenced by the AN. It wasn't just food where I tried to cut costs; I rarely bought myself clothes, preferring to wear those I owned until they were literally falling apart. I had explained that I genuinely felt it was wasteful to buy new clothes when my current ones were still in good condition, but they didn't believe me. I often felt that Mum blamed anything she didn't like about me on the AN, and that hurt, because some of those things were just me. I felt that, by blaming them on something external, she could hope they would go away when I recovered, and wouldn't feel guilty for disliking something about her daughter.

After a few days of ruminating over these thoughts, I sank into depression. And I say "sank" because that's how it felt. If I didn't have the obsessive drive to exercise and stay reasonably active to burn calories, I may not have been able to get up in the morning. I felt the depression weighing down my shoulders, I was lethargic and there was so much sadness inside me it felt as though my head was being squeezed.

My rumination caused other repressed feelings to resurface; a self-hatred and disgust so intense it hurt. Tears came to my eyes whenever the reminder of my self-hatred throbbed back into awareness. I realised I had gradually buried it over the years until I had almost forgotten it. Only a watermark remained, which coloured every aspect of my life, but I had become so accustomed to it that I didn't notice it anymore. Now that I was aware again, it was almost unbearable. It was a horrible three or four days before I gradually and unconsciously buried the self-hatred again. My awareness of it remained but at a more manageable level.

2020

I had been looking forward to 2020 for almost half of the previous year — don't laugh! — because I would finally be able to stop moving between housesits. In July 2019, Ash, a woman from one of the housesitting groups on Facebook of which I was a member, said she was looking for someone to housesit for her long term, as she was starting a job that would require her to be away for at least half of each month. I got in touch and went to meet her and her many animals. Her house had a self-contained area upstairs; it even had its own door to the outside. She had been renting it out on Airbnb but would stop when she started the new job. We got on well and her animals, (four dogs, three cats and many chickens), were lovely. I housesat for her for a few days in August, as an unofficial trial, and also because she needed someone, and she was happy with everything I had done. She said the animals were relaxed when she got home and, for her, that was the most important thing. She was happy for me to start later that year, but I had housesits booked back to back, so I couldn't come until the end of January. I was excited to be able to stop stressing about where I would be living, moving houses on busy days, planning my grocery shopping around when I was moving, and living out of a suitcase.

However, we all know what happened in 2020. Ash went to the eastern states once or twice before her employers moved their meetings online. I asked if she wanted me to move out until she started flying again, but she said she was happy for me to stay — at that point, we thought everything would be back to normal in a few weeks — and the animals could use the time to get to know me. I was relieved I wouldn't need to find another place to stay, and offered to pay her rent. When she said no, I asked what other jobs I could do around the house and garden, and for her animals, to help out and pay my way in the form of service. She couldn't think of anything, because she genuinely enjoyed watering the garden, walking the dogs and feeding them all, so I brainstormed things I could do. She had a cleaner who came once a week, so I couldn't help out there. I started weeding, vacuuming between the cleaner's visits, cleaning out the chicken coop and cleaning up the dog poo from around the house.

A week before Easter, as Covid restrictions tightened and the toilet paper shortage began, Adam and I were at Mum and Dad's for our traditional Sunday get-together. We went for the afternoon instead of dinner, so we could sit outside, (in case any of us had Covid), before it cooled down for the night. Mum, Dad and I had become increasingly nervous about going to the shops, in case we contracted Covid. Mum had pointed out that I was at a higher risk

of becoming very sick, as I was at such a low weight. I made my trips as short as possible and darted out of the way of anyone who came near me.
Woolworths and Coles had said they would deliver to immunocompromised people, but that didn't stretch to Roleystone, where Ash and I lived. The local IGA, where Mum and Dad shopped, had offered to start a free delivery service, for which they had signed up.
"We'll order your groceries with ours Hannah, so you don't have to risk going to the shops," Mum said that afternoon.
Though I was scared every time I entered the shops — this was before we had masks — I was also anxious about paying the higher prices at IGA.
"We know you feel anxious spending money on your groceries, so we'll pay for yours," she continued calmly.
I felt guilty having them pay for my food, especially since Mum had decided to stop working until Covid was under control — she's a teacher, so would be around lots of children who don't know how to socially distance. Covid had caused a lot of Dad's work had been either cancelled or postponed too, so they didn't have much money coming in. However, my anxiety was greater than my guilt, and I was tired and stressed about everything that was happening. I agreed and said thank you.

The groceries were delivered a few days later, so I went to Mum and Dad's to have a cup of tea and a chat and collect my food. They lived about ten minutes from Ash, so I wasn't worried about the petrol I used to drive there. I also gave them as much money as I would usually spend on groceries which, I soon realised, was much less than they had spent. Mum was excited to give me the box of food. She'd had fun choosing yummy things for me to enjoy. I was still embarrassed about accepting so much food from them, so I didn't look through the box until I got home.

Tears came to my eyes as I unpacked everything they had given me. I was touched by their kindness and generosity. I had never bought so many nice things for myself, yet they had given me so much in just one week. It was more than I needed. It felt far too luxurious. Included in the box were two packets of raw chicken. I'm not sure if they had assumed or just hoped that I was cooking meat for myself, but I wasn't. I considered throwing it away so they wouldn't know, but I didn't want to waste it, especially since animals had been killed. I wrote a diplomatic text to Mum:

```
Thank you so much for all this lovely food! I've
just been looking through the box and I'm
overwhelmed at how much yummy food you've given me.
It's far too generous! I've got out of the habit of
```

cooking chicken though. I'm not scared of it, I've
just got out of the habit and I can't be bothered.
It's easier to cook beans and eggs. Should I keep
the chicken in the freezer and bring it back on
Sunday?

Mum seemed to understand when she replied:

It's our pleasure. You're worth it! How about you
bring the chicken back and I'll use it to make you
some curries to take home instead?

Again, I was incredibly grateful. I knew that the curries would be more
energy-dense and have more oil than the food I made for myself — anything
is more than nothing — but, because I didn't know exactly what was in them,
I would feel ok eating small amounts with my meals.

That weekend, which happened to be Easter, I went to Mum and Dad's and
brought the chicken back. When I put it on the kitchen bench, Mum sighed
loudly.
"Oh, you're giving that back, are you?" She said angrily.
I was confused.
"I thought you were ok with it. You said…"
"We're trying to keep you alive!" She yelled, before storming outside.
I turned to Dad, feeling guilty and hopeless and trying not to cry.
"Should I just go home?" I asked. I felt the afternoon had been ruined and the
atmosphere would be tense if I stayed.
"Hmmm let's see how things go. It's up to you," he mumbled.

While Mum was outside, Dad tried to understand why I didn't want to cook
the chicken.
"I'm not scared of it, there are just so many steps to cooking it and I can't be
bothered. I eat meat when I come here though, you've seen me."
"Can you understand why that's hard for me to believe though?" He asked
gently. "We can tell you're not eating enough just by looking at you."
"I'm trying to turn things around. Everyday I'm trying." I knew it sounded
weak, a lie. I had said it so many times in the past. Each time it had been true,
but all of my trying had only led us back here.
"See, I want to believe you, but we know ED's a liar. He's lying to you and he
makes you lie to us." I still hated it when they personified the ED voice.

"You talk about it like it's a person, but the voice is me. It's coming from my head!"

"That's why we want to help you eat more. It's because your brain is starving that you're having these disordered thoughts."

"Don't you understand why it's so scary for me to eat?" I was incredulous.

He fumbled to find the right words. "Your brain is making you think those thoughts because you've been strengthening those neural pathways."

I was shocked. I already knew rewiring the brain is a big part of recovery, but for me, that wasn't all — if only! I wasn't eating more because I didn't want to put on weight; I knew from experience that I hated and was disgusted with myself at a higher weight. Being thin was the only way I could ease my self-loathing.

"What? Do you think that's all?" I asked, starting to cry.

"Tell me what it is then," Dad said.

And I started to explain, but my sobbing soon prevented me from talking comprehensibly. Dad came forward to hug me, then hesitated, remembering social distancing. Then he shook his head, deciding that consoling me was more important. But I held out my arms to prevent him from coming closer. "No don't. It's fine. I'm ok." I didn't want to risk giving him Covid if I was unknowingly carrying it.

When I had calmed my breathing, I began to explain why I was scared to eat. I was interrupted by Adam's arrival, so Dad suggested he come visit me at Ash's, so we could have a proper chat. A few days later, as we sat on my little verandah drinking tea, I told him that I found myself disgusting; how uncomfortable and gross I had felt at a higher weight when we did Maudsley; and that depriving myself of food and staying thin helped me to lessen my all-consuming, inescapable self-loathing. I was surprised when Dad took his glasses off to wipe away tears. I had assumed that he and Mum knew there was more I needed to work through emotionally, even if they didn't know what exactly. It seems they thought, up until Easter, that I just[31] needed to rewire my neural pathways in order to recover. I think learning that was quite a revelation for Mum and Dad, and it changed their attitude towards me and my recovery.

Though Mum and Dad bought me vegetables — more expensive vegetables than I would have bought for myself too — it was still less than I would usually buy. I usually went through five kilos of carrots every fortnight, because they're cheap and low in calories. If I ran out of vegetables, I would

---

[31] Actually there's no "just" about rewiring neural pathways; it is still very challenging and traumatic and can take years.

feel even more hungry than normal. However, if I gave in to my hunger and ate something more energy-dense, I would be consumed with guilt. When I couldn't find any grocer willing to deliver a few dollars worth of carrots, I decided I would need to go to the Spudshed to buy them myself. I felt bad deceiving Mum and Dad and always worried someone there would give me Covid. I was in and out as fast as possible and kept as much distance from the other customers as I could.

I watched Miss Americana[32] not long after it was released on Netflix. I had been mildly interested in it when I first heard about it, but didn't think it would be particularly interesting or life-changing. I have been a Taylor Swift fan since 2009 but I didn't know much about her other than what I read in headlines. A few months before its release, I watched a clip that showed her speaking about her disordered eating. After that, I was excited to watch the full documentary.

(BMI)

I had always been envious of how thin Taylor was, and it seemed effortless, as it often does with celebrities. I used to google the BMIs of celebrities I thought were thin and found sites that listed them. At the time, I assumed celebrities gave or sold the numbers to these sites — how else would they get the data? — and wondered if they lied, so the public would think they were thinner than they were. Now, I cynically think the sites' authors just estimate the celebrities' BMIs based on their appearance. When I had last looked up Taylor's BMI, about five years before the documentary came out, the sites gave numbers between 16 and 17. I was envious of her for having an anorexic BMI and still being able to keep up her busy schedule. Was she naturally that thin? In more recent photos and videos, I had noticed that her body was bigger, and I wondered if she had been suppressing her weight before.

One of the most helpful things for me was watching Taylor talk about making herself fast for a day or two after she had read a negative review or been fat-shamed by the media. That may seem like schadenfreude, but it wasn't. It made me feel like less of a failure for not being effortlessly thin, as I had thought she was. Hearing her talk about her struggles and thoughts around eating was validating because a lot of it was similar to what I had experienced. I didn't feel quite so alone. I had hoped I might learn something from her recovery that would help me. No such luck.

---

[32] The documentary about Taylor Swift, released in 2020.

I had been worried about contracting Covid from the students I taught at school and wanted to start teaching online straight away. We only had about 20 cases in WA, but we knew how contagious it was and that children could be asymptomatic. Piney College, the school at which I had been teaching for the last year and a half, was setting up Teams accounts so we could teach online. Once I had access to my account I asked if I could teach online the following week. I explained that I was immunocompromised and could get a letter from my GP if they needed proof. I was told we couldn't start online lessons until the following term. There was no explanation given except that that was the official decision. I could have said that I would stop lessons until the next term, as there were only two weeks until the holidays, but I didn't want to lose the income. All of my gigs had been cancelled due to Covid restrictions, so teaching was my only income. I had savings but didn't want to have to use them, because I was always worried about running out of money. I continued to teach, but made my students stand on the far side of the teaching room.

I was relieved when we started teaching online. I had been scared every time I went to school in the last two weeks of the previous term. I didn't need to worry about that at home. I also didn't have to get up so early and could wear pyjama pants to teach. Unfortunately, we only taught online for three weeks; again, that was the official decision. I emailed the school to ask if I could continue teaching online as, being immunocompromised, Covid posed a much higher threat to me. To summarise their reply: the people in charge said they were sympathetic but actually didn't care. I could have kicked up a fuss but, as I was employed as a casual, and there was another violin teacher at the school who could have taken on my students, I decided not to risk losing my only source of income. I asked to teach in the auditorium, as that was a big space no one was using — it was only used for group activities, which had all been cancelled due to Covid — and I could stand four metres away from my students.

To their credit, my students were very understanding, much more so than the admin people. Because I wanted to spend as little time in the school as possible, as that meant being around others, touching surfaces others had touched, I taught my students back to back, with no lunch break. The eating disorder loved the delayed gratification. I didn't get home until about 3 pm, so it was usually 3:30 before I had changed, cooked and sat down to eat lunch. The promise of lunch was what I clung to while I was teaching. I usually started the day already exhausted.

As we came into winter, I cranked the heater, but the auditorium was such a big space it didn't help much, even when I stood directly in the path of warm air. I felt the cold more because I was slowly starving myself and didn't have much body fat. I didn't have many warm clothes that were formal enough to wear to work either. I had decided not to use the staff room, to limit my contact with people, so I couldn't make tea. I drank hot water, and held the mug in my hands and to my chest, in an attempt to warm myself. I had to ration my water intake though, so I wouldn't be running to the toilet every hour.

When it became apparent that the lockdown would last much longer than we had originally thought, I asked Ash again if she wanted me to move out. Again, she said no, so I found myself more jobs to do to help. I tried to do an average of two to three hours of work for her each day, to pay my rent with acts of service. I brought firewood up to the house from the shed, planted vegetables, tidied up a big area of the garden that had become overgrown, took the dogs for extra walks, stacked firewood in the shed and did anything else she asked me to do.

(Exercise, food and food rules)

I was very happy to help wherever I could, but it fed the eating disorder. A lot of the jobs I had started doing for Ash were physical, especially stacking firewood. At first, I enjoyed being outside in the sun. However, the ED voice quickly noticed that I was moving more, therefore burning more calories, and loved it. As the year progressed I did more of this work, for the sake of exercise, and took the dogs for longer walks. Sometimes I took them for two long walks in one day — about an hour to an hour and a half of walking. It would have made me healthy and strong if I wasn't also gradually decreasing my food intake.

I started to think of these physical jobs as part of my daily exercise routine, so when it was too wet to garden, or I couldn't find anything else that needed to be done, I worried about being too sedentary and putting on weight. To alleviate the guilt, I did extra exercises in my room. In winter, though I was often tired, this helped me warm up, at least for half an hour or so afterwards. I also watched tv shows and movies on Netflix while I exercised, so I told myself it was a fun activity. These short exercise sessions soon became part of my compulsory daily exercise, even when the weather allowed me to garden and walk the dogs.

Because I was spending most of my days at home, my meal times weren't dictated by anyone's schedule but my own. I couldn't allow myself to eat earlier than planned, but later was acceptable; in fact, it was applauded by the ED voice. Gradually my meal times slid later. I only ate lunch later than usual for a few days, because I was gardening, before that later time became the norm. I felt greedy just considering moving lunch back to the earlier time after a few days of eating later. At the start of the year, I was eating lunch at 1 pm. It didn't take long for that to shift to 2 pm, then 3 pm. I ate breakfast at 9 am at the beginning of the year, but by the end, I wasn't allowed to eat before 10 am. Dinner was originally 7 pm but gradually moved back to 8 pm.

As I wasn't going out, the ED voice told me I could eat less. If I felt faint at home, I could find something to eat. This wasn't an option when I was out, as I rarely brought food with me — this was usually deliberate, as it forced me to restrict. At home, I made lower-calorie meals, knowing I could eat a bit more if I needed to. However, that "bit more" gradually became less. If I didn't feel as hungry one day and ate less, then I couldn't allow myself to return to my previous calorie allowance the next day. As my digestion and metabolism slowed down, my appetite decreased, and so the downward spiral continued. There were still days when I was hungry though, and wanted to eat more, or earlier, than the ED voice dictated. However, once I had decreased my food allowance, I couldn't increase it. I often went to bed hungry and sometimes had trouble getting to sleep because of the gnawing in my stomach. I lay in bed, scrolling through pictures of #loadedbrownie #sluttybrownie #caramelslice #bigbreakfast and #cheesecake on Instagram.

Even though I only taught at Piney College once a week, and had one or two gigs each week, once Covid restrictions eased, my days were full. Most days, my timetable was the same: I got up at 7 am and exercised, then fed the chickens and had a shower. Sometimes I also walked the dogs before I had a shower, if Ash couldn't. If I didn't walk the dogs, I started practising around 8 or 8.30 am. I had a break for breakfast around 9 or 10 am, then continued practising until 1 pm. Then I walked the dogs, gardened, stacked firewood, and did anything else I thought would help Ash. I allowed myself to eat lunch at 3 pm, then spent another hour or two doing jobs for Ash. After this, I did whatever uni work I needed to do and answered any emails that had come in about gigs. Sometimes I called a friend before dinner, as a lot of us came to rely on phone communication that year. After dinner, I continued my uni work and gig admin until I went to bed.

Realisations and Confusion

One surprising positive of Covid isolation was that I spoke to my friends more. I often found going to people's houses, hosting them, or meeting somewhere stressful, because of all the unknowns and the cost of petrol. Talking on the phone was much easier. There was no travel time or cost and I could talk to them while I was doing something else, such as walking the dogs, gardening, sorting gig music or cooking. I used to hate talking to people on the phone because I felt awkward, but I got used to it that year. I just had to mentally prepare myself before I called. Because I was talking to Perth friends on the phone, I started calling friends in other states too, who I usually just messaged. And because all we could do was talk, without the distraction of food, tv, shops, or anything we may have seen had we met in person, we had great conversations.

As my friends opened up to me about their own struggles, I began to feel comfortable opening up myself. I started thinking about my sexuality again; there was more time for introspection that year. I spoke to my queer friends and did some quizzes on the internet. I know most of them are made by bored teenagers and others with limited knowledge of the subject. But I figured that, if I did a lot of quizzes and they all said the same thing, then maybe they were correct. One test asked me which genders I was attracted to and included non-binary/gender-fluid in the list. I hadn't considered being attracted to non-binary or gender-fluid people before, but couldn't see any reason why I wouldn't be. The result of that quiz was pansexual. I was surprised at first, but it made sense. The friends I told weren't particularly surprised.

I still had doubts that I wasn't straight. I found men attractive, and maybe my attraction to women really was as I had told myself for years — an appreciation of their beauty. My friends kindly answered a lot of direct and very personal questions as I tried to work through this. When I asked a lesbian friend if she found any men attractive at all, she had to really think, before replying:
"Ummmm I mean maybe, if they had long hair? But even then.. hmmm..."
Another straight male friend said he could tell when other men were attractive, but wasn't attracted to them. I didn't quite understand; what was the difference?
For the rest of that year, I asked him similar questions via text, usually out of the blue.

```
Me: Do you find really good-looking men as
attractive as really beautiful women?
```

Friend: No way!

Me: What about a really good-looking man versus a woman you find unattractive?

Friend: I'd definitely prefer to look at the woman."

Me: Do you ever find a man so attractive you don't want to stop looking at him?"

Friend: No, but I definitely do with some women!

Hmmm, I probably wasn't straight then.

I had spoken to El, a non-binary friend, earlier that year about their gender dysphoria. The limited amount I had read about being non-binary sounded similar to what I experienced. When I was young, people said I was a tomboy and, even as I got older, I wasn't really interested in girly things. But I started to wonder if I was non-binary too. It didn't worry me either way, but when I spoke to El, I identified with a lot of what they were saying. They said my experience sounded similar to theirs, but that I could call it whatever I wanted. I didn't have to change my gender identity if I didn't want to.

During lockdown, while Kieran and I went on a socially distanced walk, I told him I had been thinking about my gender identity. I think he had suspected I might be non-binary. However, I was conscious that the way I dress — shorts and a t-shirt if I can get away with it — may make people think that. However, in my opinion, gendered clothing is a social construct; I wear whatever is most comfortable and practical. I considered the gender dysphoria transgender people experience. I had read a lot about the experiences of transgender people in an effort to understand how they feel. I do not, for a moment, think they're making it up; I just haven't been able to understand it. "I just can't understand how they feel; why they care about their gender so much that they feel it's wrong. They can dress more masculine or feminine. Is it that they dislike their genitals? Do I just not understand because I've never had to question my own gender?" I asked.
"My understanding is that trans people can feel so uncomfortable in their body that they feel it isn't theirs. It doesn't match how they feel inside," he explained

"Yeah that's what I read whenever I research it. But I still don't understand why gender is so important. I don't really care. I don't think being a woman is important to who I am."
Kieran was silent for a few seconds. Had I said something offensive?
"I think that's the definition of being non-binary," he said.

I first heard about Tabitha Farrar through Brittany, whose recovery account I followed on Instagram. Sometimes she spoke about things she had read in Tabitha's blog, so one day I googled her and had a read. It was there that I learnt about migration theory,[33] which explained my fear of spending money and why I hoarded food. I didn't hoard to the extreme, but I tried to make expensive food last as long as possible. I also had a very real fear of running out of food — food shortages caused by Covid didn't help. If there was ever food marked "help yourself," leftover from a staff meeting or special occasion at school, I absolutely helped myself, especially if it was a safe food. If I had a container with me I would fill it with fruit and vegetable sticks so I could take them home too. Of course, I was always worried someone would walk in and see me taking all the food for myself.

I read more of Tabitha's blogs and spoke to Brittany about the content, especially the anxiety around spending money. She said she had experienced it too, which made me wonder why it isn't spoken about more. I had thought it was only me, which made me feel very alone and freakish. I spoke to Mum and Dad about migration theory, and I think they were glad I had found it myself. They had read some of Tabitha's work already and identified with it, but had probably thought it best not to talk to me about it, in case it made me angry. I continued to read Tabitha's blogs and watched her YouTube videos for the next year or so. Learning how migration theory affected eating disorders helped me understand my own feelings and made me hopeful for recovery. Unfortunately, it didn't help me to actually eat more.

I had started speaking — I say 'speaking' not 'seeing' because most of our sessions that year were online due to Covid — to a psychologist, Anna, at uni earlier in the year. One day we were talking about the fact that I was scared to gain weight, but also didn't want to lose any more weight, because it would make gaining it back — which I knew I would eventually need to do — even harder. However, whenever I unintentionally lost weight — usually because I didn't eat enough from fear of gaining weight — I felt that my new, slightly smaller body, was the biggest body I could ever accept without hating myself. Anna suggested I write a letter to myself, which I could read if I lost more

---

[33] You can read all about migration theory here: http://tabithafarrar.com

weight and felt disgusted at the thought of gaining it back.

(Calories, weight, BMI, exercise and body-checking)

Dear future Hannah,

If you're reading this it's because you've lost weight and you're trying to convince yourself to eat more.

So, at the moment, I'm about 45kg. If I'm 1.7m my BMI is 15.57; if I'm 1.71m it's 15.39. Congratufrigginlations.

So, I'm writing this to convince you that 45kg is ok. I'm happy with my skinny body and I can see ab definition. My arms are satisfactorily thin and don't squash out at the top. I have a thigh gap and I am often surprised by how narrow my thighs are when I look front-on. My shoulder bones stick up like Guy and Lara's[34] did in year 5. My face is narrow and getting bony. I can see most ribs on my front and my boobs are pretty small. Can't remember about my back ribs... My hip bones are protruding more when I lie down.

At the moment I'm aiming for 900 calories per day. Trying to increase to 1000 but it hasn't happened that I'm aware of.

I've been exercising more. My 35-minute morning routine has become 30, with 15 minutes of squats later in the day, or in the morning as well. I'm also going for a 45-minute to 1-hour walk every day and working in the garden. This has become a habit, which would cause anxiety to stop. The extra workout time in the morning is newish, so I might be able to stop it if I make the move soon.

So, reasons to eat more:
- *Even if you put on weight, 45kg is good.*
- *Your body has heaps of repair work to do, so it will probably use the calories for that.*
- *Your metabolism has slowed down. Eating more will speed it up.*
- *You will feel more energetic and probably move more, which will burn some/all of it up.*
- *It's winter, so you'll use some to stay warm.*

---

[34] Two friends from primary school. One day, when I was ten, I noticed their shoulder bones were visible while mine were not. Even then, I felt that this made them superior in their boniness.

- *If you keep losing you'll have to go back to hospital, where you'll be on bed rest, with a tube, you'll have to gain faster, to a higher weight, uni and practice and work will stop...*

For a while, Ash and I cohabited happily. We lived in separate parts of the house, so sometimes only spoke in the morning, if I was taking the scraps out to the chickens while she was feeding the dogs and cats. That suited me well because I found it stressful living with others. Ash always seemed happy to see me, have a chat, and thank me for whatever work I had done.

From May onwards, she started getting angry with me every few weeks. It was always about something I had done with the best intention, such as walking the dogs, which had annoyed her for whatever reason. She started asking me to do or not do things in a grumpy tone of voice, as though I should have already known what she wanted. I came to feel uncomfortable living there and often avoided her, waiting until she had gone out before leaving my room. I continued to ask every month or so if she wanted me to move out, but she always said no. I did everything I could think of to be helpful and respectful. I did everything she asked but, as the year progressed, her angry outbursts increased. I considered moving out but didn't know where I would go. I figured that we would all be travelling again by the end of the year, so we could go back to our original housesitting arrangement. Then everything would be ok again.

However, it became more and more stressful living there. I never knew when I would unintentionally do something to annoy Ash. There were a few times that she yelled at me. At the time, I accepted her anger, assuming it was my fault, even though I didn't know what I had done. It was only months later, looking back, that I realised I didn't deserve to be treated that way. I did everything I could to keep the peace though, so when she asked me to walk the dogs while it was raining, I obliged, and pretended to be happy to do so. She didn't seem to think it was an unreasonable request, so I assumed that anyone else, who wasn't already exhausted and sensitive to the cold, wouldn't either.

Autism

Around the middle of the year, when some people started holidaying within the state, Ash recommended me to her friends as a house sitter. I hadn't planned to housesit anymore, because I was sick of moving around.
"Do you want me to start housesitting again so you can have the place to yourself?" I asked.
"No no, I just thought you might enjoy it," she replied.
Since I often felt stressed living with her, I decided to accept the housesits. I thought I would probably be able to relax more in a house by myself and would have more time for my uni work, as I wouldn't be gardening or walking the dogs.
"Ok sure, thanks. But let me know if you want me to drop in to feed the animals or walk the dogs if you're busy," I always offered.
It was a relief to be alone, not needing to worry about annoying Ash. I was always disappointed and apprehensive about moving back to her place when the sits came to an end.

It was during one of these sits that I started thinking about Autism. I had been pondering the genetic link between Autism and AN and it got me thinking about my conversation with Morgana, almost three years earlier, when they told me it was a myth that Autistic people don't feel empathy. What had they meant? I almost didn't message them to ask, because they sometimes take months to respond. But I'm glad I did. They responded within about ten minutes, with a few very long messages full of information, links to articles and questionnaires, and some helpful YouTube videos. They also invited me to some Facebook groups for Autistic adults.

For the next few days, I watched videos from the YouTubers Morgana had recommended, read articles, joined some subReddits, did the questionnaires and asked them a lot of questions. They explained the empathy myth, how Autism presents differently in girls and also said that, since they started learning about Autism, they had suspected I might be Autistic too. I identified with so much of what I read — not everything, but Autism is a spectrum after all.

A few days later, I messaged Mum to ask her what she thought about me being on the spectrum. She seemed excited and asked a lot of questions. By text, I explained the myth about empathy, then sent her some of the links from Morgana. We messaged about it a lot for the next few days and had a proper chat when I visited next.

Unsurprisingly, Mum had done even more reading than me since I messaged her. She was already a fan of Tony Attwood and had read some of Simon Baron-Cohen's[35] papers — I think he was already on her radar because of his work with AN. When I was a baby and toddler, Mum had sometimes wondered if I was Autistic, but accessing scientific papers was much harder then, in the early 90s. She would have needed to go to a university library and she had enough on her plate with difficult baby me. And, even if she had read the current research, it would have said that Autistic people don't feel empathy and only addressed the Autistic traits identified in boys. There wasn't much known about Autism in girls at that time.

Mum asked me about some of the things she had read and was surprised by my answers. There were a lot of everyday things I hadn't spoken about because I thought they were normal. She and Dad were shocked to learn that I rarely look people in the eye, and find it uncomfortable when I do. I usually look at different parts of people's faces when I speak to them — their eyelids, nose, eyebrows, cheeks, ears — and assumed everyone else did the same. In books, people only talk about looking into the eyes of their lover; when I was younger, Mum and Dad sometimes told me to look them in the eye, to check I wasn't lying. I thought looking into someone's eyes was a rarity.

The other big discoveries were around social cues. I learnt that Autistic girls often attach themselves to another, louder girl, whose cues they can follow when necessary, and behind whom they can hide to some extent. I realised I had done this with Adam for most of my life, and that I had struggled when he wasn't there anymore. Growing up, music was a big part of our lives and, whenever we went to new places and different group settings — music camps, performances etc. — Adam was almost always there, and I followed his lead. I knew I was doing this but assumed it was normal — he knew what to say and do because he was older. When I became older, I thought I struggled in new situations because I was a bit socially awkward. Adam was better at these things because "he's a people person," as Mum sometimes said.

Mum especially, was surprised that I thought I was socially awkward.
"You were always the one cracking jokes, before you got sick and didn't have the energy."
"Yeah, but I feel comfortable with you guys," I explained. "I've known you my whole life and I know you won't judge me if I make a mistake and say something embarrassing."

---

[35] Yep, Sacha's brother.

"But even when we're out with family friends. You used to tease everyone and joke around," Mum said.
"But you're always there too, so I feel relatively safe. And I can follow your lead if I don't know what to say or do. When I'm with others — without you there — I don't know what to do and I feel really awkward."
"Really?" Mum and dad looked shocked.
"Yeah. But you're not there to see it, so…"

For most of my life, I had felt different, but couldn't put my finger on what that difference was. It didn't bother me until I was about ten years old; try as I might, I couldn't figure out how to be "normal." After a few years, I just accepted that I was socially awkward and weird. In high school especially, I felt as though everyone else just knew how to act and what to say. I used to wonder if they all read a teen magazine I didn't know about; or if someone explained these things during the video hits show most people watched on Saturday mornings, but which I always missed because I had a WAYO rehearsal. Mum and Dad were shocked and sad to hear all of this. They asked why I hadn't told them. But I had been so confused that I didn't know how, or what, to tell them. If I couldn't comprehend my own confusion, how could I articulate it for someone else? And I would have felt embarrassed.

They also hadn't realised that this general awkwardness meant that I felt like a bit of an outcast at school, despite constantly trying to fit in.
"But you had friends at school. They came over to the house and they were lovely," Mum said.
"Yeah, they were also uncool," I replied.
I had spent a lot of time analysing the social ladder at our school, and where each friendship group ranked. My group of friends was second from the bottom. When I explained this, Mum thought I had misinterpreted things. We were pretty sure I was Autistic at this point and had been discovering just how many things, especially social cues, I had misunderstood. But I knew I was right about this one.
"Well think about it," I explained. "I was unfashionable, a bit of a nerd, I almost always did the right thing in class — a goody-two-shoes — I played violin, I didn't go to raging parties… that's almost the stereotypical loser."
Mum was still having trouble accepting this. Dad looked thoughtful for a few seconds before saying, "Yeah, that's a good point."
I wasn't offended.

We talked more about Autism from then on. I spoke to friends about it too, especially Gilbert, Jen, (a friend I met in Hobart), Lucy and Kieran. None of them were surprised. Actually, everyone I spoke to about it either wasn't surprised; said "Well I wondered, but you're so empathetic," or "But you do eye contact;" or thought I already knew and had a diagnosis. Gilbert was slightly embarrassed to admit that there had been times, a few years earlier, when I had texted him random questions without any opening chit-chat, and he and Morgana had laughed about my directness. I wasn't at all offended. On the contrary, I welcomed all evidence to support my theory that I was Autistic.

Talking to Anna helped me discover, unpack and understand a lot of the causes of my eating disorder. Growing up I was — and still am — often unsure if people were being friendly or unfriendly when they spoke to me, unless it was blatantly obvious. I learnt to assume the worst, just to be on the safe side. I didn't want to think someone was a friend, only to be rejected, so I was always cautious. This caused me to think I was socially awkward, uncool, fat, ugly, not good at whatever I was doing, unloveable, disgusting etc. My incorrect assumptions originated in caution, however, confirmation bias began to play a role. We spoke about the many occasions this had happened in my life and how I may have misinterpreted the other person's intentions.

I thought back to when I was about six years old and throughout my teenage years, when I dressed up or did something different with my hair. When Mum and Dad noticed, they would make a bit of a fuss and say "oooh" and "Don't you look grown up." At the time, I thought they were either mocking me kindly, because I had unknowingly made myself look stupid, or trying to embarrass me, to discourage me from dressing in a style too old for my age. When I voiced these thoughts to Anna, I started to wonder if I had misinterpreted their reactions. She encouraged me to ask Mum and Dad about it, so I wouldn't have to guess.

Mum and Dad seemed confused when I asked them, because they thought the answer was obvious.
"Well, we were excited that you were dressing up, wearing something different. We thought you looked lovely. What did you think we meant?"
I started to cry when I tried to speak. They were sad too when I finally got the words out and became teary themselves. We mourned for the younger me, who had felt embarrassed and confused and stopped expressing herself or trying to look nice, for fear of being laughed at.

I also (finally) realised that I had been misinterpreting comments about body size. Whenever someone said they could see Adam's ribs but didn't say anything about me, I deduced that I wasn't as thin as Adam, and therefore not as good or worthy. If Mum made a comment about herself being slim, but said nothing about me, I worried that I wasn't in the slim club with her, and was therefore "other" (in my mind: normal-sized or fat). I don't know if there were times when someone commented on my small build without mentioning Mum or Adam because I wouldn't have felt the need to worry.

Tales of Exhaustion

I had been having my violin lessons — in preparation for my Masters recital — online all year which, for the most part, had been great. I didn't need to drive to uni, I could wear pyjama pants, I felt more comfortable because I was in my own space, I could warm up until Lee, my teacher, started the meeting, so my fingers were ready to play, and I could eat breakfast just before my lesson, so I was less likely to get hungry and tired. During winter, I decided it was safe to have lessons in person again. I should have driven into uni so I wouldn't need to use public transport — even though there hadn't been any evidence of community transmission, I remained suspicious until late August, and taking public transport meant exposing myself to the respiration of a lot of people — but paying for parking makes me anxious, and I didn't want to tire myself out just before my lesson by walking for half an hour from the free parking spaces. I couldn't allow myself to eat at home before I left to catch the train, because I left before 9 am. I also worried that, if I ate before I left, I would get hungry again during the hour and a half it took to get to uni. I took my breakfast with me and ate it at uni, just before my lesson. I always hoped I wouldn't see anyone I knew, so they wouldn't hold me up or talk to me while I was eating. Often I was already hungry when I left home and had trouble concentrating on reading my book during the journey to uni. In Winter and Spring, I felt the cold even more than usual, because I didn't have any food in my belly.

Though I wanted to learn and improve my playing as much as possible, lessons became harder the less I ate. I usually had some degree of lightheadedness, so it was hard to concentrate. I often had to decide whether I should put all of my energy into playing, or save a bit, so I wouldn't need to worry about fainting on the way home. Even when I did give it my all, it wasn't much; I felt faint, as though my body was visibly fading.

In the spirit of efficiency, I tried to do everything that required me to be at uni on the days I had my lessons, so I wouldn't need to make an extra trip. This was partly to save travel time and mostly to save money on petrol and train fares. Often I went to the library and saw Anna or Krish after my lessons, even though I was usually famished and exhausted after my lesson. Krish was about ten minute's drive from uni, which was handy. However, as I took public transport in, I had to take a bus to his practice, which wasn't hard but also wasn't as fast as driving. It usually took about an hour for me to take the bus, wait for my appointment — Krish was almost always running late — and finish my appointment, then another hour and a half to get home.

I was usually exhausted and lightheaded in my appointments, but I did my best to appear energetic. Krish is usually chatty, but I was too tired to make conversation. I wanted to get out of there as quickly as possible so I could get home and eat — I never brought any food with me because, if I didn't bring anything, I couldn't eat anything. I pretended to be surprised and disappointed when my weight dropped, which it usually did. I offered vague excuses, such as being dehydrated — though I usually tried to drink at least half a litre of water before my appointments — or stressed. I'm not sure if he believed me.

One Sunday morning in September, when I was walking back to the house after taking the bins to the road, Ash came out of the house to meet me.
"Do you have time to talk later today?" She asked.
I had a gig later that day and wasn't sure how long she wanted to talk, or when she had in mind, so I stuttered for a few seconds, trying to work out what to ask or say.
"I've decided to get some backpackers in to work in the garden. If I give them a place to stay, they'll work for free. I want to give them the upstairs area so I'll need you to move out."
That was sudden.
"Oh," I said, as I felt my stomach drop and my head spin for a few seconds.
"Is there somewhere else you can move?" It wasn't really a question.
"Ummm not that I know of at the moment… How long do I have to find a place, before you need me to leave?" I asked.
"Well, it depends on when I find someone. I've put an ad up online, so it could be a few days or a few weeks." Unhelpfully vague.
The conversation ended quickly after that and I went inside to stress and try to find a new home.

After I recovered from the initial shock and anxiety about paying rent, I decided it was probably a good idea for me to move out. I had been stressed for about half the time I had been living there, always worried I might annoy Ash, or knowing that I had, but unsure how or why. I reassured myself by reasoning that I would only need to pick up a few hours of teaching to cover rent. I would also have more time to do uni work or relax if I wasn't working a few hours for Ash every day.

I started contacting friends straight away. A few potentially had rooms to rent out, but they were all either short-term, too expensive or wouldn't be available for another few months. Of course, I could have stayed with Mum and Dad, but having them see what I ate, potentially forcing me to eat more, and having to somehow hide my exercise from them, made it less appealing than living in my car and showering at the beach — yes, I did seriously consider that as an option.

One friend suggested I ask Adam if I could rent his spare room. He had bought a house two years earlier, a few months after he and Avril broke up. He had been putting off looking for a housemate since then because he didn't want to live with a stranger and all of his friends were either living with partners or had bought their own houses. He had said, not long after he bought the house, that he would happily live with me. However, at that time, I was happily housesitting and living rent-free. I didn't think he would want to live with me now though, since my eating had become so disordered again. It would put him in an awkward position with Mum and Dad, not to mention his own possible discomfort and worry. Adam would be great to live with though, so I asked him, just in case. I messaged him just before I went to sleep a few nights later and woke in the morning to two texts:

```
Heya, happy for you to stay here short term until
you find somewhere else.
```

My stomach sank.

```
Actually, I've reconsidered. You'd be a great
housemate. I don't see any reason why you couldn't
stay long-term.
```

Phew! We talked on the phone about costs and a few other things, then made a time for me to come over to see the room again.

To save petrol, I visited Adam after a violin lesson, so I wouldn't have to make an extra trip to the city. I knew I would be tired, but also knew I could struggle through. I convinced the ED voice to let me drive in because taking multiple buses to Adam's from uni would take too long. After he showed me my room, bathroom and other areas — I had only been to his house a few times — we sat down to discuss details. I was incredibly grateful that he had the wisdom to increase my weekly rent — to include average power, gas and water costs in the figure — so I wouldn't need to worry about suffering in the heat or cold to save money.

One of us had brought up the elephant in the room — my eating disorder — when we were texting about living together. Adam brought it up again while I was there. I didn't have the energy to dance around the subject or treat it with delicacy, so I just lay all the facts on the table. I told him what I usually ate for each meal, that I had strict rules regarding the times I ate, and that I exercised in my room each morning. He didn't appear too surprised and I think he was relieved to finally know the truth, instead of having to guess. He said that, aside from obviously being worried for my physical and mental health, my odd habits wouldn't bother him.

About a month earlier, Krish had sent a referral for me to The Numbat Practice. At the time, it was the only outpatient clinic in Perth specifically for people with eating disorders. CCI was still treating people, however, being government funded, they only had a limited number of sessions for each client. Unfortunately, as with CCI, The Numbat Practice has a long waiting list. I received a call from their receptionist around the time I spoke to Adam about moving in, asking if I could come in for an appointment, so they could tell me about what they had to offer and assess my situation. I was excited to start treatment and the way the receptionist spoke about the assessment made me think that people who were at a higher risk, like me, might be moved further up the waiting list. I didn't think that was fair on people who weren't as sick yet, however, if they were offering me treatment, I would take it. I felt I was ready to have another go at recovery, after all the things I had uncovered about myself that year.

I had been to The Numbat Practice not long after I got out of hospital, to see their dietician. Parking had been scarce, so I decided to take public transport this time. I was tired when I left home and navigating trains and buses tired me out more than driving would have. I was feeling lightheaded before I arrived and knew it would be a long time before I returned home and could eat again. Until then, water would have to suffice. I was also very cold. It was September so the weather was up and down.

My appointment was with Miranda, a registrar psychologist. After I recounted my eating disorder journey, which took a while, she told me about the treatment they offered.
"We use Cognitive Behavioural Therapy (CBT) because evidence proves it has the best results." She said this last part sternly; I'm not sure why. When I had done CBT ten years earlier, it hadn't been very helpful, but I was willing to give it another go. My circumstances had changed a lot since then; I was now living away from home, choosing my own food, and had come to realise just how insecure I was and why. Maybe it would be better this time.

At the end of the appointment, she measured my height and weighed me, making sure to cover the number on the screen.
"Oh gosh," she sighed, openly dismayed.

I was surprised at her reaction.
"It's not that low, is it? Surely you've seen worse?" I asked.
"I don't think I'll ever stop being shocked at what I see here," she replied.
I was worried. Maybe things were worse than I realised. The ED voice congratulated me.

A young French couple had come to look at the property and meet Ash about a week before I spoke to Adam about moving in with him. When I told her I had found a place, she said she had decided not to take the couple on, because she hadn't liked their vibe. She said I might be able to stay longer because she hadn't had anyone else respond to her online advertisement. I decided it was better to leave. I didn't want to live there in limbo, waiting to see if someone else responded to the advertisement. And Ash telling me I needed to go had made me conscious of how stressed I felt living there. I was looking forward to leaving. I had a housesit in a week or two and would move out then. After the housesit, I would go to Adam's.

I started moving my belongings back to Mum and Dad's, bringing a box or two whenever I visited. I could keep them there until I moved to Adam's. They were happy I was moving; I had spoken to them about the times Ash had gotten angry with me, and how stressed I had become. They also thought living with Adam would be good for me.

I wasn't sure what to expect when I said goodbye to Ash. She had been treating me more like an employee than a friend as the year progressed. Should I hug her? Get her a present? I decided to see how she acted and mirror her. She was in her office working when I finished packing my car, so I knocked and went in.
"I'm all packed up and ready to go. Just been saying goodbye to the dogs," I said awkwardly.
"Have you cleaned your room and the bathroom?" She asked.
"Yep. Do you want to check, in case I've missed something?"
"No, no, I'm sure it's fine."
I felt like a lowly employee might, as they said goodbye to a manager with whom they had had little contact.
"Ok. Well, let me know if there are any problems. I can come back and fix anything you need," I offered.
"Thanks, I will." She didn't make any move to get up.
"Ok well, I'll head off now. Thanks for... for everything. I'm housesitting nearby if you need anything."
"Have fun. I'll be in touch," she said in farewell.

I felt it was very strange and businesslike. But it didn't matter anymore. I was leaving. The relief I felt as I drove down Ash's driveway was similar to what I had felt the day I left Mum and Dad's eight years earlier.

I had been looking forward to housesitting; it would be my last chance to live alone for a while. The family for whom I was housesitting had bought a puppy about six weeks before they went away. When I went to meet them, they said he should be toilet trained by the time I came to stay. I agreed that six weeks was plenty of time to toilet-train a puppy. A few days before I moved, the mother of the family said the puppy wasn't quite toilet trained, but that they had lots of floor pads, wipes and disinfectant for me to use. I assumed she meant he had an accident every so often.

Unfortunately, he wasn't toilet trained at all. I think the family assumed dogs just work it out themselves, after a while — they had never had a puppy before. They had been putting puppy pads in the playpen and throughout the house, and changing them after they were soiled. When they went out they put the dog in the bathroom, with lots of pads, then refreshed them when they got home. It was not the restful week I had hoped for. It was tiring, getting up to the dog in the middle of the night when he needed to go to the toilet and stressing about dirty pads. I started toilet training him myself, in the hope it would mean cleaning up less wet pads. He improved a bit, at the expense of my energy levels. Still, it was better than being at Ash's. I was looking forward to moving to Adam's though — I wouldn't have the house to myself, but at least Adam was toilet trained!

I moved some of my things to Adam's that week. Kieran had two beds and a chest of drawers he wanted to get rid of, left behind by two ex-housemates. Dad was happy to help and it wasn't hard to borrow a ute from Grandpa, (Dad's dad) who has all sorts of utes and trucks. As Dad wanted to make the trip after he had eaten lunch, and I couldn't eat lunch before 3 pm, I decided to wait until I got home, after dropping off the beds, to eat. I felt I was making progress in recovery by bringing an apple to eat as a snack.

(Food)

It was a big expedition for my tired body. First, I drove to Mum and Dad's which wasn't far from where I was housesitting. From there, we went to Grandpa's — again not far. It was about half an hour to Kieran's, where it took some time to carry the furniture out and secure it on the trailer. Then another half hour to Adam's, where it took a while to manoeuvre everything into the house. By this time I was very hangry and had to work hard to stop myself from snapping at Dad and Adam. Everything took longer than I had hoped. It was already after 3 pm when we left Adam's. Luckily Dad was also keen to get home, probably to have a cup of tea with Mum. After we left Adam's, we drove back to Grandpa's to drop off the ute and say hello, then to Mum and Dad's where I had left my car. I declined the offer of a cup of tea and drove back to the housesit. It was 4 or 5 pm by then. I was exhausted and ravenous, but the ED voice reasoned that, if I had lunch then, I wouldn't be hungry at dinner time. I decided to wait it out, then I would be allowed to eat a bigger dinner too. I tried to distract my body from its hunger by chewing gum and drinking sugar-free cordial and soft drinks. I struggled to focus on my uni work that evening and developed terrible hunger pains, which lasted a few hours.

It was a relief to finally move to Adam's and settle. I was worried about cohabiting with someone again and having him see what I ate, but decided I would just have to see how things turned out. Adam was away with friends when I moved in and returned a few days later. I was grateful to have that time to settle in on my own. He had left a bunch of flowers and a card in my room — why was he being so kind? I enjoyed nesting and even felt ok spending money on some house necessities — a clock, toilet brush, mirror, and small whiteboard for teaching — though I compared prices between stores online first and bought everything from Kmart. It was freeing to have more time to myself too, now that I wasn't doing jobs for Ash. I went for walks to explore the neighbourhood, joined the library and worked on my thesis.

(Exercise)

As I wasn't doing any work in the garden or taking the dogs for long walks, I felt I needed to exercise more on my own. At first, I did one or two 15-minute workouts later in the day, usually before lunch and dinner. However, it didn't take long for these extra workouts to start weighing on my mind throughout the day until I had completed them. I started doing them just before breakfast and then, to eradicate all anticipatory anxiety, added them to my morning exercise. My morning workout session had grown to be about an hour long and I always dreaded it.

I wasn't quite as relaxed when Adam came home. I always thought twice about everything I did, asking myself if it would annoy him. I felt awkward if we were both cooking or eating at the same time, so I often waited until he had finished cooking before I did, and tried to make my snacks look normal if I ate when he was around. He wasn't working, because he had resigned from his job not long after all the Covid restrictions started, and was still looking —

along with everyone who had lost their job due to Covid. He was at home more than he would have been had he been working, but still went out to see friends, go to cafes, do a bit of freelance work and generally keep himself busy. I always felt much more relaxed when he was out and I had the house to myself.

It was about six weeks before my Master's recital when I moved to Adam's. I had sometimes worried, earlier in the year, that Ash might suddenly ask me to do a job or walk the dogs, just as I was getting ready to leave for my recital, so I was glad I was no longer living with her. Adam also understood the stress and work involved in putting on a recital. I prepared as well as I could for the performance. I did practice run-throughs of my pieces at home and in the auditorium where the recital would be held, even when I was exhausted. The ED voice told me it was good to practise performing when I was tired because I would be nervous and stressed during the actual performance. The voice also told me that I mustn't be too malnourished if I was able to get through the hour-long run-throughs after a day of teaching. In hindsight, I was definitely running on adrenaline and willpower. I also organised two performances at the Roleystone church and did a lunchtime performance at a hospital, so I could practise in front of an audience. I was proud of what I had managed to organise and felt that, once the recital was over, I would have the head space to focus more on recovery.

I had meticulously timetabled my preparation and eating for the day of my recital a few weeks earlier. I considered skipping my morning exercise so I had more energy to get through the day, but decided it would be less stressful to just do it as usual; I always made it through on willpower. Unfortunately, my recital was at 3 pm, which was the earliest I allowed myself to eat lunch, unless it was absolutely necessary and unavoidable to eat earlier. The ED voice suggested waiting until after the recital to eat, but luckily the healthy part of my brain won that argument. I packed my lunch, took it to uni and ate around 2 pm, just before I went into the auditorium to warm up. I was already exhausted when I left home to get the bus to uni — I decided to take the bus, partly so I wouldn't have to worry about finding a parking spot, but mostly because I didn't want to pay six dollars for parking. I had been stressed all morning and it had already tired me out. I hoped I would get another hit of adrenaline soon, to get me through the performance.

While I was waiting for my connecting bus, an old man approached me.
"What instrument is that you've got there?" He asked.
I don't have much patience for old white men — who think they're wise and want to tell me a yarn about how they used to play <insert instrument here>

back in the day and could have been a professional musician if they had stuck at it, and wasn't I lucky to be doing what I loved? — at the best of times, but I usually try to be polite. That day, I didn't.

"Violin," I said shortly, before turning away and taking out my phone. I didn't have the energy for conversation. I already felt light-headed, my stomach was empty and I wanted to be able to put all of myself into this performance, to show what I was capable of. I had worked too hard. If the man thought I was a rude, technology-obsessed youth, then good for him.

Unfortunately, I didn't get a second hit of adrenaline before my recital. However, I was used to doing full days of work with no energy and a dead brain, so I forced myself to concentrate, as I always did. About 15 minutes into the performance, I got a dopamine hit from the music instead. It was the first time in a long while that I actually enjoyed performing. Even the audience could see that I was enjoying myself at times. It wasn't perfect, but it was about as good as I could have expected. During my planning, the healthy part of me had beaten the ED voice, allowing me to pack some nuts and dried fruit to eat during the short interval. Unfortunately, when I visited the toilet, I bumped into a friend who had kindly come to watch, and we chatted for a bit. When I returned to the green room, I only had time to eat a few nuts before it was time to go back onstage. I figured it didn't really matter. What difference was one more date or nut going to make to my energy or concentration anyway?

I made it through the recital and was happy, proud, relieved, and grateful to Lee, Heidi, who was accompanying me again, and everyone who had supported me and come to watch. I was also exhausted, but somehow happiness and necessity kept me going. I basked in my success and freedom. I was truly proud of what I had achieved, especially while malnourished and after an incredibly stressful year!

A few weeks after my recital, my dog Noddy came to live with Adam and me — he had continued to live with Mum and Dad when I moved out. We had talked about Noddy living with us the day I went to Adam's to discuss everything before I moved in, and he was happy for him to come. I had wanted to wait until after my recital though, because I didn't have the time, energy or head space to think about anything else.

(Exercise)

It was nice to have Noddy living with us, and friends who visited loved him too. I started taking him for daily walks, mostly for his benefit. These walks were in addition to my morning exercise, so they usually added to my general exhaustion. On the rare occasion that the additional exercise didn't drain me, the ED voice took the opportunity to tell me that I mustn't be as sick as I thought and that it was placebo making me feel tired on the other days. As we came into summer, I started walking Noddy in the morning, just after my exercise. This made sense weather-wise, but it meant I was doing over an hour of physical activity as soon as I got up, before eating anything. I felt relieved when I got home from the walks, that my exercise was done for the day.

I didn't get much of a rest before I proceeded to the next phase of my research. I had to test and record my evaluation of the hundreds of exercises I had devised to help other violinists learn one of the pieces I had performed in my recital. It was exciting, but also time-consuming and tiring. It took about a month to test them all. I spent my mornings practising the exercises and writing a brief evaluation, and the afternoons and nights notating them. I rarely took breaks except to eat and sleep. I wanted to finish the testing as quickly as possible, so I could write the main part of my thesis. It was due in March and most of it couldn't be written until I finished the testing phase. I should have finished it in September, before my recital, but Covid had thrown a spanner in the works, so I had been granted an extension to March.

Work and Uni

Mum had asked the Western Australian Eating Disorders Outreach Consultation Service (WAEDOCS) if they could recommend any Autism diagnosticians who also had an understanding of AN. There is a crossover in the presentation of AN and ASD — such as perfectionism, rigidity, OCD and aversion to certain foods — and we wanted to make sure I wasn't incorrectly diagnosed with Autism because of my AN behaviours. They recommended Dr Khan, a psychiatrist, so I made an appointment to see him in January. I hadn't had many good experiences with psychiatrists, however, as he had been recommended, I felt positive.

"I'm confused," Dr Khan said, after I had recounted the last fifteen years of my medical and mental health history. "Anorexia is always caused by problems with the family or parents, but you have told me you have quite a good relationship with your family."
Red flag! Doctors used to think parents were the cause of eating disorders, however, that myth was debunked years ago. I decided to let it go. I was here about Autism anyway, not AN. Instead, I told him that it was Mum's comment in the changing room that had been the main trigger; it had made me determined to restrict my food properly, with strict rules, so I could lose weight as fast as possible.
"Ah yes, that makes sense," he said, smiling and nodding.

After a brief conversation about what had led me to believe I was Autistic, he got me to fill out two questionnaires, which I had already done online. He was keen for me to fill them out quickly and didn't want to answer my queries about the meaning of some of the questions. I assumed it was one of those cases where you're meant to go with your gut and answer based on your interpretation. My scores in both showed that it was likely I was Autistic. I would need to have a proper assessment, but Dr Khan said the questionnaires were usually correct.

He also asked me to fill out two questionnaires about eating, weight and shape. I used to answer the same questionnaires every month at CCI. They ask about food restriction, obsession with weight and shape, purging, binging etc. "Hmmm this score puts you in the high to severe category for a restrictive eating disorder," he commented, surveying my results.
"Ummm... yep..." Why had he asked me to do those questionnaires? Was he trying to fill up the appointment time? It was quite obvious I had AN. Krish had listed it in my referral letter and I had just told him about it, including the hospital admissions. Dr Khan said he would be in touch about when he would

be doing assessments. He conducts them with a neuropsychologist and they only do them a few times a year, when they can get their individual schedules to line up.

I had accepted a job teaching violin at Westin Primary School that year. I figured I would have more time to work now that my recital was over, and also felt that I needed to make a bit more money to pay for rent. Another friend had taught there for a long time; she said it was her favourite school and that it had a really nice community. I would have to take group classes, which I didn't know that I would enjoy, but I decided to give it a go. I really liked the atmosphere of the school when I went in at the end of the previous year, to observe the orchestra and have an interview.

Unfortunately, lessons had to be on Wednesdays — most other schools allow music tutors to choose their teaching days. This meant that, if SO offered me work again, I wouldn't be able to take it, as they usually have rehearsals on Wednesdays. I could occasionally organise a relief teacher, but they didn't want me to do that more than once a term. SO hadn't offered me any work since the end of 2019, but most casuals hadn't been offered much work in 2020, because of Covid. I decided I would accept the job at Westin anyway and see what happened with SO.

After the usual first few weeks of additional stress, as I got used to how the school operated and worked out how to run my own lessons, I settled into a routine:
9:30 am: I arrived at school half an hour before I started teaching, to make sure I got a parking spot and had enough time to get myself ready for class. After leaving my violin and books in the teaching room, I went to the main staff room. There I made myself a bottle of herbal tea and a hot chocolate, made with half skim milk and half water, cocoa and sugar-free sweetener. I put the hot chocolate in the fridge, which become a cold chocolate, by the time I drank it after school. I drank tea almost constantly while I was teaching. The fluid helped me to feel full and the taste punctuated my tiredness and hunger with a moment of happiness.

(Food rules and food)

10 am: The students in my first class were lovely, but sometimes used up all of my energy, leaving me drained for the rest of the day.
10:45 am: My first class left for recess and I got to eat breakfast. I usually ate at 10 am, but couldn't because that's what I started teaching. As I couldn't allow myself to eat earlier, I had to hold out until recess. Sometimes I didn't

have time to eat it all and would finish it at lunch. I always hoped none of the other teachers would talk to me at recess because I didn't have the energy to hold a conversation and talking prevented me from eating.
11:15 am: I had two group classes between recess and lunch, then a short break at lunch before a private student.
1:30 pm: After lunch, I had two more group classes, before school finished for the day.
3 pm: I had two lovely private students after school and I always looked forward to teaching them. It was such a treat after group classes. I was usually exhausted and just wanted to go home, but they were so lovely I made myself give them my best.

3 pm was my usual lunchtime, however, I felt it would be unprofessional to eat my usual lunch while I was teaching; hence the cold chocolate drink I prepared in the morning. I also brought a piece of fruit, chopped into bite-sized pieces for easy eating, as a substitute for the vegetables I usually ate at lunch. Eating the fruit was scary because I knew it contained more carbohydrates and sugar than vegetables, but I kept reminding myself that the extra calories counteracted the loss of the protein and fat that was in my usual lunch. It was much less volume than I was accustomed to though, and I usually felt as though I had a gaping hole in my stomach — unless I was constipated, which became more common as the year progressed. My small lunch allowed me to appreciate dinner even more than usual, unless I had stomach cramps from lack of food, which also became more common as the year progressed.

A few weeks into the school term, I received an email from SO, offering me a few weeks of work. As soon as I read it I felt butterflies in my tummy, and not the happy type. I knew it wasn't a good sign. While I loved playing with the orchestra, I had been finding the social aspect increasingly stressful towards the end of 2019. Try as I might, I always felt that I didn't fit in. I always worried that others were judging me and thought I was weird, unprofessional, boring and uncool. I don't know if anyone actually thought this; I have always had trouble interpreting people's body language and tone of voice. From the age of about eight, if ever I was unsure of the implicit meaning behind a person's words or actions, I learnt that it was safest to assume the worst. When I was working at SO regularly, I had come to accept the stress but, after over a year away, the thought of going back was daunting. I would need to organise a relief teacher at Westin too. If SO were going to start offering me regular work again, as they had before Covid, I would need to either decline the work or leave Westin. In the end, after a lot of thought, I turned SO down, explaining the clash with teaching. I was relieved. They asked me to play a few weeks later but, again, rehearsals clashed with teaching at Westin. SO stopped asking after that. They probably decided it was unlikely I would be available to play, which is fair enough.

I told everyone, and myself, that working at Westin was hard work, but rewarding. That's what all the other teachers there said, and I almost convinced myself that it was normal to be tired at the end of the day. And it probably was. However, there is a difference between tiredness and an exhaustion so heavy that only willpower allowed me to lift myself out of the car when I got home. That's not a busy day of teaching; that's malnutrition. It usually took me the whole of the next day to recover.

When I finished testing the exercises I had composed, I started writing up the rest of my thesis. Ellen suggested I request another extension to May; aiming to finish in March was not a realistic goal. For a while, I struggled to get my head around the structure of the thesis; which information belonged in which chapter. I should have gone to more of the writing workshops offered at uni, but they were always on Wednesdays, which was the day I taught at Westin.

I had some meetings in person with Ellen and Jo, but they usually suggested having them at 2 pm — probably because it was after their lunch break, however it was just before I usually ate lunch, at 3 pm — so I was always hungry, lightheaded, and struggling to concentrate. Every time I went to the meetings, I told myself to suck it up, deal with the tiredness and ask the questions I needed to ask. But I always chickened out. I worried they would think my questions were stupid or annoying, or that I was wasting their time by asking questions I should have been able to answer myself. And I was usually so tired and hungry I didn't have the brain power for the discussion that was sure to follow my query. I was also acutely aware that I still had to wait another hour after our meeting, before the bus would get me back home to eat my very late lunch.

As I wrote my thesis, Ellen and Jo often told me that certain topics and paragraphs belonged in different chapters. I didn't understand their reasoning. Was my experience in academic writing too limited, or was I just bad at it? Was my starved brain preventing me from grasping their logic or was this another case of me interpreting a situation in my own odd way, which made perfect sense to me, but no one else? I asked friends who had written theses and dissertations for advice and looked at how other theses were organised, but still couldn't work out how to apply their structure to my research. I constantly doubted myself and worried that Ellen and Jo were regretting their decision to supervise me. Was it normal for them to need to make so many corrections to my work? Did other students bug their supervisors this much?

In May, my name finally came to the top of the waiting list at The Numbat Practice. I was excited. I could only see Anna once a month or less because she had so many clients. At The Numbat Practice, I would have to pay, but the psychologists were trained to treat eating disorders specifically. I wouldn't have a limited number of sessions, as had been the case at CCI, either. I hoped we would be able to increase my food slower, and spend more time working through my deep self-hatred and building my self-esteem. I also hoped the psychologist might be able to judge, unofficially, if I was Autistic. Surely they had lots of Autistic clients there since there are so many people with eating disorders who are also Autistic.

The psychologist I was assigned, Laura, was lovely, but I worried that she would think I wasn't skinny enough to need treatment. She was so slim and glamorous herself. I took a risk though, and was open and honest, even about the things that embarrassed me. It was her job to be nice and not judge me anyway. I had looked at her profile on The Numbat Practice website and was disappointed to see that she was still a registrar. I thought the centre employed the best psychologists, who had lots of experience treating eating disorders, not people barely out of university. I wondered if they had had to lower their standards as they struggled to cater for their growing number of clients, which had increased rapidly since Covid. I had hoped they would assign me to someone with more experience, especially as I had been sick for so long. I didn't expect special treatment, but clearly standard treatment hadn't worked for me, so it was unlikely that a fresh graduate would be able to help.

It took a few sessions for me to recount my childhood, triggers and treatment history. Laura called before my next appointment to say she had been offered another job and would be leaving The Number Practice soon. We had time for one more appointment before she left, but I didn't see the point, since I would have to start fresh with someone else. Unfortunately, there weren't any psychologists there with availability for new clients at that time, so I would be put back at the top of the waiting list. Mum was angry when I told her, but it wasn't Laura's fault. If she stayed there to keep looking after her clients, she would never be able to leave.

Someone in reception sent me a standard email explaining that I was back on the waiting list and would be contacted as soon as possible. I took the opportunity to request someone who had experience using PEACE pathways, which is a type of treatment adapted for Autistic people with eating disorders.

I assumed that, as the self-professed leading treatment centre in Western Australia, at least a few of their psychologists would have been trained in this treatment method. Unfortunately, none of them had. The receptionist recommended one psychologist, who had worked in London for a few years, and had experience using a different treatment method, which she claimed was very similar, but was in fact very different. I didn't bother replying. I decided to wait and see who they assigned me. I could accept or decline then.

Though I had been granted an extension to May, Ellen recommended I apply for another. Things were taking longer than we had predicted, probably because I was so confused about the structure, and she didn't think finishing by May was realistic. As always, she was correct. I wanted to finish by August, but she suggested October, to give us plenty of time, and so I wouldn't need to apply for another extension past August. The stress was weighing heavily on me, however there was nothing I could do but keep working. I considered taking a complete break until I was mentally and physically healthier. But I knew the stress would remain until my thesis was finished, and it would take much more than a few months for me to become anywhere near well enough to improve my brain function. I also suspected I wouldn't allow myself to start eating more until I had finished the thesis.

In late April, Wendy, a lovely friend with the best sense of humour, who I had met during a rehearsal a few years earlier, posted a photo quote on Facebook. It asserted that there aren't more Neurodivergent children these days; we are just aware of more of them because we are getting better at diagnosing. It was exactly what I needed to read at that moment, so I commented "Thank you." A few minutes later, she sent me a private message.

Wendy: You said 'thank you' on my post.

Me: Yes.
I didn't know how to explain.

Wendy: Why thank you?

Me: Because I agree? And it's important.

Wendy: Awesome. it is very important.

I decided to try to explain.

Me: I only recently discovered I'm Autistic — still waiting for the official assessment but I did the screening with a psychiatrist and I'm somewhere on the spectrum. I wish I'd known earlier. Just spent most of my life feeling a bit out of place and not knowing why. And masking masking masking to fit in."

Wendy: Thanks for telling me. I kinda knew.

I was shocked. How did she know?
Me: Really? Hilarious. How? Just because I'm such an awkward turtle?

Wendy: Our son is on the spectrum.
That made sense. I wasn't sure if I should ask what specifically made her think I was Autistic. The next day I plucked up the courage to ask.

Me: Out of interest, what was it that made you think I was Autistic?
Wendy: You're a really awesome human Hannah, let's get that straight. I've never thought of you as abnormal. There are just little traits of people who sit on the spectrum that I picked up on.

Me: Haha I am a bit abnormal though. It's ok, I don't see being Autistic as a bad thing.

Wendy: Maybe I've picked up on the masking.
That was where we left the conversation. I like that it's socially acceptable to just finish a text conversation so abruptly.

That year my birthday fell on a Wednesday, the day I taught at Westin. Part of me hoped we would wait until the weekend to celebrate but, when Dad asked if they could bring dinner to our place that night, I decided it would be nice to have something to look forward to during the day. It went without question that I would need to restrict during the day, to "save up" calories for dinner, which would be hard on such a mentally and physically demanding day. But I always managed somehow, and it would make dinner so much more enjoyable, knowing I had really earned it. There was to be a red moon that night too, which was an added bonus.

By the time I got home from Westin, I had the beginnings of a tummy ache. It was probably caused by the combination of a lack of food, the stress of wondering how tired I would be and the worry that Mum and Dad would bring a particularly scary meal for dinner. I lay down, in an attempt to ease the pain, with no success. Instead, it worsened; it was one of the most painful tummy aches I had ever had. When Gran, Grandad, Mum and Dad arrived, I tried to be a good host, but I felt faint, and sitting and standing was more painful than lying down. I could already tell it wasn't going to be a good night. After trying to sit upright and pretend to be happy, I went and lay down in the corner of the room, while everyone else sat on the couch and chatted. They all asked what they could do to help me feel better, but there was nothing. I had to wait it out.

Before dinner, Mum remembered the red moon, so we went outside to have a look. She really wanted to be able to find it, to improve my night, but it was cloudy and there were buildings in the way. I was cold, tired and in pain, with a short fuse because of the cold, tiredness and pain. I gave up and went inside, just as the rest of the family were coming outside. When I got back into the lounge, Noddy was scoffing the big wedge of fancy cheese he had stolen from the low coffee table in the short time he was alone in the room. Needless to say, that only lowered my mood. I didn't mind about the cheese, but it made me sad when Noddy misbehaved. I also felt guilty; It was very kind of Adam to have bought cheese for my birthday, and it was my dog that had ruined his generosity.

I ate dinner, though it only worsened my abdominal pain. I knew it would help in the long run though, since the stomach ache was probably caused by a lack of food. Mum had made two dishes: a chicken dish and a curry she knows I love. Unfortunately, she and Dad had accidentally left the curry at home. Though I would have had to eat some rice with the curry, it would have had more volume from vegetables. The chicken dish was just chicken and sauce — both of which were fear foods for me. Extra stress. It was delicious, but too scary to properly enjoy. I argued with the ED voice before every forkful of food and it guilted me each time food passed my lips. The orange and almond cake Mum had made was also terrifying — full of fat and sugar, and nuts were one of the foods I feared the most. And I was still in pain. The dinner I had been looking forward to all day ended up being full of stress and disappointment, thanks to the eating disorder. Thursday would be better though.

Thursday was usually my favourite day of the week. Tuesday and Wednesday were my busiest teaching days, so on Thursdays, I basked in the knowledge that the worst of the week was over — while working on my thesis. Adam was also out on Thursday nights, rehearsing his choir — he had started a choir in 2012, which ran for a few years, before taking a break and restarting in 2020 — so I had the house to myself. I often felt awkward eating in front of Adam, but I didn't need to worry about that on Thursday nights.

I engaged in all sorts of disordered behaviours when I was living alone and felt peckish. Most of these involved eating strange, almost zero-calorie concoctions, or eating tiny amounts of peanut paste and honey, mixed together in a teaspoon, straight from each jar. I didn't feel comfortable doing this in front of Adam though. I wracked my brain trying to think of low-calorie food that a normal person might eat in the evening — something that didn't appear disordered — but never succeeded. Sometimes I was too self-conscious to eat anything, resigning myself to try to concentrate on my thesis with a spinning head. Other times I braved the eating disorder's wrath and ate a small amount of fruit. On Thursday nights though, I could be as disordered as I wanted and didn't even need to worry about making conversation or potentially annoying Adam.

Autism Assessment

Around the time Laura left The Numbat Practice, Kate Tchanturia's book on PEACE Pathways[36] was released. Mum bought it as soon as it was available in Australia and shared the eBook with me. I started by reading the case studies because I thought it would be the fastest way for me to understand the treatment method. It was what I had wanted and needed all along; what I had wanted since before I went to Heathgrove. I didn't know anywhere near as much about AN back then and assumed the treatment I was receiving had better results than what I felt I needed; or that the hospital didn't have the resources to provide slower, more individualised treatment. I never asked or advocated for myself because I assumed the doctors and nurses would tell me it was the eating disorder that wanted to move slower. But it was me, an undiagnosed Autistic person, talking.

Tchanturia's team found that most of the Autistic patients preferred to have one-on-one sessions with their psychologists. The psychologists also spent more time and effort helping the patient feel comfortable with them. I assumed we did group therapy in Heathgrove because paying for individual psych sessions was too expensive — though that was probably a factor.

The researchers moved much slower with food challenges, as the rituals and rules around food are usually much more deeply entrenched for Autistic patients. I assumed we had increased our food intake quickly in hospital to restore our bodies to health faster and because there was a shortage of beds — again, I'm sure the shortage of beds influenced their approach to the speed of re-feeding. Tchanturia's team started re-feeding with as many safe foods as possible. Once the patient was at a higher weight they gradually introduced fear foods. I had wanted to do this since I was in Hobart, but everyone told me these thoughts were the disorder trying to take control.

There was a strong emphasis on devising an individualised treatment plan for each patient, depending on their needs, presentation and background. Again, I assumed I hadn't experienced this in hospital because they didn't have the time or funding. And maybe that was the reason. It was reassuring though, to learn that what I had always known I needed from treatment was correct — I wasn't deluded and it wasn't the disorder talking. And maybe this treatment would help me.

---

[36] Supporting Autistic People with Eating Disorders: A Guide to Adapting Treatment and Supporting Recovery

As we got into winter, Adam and I started using the heater. When the weather wasn't too cold, it kept us warm, but as the temperature dropped, we realised the heater was a bit tired. Sometimes it even made a sighing sound, just before it stopped pumping out air. Adam didn't seem too bothered, but I was feeling the cold more and more. I often found it hard to concentrate because I was distracted by my body screaming for warmth.

Adam also had a gas heater, but it had started producing a worrying smell when he used it the previous year, so he had put it away. Mum suggested we might just need to clean the dust out, so, while Adam was on a short holiday with some friends, I decided to give it a clean. Just getting the heater and vacuum cleaner out of the cupboard and carrying them to the lounge was exhausting, but I told myself it might be worth it for the heat and comfort it would provide. There was a lot of dust inside, so I pulled it apart and gave it a good vacuum. I was apprehensive about turning it on while I was home by myself though, in case it was a gas leak, not just dust, that was causing the smell. I told Adam I had cleaned it and would wait until he was home to test it. A few days later, when I was walking back to my car after a cold, rainy day teaching at Westin, I received a message from Adam. He had arrived home that day and tested the heater. It was working and he thanked me. The news absolutely made my day. I laughed out loud, I was so relieved I wouldn't be shivering anymore.

We had been waiting since late January, to hear when my ASD assessment would be. I had called Dr Khan's receptionist a few times to enquire and had been told they were still trying to find a day when both he and Dr Hilton available. Finally, we were given a day and time in late June. It's lucky we didn't have anything on that day, as we weren't given much notice and there didn't seem to be any flexibility. We could either take the time or leave it.

As my appointment was at 8 am, I started planning how I would fit additional exercise into the preceding days, so that I wouldn't need to get up earlier than usual to do it on the day of the assessment. I was also weighing up options for breakfast. The thought of eating so early, before the assessment, made me very anxious, but I also didn't want to feel lightheaded and not be able to concentrate during such an important appointment. I decided to eat a small snack of vegetables before I went in, then have my usual breakfast afterwards.

Less than a week before the appointment, I received a reminder message from reception, informing me that my appointment was at 12 pm. I called to confirm the time change and the receptionist said it was correct. She didn't realise that she had originally given me a different time. I wondered if they were always this disorganised, but decided to excuse it. 12 pm was more convenient anyway.

Less than a week before the assessment, the receptionist sent me about 30 pages of very detailed questions for me, Mum and Dad to fill out together. As we wouldn't be seeing each other before the appointment, we arranged a video call and talked through each question. It was very slow going. After an hour, we had only answered the first five questions, so we decided to fill the forms out separately. We tried to understand why they hadn't sent us the questions back when the assessment time was made, since there was so much information to write down. Was there a reason or was it just lack of organisation?

In one of Billy Connolly's stand-up shows, he tells a story about a young boy — possibly himself? — who has trouble reading. The boy is assessed for dyslexia, after which the assessor announces: "You're not dyslexic, you're just stupid!" For some reason, our family found the combination of the story, and Billy's accent as he delivered the punch line, hilarious. We often quote it when one of us does something silly. I had worried for a while that, if I wasn't diagnosed with Autism, the line would instead be "You're not Autistic, you're just socially awkward." I would have no excuse for being weird.

We started my assessment about 15 minutes late because the previous person's appointment went overtime. For the first half hour, I was in the room with Dr Khan and Dr Hilton by myself. Dr Khan did some activities with me, which I have since learnt are usually used to assess children. I looked at a picture book about frogs and told him what I thought was happening in each picture, described how I brush my teeth, told a story using children's toys as props, and answered some questions about myself and my background.

When Mum and Dad came in, Dr Hilton asked us about my friends, any difficulties I had at school, my special interests, and my development as a baby and young child. It was a repeat of most of the questions the receptionist had sent me earlier that week. I wondered if Dr Hilton was repeating them to clarify what we had written, but he hadn't looked through our responses yet. He hadn't had time, because we had only brought them in that morning. We also spoke about the AN and the treatment I had received.

At some point, Dr Hilton asked what support we were hoping to receive from NDIS if I was diagnosed. I hadn't realised I would be eligible for any support. I don't think Mum and Dad did either. I just wanted to know if I was Autistic.

I needed closure. I didn't even care if they wrote a report. They could just tell me verbally and that would be enough.

Dr Khan and Dr Hilton were rushing through the assessment and seemed to be aiming to finish at 2 pm. However, Mum, Dad and I wanted to provide them with all the facts. Mum and Dad knew how important the diagnosis was to me and we all knew how often Autism is missed in girls. We also wanted to utilise our full two hours; there was a lot of information to get through. It wasn't our fault they had gone overtime with their previous client.

A few days before the assessment, I started to wonder if they would know if I was Autistic or not by the end of the assessment. I hoped they would be able to tell from our conversation and the activities we did, but also knew they would need to read the questionnaires we had completed. I googled it and found a blog from an Autistic man, in which he spoke about his experience with the assessment. He had to wait about five weeks to receive his diagnosis.

"Are you able to tell me now if I'm... if I'm Autistic, or do you need to go through the questionnaires?" I asked timidly, as we were being hurried out of the consulting room.
"No, not today. We still need to discuss it and score your answers from the paperwork we sent you," Dr Khan replied, as he attempted to usher us towards the door.
I wasn't surprised and didn't see the point in pushing it, so I nodded and blinked away my tears. But Mum wasn't backing down.
"It's really important to Hannah, to know either way. And it will affect the type of treatment she receives for the eating disorder."
"Yes, well, as Dr Khan has said, we need to discuss it and read through your answers from the questionnaires," Dr Hilton replied. He was polite, but there was a patronising undertone. "I have a feeling you will be borderline if you are Autistic. Try not to worry about it, even if you're not. It's not life or death." He gave a small, forced chuckle.
"It is, actually," Mum said.
I felt uncomfortable and just wanted to get out of there. We passed a small kitchenette on the way back to reception, where I saw two UberEats bags on the bench. I guessed they had a lunch break scheduled at 2 pm and were keen to eat, hence the eagerness to cut our appointment short.

"Ok, I'll just check when Dr Khan has a spot available for a follow-up appointment," the receptionist said, after I had paid.
"Do I need to have an appointment to get my diagnosis?" I asked.

"Well no, you don't, but you can use that time to go over the report together and talk about how Dr Khan can help you in the future."
I'm quite capable of reading and another appointment would cost a few hundred dollars. I didn't need help from a psychiatrist either.
"Oh, ummm, that's fine. I can read it myself and, if I need to, I'll make an appointment. Is that ok?"
"Yes. You'll need to come into reception to collect your report though. We can't email it directly to you due to confidentiality reasons. We'll fax one to your GP but we can't send it to you securely."
I was worried about how much petrol I would use, driving there again to pick up the report. Better than paying for an appointment though.

Once we were outside, Mum, Dad and I discussed how rushed the assessment had been and how there was still so much information we hadn't covered.
"Maybe we should ask for another appointment, so we can talk about everything we missed," Mum suggested
"We'll probably have to wait another six months or more to get them both in the same room again though," I replied.
That afternoon, Mum started drafting an email to send to Dr Khan, containing everything we hadn't had time to talk about.

Over the next week, Mum messaged me with questions about my childhood and teenage friends, my current friends, special interests, and anything else we hadn't covered in adequate detail in the questionnaires or appointment. The previous year I had discovered that one of my best childhood friends had since been diagnosed Autistic. I was his only true friend at that school, so some other children teased us about getting married. Out of interest, I asked my other best friend from that age, with whom I rarely speak now, as she moved interstate when we were six, if she was Neurodivergent. It turns out she has Bipolar and Borderline Personality Disorder.

While I was waiting the compulsory 15 minutes after my first Covid vaccine, Mum messaged, asking how many of my current close friends are Neurodivergent. I hadn't actually counted before, so I was surprised when I discovered that seven of my nine closest friends are Neurodivergent. The two who are Neurotypical — as far as they know — both have generalised anxiety and have had other mental health problems in the past.

About five weeks after the assessment, I had an appointment with Krish. He had just received the report from Dr Khan's office. They had decided that I was not Autistic. I had spoken to Krish about the possibility that I was Autistic before getting the assessment, and he knew how important the diagnosis was to me. We had also spoken about my Autistic traits, my masking and how difficult it is to diagnose girls.

"I recommend you get a second opinion," he said. "Find someone else. It sounds like it was very rushed, and he doesn't do Autism diagnoses very often anyway. Should we find someone who is more experienced?"

"Yeah, I don't know who to go to though. WAEDOCS recommended him because apparently he knows about eating disorders, but I would question that too… Maybe I'll ask WAEDOCS again?"

"Ok, yes, let's start there, and if they don't have anyone else I can ask my contacts. Shall we do that?"

"Yep, sounds good," I replied, doing my best to hide my devastation at my lack of diagnosis.

"Ok, and do you have a copy of this report? Do you want me to print it out for you?"

"Yes please. They said they couldn't send it to me. I don't know why…"

"All good, I'll print one off for you."

Dr Khan's receptionist never contacted me about coming to pick up my report, so I'm glad Krish gave me a copy!

I waited until I got home to message Mum and Dad about the report. I would have been completely distraught, heartbroken and bawled my eyes out, if Wendy hadn't told me she knew I was Autistic a few months earlier. Instead, I was furious at Dr Khan and Dr Hilton for pretending to be competent diagnosticians when they were clearly not. Mum was as angry as I was.

There were so many inconsistencies and errors in their report it would have been laughable if it wasn't real life. In the Psychosocial History section, they had written "Hannah has a variety of friends, and always has; she says that are very supportive and close." Aside from the typo, which suggests it was written in a hurry and not proofread, they failed to mention that almost all of my friends are Neurodivergent which, in the context of this report, is incredibly important.

In the following paragraph, they wrote that I had been seeing a psychologist at The Numbat Practice, "who is going on maternity leave." That was news to me. I wondered where they pulled that erroneous story from. They also said I was in hospital at Governor in 2020. Again, I wasn't aware of a hospital admission that year. The remainder of their report exhibits a complete lack of understanding of Autism in girls, but these two claims show that they also weren't listening properly during the assessment. They were more interested in their lunch.

Under the heading Features Not Suggestive of Autism, they listed my self-identification as a sympathetic person. People used to think this was true of Autistic people, until sometime in the 1990s, when they discovered that most Autistic people are highly sympathetic, but can be unaware of another person's distress due to Alexithymia. Everything else they had listed under that heading was either incorrect or showed their lack of a deeper understanding.

The remainder of the report had a similar lack of depth of understanding of Autism. A few days after Krish gave me my report, I decided to leave a Google review for Dr Khan. He didn't have any reviews at that point, so I left him with a one-star average. I wrote:

Do not go to Dr Khan for eating disorder or Autism treatment/diagnosis. His knowledge of EDs is lacking and out of date. His ASD assessment was not at all thorough; it was rushed, with the goal to complete it in 2 hours. He didn't take the time to understand what I was saying, and therefore misunderstood, which was reflected in the report. His secretary rarely answers the phone. If you leave a message on their answering machine, it is unlikely they will call back. If you are lucky enough to speak to the receptionist and ask her to pass a message/question to Dr Khan, don't expect a response. Approximately 50 pages of in-depth questions were emailed to me three days prior to my ASD assessment, even though it had been scheduled about a month earlier. It's a shame that someone so incompetent is "qualified" to practice.

The report posed another problem. In the Background section, Dr Khan had written that I was exploring my sexuality — which, by the way, is another common Autistic trait. I had planned to show the report to Mum and Dad and talk it through with them, but I still hadn't told them about my sexuality and didn't know if I was ready to do so. I considered sending them photos of the report, omitting that paragraph that mentioned exploring my sexuality and keeping the hard copy to myself. However, after a few days, I decided I might as well tell them. I had been considering it for a while and knew they would be completely accepting and supportive. I had only held off telling them because I felt that their knowing would make it final, and I was still unsure.

Mum and Dad were going down south for a holiday the following week and I would be looking after their house and dogs. We decided to go through the report together at their house in the morning before they left. I had circled the biggest errors in the report and told Mum beforehand that there was one thing in particular that I needed to talk to them about. I was a mixture of nervous, not nervous, a little bit excited, and looking forward to the relief I would hopefully feel after I told them.

I showed them some of the almost-funny parts of the report first, such as my sympathetic nature suggesting I'm not Autistic. Eventually, Mum said, "You said there was something in the report you needed to talk to us about.."
I was grateful she had brought it up. I'm bad at introducing sensitive topics. I had thought about how I would word it, because I'm bad at that too, when put on the spot. I thought it would be best to say it plainly, before explaining the details.
"I'm not straight," I said.

It took them both a few seconds to work out what I meant, then question themselves internally, to check they had understood. "What do you mean?" Mum asked, to triple-check.
I sighed. "I think I'm pansexual."
As I had predicted, Dad asked, "Which one's that again?"
I had to laugh. "I knew you'd say that!"
After doing my best to explain the difference between being pansexual and bisexual, I told them I had decided I was probably non-binary, but that I was still working it out. At some point, I started to cry. Then I apologised for delivering such a bombshell just before they went on holiday.

We talked for another hour or so after that. They were every bit as supportive as I knew they would be. They asked how long I had known and how I had worked it out. They were infinitely grateful to the friends I had spoken to while I was figuring it out. They cried themselves, for all the times they wished they could have helped me, when I felt that I was a lesser person, and disgusting, for not being straight.
"But why were you worried about not being straight?" Mum asked. "We told you and Adam, from when you were little, that there was nothing wrong with being gay. Did you think we wouldn't love you?"
"I always knew you would accept me. Actually, Lucy says you've got an oddly large number of gay friends for a straight couple," I laughed.
"Do we?" Dad asked, confused.
"Apparently… But the rest of society… I mean, gay marriage only recently became legal."
Mum and Dad both looked thoughtful. They hadn't considered that point of view until I voiced it; then they understood perfectly. I was glad I had told them. We were all much closer for it.
"Have you told Adam?" Mum asked.
"No… I haven't found a good time to bring it up."

"Are you worried about telling him?"
"No, I just… It's not something you can bring up out of the blue is it? Oh by the way I'm pansexual, see you later…"

Later that day a few friends checked in on me, to ask how the conversation had gone with Mum and Dad. I had mentioned that I was going to tell them and was feeling nervous. Mum and Dad also messaged a few hours later, to check I was feeling ok after such an emotional morning.

Marissa and Malnutrition

The daughter of Mum's friend Sally had developed an eating disorder a few years earlier, so Mum and Sally often spoke about the difficulties, dangers, new research and treatment of eating disorders. Sally's daughter Jo had recently found a psychologist she really connected with, who had been very helpful. After our disappointment at The Numbat Practice, Sally recommended Jo's psych. Mum called the practice where the psych worked, and spoke to Marissa, the owner, who was incredibly lovely and understanding. She sounded like she really knew what she was talking about, was passionate about helping others, and knew about the connection between eating disorders and Autism. Mum asked me if I would consider seeing Marissa. Since Jo was happy with her psychologist, I thought it was worth a try. Mum and Dad had a Zoom appointment with Marissa while they were on holiday, so they could talk to her about Autism, Kate Tchanturia's PEACE pathways treatment method, and some of my background.

I started seeing Marissa a few weeks later. My appointments were usually at 9 am on Thursdays. In some ways this was great. Tuesday and Wednesday were my busy days and on Thursday I could take things a bit easier until I started teaching in the afternoon. However, since I couldn't eat breakfast until 11 am, I had to go to the appointment on an empty stomach. If I was a bit constipated, this was ok, but on some weeks I felt lightheaded throughout the appointment and the drive home. Sometimes I struggled to concentrate and just wanted the appointment to end so I could get home and eat. At the same time, I wanted to continue our conversation, so I could make sense of my thoughts. I started bringing some apple slices with me, to eat on the way home if I felt lightheaded. Even eating that small amount before 11 am was a huge step for me, especially since fruit was a fear food.

Hunger and dizziness aside, my sessions with Marissa were very helpful. I knew I needed to improve my self-esteem before the ED voice would allow me to start eating more, and she helped with that. We talked through all the things that had contributed to my low self-esteem: the worry that I was gay; feeling that I didn't fit in but not knowing why; my academic and musical achievements dropping when I had Chronic Fatigue Syndrome; feeling embarrassed for having gross bowel movements caused by my food intolerances and IBS; thinking Mum wouldn't love me if I wasn't thin; thinking being thin was the ultimate realisation of selflessness and willpower; feeling that I needed to utilise thin privilege to make up for my social awkwardness, and much more. There were so many facets to the cause of my eating disorder, many of which I had never even questioned, such as my belief that being thin was the ultimate achievement in life.

(Food)

Over the past year and a half, I had been given some vouchers for a hotel's restaurant, in exchange for performing there at a discounted rate every Sunday. I gave some of the vouchers away, sold some online and was slowly using the rest to take friends out. The restaurant did a lunch buffet on Thursdays and Fridays, so I asked Siena if she wanted to check it out. The buffet started at 12 pm and finished at 2 pm, so we decided to get there at the beginning, so we had as much time to eat as possible. I was anxious about eating lunch earlier, so I omitted the protein from my breakfast and just ate the vegetables. That way, I reasoned, it was more like having a late breakfast, or skipping breakfast and having a big lunch.

Each time we went, I was ravenous, lightheaded and getting hangry when I arrived. I was so anxious to eat that I was sweating and had to force myself to walk to our table and the buffet at a normal pace, instead of power-walking. I had been worried that there would be lots of energy-dense food and not many vegetables to fill me up. However, I was relieved to find that there were lots of salads, vegetable curries and fruit platters.

As when I ate at the breakfast buffets in China, I struggled to control myself. There was so much food on display. I wanted to eat it all since I had paid to eat as much as I wanted. Would it be thrown out if it wasn't eaten? There was still so much food the dishes when we left. I hoped they gave it to the staff. I wanted to try everything and take bigger servings because it all looked so good, but I didn't want the staff at such a fancy restaurant to think I was making a pig of myself.

While I ate, I was torn between eating as fast as possible so I could get more food, and eating slowly to savour the taste. I didn't feel too guilty about eating more because I was mostly eating vegetables. I knew there was oil and other ingredients that may have been more calorie-dense in the sauces, but I told myself it would be ok, as long as I didn't have "too much." Siena loves good food, but also wanted to catch up and asked me lots of questions. She was there on a social outing, not to have her first decent meal of the week. Her questions annoyed me because I had to stop eating to answer them. I made my answers as short as possible and sometimes talked with my mouth full. When I finished my plate I was itching to go back to the buffet for round two.

We usually stayed there until almost 2 pm. I was always uncomfortably full and bloated, regretting my last plateful and starting to worry about how many calories I had actually consumed. I would start guessing at what the sauces contained, what measurement I had had and what I should have resisted. I always berated myself for eating so quickly, promising the ED voice that next time I would work harder to slow down and enjoy the different tastes.

My bowel movements were usually slow and sluggish for the next day or so, as my body struggled to process a day's worth of food in one meal. Sometimes I would get a stomach ache later in the afternoon, which was particularly uncomfortable when I started teaching on Thursday afternoons. At least I had the energy to teach though.

(Food)

I skipped breakfast almost completely — aside from a few bites of vegetables — the last few times we went to the buffet, so I would have more room in my stomach. Unsurprisingly, I was even more tired and antsy while I waited to go into the restaurant. I was lightheaded, dizzy and cold while I sat on the bus on the way there, trying and failing to concentrate on reading my book. The walk from the bus stop was also exhausting and I was torn between wanting to quicken my pace, to arrive sooner, and being too tired to walk much faster.

As the year progressed, I found it harder to summon the energy I needed to teach before I ate breakfast at recess, on the days I taught at Westin. I often ate some slices of apple or cherry tomatoes before I left the house in the morning. I told myself this was a step towards recovery, breaking my strict rule of not eating so early in the morning.

(Food)

I felt increasingly lightheaded when I drove to school in the mornings, and found it difficult to concentrate. It was lucky I knew the route well, otherwise I would have struggled even more. The ED voice rebuked me for my lack of focus, telling me I just needed more willpower to maintain concentration. And that, if I had been able to wait until recess to eat earlier in the year, I could do so now. I had lowered my food intake since then, but I had had a snack before I left home. Yes, that snack contained about ten calories, but if I had a stronger will, I would be able to wait to eat.

Sometimes I worried about blacking out while I was driving, but I told myself I wasn't that unwell yet. Anyway, I had eaten a few pieces of apple before I left the house. I often thought it wouldn't matter too much if I fainted anyway, even if I died. I had been feeling hopeless about my life prospects. I didn't know how I would ever be able to convince myself to eat more and accept myself at a higher weight. Just the thought disgusted me. And even when I finished my thesis, what would I do? I had planned to do a PhD, but I knew that wouldn't be a good idea until I could concentrate properly. Would I just keep teaching, struggling through each day? After so much practice and hard work, was this all I had achieved? I just hoped I didn't injure anyone else if I fainted. Hopefully, my car would just coast to a stop when my foot came off the accelerator.

In term four, the high school music teacher at Westin started overseeing the primary music program. She suggested we have a fortnightly meeting before we started teaching on Wednesdays, so she could keep us in the loop about everything happening in the music department. I was happy to be paid for an easy 45 minutes of listening and talking, but had to change my morning plans in order to get to school before 9 am. From then on, I got up half an hour earlier every fortnight, so I would have time to fit in my exercise and shower before leaving. I'm the first to point out that getting up at 6.30 am is definitely a first-world problem. However, it's much harder in winter, especially if you are feeling the cold more than you should, due to near-depleted energy reserves and low body fat; your sleep was interrupted by trips to the toilet during the night, thanks to your malnourished body; and you only have a gruelling exercise routine and a long day of teaching to look forward to.

Though I was getting up earlier, I still wasn't eating until recess — aside from the small amount of fruit and vegetables I sometimes ate before I left the house or during my drive to school. The meetings should have been more relaxing than teaching, however, we often had them outside — the other teachers thought the icy air was "refreshing" — or in an unheated room. I shivered through these meetings, often sweating from the cold, and unable to move to get my blood flowing. I made tea in an attempt to keep myself warm, but often finished it in the first 20 minutes. I was usually dizzy during the meetings, after less sleep than usual and possibly because my body was using up even more of its dwindling energy reserves, trying to keep me warm enough to stay alive in the winter temperatures. I found that blinking lots, or squeezing my eyes tightly when I blinked, helped me to concentrate for a second or two after the blink.

One night I finally found a loose segue, during a conversation with Adam, to tell him that I'm non-binary and, from there, that I'm pansexual.
"Wait, which one is pansexual again?" He asked.

"I knew you'd ask that. That's what Dad said!" I exclaimed.
He didn't seem as interested in the news as I had expected. Maybe he had suspected I wasn't straight, but didn't know what brand of queer I am. He was more interested in why I felt ashamed and embarrassed, given the entirely un-homophobic household in which we were brought up.

A month or so later the topic came up again. As we hadn't spoken about it since I had told him, I asked if he had been hesitant to bring it up, fearing I might not want to talk about it.
"No, I just didn't feel the need. It's not like you're a different person because of it."
And that right there is so beautiful in its simplicity and unplanned honesty. He didn't even intend for it to be a deep statement. Blissfully unaware, just speaking his mind.

Later in the year, Adam was offered a job working at the Type 1 Diabetes Family Centre — he's a Type 1 diabetic himself. When he was describing the position, he said it sounded like he would mostly be working independently, aside from a few meetings and check-ins with his boss.
"Oh, that's great! You can probably work mostly from home then," I said.
"Mmm maybe. I prefer to be around people though," he replied.
"How are we related?"
I swear Adam stole all of the confidence genes when he was born. Yes, I know that's not how biology and genetics work.

I started teaching at Oldham College in term three. It was closer to home, had a better music program, and had more students than Piney College. I taught at all three schools — Piney, Oldham and Westin — in third term then, as Oldham was happy with me and wanted me to continue, I resigned from Piney College before term four.

I had about seven hours of teaching to fit in at Oldham. The head of music recommended I split it over two days, but I didn't want to drag it out. I preferred to squash it all into one horrible, tiring day, so I could have a full day at home in my pyjamas, working on my thesis.

Because of my morning exercise, which continued to grow in length, I said I couldn't start lessons until 9 am — the healthy part of my brain didn't want me to have to get up too early, especially as it was winter when I started in term three. I taught my first few lessons before I ate breakfast, which I learnt to eat after recess, so I wouldn't have to make conversation with other members of staff.

My energy changed from week to week, but I was usually lightheaded and short-tempered during the first few lessons of the day. On some days I was, somehow, full of energy in the morning, until I crashed in the afternoon and had to drag myself through until I finished at 5 pm. The last few lessons were usually a test of willpower. I tried to make myself stand up — as I always did to teach; it's a compulsion I've had since the AN started — but sometimes my legs were too weak. The students were tiny year ones and twos, so it was probably better that I sat anyway, so we were the same height. When I needed to stand, I had to concentrate to prevent my legs from folding underneath me. My head always spun faster and felt lighter for a few seconds too.

In my sessions with Marissa, I continued to realise things that felt like epiphanies but were actually just truths that should have been obvious to me. The day I first considered that maybe being thin isn't the most important thing in life, it felt like a huge breakthrough. And for me, it was. Unfortunately, the discovery was ultimately unhelpful to my recovery. I knew that most people still value thinness a lot, revere people who are thin and unconsciously judge others based on their body size. I had come to realise that I used my thinness as a shield of sorts. Even though I was socially awkward and boring, I felt that being thin helped protect me from being bullied and made me generally more acceptable as a person. And sadly, I wasn't wrong.

I often felt, and still feel, like a gullible fool for believing these lies in the first place, but I have to remind myself that I was an undiagnosed Autistic child, desperately trying to fit in. I was always searching for information that would help me to do so. Almost everyone — the media and the general population — told me that being thin is better, being overweight is caused by laziness and greed, eating healthy and exercising is a display of willpower, the list goes on. Autistic me thought that doing all of this perfectly would allow me to fit in and make me likeable, even if I was socially awkward and physically unattractive.

Another important conversation started when I told Marissa what Michael had said, back when we were at uni, about me being similar to a religious person, who believes in God even though there is no proof. Marissa built on that, suggesting that diet culture is the religion, or cult, that most of us believe in. I went home and brainstormed what diet culture would look like as a religion. Thin people, obsessive exercisers and diet culture as a whole would be the deities to which followers prayed or revered. The clergy would be "wellness" influencers, The Kardashians and Pro-Ana sites. I also wrote 11 commandments, which were signs of diet culture "enlightenment." The more I think about it, the more I realise that diet culture really is a cult. Emaciation isn't healthy. That belief is kept alive by the clergy and their followers.

Though talking to Marissa helped me to unpack a lot of false beliefs, self-hatred and trauma, it still wasn't enough to make me feel ok about eating more. Even though I didn't quite see it as greed and a lack of willpower anymore, I knew that eating more would lead to weight gain and I didn't want to lose my thin privilege. Aside from hating myself, I thought others would reject me too. I knew my friends and family wouldn't, but couldn't be sure that other acquaintances, people I worked with, and general society, wouldn't judge me.

Teaching became increasingly exhausting. I often felt that my legs were about to give way beneath me, but still rarely allowed myself to sit. I dreaded teaching, even at home, because I knew it would be an exhausting slog. I wouldn't even be able to eat something that might fill me up, if not provide energy, such as vegetables, because I rarely had breaks between students.

Gigs were similarly exhausting, as well as stressful. We mostly performed at weddings and corporate functions. Because I owned the company and organised the logistics, the blame would fall on me if something went wrong. Usually, everything went well, even when the wedding party changed their plans at the last minute without telling us, and we had to guess when to play. However, the short surge of adrenaline caused by these stressful surprises always sapped what little energy I had; my head felt so light it could float away.

For me, each gig felt like a big, exhausting, stressful mission. I had to drive to the venue, which was sometimes somewhere I had never been before. Luckily I had started using Google Maps navigation while driving earlier that year, which reduced my stress a lot. Finding parking and the exact location within the venue was something I worried about for at least a week leading up to a gig, so I always found out as much as I could beforehand, getting maps of venues and deciding where to park.

I was usually the one to bring the music files, which were so big and heavy I transported them in a big box on wheels. It works well on paved ground, but it's awkward to carry up steps and wheel over long stretches of uneven ground. Especially when I'm also carrying a violin, music stand and trying to look clean, neat and professional.

Even when things ran smoothly, I worried about anything that could go wrong. If someone played a note out of time, I felt it was my job to get us all back together. If the rest of the group was getting tired, I felt that I needed to be the one to keep their spirits up — even though I was probably the person with the least energy or enthusiasm. I started most gigs lightheaded, tired and hungry and became moreso throughout the gig. It worsened when we stopped playing during speeches or wedding ceremonies. Without anything to occupy my concentration, I became acutely aware of my lightheadedness. Overshadowing all of this was the knowledge that, even when the gig was finished, I would need to pack up, carry everything back to my car and drive home before I could rest.

Malnutrition was making it harder and harder for me to concentrate on my thesis. Pulling together ideas from different sources, describing violin techniques clearly and concisely, structuring paragraphs, explaining others' findings in my own words, and bringing together the different aspects of my own research — it felt like an F45 marathon on a tightrope for my brain. I couldn't hold multiple ideas in my head for long enough to work out how to order them, let alone put them into words. Often, when I tried to think through an idea or concept, I either felt that I was hitting a wall inside my head, or that there wasn't even a wall; just emptiness. I know it isn't unusual for postgraduate research students to feel as though they are drowning, but I'm sure that, in my case, the feeling was magnified.

It didn't help that I was constantly second-guessing the meaning behind Ellen and Jo's emails. Were they sick of me? Was my writing actually terrible, however politely they worded their advice? Was I the worst Master's student they had ever had? Were they complaining about me to each other? Were they regretting taking me on and hanging out for me to submit so they wouldn't have to hear from me again? I hadn't seen them in person since the beginning of the year, so I only had their words to scour for clues. Even if I had seen them I doubt I would have been able to read their feelings.

As I write this, I don't remember how I was feeling at that time, well enough to relive it now. I've forgotten just how desperate, stressed and exhausted I was. Possibly because my body is protecting me from reliving that trauma; possibly because I was so malnourished that the memories just haven't survived. My memories leading up to both hospital admissions are similarly vague and patchy. I knew I was close to being ready to submit my thesis and just needed to persevere for a bit longer. It wasn't long until the end of term four, when I would be able to have a proper, well-deserved relax over the holidays.

I worried my body would give out before I finished though. I knew it wasn't at all healthy but, because I was eating more than when I was admitted to hospital in 2017, and because my weight was higher, I thought I must still be kind of ok. In hindsight, my lack of perspective was disturbing. Just because my BMI wasn't quite as shockingly low as it had been in the past, I thought that I was pretty much healthy. I was greedy and lazy to think I needed to eat or rest more, or give myself a break from working.

Finally, I was finished. Ellen and Jo gave me the green light to submit. I timed my submission carefully because the ED voice didn't allow me to eat breakfast until 11 am, but the Graduate Research Office reception is closed from 12-2 pm, presumably for the receptionist to have a lunch break. I also needed to print some things and get one more signature before I submitted it. I spent a long time deciding whether I should take my breakfast to uni, so I could eat it there at an acceptable time — after 11 am — or eat very late when I got home. I can't remember what I decided, due to my afore-mentioned patchy memories of that time.

I was excited, but not as excited as I had imagined. It hadn't sunk in yet. I was proud of myself though, and enjoyed having my Polaroid taken, posing with my complimentary mug, for the photo board. My celebration was not writing my thesis that afternoon.

Dad said he wanted to take the family out to dinner to celebrate my hard work and achievement. I was excited to have a meal out, since I never allowed myself to spend money on eating out. I started looking at menus online but, while everything sounded delicious, almost everything was a fear food. I didn't want to have to restrict at my celebration dinner; nor did I want to feel guilty during and after the meal. As much as I wanted to celebrate, there was no solution to my ED-imposed dilemma.

Crash

Two weeks before the end of term four — I was nearly there! — I booked myself to play at three weddings on one day. Coincidentally, the first two weddings were at the same venue and both had booked a string trio, so I thought it made sense for me to play for both. About an hour and a half later, Krista, who played cello in the trio for the first two weddings, and I were booked as a string duo for the third wedding, about 45 minutes away. I could have booked someone else to play at the third wedding, but figured I might as well do it. I would need to give the music files to someone else if I didn't play, and the extra money would be nice. The first two weddings were inside, in a venue I had been to many times before, so I wouldn't need to stress about finding it. I knew it would be tiring, but I promised myself a nice dinner at the end of the day, which I would enjoy even more than usual, knowing that I had really earned it. I would have the house to myself too, as Adam and Emily, his girlfriend, were away for the weekend.

I maintain that I probably would have been ok if we hadn't had a maximum of 42 degrees Celsius that day. I had seen the forecast earlier in the week but reasoned that, as the first two weddings were inside, we wouldn't be hot, and it should be cooling down by the third wedding, which was outside. Wrong on both accounts. The first two weddings were in a Catholic Church which, along with their hard seats, are also famous for their lack of air conditioning — this same church is also freezing in winter. The fans positioned along the walls helpfully blew hot air around.

The first wedding started at 10.30 am, which was before breakfast time, so I decided to wait until it ended at 12 pm, to eat. I knew I would feel lightheaded until I ate, but I had eaten that late before and survived. I kept myself hydrated and finished my half-litre bottle of water before the end of the first ceremony. While we were playing during the signing of the register, the lightheadedness became much worse. It felt as though the spinning in my head was getting faster, and travelling wider circles. We had about a minute after the signing before we had to play again for the recessional. The dizziness was so intense, I was worried I might faint, so I frantically motioned to Nina, the other violinist, to ask if I could drink some of her water. I felt guilty asking to drink her water on such a hot day, and was planning to pour some into my own bottle — Western Australia may have been Covid zero at that point, but most of us had remained hyper-aware of germs — but she waved her hand and motioned for me to drink straight from her bottle. What an angel. I don't know if I would have fainted without that extra half cup of water, but it marginally decreased my lightheadedness.

After the first wedding, I had breakfast. Nina and Krista thought it was my lunch. They were also eating lunch, so luckily I didn't feel out of place. I tried to fill up my water bottle from the tap in the bathroom, but the sink was so shallow that I could only fit my bottle underneath if it was almost horizontal. I could only get about a cup of water inside before it started flowing out again.

I wasn't as lightheaded during the second wedding — my head was still spinning but that wasn't unusual — so I hoped it would improve as the day progressed. It was really heating up, so the church was very hot and humid when we finished the second wedding. I wished I could go home to the air conditioning and have a relaxing lunch.

I also needed water — more than a cup this time. I asked the lovely woman who works at the church if there was a tap, somewhere other than the toilets, that I could use.
"Unfortunately not sorry. But, you know what, I've got a lovely cold bottle of sparkling water in the fridge you can have. It's only half full though."
"Is it yours though?" I asked.
"Yes, but I'll be fine, it's ok," she replied.
"No no, I can't take yours. It's yours. It's ok, I'll find water at the next venue."
"No, I can't let you get dehydrated. You look like you're melting!"
We continued in this manner a little longer, before I gave in. The cold, fizzy water was bliss! I am eternally grateful to her. I finished the whole bottle before I reached the next venue.

I had brought lunch to eat when I got there. I was hungry when I left the church, but I always eat as close to a gig, performance, rehearsal or teaching, as possible, so the energy from the food isn't wasted while I'm sitting waiting. That's my illogical reasoning anyway. I don't know if it holds up to science. I knew my lunch wasn't very calorie-dense, but I hoped it would be enough to keep me going until I was finished for the day.

I met the florist the couple had hired not long after I arrived. She was lovely and very friendly, but I wasn't in the mood for talking. I needed to conserve energy and eat my lunch. It was still about 40 degrees and I couldn't sit inside, because they were setting up for the reception. I sat in the shadiest spot I could find, while the florist chattered away. She really was lovely.

If it had been ten to 15 degrees cooler, I would have still struggled through that day, but nowhere near as much. Sitting outside, eating my vegetables and tinned tuna, the heat sapped what little energy I had. My tiredness and lightheadedness were magnified by the heat. I was drinking so much I was worried it was too much — I didn't want to drown my brain or dilute my electrolytes. Needless to say, I made it through the wedding fuelled entirely by willpower — and the ED voice telling me that if Krista was able to keep playing, then I should be too.

I hoped my energy would improve when I drove home, with the stressful part of the day over. I even turned the air conditioning up to level two, which I rarely do, because someone once told me that running the air conditioner uses petrol. At home, I turned the air conditioner up high and lay underneath it, however the dizziness continued.

I was starting to worry that it would never go away. This had persisted all day with no reprieve. I had a strict rule that dinner could not be eaten until 8 pm at the very earliest, and had planned to go to the Spudshed to buy broccoli before dinner. But I didn't know if I would be able to. I knew had the willpower to make myself go to the shop, but I was (finally) seriously worried that I might collapse. After arguing with the ED voice, I made what felt like a life-changing decision — honestly, deciding to move to Hobart was easier — to eat dinner before 8 pm. I ate around 7.30. I felt guilty, but nowhere near as much as the all-consuming self-loathing as I would have experienced had I not truly believed that I was close to losing consciousness.

I still felt dizzy and weak after I had eaten. It was a different type of lightheadedness to that which I had become accustomed. It was more intense and it felt dangerous to move, as though moving would put too much strain on my body, causing me to fade into unconsciousness or worse. I was worried my heart was struggling; my heartbeat felt weak.

I went to the Spudshed after dinner. I hoped I would feel better afterwards. Maybe the stress of knowing I still had an errand to run was causing the lightheadedness. Sometimes, after feeling lightheaded for a long time, it went away if I distracted myself. I relate it to being overtired — you know, when you're so tired that you become hyperactive and laugh at everything? Sometimes that happens when I'm lightheaded. That night though, it didn't.

After a long discussion with the ED voice, I called Mum and Dad as I was walking back to my car. I hadn't wanted to, in case they made me go to hospital, but I was genuinely scared that maybe I needed to. I hoped they would know what to do. Maybe just having them there would help me feel better. If something happened they could call an ambulance. I just had to hope they wouldn't make me go straight to hospital, because I knew I fit the criteria for an involuntary admission. Again. The fact that I called Mum and Dad is proof of how desperately worried I was about my well-being. Better late than never.

They didn't answer when I rang, but phoned back about a minute later. Mum knew there was something wrong almost straight away.
"Hannah, are you ok?"
"I don't know. I'm not feeling quite right and I don't know what to do." I was trying not to let them hear my tears.
"We'll come over now. But Hannah, do we need to call an ambulance?"
"I don't think so."
I didn't tell her I had been wondering the same thing all night. I didn't even try to convince them that they didn't need to come over. I hadn't wanted to ask them to drive all the way to our house at night, but I hadn't; they had offered. And I was too scared and desperate to brave this alone. I was finally worried I might die.

"Ok, Dad's getting dressed now. We'll be there in about 40 minutes. Will you be ok until we get there?"
"Yes. Thank you. I should be fine."
"Ok. We'll have Dad's phone with us, so just call if you need anything."
I felt it, and I think Mum did too. We were at a turning point. Was tonight the night that I would sink or swim? Do or die? (Eat or die?)
"Mum..." I hesitated.
"Yes?"
"Could you please bring my groceries over with you?" I felt terrible asking. "I don't know if I'll be up to coming to dinner tomorrow night."
I didn't know if my body would be able to cope with the extra restrictions I usually imposed upon myself on Sundays, in anticipation of a bigger dinner at Mum and Dad's. And it was always Sunday nights that they sent me home with my groceries. Yes, a year and a half later they were still buying my groceries, even though we were no longer in lockdown. I had suggested to Mum, more than a few times, that I start buying them again. Every time, she asked if I would be able to make myself spend the money on buying everything I needed. Every time, I said no. I felt guilty, embarrassed and ashamed that, at 29, with a huge amount of savings in the bank, my parents were still buying my groceries. But it was also one less thing I had to worry about.

I can't remember much of what happened when Mum and Dad came over — again, patchy memories. They were, understandably, incredibly worried, and seriously considered taking me to the Emergency Department. Thankfully though, they agreed that a forced admission wouldn't be helpful. We all knew that's what would happen if we went to hospital. I cried, but I didn't sob. Quiet, desperate, hopeless tears escaped from my eyes and rolled down my cheeks as I described my day to them. Then Dad asked if he could make a cup of tea — classic Dad — and we chatted.

They insisted on staying the night so they could check on me every hour or so, and be there if things got worse.
"But... I'm worried... I don't want you to see what I eat for breakfast." My desperation and exhaustion had rendered me completely honest.
"It's ok. We'll leave not long after we get up tomorrow, if you're feeling ok" Mum said gently. "We were thinking of going out for breakfast tomorrow anyway."

I didn't do my exercises that morning. Instead, I slept in and was surprised that I didn't feel too guilty. But I knew I had really pushed my body to its limit the day before. For a long time, I had held the view that making my body so weak that I fainted, would be a sure sign that I had succeeded in making myself "sick enough." I knew I wasn't eating enough, my weight was dropping and I was often hungry and tired. However, because of my body dysmorphia, and because I was still able to work and mostly look after myself — even if it was a constant struggle and left me exhausted — I didn't think I was sick enough. It would be an achievement if I fainted though. Then I would let myself eat a bit more — or that's what the ED voice told me anyway. I think I came close to fainting that day. However, while the ED voice would have congratulated me if I had, I was glad that I hadn't. I didn't have time to be sick, now that I was an adult with work and bills.

Mum and Dad suggested I cancel my teaching that day, but I was worried about losing the income. It tired me out even more than usual, but I pushed through. It probably helped that I was eating more than I usually would on a Sunday, since I had decided not to go to Mum and Dad's for dinner. They checked in on me during the day and made it very clear that they would drop everything and come over if I needed them. I was still feeling weaker than usual on Monday, but I did my usual exercise anyway; I couldn't skip two days! I ate slightly more than usual though, but only slightly. On Saturday night I had finally accepted that I needed to eat more, but what felt like a lot more to me was, in reality, negligible. Eating one extra apple over the whole day felt like a huge step for me.

On Monday night, I began to feel more faint and lightheaded than usual, while I was trying to get to sleep. It was almost as bad as it had been on Saturday.

Was I about to faint? I knew I still wasn't eating enough. All I could think to do was check if my blood sugar was low — lucky I was living with a type one diabetic. It wasn't too late; not yet midnight. Adam's bedroom light was still on; it sounded like he was watching TikToks in bed. I knocked.
"Adam?"
"Yeah? Come in."
I opened the door, already feeling guilty for disturbing him.
"You ok?" He asked.
"I don't know. I feel faint. Could I do a BSL?"[37]
"Yeah sure. My kit's on the chest of drawers there. You ok?" He asked again, his gaze intensifying. We hadn't spoken about Saturday, but I assumed Mum and Dad had told him. I sat on his bed to set up the equipment and prick my finger.
"Ahaaa always perfect," I joked, when the machine displayed my sugar level reading.
"Wish mine was that good," Adam grumbled good-naturedly.
That didn't rule out organ failure though.
"Are you still worried?" He asked.
Terrified. I started to cry. I didn't know what to do. I knew I was killing myself. I could feel my body struggling, even more than before, which I hadn't thought possible, but I didn't know what to do. He comforted me but I don't remember what he said. I just remember him gently stroking my shoulder while I sobbed and apologised for bothering him. I went back to bed after a minute or so. I needed to try to sleep because I was teaching at Oldham the next day. I still felt dizzy, but eventually, I fell asleep.

I literally staggered through my seven hours of teaching on Tuesday. It took constant willpower and concentration to keep going. It was my last day there for the year; nearly there. Wednesday was similar. I sat down for all of my lessons and the students were happy to do so too. It was a relief to finish at the end of the day.

I had an appointment with Marissa on Thursday, but asked if we could have it online because I didn't feel up to driving. I felt very weak during the session, probably because I hadn't eaten breakfast yet. I never ate before our appointments, but I was feeling the effects more than usual that day. I told her what had happened on Saturday and she was worried, especially as I hadn't felt up to driving in. She kept suggesting I go to hospital, but I resisted.

---

[37] Blood Sugar Level

Mum had told me that she wouldn't accept any work that week, in case I needed her — she's a relief teacher. After my appointment, I asked if she could come over. Again I felt guilty for asking her to drive over when she could have been doing something fun, but desperation made me put my own needs first for once. I felt hopeless. I was still exhausted, Marissa had made me feel even more scared about my mortality, but I didn't know how I could convince myself to eat more. Mum came straight away, and at first, I was relieved to see her.

However, when she saw how weak I was she started talking about going to hospital again. I was relieved when I managed to convince her to let me stay home unless my symptoms worsened. I could see she still was questioning her decision, even as she spoke. Possibly ruin our relationship and destroy any trust I had in her by forcing me to go to Emergency — which we both knew would lead to an emotionally detrimental and long hospital admission — or possibly enable my death?

Mum stayed with me for the rest of the day and Dad came over when he finished work. I could hear them talking in quiet, concerned voices in the lounge room while I read. I knew I wouldn't be able to put up a fight or run away if they decided I needed to go to hospital. Luckily they didn't. It was still on the table, but they agreed to let me stay home unless I went downhill. Unfortunately, they also wanted to keep an eye on me at all times, in case I collapsed. As Adam was at work during the day, this meant having one of them with me. I regretted calling Mum for the next two months.

Refeeding

For the next month or so, we went back and forth between Mum and Dad's house and Adam's, depending on what we needed to do that day. Mum and Dad didn't allow me to drive in case I collapsed. In some ways it was a relief to be driven around again, like a child, not needing to worry about directions or changing lanes. I started seeing Krish weekly and had a blood test every day. Krish organised for my blood analysis to be fast-tracked and called to tell me my results every afternoon. I have appreciated Australia's health care system, (aside from mental health), since I was very young — probably since I was eight and Adam was diagnosed with diabetes — but I appreciated it even more during this period. To think that we could get these results so quickly and it was free!

My already small and uncooperative veins took a beating over the summer. Luckily there were two amazing phlebotomists at the local collection centre, who were incredibly skilled as well as being beautiful humans. They always made sure it was one of them who took my blood, as the others who worked there could never get the blood to flow.

I stopped exercising after the Thursday when I asked Mum to come over. Feeling that weak without having done anything rigorous, aside from my morning exercise, scared me into stopping. We were still in limbo about hospital though. I didn't mind Mum and Dad being around — I wasn't up to doing much more than reading and colouring in anyway, and they were letting me eat what I wanted — but going into hospital would be horrible. It had only been bearable a few years before because I had felt so positive about recovery. I was not at all positive this time.

I started eating more but had to increase my intake slowly, in case I got refeeding syndrome.[38] I genuinely wanted to eat even more — I must have almost completely depleted my energy reserves; I felt so faint and frail that I wondered if my body was shutting down — but was worried about refeeding syndrome. That was the main reason for the daily blood tests.

Marissa recommended seeing a dietician, mostly to talk about refeeding syndrome. In hospital I took phosphate every day for the first two or three weeks, to help avoid refeeding syndrome, but the amount of phosphate I needed depended on how much I was eating. This was all calculated and

---

[38] The early days of refeeding are dangerous because refeeding syndrome can cause heart failure. Google it.

monitored in the hospital setting, which we couldn't do at home. Unfortunately, the lovely dietician I had seen when I first got out of Governor, was booked up for about a month, as was the dietician at Marissa's clinic. Luckily I was able to get an appointment a day or two after I called, at a place Siobhan recommended. I was very apprehensive about going. I knew going to hospital was still a possibility and that the dietician would have a strong influence on Mum and Dad's decision. If she thought I was at high risk of getting refeeding syndrome, I was almost certain they would take me straight to hospital.

"Now, you're going to need to be completely honest with the dietician about what you're currently eating, and what you were eating up until last week," Mum said, after I booked the appointment.
"Yeah, I was planning to." I was happy to do that. I had been (almost) completely honest with everyone since that day anyway.
"I've done some rough calculations, based on what I've seen you eat; the number of calories you're getting each day is below the WAEDOCS criteria for an involuntary hospital admission."
I didn't know that, within the WAEDOCS criteria, there is a list of behaviours and symptoms, of which only one needs to be fulfilled to require an involuntary admission — I googled it after my conversation with Mum, to check. One of these is having eaten below a certain number of calories for five or more consecutive days. I had been eating below that number for months.
"In some ways, I'm colluding with the eating disorder by not taking you straight to hospital," she continued. "But I understand that, at the moment, hospital would be harmful for you emotionally. I want to help you increase your food and get better at home, but only if we can do it safely."

Kara, the dietician, seemed nice, and seemed to understand my discomfort. "This is a no judgement zone," she said at the beginning of the appointment. I appreciated that, but also wondered if she meant it. It was sometime after I told her what I ate in an average day — which I always find incredibly embarrassing — that she handed me a hard copy of the WAEDOCS document.
"Do you fulfil any of the criteria listed there?" She asked.
It was the same list I had found online. I hoped the calorie limit would be lower than what I had read. It wasn't.
"No," I lied. Why would I say yes?

We spoke about refeeding syndrome and she said it was very uncommon. She had only seen it in South Africa when they were refeeding babies and children who had suffered severe malnutrition. Though maybe I fit into that category.

Then she took me through what I would need to eat at every meal after I left the appointment. It was a huge increase from what I had been eating — so much rice! I was completely overwhelmed. I was honest with her.
"I can't eat that much straight away. It's too fast. Can I build up to it?"
"Just do your best," she said, to my surprise.

When we had talked through everything, Kara asked if I was happy for Mum to come in, so she could fill her in.
"Umm not really. I can tell her anyway." I was terrified Kara would say something that would cause Mum to decide I needed to go to hospital. I also felt so weak and shaky from that fear, I was worried I would faint. Then they would definitely want me to go to hospital!
"Your Mum will feel better if she's included. She's very worried," Kara pushed back. "Shall I go get her?"
"I'd really prefer not. I don't want her to be involved," I said uncertainly, scared to stand up for myself.
"But if we leave Mum out of this, she'll continue to worry. If I talk to her, she'll feel better, knowing what's going on."
I didn't have the confidence to assert my rights. And she may have a point about alleviating some of Mum's anxiety.
"Ok," I conceded. As long as Mum didn't start controlling my food, adhering to the terrifying eating plan Kara had given me, it would be ok. Kara had said I didn't need to go to hospital, so it would probably help for Mum to hear that from her.

It didn't take long for Mum to tell Kara that I fulfilled one of the WAEDOCS criteria.
"Well in that case I agree, you should go straight to hospital," Kara replied. My stomach dropped.
"But you said I could do this at home and refeeding syndrome was really unlikely," I said weakly. I was terrified. The possibility of hospital suddenly felt very close.
"But you said yourself, you won't be able to stick to this plan," Kara said.
"Then what was the point of going through it all?" I asked. "Why didn't you just tell me to go to hospital?"
"Because I wanted you to see how much you would need to eat. You're already overwhelmed."
I didn't buy it. If Mum hadn't come in, she would have sent me on my merry way with the meal plan and information leaflets.

We talked in circles for the remainder of the appointment.

"Please, can you let me know what you decide, about hospital?" Kara asked, as we were leaving her office.
"Absolutely, we'll do that," Mum said earnestly.
I never did. I decided that, if Kara followed up I would tell her, but I couldn't be bothered calling. I felt she had been dishonest, but I couldn't work out her motive. Mum was confused too. She felt that, if she hadn't told her that I fulfilled the criteria for an involuntary admission, Kara would have continued to support us with refeeding at home. She also felt it was odd that Kara had suddenly changed her advice, but neither of us could work out why.

The drive home was tense. I didn't know if Mum was going to take me to hospital and I don't think she did either.
"What are you going to do about hospital?" I asked timidly, terrified that Mum would yell at me.
She sighed. "I'll need to think about it. And also talk to Dad." She was stressed and struggling to contain it.

Not long after we got home, the fear Mum had been bottling up over the last week, spilled out and she started directing her anger at me. I always get scared when Mum yells, even if it's not directed at me, and that afternoon I was already on edge. I started sobbing uncontrollably. Everything was coming out; all my fears and insecurities. I was able to articulate some of them, but everything else flowed out in my tears and wailing. I don't think Mum had realised the depth of my despair, or how much I had been holding inside. She started to sob too; it hurt her to see me so utterly distraught. I didn't want to worry her, so I tried to stop crying, in an attempt to make her feel better.

When I was able to speak more clearly, I told Mum about some of the things I had unpacked with Marissa — the insecurities that had contributed to the development of the eating disorder, and my intense, all-consuming self-hatred. She was shocked and incredibly sad that I had been dealing with so much on my own for most of my life. I hadn't realised the information was new to her. I thought we had spoken about these things in the past year, but maybe I hadn't been able to impart the depth of my trauma until that moment.

Mum called Dad later that afternoon. I lay on the couch in another room, reading and eavesdropping.
"We've had an emotional afternoon. It's been rough, but we're both feeling better now…" I heard her say. It was another week or two until I felt I could almost stop worrying that they would take me to hospital. The fear was still there for a while though, in the background, especially when I felt faint.

That summer was not the well-deserved, relaxing, celebratory break I had been looking forward to. I understood why Mum and Dad wanted to keep an eye on me for the first few weeks. I appreciated them giving up their time, and driving me around to appointments; it was definitely better than being in hospital. However, I started to find their constant presence stressful. I can never completely relax unless I'm alone, even with family. Although Mum and Dad occupied themselves, took care of their own food and pretty much left me to my own devices, I was always slightly on edge. Moving back and forth between houses didn't help either. We often didn't decide which house we would sleep at until the afternoon and I don't deal well with uncertainty. For a week or so I had awful stomach aches, presumably caused by stress, which usually started in the afternoon and lasted until after I went to bed.

About two weeks before Christmas I had an appointment with Sam, one of the clinicians in my care team. I was hoping she would say I was well enough to return to normal life, without Mum and Dad's supervision, but with more food. Instead, she said she wanted Mum and Dad to continue monitoring me until at least mid-January. I was shocked. I tried to convince her that I was out of danger, but she said she was still worried. I had been trying to convince Mum and Dad that I was well enough to be on my own and had hoped that, if Sam said I was ok, they would believe me. Without Sam's support, I would have to convince them myself. Surely they wouldn't feel the need to keep this up for more than another week. I didn't need to tell them that Sam wanted them to continue monitoring me for another month.

After our appointment, she came out to speak to Mum, who had driven me there. Sam told her what she had told me, that she recommended having someone with me at all times for at least the next month. My stomach dropped. I couldn't believe she had told Mum. What happened to patient confidentiality? I was angry, but didn't know if I had the right to speak up. Would it be rude? I didn't want to make things awkward. So I stayed quiet and tried not to cry.

I hardly spoke to Mum on the drive home after the appointment with Sam. I felt hopeless and could see no way out. I had done it again; made myself too sick to be allowed to turn things around on my own. Whenever others had become involved in the past, they always forced me to do things their way, or too fast, which never helped my long-term recovery. They put a bandaid on, but it quickly peeled off. Mum hardly spoke either. She was worried about me and didn't know how to help. At the time, I thought she was angry at me for not talking.

When Adam found out how much I, (and Mum and Dad), was struggling, he started helping out whenever he could. He worked at home for one or two days, so he could be the one to keep an eye on me, giving me some space from Mum and Dad. They started letting me sleep at home, while they slept at their house, if Adam was home. Adam was great, and I think he tried to organise things so that he and Emily, his girlfriend, slept at our place instead of hers where possible. He even came to look at two houses with me one afternoon — I was hoping to buy my own place as soon as possible, while interest rates were low and before house prices went up.

About a week after Adam started helping out, Mum and Dad decided my friends could monitor me too, if they felt comfortable. Michael, Gilbert and Kieran came to visit at different times. I felt bad that I wasn't well enough to go out and do something exciting with them. I worried they would be bored just sitting in the living room chatting, but they didn't seem to mind. They were nothing but understanding and supportive.

Another day Lucy and her girlfriend Gideon came to visit. When they arrived, Lucy handed me a gift bag.
"This isn't your Christmas present," she said. "I'll give you that when I see you next."
"What's this for?" I asked.
She shrugged self-consciously. "Just because, you know.."
I was filled with gratitude that they had wanted to put together this collection of gifts, to help me while I was struggling. I was moved again when I found such thoughtful gifts inside. I hadn't realised they cared so much. I can't put into words how surprised, disbelieving, appreciative and loved I felt. #blessed.[39]

It was around that time that I started exercising again, though not as much as I had previously. I had been worried to do so when Mum and Dad stayed the night at our place, or when we slept at their house, in case they heard me moving around in the morning. Once I started exercising again, I couldn't stop. Even when Dad stayed the night at our place, I took a chance and exercised. Luckily he didn't come in to check on me until I had finished.

"I'm not sure if it's worth asking you this, because you can just lie... Have you started exercising again?" Mum asked one day, when we were driving home from an appointment with Krish. How did she know? Maybe she just suspected. Maybe Dad had heard me the morning he came in to check on me,

---

[39] I use this facetiously. It is possibly my least favourite hashtag.

and that's why he had come in. Should I tell her the truth? She probably wouldn't believe me if I lied anyway.

"Yeah," I said quietly. "But it's nothing strenuous. Just some bodyweight exercises," which was true.

She sighed.

"I'm not going to force you," she said, "but I want you to consider stopping, for your health. You're not out of the danger zone yet, and if you go backwards, you may need to go to hospital."

It only took me a few seconds to consider, before deciding to continue.

I will admit I was a bit of a brat to Mum and Dad during this period. For the first few weeks, I did my best to stay upbeat and work with their schedules. I appreciated them giving up their time to look after me and for caring so much. I often thought I would have preferred they didn't care quite so much, so I could be by myself, but at least they hadn't taken me to hospital.

However, when Sam said she wanted Mum and Dad to continue looking after me for at least another month, it was too much. I couldn't live like that any longer. I felt suffocated, stressed, worried and hopeless. How long would this continue? I wanted to get back to my life. I had waited for so long, and worked so hard, to be able to enjoy this time off, but it had been snatched away. During this period, I often thought being in hospital would be preferable. I also wondered if Mum and Dad were continuing to monitor me for their own peace of mind. If they weren't with me they wouldn't know if I had collapsed, so they would always be worried. If they left me alone and I died, I knew they would never recover. They would always regret it.

Sometimes I got angry at them when I felt they were being unreasonable. Sometimes I didn't even try to be flexible if I wanted to sleep at my place instead of theirs. Sometimes I skipped a snack if I wasn't too hungry, just to spite them. Sometimes I gave them the silent treatment. On the whole though, I did my best to stay positive. I knew Mum and Dad were acting out of love and fear. And it was better than going to hospital again.

It wasn't until late January that I finally asked Sam why she had told Mum.

"Oh my gosh, I'm so sorry. I thought you were ok with me telling her," she said.

"Why would I be ok with that? I didn't want them to keep hanging around. If you hadn't told Mum she wouldn't have known…" I replied weakly. I felt awkward causing conflict.

"I'm so sorry. I really thought you were happy for me to tell her. Oh gosh, I'm so sorry. That's terrible."

Sam continued to apologise while I shrugged, embarrassed. "It's ok," I said eventually, even though it wasn't, so she would stop apologising. I wish I could say that was the first time a clinician has broken patient confidentiality.

A New Perspective

As my blood results and blood pressure normalised, and my heart rate and weight increased slightly, Krish said it was safe for me to be alone for short periods. This gave me a window of a few hours between Adam leaving for work and Dad coming over, when I could be by myself. I relished that time alone. Krish also said I could start doing short drives. Each week he allowed me more freedom until finally, less than a week before school started for the year, I was granted full independence.

It must have been late January when I first learnt of Grace Tame's existence. The famous photo of her and Scomo at the Australian of the Year Awards showed up in my Instagram feed. I had never watched or followed the awards, so I had missed Grace's win the previous year — I had been too busy working on my thesis then anyway. A quick Google told me about her sexual assault and campaign to change the gag law. She was also Autistic, had anorexia nervosa as a teenager and was from Hobart. I had even lived at her school for about a week at the beginning of my third year in Hobart. I started following her on Instagram and she became an inspiration and a role model.

Our family was worried about the impending opening of the national and state borders. Mum, Dad and I had been wearing masks since not long after Christmas — a few sneaky Omicron cases were detected on Christmas Eve and quickly spread. Mum had already decided she would stop teaching until case numbers were low again, though we didn't know if that would ever happen. I was worried about teaching, however, that was my main income, and the risk of Covid would be everywhere, including at gigs, which was my only other source of income. Mum kept telling me it was dangerous for me to teach, given how weak my body still was, but I didn't know what other option I had, if I wanted to maintain my financial independence.

I knew Mum and Dad would be happy for me to move back home if I had to stop working while Covid raged through the state, but I didn't want to do that. As I gradually felt physically stronger, the ED voice told me I didn't need to increase my food intake anymore and could start exercising again. If I stayed at Mum and Dad's they would be watching. I felt I was starting to get my life together — laughable in hindsight — and living at home again, far away from my friends, with no work, felt like a few steps backwards.

Luckily, a week or two before school went back, Krish said my blood results had normalised enough that I probably wouldn't become seriously ill if I contracted Covid. I knew that a white blood cell count that was only just inside the normal range wasn't worth much against Covid while my weight was still so low, but I didn't care. I just wanted to get back to normal life, whether or not I would actually be safe. I dreaded having to worry about contracting Covid every time I went out in public after the border opened though. I expected Mum and Dad to say that I still wasn't well enough to teach and try to stop me from going back to work. I didn't know what I would do if they tried; I didn't know if I had it in me to put up a fight. Luckily they didn't.

Though he had said it was safe for me to work, Krish suggested I stop teaching the group classes at Westin, because there wasn't enough room to socially distance, and the students wouldn't be wearing masks. To be honest, I was relieved. I would have been working nine-hour days there, with hardly any break, including the private students I taught after school. I was worried about telling Westin so close to the start of term, but luckily they were understanding. They even allowed me to use an empty room to teach my private students after school, and held my position for me to return in term two.

When I arrived at Westin in the first week of term, I bumped into Liz, the mother of Sophie, who was one of my private students.
"I'm glad we bumped into each other actually," she said, after exchanging the usual pleasantries. "It might be good to warn you, Sophie has become quite anxious, since late last year, and it got worse over the holidays. Just so you know, in case she gets anxious during lesson."
I was surprised and sad. Sophie is a lovely girl; very intelligent — I would say wise beyond her years — caring and well-spoken. After teaching her for a year, I had formed the belief that she was mostly comfortable in her own skin, and wasn't afraid to be different.
"Oh gosh, I'm sorry," I said sincerely. "Should I talk to her about it?"
"Oh no, no, please don't mention it. Just so you're aware, if she gets stressed in lesson."
"Of course. I'll be gentle," I smiled.
"Actually, would it be ok if Sophie sits in on the lesson before hers? She might need to rest of be out of the heat."
"Yeah of course. Maybe she can play with us too." I was more than happy for her to join us. I knew she wouldn't disrupt the lesson and it would be lovely to have her there.
"Maybe. Playing with someone else might make her anxious…"
"We'll see how we go. Whatever she wants to do," I assured her.

As soon as Sophie walked into the teaching room I noticed that she had lost a lot of weight. Did she have a restrictive eating disorder? Surely not; she didn't seem the type. But then neither had I, when I was younger. Sophie sat in the corner, looking outside anxiously. After a few minutes, she went back outside, returning in time for her own lesson.

I became increasingly worried during her lesson. It wasn't just that she had lost weight; she looked frail and breakable. She was anxious too, almost irritable, and was having trouble concentrating. Near the end of the lesson, she said she was finding it hard to focus because she was tired.
"Did you have a snack after school?" I asked, offhand.
"I'm not really hungry," she mumbled self-consciously.
How many times had I used that lie as an excuse for not eating? I sent Liz a message, while Sophie was playing one of her pieces, asking if she could come back a few minutes early, so I could speak to her. I was trying to work out how to tell her that Sophie might have an eating disorder.

I spoke to Liz outside, while Sophie was packing up.
"How was she?" Liz asked.
"Very anxious… And… I noticed she's lost a lot of weight," I replied.
"Yes… We've noticed she's been restricting her food."
"I wondered," I said, relieved I wouldn't have to be the one to break the news.
"We're on the waiting list at The Numbat Practice."
"Oh good. It's a long wait though, about six months at least," I said, speaking from experience.
Liz looked worried. I wondered if she thought it odd that I knew about The Numbat Practice, let alone how long the waiting list was. I didn't care though. I had to help Sophie however I could. It broke my heart to see her looking so unsure and afraid, and to think of her fighting with the monster inside her head all day — the monster I knew all too well.
"I've… I've been there… the eating…" I tried.
"Oh right… And did they cure you, at The Numbat Practice?" Liz asked
"Oh, no… No, they didn't help me…" There was so much to explain. Sophie had finished packing up and was walking towards us. She would be within hearing range soon.
"I'll message you," I said. "I'll do everything I can to help, really. I don't want her to have to go through this."
Liz tried to say more, but Sophie had reached us and was looking at us questioningly, probably aware that we had been talking about her.
"I'll message you," I said, as I walked back to the classroom to teach my next student.

I struggled to hold myself together for the rest of the afternoon. I couldn't stop thinking about Sophie. I wished I could hug her and make it all better. I worried about her all the way home. I was starting to understand how Mum and Dad felt, watching me starve myself. I sobbed on and off, wondering if I should be driving while I was crying. It was almost a physical pain, combined with a longing too huge and strong to contain inside myself. I wondered why Sophie's sickness was affecting me more than my other friends who have had anorexia nervosa. I know a lot of people, mostly from hospital, who have suffered for much longer and been in greater medical danger than Sophie. After over a year of contemplation, my conclusion remains the same: I knew Sophie before she got sick, and seeing how much the illness changed her, in such a short amount of time, is nothing short of tragic.

I texted Liz on and off that week and offered to catch up so she could pick my brain. When I visited Mum and Dad that weekend, I asked if they had any books Liz might find helpful. Mum has collected quite a few books on anorexia nervosa over the years. She sent me home with two books and also wrote a note to Liz, who she has never met, offering to answer any questions and to help in any way she could. I cried again when I left their house that night. I desperately wanted Sophie to get whatever help she needed before she spiralled down any further.

Liz and I messaged quite a bit those first few weeks and for the rest of the term. Sophie didn't come to her lesson the next week because she was too tired. She went into hospital a few days later. I felt as though I had been punched in the guts when Liz told me. I had hoped it wouldn't come to that. I worried about Sophie a lot and gave Liz as much support as I could. I wanted to visit her in hospital, but she only felt comfortable seeing her family.

Given how ineffective and traumatic "treatment" has been for me, my best advice is to catch the eating disorder early, to turn things around before the disordered thinking becomes too entrenched. And see a psychologist. I tried to think of what I could do to help Sophie. What would have helped me, 15 years earlier? Aside from early intervention, which Sophie was now getting, and psychological treatment, which I couldn't provide, I realised what may have helped me was to know, without any doubt, that my friends cared about me.[40]

---

[40] Again, Dad has had to point out that my friends often showed me how much they cared, by visiting me in hospital and bringing thoughtful gifts and cards. However, it never occurred to me that they actually cared. I assumed they did these things because they were nice people, not because they truly cared about me.

Every week or two, I made Sophie cards and little presents, which I gave to Liz to pass on, when I came to Westin to teach. She asked me not to mention the eating disorder in my cards to Sophie, so I wrote silly poems and referenced jokes we had shared the year before. I hope they helped.

I spoke to Marissa about Sophie, telling her how much I cared and how it hurt me, knowing what she was going through. Thinking about it as an outsider made me view my own circumstances differently. Maybe I didn't deserve this either. If I thought Sophie looked frail, maybe that's how I looked too. I viewed my build as somewhere between average and slim, but maybe the body dysmorphia was still warping my perspective. Marissa and I discussed how I might be able to use these new thoughts to help my own recovery, but we didn't come up with anything.

Around that time, Mum told me that Jo[41] was also struggling. She had been having heart problems and had been to the Emergency Department a few times. The ED voice asked ne why I had never been sick enough to have heart failure. Instead, I was the failure for ever working hard enough to lose weight. The healthy part of me was able to remind myself that, after my scare the previous year, I didn't want heart problems. I wanted to be able to live my life. I also wanted to stay thin though, but... I digress.

I had wondered for a while if Mum and Sally were deliberately keeping Jo and me from meeting, in case one of us accidentally triggered the other. One day I asked Mum if this was the case, and she confirmed my suspicion. I said I had wondered if I would trigger Jo but didn't think there was much that would trigger me these days that I hadn't already seen. Seeing thin people and hearing others talk about restricting food is triggering, but it's nothing new. I asked if there was anything I could do to help Jo from afar. Mum suggested I write her a letter. I could send it to Mum, who would read it to check for potential triggers before sending it to Sally, who would also check for triggers, before giving it to Jo, who could decide if she wanted to read it or not.

I tried to think of something to write that would be helpful. How much help could one letter provide? I doubted I could change her mindset if I couldn't change my own. After a week or two of pondering, I decided not to write to Jo. Not knowing what to write felt overwhelming. Mum had said I didn't need to anyway; only if I wanted to. A few days after I made that decision though, Mum asked how I was going with my letter.

---

[41] The daughter of mum's friend Sally, who has an eating disorder and recommended Marissa's clinic to us.

"I can't think what to write that will actually be helpful," I said. "If I knew that…" I trailed off.
"How 'bout you write about some of the realisations you've had that have helped you?" Mum suggested.
That sparked an idea. It took me about 15 minutes to write. I was surprised at how quickly and easily the words flowed.

Dear Jo,

I've been wanting to talk to you for a while, but I know it may not be the best idea, for either of us because anything can be triggering… So Mum suggested I write a letter. It's hard to put everything into a letter, but I'll do my best.

I think the best treatment is early intervention because recovery only gets harder. So here are some things I wish I had known and believed when I was 18.

It will actually never be enough. When I first went into hospital I thought that was an achievement. I'd made myself so sick I needed to be hospitalised. But then I found out there were people in there who had been sick for longer, were at lower BMIs, had had multiple hospitalisations, needed the tube, exercised more or ate less prior to hospital. So then I thought if I had two hospital admissions then I would have earned recovery. But that didn't happen until much later.

Before my second admission though, I had a bit of an epiphany. I'd been reading Lily Collins' book (which you're welcome to borrow by the way). She had AN and bulimia in her teens/twenties, which is why she was in 'To The Bone' — a movie about a girl with an ED. Anyway, there was a quote in there which at first I brushed off as motivational instaquote fluff. But then I was thinking about it again while I was entering the freeway one day - yes I still remember. And I realised how true it is. This is the quote:

"There is a greater happiness to be attained — the happiness of enjoying myself to the fullest during the one life I have and accepting myself for who I am."

I can't remember now if she explains the quote, but this is what it means to me. You know how you feel really good about yourself when you've eaten less at a meal or you're less hungry or you've worked out for longer than usual, because the ED voice congratulates you for your hard work and willpower? She's saying there's a greater happiness than that false, short-lived, shallow happiness; the real happiness of not hating yourself, enjoying actual life things like hanging out with friends, being spontaneous, laughing at a joke because you have the energy to laugh and feel real emotions.

And then I realised — this was an important car trip — that, even though I hadn't had a heap of hospital admissions or been to emergency because of a failing heart or reached a BMI as low as others or run 10km every day or been sick for as long as others, I could easily do that if I let myself keep going. And I'm not saying that's an achievement. I'm saying that, because of how my brain is wired and how low my self-worth is, it would be easier for me to keep restricting and exercising, which would lead to all of those things I hadn't yet "achieved" without really trying. It would be easier than "giving in" and eating more. Because actually eating more and stopping the exercise is way harder, as you know. So if you think you're not sick enough or haven't been sick long enough, give it ten years and you will have done all those things your ED tells you you need to "achieve" to be worthy of recovery. But please don't actually give it ten years. Just realise now that you could, because you have the willpower. I hope that makes sense. And I hope it doesn't sound like I'm encouraging you to stay sick to tick off the ED goals. I'm saying the opposite.

Here's an analogy I used to explain the paragraph above to Dad, who often can't even comprehend my disordered thinking because it's so messed up. A person, let's call her Nadia, could have gone to uni and studied medicine because she was really clever. But she didn't want to be a Doctor. She wanted to work in the family business as a secretary. You have the willpower to kill yourself - that's what I realised. I could keep doing this until I killed myself if no one intervened. Morbid I know, but it's true. But I could choose not to, and become a secretary/healthy person. Does that make sense?

Also, you may think you're not sick enough because you feel fine. But I've often felt fine even in the weeks before a hospital admission. I could be full of energy and not even very hungry, so I believe I don't need to eat as much as others to survive. Maybe none of us do. But it's actually just my body running on adrenaline and taking energy from my vital organs to help me move around. I know it's hard to believe it at the time. You probably feel fine too. The body is amazing.

So topic change - if you need any motivation to make even a few healthy choices right now, know this: hospital may seem like an achievement, but that changes very quickly. Outside of hospital, you can kind of go at your own pace. Yes, it's a constant battle with that horrible voice in your head that makes you think it's helping you, but at least you're at home with your friends and family and, once again, you can go at your own pace. In hospital, you pretty much lose all your rights. You have to eat what they tell you and, if you don't, they stick a tube so far up your nose it makes the Covid test seem like a walk in the park. If you're on a medical ward you'll have a nurse with you 24/7, which is fine if they're nice, but if they're not you're stuck with them for 8 hours... And, no joke, they will watch you shower and go to the toilet. There you go, 2 good reasons to stay out of hospital: avoid the tube and keep your privacy.

One more thing that may or may not help. I realised when I was watching the first Hobbit movie, how similar Gollum is to a person with an ED. He's so obsessed with the ring that he stops caring about anything else. He loses his friends — ok, I haven't killed any of my friends — he hardly eats, he freaks out when he loses the ring and he lives in a cave alone because he doesn't trust other people. I don't know if that helps... It hit home pretty hard when I realised it.

That's all I can think of to say at the moment, but I'm happy to answer any questions. I'm not a fan of inspirational quotes, like "life isn't about waiting for the storm to pass, it's about learning to dance in the rain," — that one makes me want to scream — but here are some that I've actually found helpful because they are so true. Don't speed through them, think about each one.

If we wait until we're ready, we'll be waiting for the rest of our lives.

The food you choose to eat or not eat does not make you good or bad.

The voices in my head are trying to kill me.

Quit measuring your weight and start measuring your quality of life.

Losing weight is not your life's work and counting calories is not the call of your soul. You surely are destined for something much greater.

Recovery is a fight. And losing means death.

Eating isn't something that you have to earn. It's a necessity to survive and a right that you have.

You have a 100% chance of getting better if you put as much work and energy into recovery as you do into the eating disorder.

Being thin will not magically solve all your problems.

You are not fat. You have fat. You also have fingernails. But you are not fingernails.

Recovery is hard but it's far better than dying from anorexia.

You would have to hate some a lot to starve them to death.

I never thought I was a bully until I listened to how I spoke to myself

I hope these help.

Hannah

Wisdom Teeth and Another Assessment

A few weeks into term I had an appointment to see a dental surgeon. I had gone to the dentist for a check-up in January, and been told that I would need to have my wisdom teeth taken out within the next six months. That wasn't what I wanted to hear; I had enough to worry about already. The dentist recommended a dental surgeon, who would be able to provide more information and talk through options with me. I hoped he would say I could wait a few years to get them out. Maybe I would be in a better place then, physically and mentally. Unfortunately, the dental surgeon agreed that all four needed to be taken out that year, sooner rather than later. He was leaning towards general anaesthetic, as one or two teeth looked like they would be particularly difficult to remove. Being asleep sounded good to me too.

I asked him if it was safe for me to be given anaesthetic, as I was still underweight and had had AN for a long time. He said it should be fine and that he had operated on other patients under general anaesthetic, who also had anorexia. I got the feeling he didn't really understand the risks and also just wanted to end the appointment, so I decided to do my own research. I have come to assume that most people, including medical professionals, have no idea about eating disorders.

I asked for advice about wisdom teeth removal and anaesthetic in some eating disorder communities on Facebook but received conflicting responses. Mum was adamantly opposed to it when I told her and Dad I would need to have the operation later that year. I had almost convinced myself it would be safe, but Mum's reaction made me start worrying all over again. I knew that, while she always errs on the side of extreme caution, she also usually knows what she's talking about, because she researches everything thoroughly. I had hoped to have the operation during the first term school holidays but would need to book soon. Mum wanted to research the dangers herself and speak to Marissa and the people at WAEDOCS first, all of which would take time.

Mum, Dad and I had continued looking for someone to do another Autism assessment. They needed to have experience diagnosing girls and also understand the similarity in presentation with AN. I had been given a few recommendations for clinicians from people in the Autistic community, but Mum discovered Autism WA. They have three experienced assessors on the panel, so we figured they would understand the different presentation in girls.

I contacted them and they sent me pages and pages of detailed questions, similar to those we had filled out the the previous year. It was a pre-screening of sorts, from which they would decide if they would assess me. They also asked us to send them any school reports that mentioned Autistic traits. We saw this as a good sign; they were being thorough. Some of the questions were directed at me; others at Mum and Dad. Mum spent days typing comprehensive, detailed responses. She spent at least 40 hours writing. She had to move her answers to a separate document because there wasn't enough space for all of her writing in the PDFs Autism WA had sent. She wanted to make sure they had all the information they needed, so we didn't have a repeat of the last assessment.

One question asked if I had had a previous assessment and, if so, to attach the report. I did so, assuming the information within would help them understand if I was likely to be Autistic. About a week after I sent in the completed questions, I received a reply informing me that, as I had already had an assessment, they couldn't do another. I was confused. I emailed back, explaining that the people who had conducted the first assessment were inexperienced. Their reply explained that, as they are government-funded, they can't assess everyone. As I had already had an assessment, they wouldn't do another. While I understood their reasoning — not that I completely agreed with it — it would have been helpful if they had asked about any previous assessments before sending all of the other questions. Mum had wasted hours typing her answers.

I returned to the Autism groups on Facebook, requesting recommendations for assessors. In my post, I said that, as I had had an assessment the year before, I had been knocked back by Autism WA. Another group member, Selina, commented:

```
Selina: I think I know who did your first
assessment. I had a similarly terrible experience.
Did his surname begin with K?

Me: Yes! How did you know?

Selina: I'll send you a private message.
```

Selina had also been to see Dr Khan for an Autism assessment. In her initial appointment, he had told her she wasn't Autistic, and that she was wasting her money. He then told her about my Google review, saying I had slandered him because he told me I wasn't Autistic. She had three appointments with him and he had apparently spent the majority of the time complaining about me.

He never mentioned my name but, as he only had three Google reviews at the time — two people wrote reviews soon after I did, which made me wonder if they were fake, or if Dr Khan had started asking his clients to leave a review to improve his one-star rating — it wasn't hard to identify mine. It makes me wonder how often clinicians actually break patient confidentiality, hoping they won't be discovered.

I had a stressful start to the year. I was scared every time I went out in public, which I did as little as possible, even though I was wearing an P2 mask, in case particles of the virus slipped through a tiny gap between my skin and the material. I had finally started buying my own groceries. I used click and collect for most things but still went to the Spudshed for my fruit and vegetables because they were so much cheaper. I was in and out as quickly as possible and felt anxious if I had to wait in a long queue, where I was possibly exposing myself to Covid. Most of my students wore a mask to lessons, but I flinched whenever they fidgeted with it, or pulled it down to talk.

I was waiting for an appointment with Krish when I saw the announcement that Putin had invaded Ukraine. I watched in horror as the war dominated the news for the next month or two. I didn't know what I could do to help, so I donated to the Red Cross. I felt as though there was chaos everywhere. When would it end? And what could I do to help?

One night Gilbert messaged to tell me that he and his girlfriend had broken up. I almost cried. I was so sad for him. I had thought she was "the one." They had been so happy together. It stayed on my mind. Only a week or two later, he messaged to tell me his dad had stage four pancreatic cancer. Again, I almost cried. I didn't know what to do except be there for him. I supported him as much as I could and worried that it wasn't enough. I was sad for him, his dad and their whole family. A few weeks later, he told me he had just found out his mum had breast cancer. She had been keeping it to herself because of his dad's diagnosis. I was angry at the world for hurting one family so much, though I know others have it even worse.

I knew I had put on weight since the day I had almost collapsed. It was hard to know how much though, because of body dysmorphia, weight fluctuations and because I still drank as much water as I could before Krish weighed me. I told myself that it couldn't be very much, since my clothes still fit. As I had four years earlier, I tried to convince myself that it was worth it to have more energy. Deep down though, I didn't believe it. Seeing thin people made me hate myself even more than it had a few months earlier. Even my students, many of whom are younger than ten, triggered me. I stared at their thin arms and tiny waists while I was teaching them. Why couldn't I be that small again? Had I been that skinny when I was their height? Would my arms be that thin if I was scaled down to their height? Did they think I was fat?

When I told Marissa about Autism WA falling through, we started talking through other options. A lot of Autistic women had recommended one particular clinical psychologist in Perth, which confused me, as my understanding was that assessments needed to be conducted by a psychiatrist and one or two other clinicians. Marissa explained that, as an adult, I could be assessed by a clinical psychologist.
"Could you assess me then?" I asked.
"Me?"
"Yeah.. or do you need to specialise in Autism or something?"
"No, I'm a clin psych and I've been on panels for Autism assessments, so I'm qualified."
"Well, could you then?"
We talked through the pros and cons. I had been seeing Marissa weekly for about eight months, so she knew me much better than anyone else I would go to for an assessment, who I would speak to for three or four hours at most. In the end, Marissa agreed. She suggested we spread it out over three or four sessions, so we could do it thoroughly and no one could question the validity.

We finished the assessment on March 31, just in time for Autism Awareness month in April.
"Are you able to tell me today if I'm Autistic or not, or do you need to go through your notes and score the questionnaires?" I asked hesitantly at the end of our appointment.
Marissa chuckled. "Hannah, you're definitely Autistic. I don't know yet if you're level one or two, but you're Autistic."
My heart soared as I smiled and tears filled my eyes.
"How do you feel? Are you ok?"
"Yes. I'm just so relieved. I knew I would cry if I got my diagnosis," I laughed.
""They're happy tears, right? You're not regretting doing this?"
"Oh yes, definitely happy tears! Thank you for diagnosing me."

That was one of my happiest days. I told my family and close friends I finally had a diagnosis. They were happy for me and some jokingly congratulate me on "passing the test." Mum and Dad had bought me an assortment of badges and pins for Christmas the previous year; most advocated for queer pride, feminism or Autism awareness. I had been wearing one or two each day when I remembered, but there was one I decided I wouldn't wear unless I was diagnosed. It says "actually autistic." After my appointment with Marissa, I put the badge on.

The next day — I waited because March 31 is transgender awareness day and I didn't want to take the focus away from them — I wrote a Facebook post.

I'm not one for making personal announcements on Facebook but I feel it is important that this one is made.
Yesterday I was officially diagnosed with Autism. It would have been awesome to have known 20 years ago, even ten. But, as with most things, the diagnosis criteria were modelled on boys, so there you go...
I'm sharing this for two reasons:
1. *I try really really hard to read social situations and fit in but sometimes I get it wrong. Please tell me if I offend you because chances are it wasn't intentional. I'm too busy trying to be accepted to ruin it by insulting anyone!*
2. *If you have any questions about Autism, feel free to ask me, particularly if you think you, or someone in your life, may be Autistic. There's so much misinformation on the internet these days that it's hard to know what is true.*

It would take too long to describe the relief, which is still sinking in, after years of anxiety, confusion and self-blame, so I won't try. Instead, I want to thank everyone who accepted me for the awkward turtle I am, even without the diagnosis, just as Hannah.
I also want to thank Kieran and Callum, for hinting I might be Autistic; Morgana for spending hours answering my questions and sending me helpful information; Mum and Dad for spending even more hours reading all sorts of research papers, books and watching videos to understand the condition; Suzanne and Asusa for also answering all my random questions; Wendy for secretly diagnosing me and telling me when I needed the validation; Rhiannon for assuming I already had a diagnosis; and everyone else who has talked this through with me for the past 20 months.

No, this is not an April Fools. If it was, it was over 2 years in planning. Which yes, is the kind of thing I would do, but not this time.

I made the post because I thought it would help people to know, so I wouldn't accidentally offend anyone (again). I also hoped to raise awareness so that, if anyone was wondering if they were Autistic themselves, they would know they could talk to me. I was astounded by people's comments. I hadn't been expecting such kind words and support. A few people also sent private messages, thanking me for sharing the news. One friend had only been diagnosed a week earlier and said they were crying as they read my post.

I didn't understand why my friend was crying until later that day. I had known I would cry when I was diagnosed, but I thought it would just be one little happy cry. However, for the next week, I found myself spontaneously sobbing my heart out, for a few minutes at a time. They weren't sad tears. They were kind of happy tears, but I think that, mostly, they were tears of relief. I had been waiting for this day for almost two years. But I had also been waiting since I was about ten years old and had started feeling different without understanding why.

Later that day, I played at a wedding with Krista, with whom I had been discussing Autism for the past year.
"Hey congrats on your diagnosis by the way!" She said, as we were packing up.
I laughed. "I love that you think it's something worth congratulating!"
She looked uncomfortable. "Isn't it though? I thought it's what you wanted…"
"No no, it is," I assured her, "and I love that you know that."
The Sunday after my diagnosis, when I went to Mum and Dad's for dinner, Mum made a special dessert, to celebrate my diagnosis. As with Krista, I was touched by her care and her understanding that this really was something to celebrate.

Panic Attacks

I had been ready for school holidays since about the fifth week of school term. Only in hindsight did I realise what a stressful term it had been. However, at the time, I thought I was coping well. This was possibly due to my lack of interoception. The stress of the war in Ukraine, rising Covid cases, understaffed hospitals resulting in ramping and a shortage of beds, Sophie having AN, Gilbert's parents both having cancer, worrying that Marissa wouldn't find sufficient traits to diagnose me with Autism, and completing the paperwork to buy a house, all eventually built up.

About a week after receiving my diagnosis, I woke during the night with diarrhoea. For the rest of the night, I went back and forth between my bed and the toilet. A few times I felt as though I was about to vomit; luckily I didn't. My sleepy brain decided that it was my body reacting to the built-up stress, as it had three years earlier. Though my energy levels that term had been better than the previous year, my mental and emotional recovery hadn't progressed much since the initial health scare four months earlier. Now, feeling weak from diarrhoea and a night of broken sleep, I was scared my body was sicker than I had realised. The fear that I might collapse or have a heart attack returned.

The next day, I experienced the exhaustion and bottomless hunger I always feel after clearing out my insides. I still did my morning exercise though, tiring myself even further. The depth of my exhaustion exacerbated my fear. The vomiting and diarrhoea a few years earlier hadn't been fun, but my body had bounced back. This time, my body was still recovering from nearly dying only a few months earlier; it was nowhere near being healthy. What if it couldn't cope and I collapsed? Or, if I didn't collapse, what if I was exhausted for weeks, as I had been over the summer? I was scared to take that much time off work. I still wasn't eating enough and felt tired more often than I should.

Though I was almost certain the diarrhoea had been caused by stress, it occurred to me that it could be Covid. I had been very careful, but I knew that my P2 mask was only 98% effective. I did my first-ever RAT that morning. I hadn't needed to do one until then, because I hadn't had symptoms. I had been dreading it though — aside from being uncomfortable, it also brought back memories of the NG tube. Luckily, it was negative.

I had to teach at school that day and was also meeting Harriet[42] in the car park before I started, to give her some music for a gig. Breakfast hadn't improved my energy levels at all, so I was still feeling incredibly weak when I arrived at school, and was dreading the next five hours of teaching. Willpower can get me through exhaustion and dizziness, but I was worried it wouldn't be enough to keep me conscious. I laughed about my exhaustion with Harriet — though the laughter was forced — as we commiserated about what a joke the year had been so far. When I saw her a few weeks later, she told me I had looked absolutely dead on my feet.

I made it through teaching, but the following day would be even busier. And I was still exhausted. I had diarrhoea again that night, which increased my anxiety. What would happen if it never stopped? My body would be drained of electrolytes and I would eventually need to go to hospital. They might keep me in to "treat" the eating disorder.

On Wednesdays, I usually taught for two and a half hours at one school, before driving to Westin, eating lunch in the car park, and teaching for another three hours. Unfortunately, on this particular day, I also had an appointment with Pari, the psychiatrist in charge of the eating disorder program at the Heathgrove Clinic, before I started teaching that morning.[43] I was worried she would be running late, as doctors often do. Even if my appointment finished on time, I would need to rush to get to school on time. However, if I hadn't taken that appointment I would have had to wait another month.

As (bad) luck would have it, Pari was running very late. I was trying not to think about the time because stress saps my energy and I already felt lightheaded, weak and slightly shaky. Again, I wondered if I would make it through the day without collapsing. While I waited, I texted Jen,[44] who offered what moral support she could from Melbourne. I had told her how exhausted I had been the day before, and my worries about the busy day ahead.

---

[42] Remember Harriet? We rented together for a bit in Hobart.

[43] I was on an eating disorder mental health care plan, which allowed met to get a Medicare rebate on 40 psychology sessions per year. However, I needed a report from a psychiatrist after the first 20 sessions in order to get a rebate for the next 20. I had already had more than 20 sessions, so I had been paying the full amount for about two months already, while I waited to see Pari.

[44] A close friend I met in Hobart.

The receptionist knew I needed to leave on time so, when it was 30 minutes into my appointment time and I was still waiting, she emailed Pari. A few minutes later, Pari and her client came out to the waiting room.
"I'm sorry, I was talking too much," said the client, who didn't look sorry at all. I deduced that Pari had told him she needed to finish their session because I was waiting. I was wearing a mask so I didn't bother faking a smile at the man. Silver linings.

When Marissa told me I needed a psychiatrist to "sign off" for me to get my next 20 sessions, I thought she meant they literally just needed to sign a form — that's Autistic literality right there. It turned out Pari needed to write a report, which meant me recounting the history of my eating disorder. I told her as much as I could in the half hour we had remaining until I needed to leave. In the last five minutes, she talked to me about recovery and tried to give me hope that it was possible. I just nodded because I really needed to leave. Finally, she said she wanted to offer me a place in the inpatient program at Heathgrove.
"We don't usually accept patients with severe and enduring eating disorders, which is what you have, because they are unlikely to recover. But you seem positive; you've improved almost on your own since the end of last year. I think you could recover and I would like to offer you that opportunity."
Again I just nodded and said "Thank you," because I needed to get to school.

My head was reeling with questions though — would they cater to my food sensitivities this time, or would they tell me I needed to go see an immunologist? Why don't they take people who aren't likely to recover? What are those people meant to do? If they can't help people with severe and enduring eating disorders, is their program actually any good? Did she really think she was doing me a favour by offering me a place in the program?

I arrived at school just in time for my first student and somehow made it through the day. I felt as though every single cell in my body was running on empty; there was no part of me that possessed any energy. It was as bad as the complete exhaustion I had experienced at the end of the previous year. I was constantly terrified I would collapse. Messaging Jen between students got me through the day. Receiving her replies was my one source of hope and happiness on that seemingly unending, bleak day.

A week or two earlier, I had asked Krish what he thought about me taking anti-anxiety medication. I had been feeling increasingly stressed in situations that should only have been mildly stressful, such as gigs and teaching. He gave me a prescription for Zoloft and recommended I start on half a tablet, in case I experienced side effects. I had been hesitant to take it, as some of the side effects were serious, so I asked Pari her opinion as we were finishing the session. She agreed that it was a good choice of medication and that the side effects were rare. I started taking it that night. I had been worried that, if I experienced side effects, I would be too sick to work, but that was my last day at school for the term. I was teaching from home for the next two days, but wouldn't need to drive anywhere, so I wasn't as worried.

That night, while I was brushing my teeth, I noticed a grey line at the base of one of my molars, where it met the gum. I had needed to have a crown put on that tooth a few years earlier, so I wondered if it was coming loose. My first emotion was pride. The ED voice congratulated me on making myself so unwell that my teeth were starting to fall out. I had heard of malnourishment causing gum problems, which allowed teeth to come loose. After a few seconds, however, my pride was immediately replaced with fear. I didn't want my teeth to fall out. Being cold and tired was one thing, but this would be a huge hassle. I would need to get false teeth, which would mean going to special dentists, which would cost who knows how much. My mind ran away, exploring all the horrible outcomes of my teeth falling out. I felt I was back where I had been at the end of the previous year. Why hadn't I learnt my lesson then? I still wasn't eating enough and now my teeth were falling out. I was destroying my body.

I was worried about my tooth — I started chewing very carefully on the other side of my mouth — and exhausted from a stressful few months, two nights of broken sleep and a lack of electrolytes and whatever else the diarrhoea had expelled from my system. I worried that I was dangerously unwell. It wasn't an unreal fear; most people would agree that I was sick. The anxiety was even worse at night because I was scared I would vomit or get diarrhoea again, and that it would never stop. Luckily it didn't happen again after the first two nights, but that didn't stop me worrying.

The constant fear was exhausting, which only fed the fire; the exhaustion confirmed to me that I really was sick. Luckily, as it had the year before, my fear of death outweighed my fear of gaining weight. I allowed myself to lie on the sofa and read or colour-in during the day. I also allowed myself to eat more; not much more, but a small amount. However, the lightheadedness persisted throughout the day. I remembered what Dad had said over the summer; he and Mum were happy to look after me, but they probably wouldn't be able to do it again. If I got that sick again, I would need to go to hospital. I also knew that, if I fulfilled the criteria for an involuntary admission again, the doctors would want to get me to an even higher weight than I had been four years earlier, before they discharged me. I had to get better on my own.

It wasn't just the fear of another hospital admission that was worrying me. Since being told that I was out of immediate medical danger a few months earlier, I hadn't worried too much if I felt lightheaded or tired; I knew I would probably be ok. And if I wasn't, maybe it was for the best; I felt I had no direction in life. Even though almost collapsing had scared me into eating a bit more, I hadn't made any further progress in my recovery. Maybe I was meant to die young — not that I believe in fate, destiny or a greater plan. I felt guilty thinking that way though; I knew Mum and Dad especially would be distraught. But maybe it would be better in the long run; they could stop worrying about me. Since getting an official Autism diagnosis though, I felt I had permission to be my quirky self. And I was excited to explore the things I had been trying to suppress. I didn't want to die now. What a waste, to die when I had just been validated; just when I had been given permission to be me, and to stop beating myself up for not being able to be normal.

I was so worried about the strength of my heart that I stopped exercising for a few days. Exercising made me anxious, because I was worried I was seriously harming my body. The chronic lightheadedness made me increasingly anxious, and the resulting nervous energy tired me out, making me feel even weaker and continuing the spiral.

Reading, which has always been something that calms me, only added to my anxiety. I was reading The Ballad of Songbirds and Snakes, the new Hunger Games book, and I found myself worrying about the characters. Not the fun sort of worry though, when you become so absorbed in the story that you feel you're a part of it. Instead, I had constant butterflies in my stomach, the type that come alive when you're on the train alone at night and a few thugs get onto your carriage.

I had started learning about the pyramids of Giza through an online course and also had some admin to do for the business. However, just thinking about doing either of these, which I would usually find relaxing, agitated the butterflies into a whirl of chaotic flight. The most calming activity I could find to fill my time was colouring in, while watching The Big Bang Theory. Even then, the butterflies in my tummy were active all day, my chest was tight, my heart was beating harder and faster than usual, I was lightheaded and still felt weak. What was wrong with me?

I had started meditating at the end of the previous year. I only meditated for five minutes at a time, because I got bored, but I reasoned that a small amount was better than nothing. However, after a few days of constant, terrifying anxiety, I decided to increase the length of my meditations. I looked for guided visualisations on YouTube too, because Mum and Dad used to play them for me when I was younger and couldn't get to sleep.

I asked Mum for advice about meditation too. I didn't want to tell her about the anxiety, diarrhoea or general exhaustion, in case she came over to babysit me for the next two months again, or took me to hospital. So as not to worry her more than necessary, I only told her about the anxiety. I knew she would understand because she had panic disorder when she was pregnant with me. As always, she came to the rescue. She said it sounded like what I had been experiencing were panic attacks and that they had developed into panic disorder — all of this via text message, because she knew I found talking on the phone stressful. Later that day, Dad sent me digital files of the guided visualisation tracks I listened to as a child. It was comforting to hear them again.

I had been in an almost constant state of anxiety — the only relief was when I managed to fall asleep — for about a week when it reached its peak. I'd had a particularly rough day and spent about an hour meditating. I had become so anxious that I was worried I would have a heart attack if I didn't calm down. Luckily, the meditation helped reduce the anxiety, but only while I was actually meditating. Adam had been staying at Emily's for the past few nights, which was helpful in some ways, because I didn't have to pretend I was ok. That night, however, being alone only strengthened the anxiety. The worst thing was that I didn't even know what I was scared of. The only times I have experienced this level of fear is when I have been seriously scared for my life. But the threat was unknown, so I didn't know how to fix it. This lack of control probably added to my anxiety.

I considered asking Mum and Dad to come over. I was almost 30, but I just wanted my parents. However, covid cases were reaching their peak, and I felt that wearing a mask — which we always did when we saw Mum and Dad indoors — would be more stressful than being alone. I didn't want to bother Adam, but I could see, on the Find My Friends app, that he was still at work, so I called to ask if he was coming home or going to Emily's that night. He knew, almost immediately, that I wasn't ok. Maybe it was because I was calling him, instead of texting, or maybe he could hear it in my voice.
"Are you ok?
I started to cry. "I've been anxious all week and it's getting worse," I sobbed.

"What are you anxious about?"
"I don't know. I don't know what to do. Don't worry, I'll be fine when I go to sleep. I'll just meditate."
"Hmmm well I've hit a wall here at work anyway, so how about I come home now. Will that help?"
"No it's ok, you don't need to. I'll be fine. Stay there if you need to work." I wasn't playing games, I honestly didn't want to put him out. It wasn't his fault I was a mess and I didn't want to prevent him from doing his job.
"You don't sound fine… It's ok, I should have finished for the day anyway. I'll leave now. I'll pick up some dinner on the way, but I should be there in about half an hour, ok?"
Classic Adam and his Guzman y Gomez addiction.

Having Adam there with me helped a bit, but I was still feeling uneasy. I told him about the anxiety I had been experiencing for the past week. I think he had trouble understanding the nameless fear, as I had when Mum used to tell me about her panic attacks. However, as I had with Mum, Adam believed me and did his best to understand. We had a long chat that night. Sometimes we talked about my anxiety and eating disorder; other times about everyday things, such as what Adam had been doing at work. I cried on and off, and Adam held me while I sobbed helplessly. He also told me that it's normal to be able to see that grey line at the base of a crowned tooth, and for it to feel a bit strange sometimes while chewing.

Not long after 11 pm, I was only feeling marginally better. However, I was exhausted from the anxiety and crying and hoped to find peace in sleep. Adam said to come and get him if I needed anything. I thanked him for everything and apologised for using up his free time when he could have been relaxing. As always, the anxiety worsened when I went to bed. My heart was racing, I was sweating and there was a big, tight knot in my stomach. It had been the same every night since I woke up with diarrhoea. Eventually, I fell asleep.

The next day, when Mum messaged to ask how my meditation and anxiety were going, I told her what had happened the night before.

Mum: Why didn't you call Dad and me? We would have come over.

Me: I didn't want to potentially expose you to Covid. And wearing masks would have made me more anxious.

Masks reminded me that we were in constant danger of contracting a potentially life-threatening virus, about which we knew very little.

```
Mum: We could have not worn masks, given you were in
such a state. Just call us if you feel like that
again, ok? We'll come straight over.
```

I thanked her. I knew how much she and Dad cared, but they — Mum especially — were meticulous in their Covid precautions.

My anxiety began to subside a day or so later. It returned at night, but during the day I was almost anxiety-free. Maybe the Zoloft was starting to work. Maybe all the crying and resting had helped. In an ironic twist of circumstances, I started to worry if I *didn't* eat a meal or snack at the scheduled time. The slightest hint of lightheadedness reawakened my anxiety. I tested myself a few times, thinking it would be ok to skip one snack, but my nervous reaction was enough to make me cease the Russian roulette.

(Calories)

By the end of the school holidays, the panic attacks had mostly stopped. I continued meditating every night and reduced the stress in my life as much as possible. I also made sure I ate all of my meals and snacks. I had made new food rules when the panic attacks started, allowing myself a higher daily calorie intake. So far I hadn't felt guilty and planned to make another small increase in a week or so. If I increased my intake incrementally every few weeks, I could be eating 2000 calories a day by the end of term two. Surely then it would be safe for me to be put under general anaesthetic while they took my wisdom teeth out.

I surprised myself with how well I coped during term two. I moved house without too much stress. I also had a slightly higher teaching load, but wasn't getting too tired because I was eating more — though still not enough. I never managed to increase my calorie intake again, but nor did I decrease it, even though I hated how I looked. I had found something worse than hating myself — living in constant fear. I was unsure if I had actually put on weight though. Was it body dysmorphia?

Near the end of term, when I knew my operation was looming, the panic attacks returned. I wasn't scared of the pain or discomfort; I was scared Mum's fears would be confirmed and the anaesthetic would cause my malnourished body to shut down completely. Even when WAEDOCS assured us it was safe, the worry seed, which had already been planted, grew in another direction. I wondered if, as I would be on a lower dose of anaesthetic, I would be unable to move, but would feel everything — someone had told me, years earlier, that this sometimes happened. I didn't know if it was true, but my mind decided to dwell on it. I was also worried that, if I was in pain or discomfort after the operation, I would have trouble eating enough. I didn't want to be tired or lightheaded when I was teaching. And I knew that, if I dropped below my new calorie limit, it would be hard to increase it again.

One Saturday afternoon, when I found myself in the unusual situation of having a few hours free, I started worrying about how to fill the time. The worry quickly became general anxiety and the feeling of doom returned. By the time I had talked myself into asking Mum and Dad if we could FaceTime, I was terrified. I couldn't hold back my tears when they asked how I was. I hadn't realised quite how *not* ok I was.
"Do you want one of us to come over?" Mum asked.
"But.. we'll have to wear masks and that will just make me more anxious."
"It's ok, we can make an exception. Dad and I haven't been anywhere since last weekend so we won't have it."
"But what if I have it?"
"Do you think you have it?"
"No. I've been wearing a mask everywhere. But… I don't want you to have to come over. It's already late.."
"Hannah, we're your parents. We love you and we will do whatever it takes to help you."
I felt guilty asking them to drive over. Petrol prices had spiked since Putin invaded Ukraine.
"Do you want Dad to come over? He can leave straight away."
Eventually, I gave in to their kindness. Again, my fear outweighed my eternal goal to not put anyone out.

Dad arrived about 40 minutes later. Just knowing he was on his way made me feel better. We ate dinner together; he had brought his with him and didn't comment on what I cooked for myself. After dinner, we chatted and worked on a Harry Potter jigsaw until we went to bed. Dad refused to take my bed and I didn't have a spare, so he arranged sofa cushions and a beanbag into something resembling a bed on the floor. He said to come get him if I needed anything during the night. My anxiety increased when I went to bed, but meditation and the knowledge that Dad was there if I need anything, calmed me enough to get to sleep.

My anxiety fluctuated for the next week or so, before settling back into panic disorder, with nightly panic attacks. I usually felt fine during the day and was able to work and even enjoy myself. But when the sky began to darken, I started to feel uneasy, which worsened as the night progressed.

I started colouring in again while watching light-hearted TV shows and movies in the background. I also started some craft projects in which I could become completely absorbed — the life-size Mirror of Erised took at least a month. I read as much as I could, but some books worsened my anxiety. When I wasn't working, I filled my time with these mindful, calming, low-stress activities. Mum recommended yoga, partly to help my digestion and partly for mindfulness. It helped for about two weeks before it started making the anxiety worse. For some reason, moving my body through the asanas brought back the feeling of impending doom. I messaged Mum a lot too, especially at night. Usually, we just talked about whatever we were doing, or interesting things we had read. It comforted me to have that small amount of human contact, without the stress of someone actually being there in person.

Some nights, text messages weren't enough; my fear was too great. Dad was always willing to come over to fight away the monsters beneath my bed. Aside from the first night that he came, when the anxiety lingered, I felt completely calm having Dad there; no more anxiety. But I didn't want to rely on him. I wanted to be ok on my own and for him to be able to sleep at home in a proper bed. I also wanted to be able to exercise in the morning without him knowing. I always did it as quietly as I could in my room, but I worried he would hear.

As always, my friends helped as much as I would let them. One night, Siena messaged to see how I was going. We hadn't spoken for a while so she was checking in. I could feel a panic attack beginning, so I told her. She offered to come around, but I worried that might make things worse. I was already a mess and knew I would try to act normal if she was there. She understood my need to be alone and was happy to continue texting, to keep me company.

Another night I spoke to Gilbert, over Facebook Messenger, about the panic attacks. Like Adam, he tried to understand how I could be scared without knowing what I was scared of. I did my best to explain.

```
Gilbert: Yeah, well Harry Potter's got a quote for
that.

Me: What's that?
```

Gilbert: "What you fear most of all is fear itself."

Me: Wow!
Very true
Just need a patronising
*patronus

Gilbert: Haha I can do that
You do know Hannah that if you get therapy that would probably help with your anxiety.
You just need to do breathing exercises.
And need to do mindfulness.

It took me a few seconds to realise he was making fun of my autocorrect; patronising me.

Me: And quit sugar. Drink more green tea.

In the last week of school term — I know, it's always the last week — my anxiety worsened as the wisdom teeth operation approached. As often happens when I'm particularly stressed, I became constipated. On Tuesday night, I woke up a few times with diarrhoea. On my final visit to the toilet, I felt so weak that, as I sat there, my right leg was shaking. On Wednesday morning — yes, Wednesday again, my busiest day — I felt nauseous and dry-retched into the toilet bowl. Nothing came out. I wondered if I should cancel my students, but decided it would be better to struggle through the day than reschedule the lessons. I would have enough to worry about in the holidays.

An hour or two before I left the house, a pain bloomed on the right side of my lower abdomen. It felt like a bubble of trapped air, so I assumed it would sort itself out. I'd had countless stomach pains similar to this throughout my life. I took a heat pack to school with me though, because the pain was worse than usual. It was also a cold day. Something made me do a quick Google, to check which side my appendix is on — my right. My symptoms also matched those of appendicitis. Wonderful.

When the pain hadn't moved or lessened by the early afternoon, I called Krish from school. We talked through my symptoms and, while they pointed to appendicitis, I didn't feel any additional pain when I pushed my hand into it, which suggested it *wasn't* appendicitis. He sent me a form to get an ultrasound anyway, to see if there was anything else in that area. I felt slightly better after speaking to Krish, but was still worried. I was also still in pain and feeling very weak from my nocturnal toilet adventures.

Luckily, that was my last day teaching at schools for the term. However, the diarrhoea and stomach pain brought back my fear of vomiting. I knew I was healthier than I had been three months earlier, but if I vomited every night I wouldn't be well enough to have the operation. Then I would have to wait until the next school holidays. I just needed it to be over; hopefully then the anxiety would dissipate. I worried that, if my gastro symptoms had been caused by stress four years earlier, surely they would return now. I was much more stressed than I had been back then. I put a bowl beside my bed so that, if I woke up in the middle of the night needing to vomit, I wouldn't have to groggily run to the toilet. The bowl is still there. Murphy's Law prevents me from putting it away.

A long and uncomfortable ultrasound showed that I didn't have appendicitis, and there was nothing out of the ordinary in the area. The pain remained in my lower abdomen for over a week, before slowly fading to nothing. I can only guess that it was an innocent pocket of air that overstayed its welcome because I was so anxious.

While I remained relatively calm during the day, my nighttime panic attacks worsened as the operation approached. Dad stayed the night quite a few times. While I always felt safe when I knew he was on his way, I felt bad asking him to come.
"You're not asking. We're offering," Mum always said.
"Yeah, but you shouldn't need to keep looking after me like this."
"Hannah, we're your parents. We will *always* be your parents. We will *always* look after you. It is our honour."

I decided to write Mum and Dad a letter, straight from the heart, telling them how much I appreciated their unending and selfless care. I told them what wonderful role models they had been for me. They had taught me, through their own actions, to always treat people with respect and do the right thing, and for that, I am incredibly grateful. They both cried when they read it. Even though I had thanked them profusely each time they came to my aid, I wanted to write it down. Sometimes writing is more meaningful than speaking; letters can be kept.

One night when I was at Mum and Dad's, not long before the operation, we were talking about my panic attacks. I knew Dad was happy to come over whenever I needed him, but I didn't want to become dependent on him. Each time he came, it reinforced my belief that the anxiety was bigger than me. Conversely, when I was able to get through the night by myself, even if I was terrified, it gave me hope that I could do so again.

After our conversation, Mum and Dad went inside briefly, to check on the dinner and feed the dogs. I stayed outside because I would have had to put my mask on if I went in. As I sat there, looking out at the darkness, my thoughts turned to the drive home and the dark, empty house awaiting my return. Thoughts of spending another night there, alone, fighting my unknown fears, welled up and overwhelmed me. My face crumpled as I started crying quietly. I didn't care if Mum and Dad saw. They were inside. Maybe they would, maybe they wouldn't. My deep, intense anguish twisted my face and squeezed my eyes shut. I heard the door open, and then Mum and Dad were on either side of me, holding me as I sobbed. They had me. They would always look after me.

That was about a year and a half ago. Needless to say, the general anaesthetic didn't kill me. I was terrified the night before the operation though, and sobbed into Dad's shoulder. I could feel adrenaline pulsing through my body when I went to bed. I was clammy and cold. I worried I would vomit from the stress which, I assumed, would make it unsafe to anaesthetise me.

I had hoped the panic attacks would stop after the operation. Three or four months later, though I had continued taking Zoloft, meditating every night and reducing the stress in my life wherever possible, I was still having one or two attacks each week, though they weren't as bad as they had been earlier in the year. One night, Mum asked me how I meditated. I think she wanted to check that I was actually meditating, not just letting my thoughts wander. Her panic disorder had dissipated about three months after she started meditating, but it had been longer than that for me. I don't know the answer; everyone is different. However, without diminishing Mum's experience, the circumstances that caused her anxiety were relatively short compared to my 15 years with anorexia nervosa and 20 or more years of almost constant masking.

A few weeks after the operation, I started seeing a psychologist who specialises in helping Autistic people do life. Aside from reviewing my Autism report and amending it to a level 2 diagnosis, she has helped me understand how Autism affects my life. She also told me that she read about a virus that caused gastro symptoms, then remained dormant in the body for a few months or weeks, before becoming active again. Maybe the lady at SO was correct. The vomit bowl is still beside my bed though, just in case.

This may seem an odd place to end the narrative. Getting my wisdom teeth taken out isn't much of a climax and I still haven't recovered from AN. But this is real life, not Hollywood. I wrote this in the hope that it will give clinicians, carers, friends and anyone who is interested, a better understanding of what it is like to have anorexia nervosa. Having said that, everyone's story is different. I also hope that it will help anyone suffering from an eating disorder to feel less alone. Lastly, I hope it will help anyone who is wondering if they, or a loved one, are Autistic. I don't like over-emotional, drawn-out book endings and, being Autistic, I'm going to abruptly finish here.

Thank You

Firstly, thank you to the people who helped me to still be alive and (relatively) well today: Mum, Dad, Adam, Shannon, Dorothy, my friends, (the few helpful) clinicians, and people I have only ever interacted with on social media, but who helped and inspired me nonetheless.

Thanks also to Brittany, Bryn, Dad, Ellie, Isaac, Jen, Lydia, Euphina and Suzanna for giving me feedback on my drafts. It was helpful to know my disordered thoughts made sense to others.

Finally, thank you to these special people for your generous contribution to my campaign.

Jemma Armstrong
Siri
Maree Clark
Laura Doyle
Siobhan Finn
Avril Hughes
Alison Jones
Ruth Klein Cook
Lloyd Owens
Tim Rennie
Sophie Reynolds
Mark Schmalfuss
Ciara
Jessica Taylor
Jeanette Teh
Emma Townsend
Noelle Zhao

Recommended Books & Social Media Accounts

Autism
Different, Not Less - Chloé Hayden
Rainbow Girl - Livia Sara
Strong Female Character - Fern Brady
Supporting Autistic People with Eating Disorders - Kate Tchanturia
The Ninth Life of a Diamond Miner - Grace Tame
Ten Steps to Nanette - Hannah Gadsby
Unmasking Autism - Dr. Devon Price

@_anniecrowe
@akindofspark
@autibiographical
@autisticflair
@autisticgirlsnetwork
@awfulslothofficial
@chloeshayden
@drdevonprice
@edneuroaus
@littlepuddins.ie
@livedexperienceeducator
@livlabelfree
@mooseandfreckles
@neurodivergent.reflections
@neuroqueering_nutrition
@princessandthepeapodcast
@purpleella
@spicylittlebrain
@squarepeg.community
@theneurodivergentot
@yellowladybugs_autism

Body Image & Eating Disorders
8 Keys to Recovery from an Eating Disorder - Carolyn Costin & Gwen Schubert Grabb
Beautiful Monster - Kate McCaffrey
Different, Not Less - Chloé Hayden
Goodbye Ed, Hello Me - Jenni Schaefer
Life Without Ed - Jenni Schaefer
Living Full - Brittany Farrant-Smith
The Ninth Life of a Diamond Miner - Grace Tame

Supporting Autistic People with Eating Disorders - Kate Tchanturia
The Opposite of Butterfly Hunting — Evanna Lynch
Unfiltered - Lily Collins
You Are Not a Before Picture - Alex Light

@_anniecrowe
@alexlight_ldn
@awfulslothofficial
@ccicoaching
@chr1styharrison
@diet.culture.rebel
@edneuroaus
@emilymurray.rd
@i_weigh
@jameelajamil
@livlabelfree
@meerchatter
@mentally_fitt
@neuroqueering_nutrition
@realistic.body.therapist
@stuff_my_ed_never_says
@oh_hi_han
@ohobjectivehealth
@theantidietplan
@yrfatfriend
@zoameliaa

LGBTQIA+
Annie on My Mind - Nancy Garden
Growing Up Queer in Australia - Benjamin Law
Heartstopper Collection - Alice Oseman
The Spectrum of Sex - Hida Viloria & Dr. Maria Nieto
Ten Steps to Nanette - Hannah Gadsby
Testosterone Rex - Cordelia Fine

@abcqueer
@kaleidoscopenews
@lgbt
@pinknews
@sockdrawerheroes
@transfolkofwa
@trevorproject

www.ingramcontent.com/pod-product-compliance
Lightning Source LLC
Chambersburg PA
CBHW011149290426
44109CB00025B/2540